New York City

David Ellis

LONELY PLANET PUBLICATIONS
Melbourne • Oakland • London • Paris

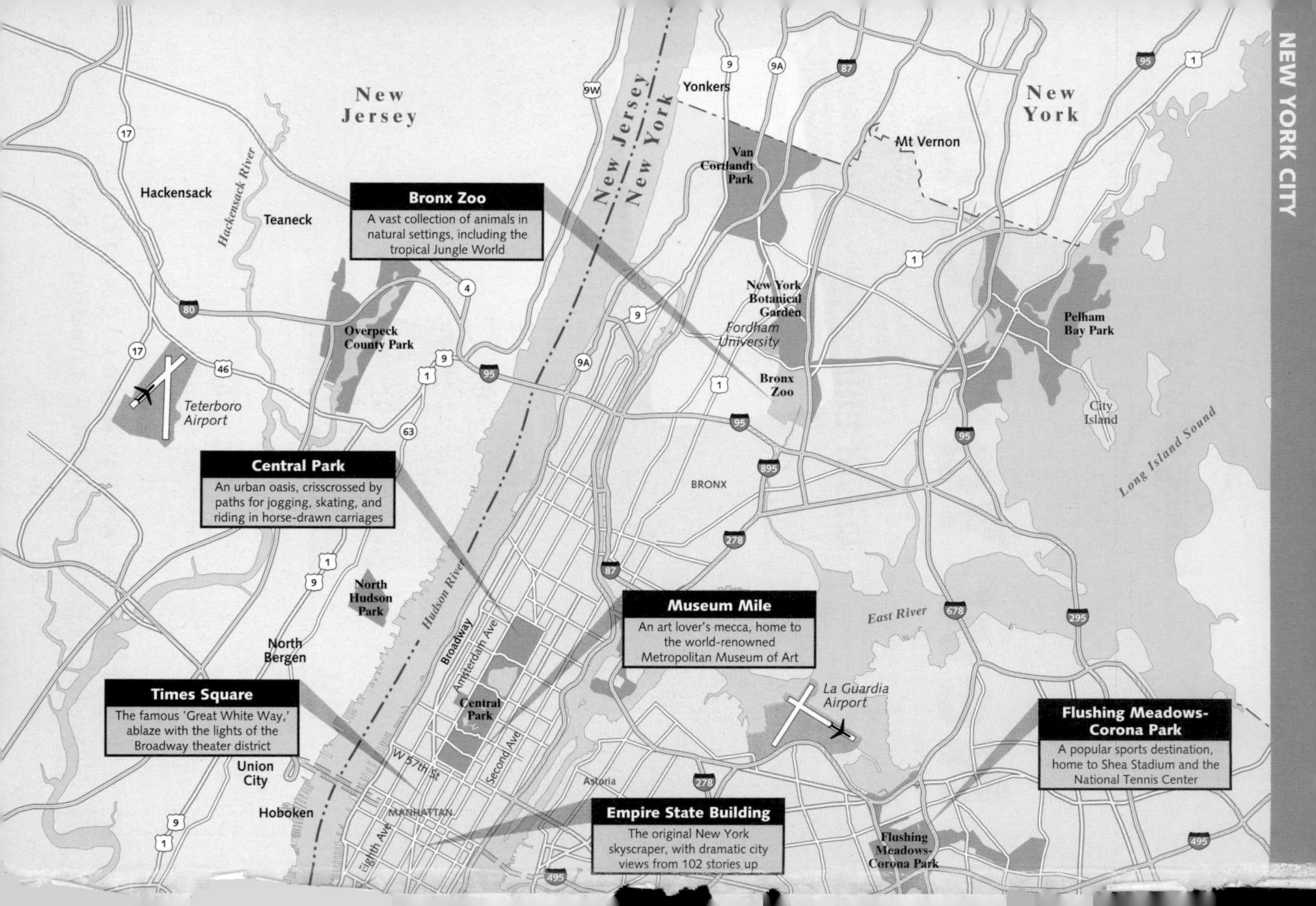
New Jersey
New York
Hackensack
Hackensack River
Teaneck
Bronx Zoo
A vast collection of animals in natural settings, including the tropical Jungle World
Yonkers
Van Cortlandt Park
Mt Vernon
New York Botanical Garden
Fordham University
Bronx Zoo
Pelham Bay Park
City Island
Long Island Sound
Overpeck County Park
Teterboro Airport
Central Park
An urban oasis, crisscrossed by paths for jogging, skating, and riding in horse-drawn carriages
BRONX
North Hudson Park
Hudson River
North Bergen
Broadway
Amsterdam Ave
Museum Mile
An art lover's mecca, home to the world-renowned Metropolitan Museum of Art
East River
Times Square
The famous 'Great White Way,' ablaze with the lights of the Broadway theater district
Central Park
La Guardia Airport
Flushing Meadows-Corona Park
A popular sports destination, home to Shea Stadium and the National Tennis Center
Union City
W 57th St
Second Ave
Astoria
Hoboken
MANHATTAN
Eighth Ave
Empire State Building
The original New York skyscraper, with dramatic city views from 102 stories up
Flushing Meadows-Corona Park

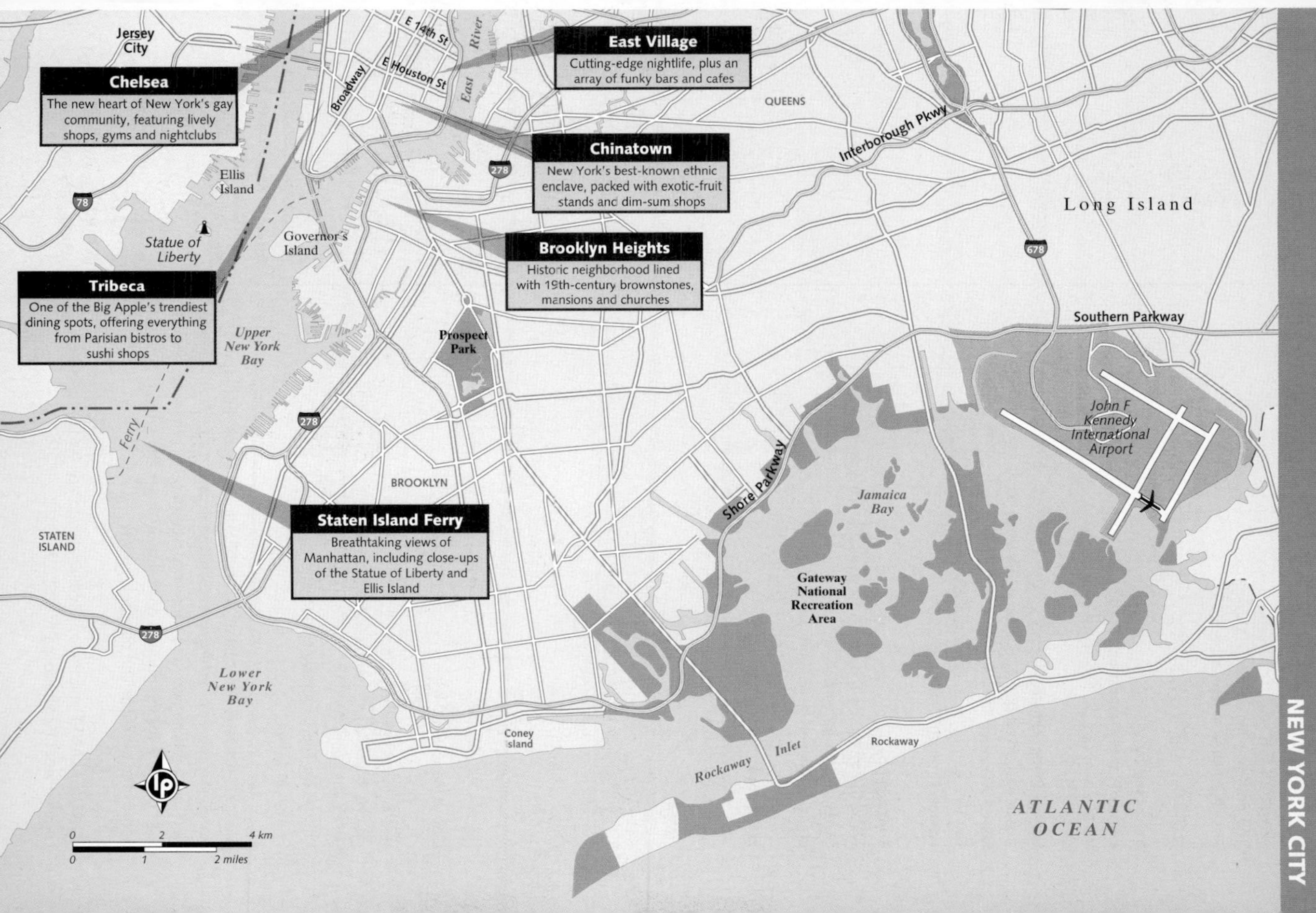
Jersey City
Chelsea
The new heart of New York's gay community, featuring lively shops, gyms and nightclubs
East Village
Cutting-edge nightlife, plus an array of funky bars and cafes
Chinatown
New York's best-known ethnic enclave, packed with exotic-fruit stands and dim-sum shops
Brooklyn Heights
Historic neighborhood lined with 19th-century brownstones, mansions and churches
Tribeca
One of the Big Apple's trendiest dining spots, offering everything from Parisian bistros to sushi shops
Staten Island Ferry
Breathtaking views of Manhattan, including close-ups of the Statue of Liberty and Ellis Island
E 14th St
E Houston St
Broadway
East River
QUEENS
Interborough Pkwy
Long Island
678
278
78
Ellis Island
Statue of Liberty
Governor's Island
Upper New York Bay
Prospect Park
Southern Parkway
John F Kennedy International Airport
Ferry
BROOKLYN
Shore Parkway
Jamaica Bay
STATEN ISLAND
Gateway National Recreation Area
Lower New York Bay
Coney Island
Rockaway Inlet
Rockaway
ATLANTIC OCEAN
0
2
4 km
0
1
2 miles

New York City
2nd edition – November 2000
First Published – September 1997

Published by
Lonely Planet Publications Pty Ltd ABN 36 005 607 983
90 Maribyrnong St, Footscray, Victoria 3011, Australia

Lonely Planet Offices
Australia Locked Bag 1, Footscray, Victoria 3011
USA 150 Linden St, Oakland, CA 94607
UK 10a Spring Place, London NW5 3BH
France 1 rue du Dahomey, 75011 Paris

Photographs
All of the images in this guide are available for licensing from Lonely Planet Images.
email: lpi@lonelyplanet.com.au

Front cover photograph
Lady Liberty through the looking glass (Stone/Hugh Sitton)

ISBN 1 86450 180 4

Printed by The Bookmaker International Ltd
Printed in China

Contents

The Author

David Ellis

This second edition of *New York City* was updated by David Ellis, who wrote Lonely Planet's first *New York City* guide. He also worked on the first two editions of *New York, New Jersey & Pennsylvania* and reviewed restaurants for *Out to Eat – London*.

A native New Yorker, David was born in Greenwich Village and has lived in three of New York City's five boroughs (Manhattan, Brooklyn and the Bronx). Over the last 15 years, he has reported on politics, business and culture at *Time* and *People*. His work has also appeared in the *New Republic* and *New York* magazine and on the BBC. He currently works as an editor at the *Wall Street Journal* in London. David is now working on a book of photos and essays about the culture and history of the New York City bar scene.

From the Author

First, thanks go to my wife Jane Lloyd Ellis for her companionship in researching the first edition and for her help with this update, which wasn't always as enjoyable a job as revisiting favorite restaurants.

Many sources provided information and support, and I would like to thank specifically the staff at the New York City Convention & Visitors Bureau. Most knew me only as a 'lost tourist' but provided comprehensive help in an unfailingly polite manner. (So much for the gruff reputation of New Yorkers.) Laura Otterbourg's staff at the New Jersey Division of Travel & Tourism also helped guide my update. Over the summer months in New Jersey, David and Lisa Furrule provided invaluable support.

I would also like to thank Bud Kliment of Columbia University for background help and advice, Daniel Levy for his insights on architecture, especially in Lower Manhattan, and Tom Lloyd for his history of contemporary New York music. Journalists Rob Walker, Richard Lacayo, Larry Mondi, Larry Hackett and Mark Solomon provided companionship and, in some instances, contributed spare beds and phone lines to this effort.

At Lonely Planet, I'd like to thank editor Tom Downs for his great work on the first edition of the book, as well as the whole team in Oakland for their help.

Most of all, I thank my grandparents, Ruth and Bernard Wynne, for helping me discover New York City's many hidden glories.

This Book

David Ellis wrote this second edition of *New York City*.

The hardworking LP team (clockwise from lower left): Heather Haskell, Amelia Borofsky, Valerie Sinzdak, Kevin Anglin, Erin Corrigan

From the Publisher

Lonely Planet's Oakland office churned out this Big Apple guide. Valerie Sinzdak edited the book, but she could never have done it without the help of a tireless team of editors and fact checkers, including Erin Corrigan, Kevin Anglin and Amelia Borofsky, who never balked at phoning any New York establishments, not even a place called Hell. China Williams, Paul Sheridan and Valerie proofed the text, and Susan Derby painstakingly proofed the intricate maps. Senior editors Maria Donohoe and Brigitte Barta pitched in with plenty of advice and encouragement along the way. Thanks, too, to Mariah Bear, Kate Hoffman and expert stand-in editor Robert Reid, who saw the book through a critical week while Valerie flew off to Manhattan and fell prey to some savvy New York hucksters who can see a tourist coming from miles away. But that's another story.

Cartographer Heather Haskell performed the Herculean task of drawing the maps for this edition, breaking Oakland office records for the greatest number of key items on a single map (216). Best of all, she brought the doughnuts. Guphy, Patrick Phelan, Rachel Leising, Matt DeMartini, Chris Gillis, Eric Thomsen and Mary Hagemann also helped with the maps, with guidance from senior cartographer Monica Lepe and the inimitable Alex Guilbert.

Designer Wendy Yanagihara wrestled an unruly Manhattan onto the page, with help from design manager Susan Rimerman. Beca Lafore headed up the team of illustrators, including Jennifer Steffey, Rini Keagy and Justin Marler. Simon Bracken designed the quirky cover for the book, and Paul Sheridan gets credit for the pithy front-cover banner.

Dani Valent, author of Lonely Planet's *New York City Condensed*, improved this edition with some additional coverage, as did freelance writer Sandhya Rao, who worked late into the night hopping from club to club throughout the city. Ken DellaPenta created the index. Thanks to everyone for a lot of hard work.

Foreword

ABOUT LONELY PLANET GUIDEBOOKS

The story begins with a classic travel adventure: Tony and Maureen Wheeler's 1972 journey across Europe and Asia to Australia. Useful information about the overland trail did not exist at that time, so Tony and Maureen published the first Lonely Planet guidebook to meet a growing need.

From a kitchen table, then from a tiny office in Melbourne (Australia), Lonely Planet has become the largest independent travel publisher in the world, an international company with offices in Melbourne, Oakland (USA), London (UK) and Paris (France).

Today Lonely Planet guidebooks cover the globe. There is an ever-growing list of books, and there's information in a variety of forms and media. Some things haven't changed. The main aim is still to help make it possible for adventurous travelers to get out there – to explore and better understand the world.

At Lonely Planet we believe travelers can make a positive contribution to the countries they visit – if they respect their host communities and spend their money wisely. Since 1986 a percentage of the income from each book has been donated to aid projects and human-rights campaigns.

Updates Lonely Planet thoroughly updates each guidebook as often as possible. This usually means there are around two years between editions, although for more unusual or more stable destinations the gap can be longer. Check the imprint page (following the color map at the beginning of the book) for publication dates.

Between editions, up-to-date information is available in two free newsletters – the paper *Planet Talk* and email *Comet* (to subscribe, contact any Lonely Planet office) – and on our website at www.lonelyplanet.com. The *Upgrades* section of the website covers a number of important and volatile destinations and is regularly updated by Lonely Planet authors. *Scoop* covers news and current affairs relevant to travelers. And, lastly, the *Thorn Tree* bulletin board and *Postcards* section of the site carry unverified, but fascinating, reports from travelers.

Lonely Planet gathers information for everyone who's curious about the planet – and especially for those who explore it first-hand. Through guidebooks, phrasebooks, activity guides, maps, literature, newsletters, image library, TV series and website, we act as an information exchange for a worldwide community of travelers.

Correspondence The process of creating new editions begins with the letters, postcards and emails received from travelers. This correspondence often includes suggestions, criticisms and comments about the current editions. Interesting excerpts are immediately passed on via newsletters and the website, and everything goes to our authors to be verified when they're researching on the road. We're keen to get more feedback from organizations or individuals who represent communities visited by travelers.

Research Authors aim to gather sufficient practical information to enable travelers to make informed choices and to make the mechanics of a journey run smoothly. They also research historical and cultural background to help enrich the travel experience and allow travelers to understand and respond appropriately to cultural and environmental issues.

Authors don't stay in every hotel because that would mean spending a couple of months in each medium-size city and, no, they don't eat at every restaurant because that would mean stretching belts beyond capacity. They do visit hotels and restaurants to check standards and prices, but feedback based on readers' direct experiences can be very helpful.

Many of our authors work undercover; others aren't so secretive. None of them accept freebies in exchange for positive write-ups. And none of our guidebooks contain any advertising.

Production Authors submit their raw manuscripts and maps to offices in Australia, the USA, the UK or France. Editors and cartographers – all experienced travelers themselves – then begin the process of assembling the pieces. When the book finally hits the shops, some things are already out of date, we start getting feedback from readers and the process begins again....

WARNING & REQUEST

Things change – prices go up, schedules change, good places go bad and bad places go bankrupt – nothing stays the same. So, if you find things better or worse, recently opened or long since closed, please tell us and help make the next edition even more accurate and useful. We genuinely value all the feedback we receive. Julie Young coordinates a well-traveled team that reads and acknowledges every letter, postcard and email and ensures that every morsel of information finds its way to the appropriate authors, editors and cartographers for verification.

Everyone who writes to us will find their name in the next edition of the appropriate guidebook. They will also receive the latest issue of *Planet Talk*, our quarterly printed newsletter, or *Comet*, our monthly email newsletter. Subscriptions to both newsletters are free. The very best contributions will be rewarded with a free guidebook.

Excerpts from your correspondence may appear in new editions of Lonely Planet guidebooks, the Lonely Planet website, *Planet Talk* or *Comet*, so please let us know if you *don't* want your letter published or your name acknowledged.

Send all correspondence to the Lonely Planet office closest to you:

Australia: Locked Bag 1, Footscray, Victoria 3011
USA: 150 Linden St, Oakland, CA 94607
UK: 10A Spring Place, London NW5 3BH
France: 1 rue du Dahomey, 75011 Paris

Or email us at: talk2us@lonelyplanet.com.au

For news, views and updates, see our website: www.lonelyplanet.com

HOW TO USE A LONELY PLANET GUIDEBOOK

The best way to use a Lonely Planet guidebook is any way you choose. At Lonely Planet, we believe the most memorable travel experiences are often those that are unexpected, and the finest discoveries are those you make yourself. Guidebooks are not intended to be used as if they provided a detailed set of infallible instructions!

Contents All Lonely Planet guidebooks follow the same format. The Facts about the Country chapters or sections give background information ranging from history to weather. Facts for the Visitor gives practical information on issues like visas and health. Getting There & Away gives a brief starting point for researching travel to and from the destination. Getting Around gives an overview of the transport options available when you arrive.

The peculiar demands of each destination determine how subsequent chapters are broken up, but some things remain constant. We always start with background, then proceed to sights, places to stay, places to eat, entertainment, getting there and away, and getting around information – in that order.

Heading Hierarchy Lonely Planet headings are used in a strict hierarchical structure that can be visualized as a set of Russian dolls. Each heading (and its following text) is encompassed by any preceding heading that is higher on the hierarchical ladder.

Although inclusion in a guidebook usually implies a recommendation, we cannot list every good place. Exclusion does not necessarily imply criticism. In fact, there are a number of reasons why we might exclude a place – sometimes it is simply inappropriate to encourage an influx of travelers.

Entry Points We do not assume guidebooks will be read from beginning to end, but that people will dip into them. The traditional entry points are the list of contents and the index. In addition, however, some books have a complete list of maps and an index map illustrating map coverage.

There may also be a color map that shows highlights. These highlights are dealt with in greater detail later in the book, along with planning questions. Each chapter covering a geographical region usually begins with a locator map and another list of highlights. Once you find something of interest in a list of highlights, turn to the index.

Maps Maps play a crucial role in Lonely Planet guidebooks and include a huge amount of information. A legend is printed on the back page. We seek to have complete consistency between maps and text, and to have every important place in the text captured on a map. Map key numbers usually start in the top left corner.

Introduction

ANGUS OBORN

Only one city on the globe has had the arrogance to hang banners saying 'Capital of the World' along its avenues. It's not an empty boast, though: Long after New York City ceased to be the geographic and political center of the USA, the Big Apple's romantic reputation has continued to loom large in the popular imagination. Over the years, it has gained, then lost, its leading role in many different arenas, including politics, agriculture, manufacturing and shipping, as well as film and TV production. But history has taught New Yorkers that their city will soon find a new activity to exploit, and they remain forever confident that no rival will ever equal it as a center for cultural and intellectual pursuits.

At the beginning of the 21st century, the city may be standing at the height of its influence, with more money in its coffers and more cultures represented in its population than just about any other time in its history. A longtime favorite with foreign visitors, New York City has begun to look more and more appealing to other Americans, who now see it as a fun, invigorating destination. About 35 million visitors pass through New York in a single year, all seeking success, education or merely entertainment. Tens of thousands more come to stay (legally or illegally), and all of them, if they look hard enough, can find people just like them already at home here.

EB White remarked drolly on New York's hold over its residents when he observed that many English sparrows had chosen to live in the Big Apple: 'It is a sign. Why these birds deliberately endure the hardships of a life in town when the wide, fruitful country is theirs for the asking, is a matter for some comment.'

With seven million residents, New York City has more than twice as many people as Los Angeles, the second-largest US city. Without nearly as much space to sprawl as Los Angeles, though, the Big Apple packs all of its people into 309 sq miles. (It's no wonder the city has had to look skyward, erecting skyscrapers so that New Yorkers can live and work on top of each other. Not that the natives do much looking up, though – every day, they blithely stroll past towering buildings that command drop-jaw gazes from many visitors.) Yet from this density comes New York's intensity. The crowding of so many colors and cultures within its borders is just what makes New York City one of the most exciting spots in the world.

Yes, some of the clichés are true: A New Yorker talks faster – and closer to your face – than just about anyone else. And some of the habits of the city's denizens can seem a little rude; sometimes they bury their faces in books, stare into space on the subway trains or stand right in the middle of escalators, blocking those who are trying to pass. Think of these annoying tics as survival instincts – in this crowded metropolis, people need to tune out their neighbors every once in awhile. But contrary to New York's tough-guy image, the locals are often gracious and helpful to tourists, sometimes even excusing themselves if they bump into you. And they love to give directions, if only because visitors' questions make them feel like experts on their beloved city.

For tourists, New York can be an exhausting holiday destination. This mega-city demands that you assault it with a game plan. Define your sightseeing priorities and get to those spots ahead of anyone else. But you won't need a plan to experience the real, everyday New York. Along the way, serendipitous occurrences will unfold, because some of the city's best entertainment can be found for free on the streets.

Facts about New York City

HISTORY

Native Peoples

For more than 11,000 years before the Europeans arrived, Native Americans occupied the area now known as New York City. These early residents spoke a language called Munsee, common in the area all the way down to Delaware, and called themselves the 'Lenape' – or 'People' – of the region. The Munsee language had several names for the area, including *Manahatouh* ('place of gathering bow wood'), *Manahactanienk* ('place of general inebriation') and *Menatay* ('the island'). The name 'Manhattan' can be traced to any one of these words.

From the dozens of settlements that archaeologists have identified in today's New York, and from the accounts of the early 16th-century European settlers, historians have pieced together a picture of how the native Lenape lived. They were a transient people who lived off the land, dwelling along the banks of the local waterways in the summer and moving inland to the woods during the colder months. They hunted the plentiful small native game (turkey, rabbit, deer) and enjoyed shellfish (oysters mostly), berries and corn. While they used the bow and arrow, they shunned the heavier planting and cooking equipment that the Europeans offered them in trade.

Some of the roadways in New York still follow the old Lenape paths. That's why Broadway cuts diagonally across the island and continues all the way to Albany, in one form or another.

The Europeans Arrive

Giovanni da Verrazano, a Florentine hired by the French to explore the American northeastern coast, hit these shores in 1524. Though history records that a black Portuguese man named Esteban Gomez sailed part of the river two years later, no serious attempt was made to document the topography of the area or its peoples until

NEIL SETCHFIELD

September 1609. That's when English explorer Henry Hudson, on a mission to find the Northwest Passage, anchored *Halve Maen (Half Moon)* in the harbor for 10 days before continuing up the river. 'It is as beautiful a land as one can hope to tread upon,' reported Hudson.

The Struggle to Control New York

By 1625, the first Dutch settlers were dispatched to establish a trading post they eventually called New Amsterdam, the seat of a much larger colony called New Netherland. Historians generally agree that the story about the purchase of the island from local tribes for goods worth 60 guilders ($24), while sounding like a myth, may actually be true (though a more accurate exchange rate for the goods would be about $600 – still a bargain).

In 1647, a new governor named Peter Stuyvesant arrived to impose order on what the Dutch government considered an unruly colony. His ban on alcohol and curtailment of religious freedoms caused unrest among the settlers, and few regretted the bloodless takeover of New Amsterdam by the British in 1664.

Renamed New York, in honor of King Charles II's brother the Duke of York, the port town retained much of its Dutch character well into the mid-18th century. By that time, opposition to the excesses of British colonial rule had developed, and New Yorkers voiced their frustrations in John Peter Zenger's influential newspaper, the *Weekly Journal*. Though many influential New Yorkers resisted a war for independence, New York's Commons – where City Hall stands today – was the center of many anti-British protests. King George III's troops controlled New York for most of the Revolutionary War and took their time going home, finally withdrawing in 1783, a full two years after the fighting stopped.

Boom Years

By the time George Washington was sworn in as president of the new republic on the balcony of Federal Hall on Wall St in 1789, New York was a bustling seaport of 33,000 people. The new US Congress abandoned the city after establishing the District of Columbia the following year. The move was probably driven by the founding fathers' dislike of the city – Thomas Jefferson later said that he regarded New York to be a 'cloacina [sewer] of all the depravities of human nature.'

New York boomed in the early 19th century, and by 1830 its population approached 250,000, though it had no police force to speak of until the Civil War period in the 1860s. The Croton Aqueduct, completed in 1842 at a then-phenomenal cost of $12 million, brought 72 million gallons of fresh water to the city each day. This development not only improved public health conditions but finally allowed residents the opportunity to bathe regularly.

The years following the Union victory in the Civil War became a time of prosperity for both private and public figures. William Magear Tweed, notorious boss of the city's Tammany Hall Democratic organization, used public works projects to steal millions of dollars from the public treasury before being toppled from power. Meanwhile, robber barons like railroad speculator Jay Gould were able to amass tax-free fortunes that approached $100 million.

Growing Pains

Widening gaps between the rich and poor and tensions between different racial groups made for an occasionally explosive atmosphere in the mid-19th century. In the summer of 1863, poor Irish immigrants launched the 'draft riots,' in large part because of a provision that allowed wealthy men to pay $300 in order to avoid being conscripted to fight in the Civil War. Within days, the rioters turned their anger on black citizens, whom they considered to be the reason for the war and their main competition for work. More than 11 men were lynched in the streets, and a black orphans' home was burned to the ground.

Economic and racial tensions continued to fester as the city filled with different ethnic groups pouring in from Europe. New

York City's population more than doubled from 515,547 in 1850 to 1,164,673 in 1880, as southern blacks arrived in search of a better life and waves of poor immigrants from Ireland and Central Europe came seeking the storied 'streets of gold.' But for those with little money, there was merely a life of manual labor and isolation at the end of the journey. Inevitably, a tenement culture developed; the poorest New Yorkers invariably worked in dangerous factories and lived in squalid apartment blocks. The work of crusading journalist Jacob Riis, who chronicled how this 'other half' lived, shocked the city's middle class, leading to the establishment of an independent health board and triggering a series of workplace reforms. Meanwhile, millionaires like Andrew Carnegie, John D Rockefeller and John Jacob Astor began pouring money into public works and created such major institutions as the New York Public Library in 1895.

In the late 19th century, the burgeoning of New York's population beyond the city's official borders led to the consolidation movement, as the city and its neighboring districts struggled to service the growing numbers. Residents of the independent districts of Queens, Staten Island, the Bronx and financially strapped Brooklyn voted to become 'boroughs' of New York City in 1898.

This new metropolis absorbed a second huge wave of European immigrants, and its population exploded once again, from just over three million in 1900 to seven million in 1930. During this period, horse-drawn trolleys were abandoned as a major network of underground subways and elevated trains ('els') made the city's outer reaches easily accessible.

During the Great Depression in the 1930s, crusading mayor Fiorello La Guardia fought municipal corruption and expanded the social service network. Meanwhile, civic planner Robert Moses used his politically appointed position as a parks commissioner to wield power without the obligation of answering to voters. He used that influence to remake the city's landscape through public works projects and highways that glorified the car culture and disdained public transportation. Unfortunately, Moses had the power of a modern-day Baron Haussmann (who redesigned Paris for Napoleon) but none of the master's aesthetic sense; his schemes (which included the Triborough Bridge, Lincoln Center, several highways and Lower East Side projects) often destroyed entire neighborhoods and routed huge numbers of residents.

The Big Apple Gets Its Name

It has long been thought that New York City was dubbed 'The Big Apple' by jazz musicians who regarded a gig in Harlem as a sure sign that they had made it to the top. But Barry Popik, an amateur historian, did extensive research into the phrase and came up with a surprising answer. He discovered that the term first appeared in the 1920s, when it was used by a writer named John FitzGerald, who reported on the horse races for the *Morning Telegraph*. Apparently, stable hands in a New Orleans racetrack called a trip to a New York racecourse 'the Big Apple' – or greatest reward – for any talented thoroughbred. The slang passed into popular usage long after the newspaper – and FitzGerald – had disappeared.

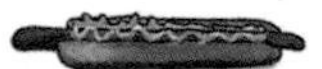

Tailspin & Renewal

In 1945, New York emerged from WWII proud and ready for business. It was one of the rare world capitals undamaged by war, a major port, the center of culture and home of the burgeoning television industry. It seemed wholly appropriate that the headquarters for the fledgling United Nations should be located here.

But throughout the 1950s, the middle class began abandoning the city for its suburbs, and New York began a slow but steady decline. Television production, manufacturing jobs and even the fabled Brooklyn Dodgers baseball team moved to the West Coast, as did with the Dodgers' crosstown rivals, the New York Giants. Manufacturing plants shut down, and it was years before a service economy took hold and replaced heavy industry. Hardly a month went by without some city institution – be it a restaurant, famous nightclub, department store or architectural landmark – being shuttered, abandoned or torn down.

By the '70s, the unreliable, graffiti-ridden subway system became an internationally recognized symbol of New York's economic tailspin. Only a massive federal loan program saved the city from bankruptcy. The summer of 1977 marked New York City's social nadir. During those months, while the city was gripped by an infernal heat wave, a serial killer later dubbed 'Son of Sam' stalked and killed young people. In the midst of it all, the city suffered a massive power outage (just days after a power company official had stated that a wide-scale blackout was impossible). Throughout the night, thousands of rioters stole millions of dollars worth of store goods. This was the city at rock bottom, out of control and forbidding.

Yet New York's prominence as a world financial center also provided a lifeline – and set the stage for the booming '80s. Culturally,

Gay & Lesbian New York

San Francisco's reputation notwithstanding, New York City has long been the true center of gay culture in the USA. At least two neighborhoods – Chelsea and Greenwich Village – have become synonymous, in popular consciousness, with gay life. Gay and lesbian visitors should feel extremely comfortable in these areas and practically anywhere else in the city.

At the beginning of the 20th century, gays and lesbians were widely known to meet in hidden clubs around the Bowery. Later, gay men gathered in the theater district, while lesbians attended drag clubs in Harlem. After WWII, Greenwich Village (once the city's largest black neighborhood) became the city's prime gay enclave, though quiet clubs and bars could be found uptown.

Throughout the '50s, the police regularly arrested gays and lesbians on morals charges, leading to the establishment of the Mattachine Society, the country's largest gay political organization. At one time, it was illegal for women to dress in men's clothing, and lesbians in drag were often arrested and transported to the Women's House of Detention on Sixth Ave and 8th St, now the site of the Jefferson Market public library. Gay men would gather in so-called tea houses in Times Square and cruise each other on the Midtown avenues well into the late '60s.

The signal moment of the modern gay rights movement occurred in New York on June 27, 1969. That night, the police launched a raid on the Stonewall Inn, a Christopher St men's bar. Its patrons were mourning the death of self-destructive singer Judy Garland, an icon for the gay community, and many angrily resisted the bust. Three nights of riots followed. The Stonewall rebellion and other protests led to the introduction of the first bill designed to ban discrimination on the basis of sexual orientation in 1971. The controversial measure was finally passed by the city council in 1986, and seven years later gay couples won important legal protections when New York allowed the registration of 'domestic partnerships.'

Today, the Gay Pride parade, held on Fifth Ave on the last weekend of June, attracts visitors from around the world, and gay Greenwich Village has become a visitor attraction. Even local gay residents complain that the area around Hudson and Christopher Sts is being ruined by day-tripping partygoers and tourists intent on getting a glimpse of gay life. That helps explain why Chelsea is now the hottest gay neighborhood in the city, with clubs, cafes, gyms and restaurants that cater to the community clustered around Eighth Ave between 14th and 23rd Sts. You'll find lesbian clubs and restaurants on the 10 blocks of Hudson St north of Houston St. There's also a thriving gay club scene in the East Village, along with a host of gay bars scattered uptown. For more information, see Gay & Lesbian Venues in the Entertainment chapter.

the city began a minor revival right after 1977, with films being shot on the streets, Broadway musicals staging a comeback and the Yankees, the town's storied baseball franchise, winning two consecutive World Series. Yet the city faced an unanticipated health crisis in the form of AIDS, and the emergence of crack cocaine led to a jump in crime. Both issues taxed the city's already overextended welfare and law enforcement resources.

The era was presided over by Ed Koch, the colorful and opinionated three-term mayor, who seemed to embody the New Yorker's ability to charm and irritate at the same time. During these anything-goes Reagan years, the city regained much of its swagger as billions were made on Wall St. But in 1989, Koch was defeated in a Democratic primary election by David Dinkins, who became the city's first black mayor. Dinkins, consistently criticized for merely presiding over a city government in need of reform, was narrowly defeated for a second term by moderate Republican Rudolph Giuliani.

Rudy cleans up the city.

A City Emergent

The Giuliani era, helped by the nationwide economic boom, has fashioned New York into the city of today's popular imagination. The current mayor, now in his second and (legally mandated) final term, conveys all the charm of a high school detention officer, and he's drawn both praise and criticism for cracking down on so-called 'quality-of-life' offenses, which range from urinating in public to sleeping on the streets. During Guiliani's reign, the crime rate has fallen sharply, the subway has remained efficient and cheap, and statistically speaking, New York has become just about the safest big city in the US.

To help matters even more, the '90s stock market boom has fueled building and spending. The city may even get around to making a huge investment in infrastructure and building a much-needed new subway line under Second Ave. To be sure, New York is by no means nirvana: The gap between rich and poor has widened, and some sectors have complained that the city has become a much meaner place for the homeless and other downtrodden New Yorkers under Giuliani's administration. Plus, the phenomenally expensive housing continues to hamper the influx of new residents. Still, with great bargains, great food and world-class cultural attractions, New York remains a prime destination.

GEOGRAPHY

New York City, a 309-sq-mile area, is largely made up of some 50 islands besides its most famous one, Manhattan. Some islands are mere clumps of land set in the water, but others include the borough of Staten Island, as well as Queens and Brooklyn, which together comprise the westernmost end of Long Island (a fact not made clear by maps of the city). In fact, only the borough of the Bronx is physically connected to the US continental mainland, though its official borders include the offshore fishing port of

City Island. In all, New York City contains 6,374 miles of streets and over 500 miles of waterfront.

The water gap between Brooklyn and Staten Island – the 'narrows' through which the first Europeans entered the area – serves as the entrance to New York Harbor, which is also accessible to ships from the north via Long Island Sound. Manhattan itself is bordered by two bodies of water: the Hudson River in the west and the East River in the east, both technically estuaries subject to tidal fluctuations.

CLIMATE

Books will usually tell you that New York's weather is 'temperate,' but the yearly averages do not convey the temperature extremes that can make life unbearable sometimes. It's unbelievably hot and humid for days on end in summer, then glacially cold and windy in December, January and February, with the odd day of warmish weather.

Each year, about 45 inches of rain fall on New York, with long wet stretches common in November and April. Snow and freezing ran fall almost exclusively from December to February, and the average total is about 30 inches, though major blizzards occur about once every four years.

In winter, high winds and Canadian weather fronts can combine to drive temperatures well below the freezing mark of 32°F (which happens to be the mean daily temperature in January). These winds are especially strong on the West Side of Manhattan off the Hudson River, and local weather reports invariably estimate the windchill factor on these days.

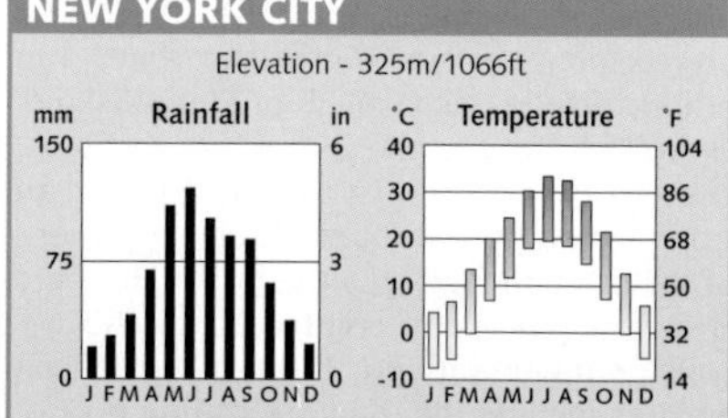

In summer, the mean daily temperature is 77°F, and days can be comfortable until the humidity rises to about 60%. In general, temperatures tend to be a bit higher in Manhattan, because the heat is absorbed by concrete and asphalt. On particularly bad days, New Yorkers will complain that 'it's not the heat, it's the humidity' that's driving them to sweat-drenched distraction.

ENVIRONMENT

In recent years, New York has come a long way in improving the quality of its air and waterways. Prior to these environmental changes, the city's docks suffered decades of decline while heavy shipping moved away from Manhattan to a 'superport' in New Jersey. But visitors will note that the city's narrow streets are anything but pristine, and its infrastructure is in desperate need of improvement (potholes riddle the streets, and flooding from century-old water mains that crack are nearly a biweekly occurrence). The city also needs to find a new spot for its garbage now that Staten Island's dump – the world's largest – has finally been closed.

The Hudson River, where kids swam off piers as recently as the 1950s, used to be a dumping ground for 200 million gallons of sewage daily. But that changed with the opening of a new sewage treatment plant on W 125th St in 1986. The worst pollution actually came from two now-closed General Electric manufacturing facilities near Albany. These factories dumped PCBs (polychlorinated biphenyls) into the river and poisoned the fish supply. Today, it's actually possible to catch striped bass, blueback herring, yellow perch and blue crab in the Hudson, and health officials say they're safe to eat if you're so inclined.

Whatever the conditions of the air and water, visitors will probably suffer most from the 24-hour noise pollution in New York – car horns, sirens and trucks bedevil those used to quieter corners of the world.

GOVERNMENT & POLITICS

New York has a long record of voting for the Democratic Party, though there are conservative pockets in the blue-collar sections of Queens and Brooklyn, and suburban Staten Island is almost exclusively Republican. Despite the Democratic tradition, socially liberal Republican reformers can be elected mayor, as proven by two-term activist mayor Rudolph Giuliani.

A former federal prosecutor, Giuliani was elected to City Hall on his second attempt in 1993, defeating the beleaguered David Dinkins. Giuliani has shaken up the city bureaucracy and taken credit for the continuing drop in crime, but he also has a well-deserved reputation as a control freak who cannot allow his administrators any independence but who also doesn't want to take the blame for administration failures. In recent years, he has run both the public schools' chancellor and the police chief out of town when they began garnering credit for good performances and threatened to diminish Giuliani's own ability to take credit for innovations in the education system and law enforcement.

In 1997, Giuliani ran for reelection and won big, due to a combination of his genuinely decent record and the great weakness of his potential Democratic opponents.

The city's political structure also includes five borough presidents, who have their own local staffs and smaller budgets for community-level works and patronage. Historically, these positions are held by career political hacks and/or mayoral candidates in waiting. The administration also includes a citywide comptroller (who serves as budget administrator and auditor) and a public advocate (who largely is concerned with consumer affairs).

New York also has a 51-member city council. These elected officials, who are paid over $70,000 a year, are meant to represent individual neighborhoods and serve as a check on mayoral power. But in reality, city council members spend little time on their four-year jobs, and many of them are lawyers who conduct full-time legal practices.

In 1994, a law was passed limiting city council members, the mayor and major office holders to just two terms. The council members unsuccessfully tried to fight the law in court and then sponsored a 1996 ballot initiative allowing current members a third term before dismissal. Although the politicos cleverly worded the ballot item so that a 'yes' vote on the measure actually meant approving the term extensions, it was convincingly rejected, and most current city council members clear out in 2001, creating an entirely new crop of local politicians.

ECONOMY

With a city budget of more than $35 billion annually, New York could stand alone as its own city-state. It is either the nation's leader or a major player in the worlds of finance, tourism, shipping and transportation and is still a prestigious address for major US corporations and nearly all prominent foreign companies.

Though the city fell seriously behind in manufacturing in the post–WWII era, it is still the country's leading producer of clothing, as well as the world's communication center. And in the global marketplace, New York remains the major financial center. In fact, the market's success has a major impact on the local economy – though it is responsible for only 4% of city jobs, Wall St tax payments account for 17% of city revenue. Plus, restaurants, bars and real estate brokers all benefit when local fat cats are doing well.

The importance of tourism to New York's financial health cannot be overstated. Some 30 million visitors come to the city each year (10 million in the Christmas holiday season alone), and they pour $18 billion into the local economy. In all, some 25,000 different New York businesses directly benefit from the tourist trade.

POPULATION & PEOPLE

Approximately half of all New York state residents live in the New York City area, with the majority of those belonging to major ethnic groups. The latest census count (1990) indicates that some 52% of the population is white, though immigration patterns in the middle of the decade virtually guarantee that non-Hispanic whites are now no longer in the majority. Blacks make up 29% of the population, and Asians account for 7%. People of Hispanic origin (all races) comprise 24%. About one million people fall into other racial categories.

Of the city's 7,322,000 residents, 28% are foreign-born, buttressing its reputation as the nation's 'melting pot,' though that term seems somewhat quaint and misapplied in this era of increased ethnic identity and, sometimes, division. Official estimates indicate that in the early '90s, the largest group of immigrants came from the Dominican Republic (about 25,000), and most settled in Washington Heights, believed to be the neighborhood with the largest recent influx of foreign-born residents. In the late '90s, an as-yet-uncounted number of West African blacks have also migrated to Harlem, the city's most famous African American neighborhood. At the same time, about 20,000 people from the former Soviet Union flooded into the Brighton Beach section of Brooklyn. A like number of immigrants from China, Taiwan and Hong Kong settled in Chinatown, pushing the borders of that neighborhood north toward the East Village.

LIZ BARRY

Young Hasidic Jew

Moreover, federal lotteries in the '80s and '90s handed out a disproportionate number of resident visas to immigrants from Ireland and Poland. As a result, many Poles moved to the already established Eastern European neighborhoods of Williamsburg and Greenpoint in Brooklyn, while the Irish (who are basically everywhere) have added to their traditional stronghold in the Riverdale section of the Bronx.

Some of the new subcultures may be here just temporarily. Some estimates suggest that more than 5000 young middle-class Japanese are currently living in the East Village. They've been attracted by the neighborhood's cutting-edge reputation and the fact that a cheap dollar takes the sting out of ever-increasing rent rates. Walking around the East Village, you'll see these young Japanese even adopting 'hip-hop' style and wearing outrageous Afros in a weird clash of retro styling.

Taken as a whole, New York City is a singular example of racial diversity. Visitors from abroad are often stunned at the variety of color in a single subway car. The city is home to the largest Chinese population in the US, along with the country's largest bloc of Asian Indians. On Labor Day, hundreds of thousands of Caribbean-born immigrants attend the Caribbean Day parade in Brooklyn. New York City claims to have more Jews than anywhere outside of Israel, more native Greeks than anywhere outside of Athens, more native Russians than anywhere outside of Moscow, and perhaps more native Irish than anywhere outside of the British isles. Differences in culture and undocumented immigration may make some of these boasts statistically unprovable, but a walk through several of the city's neighborhoods leaves the impression that the statement is probably not far off the mark.

Blacks

There are about two million blacks living in New York City. African slaves first arrived in New York in 1644, when it was still part of the Dutch colony of New Netherland. By the time the American colonies went to war with Britain, New York's black population numbered about 2000, and slaves fought on both sides of the conflict in the hope of winning their freedom. (After the war, the state of New York freed those who fought in the local armed forces.) By the early 19th century, the abolitionist movement had been established in New York City, along with *Freedom's Journal*, the nation's first black newspaper. But voting rights were not bestowed on black males until well after the Civil War, in 1870. At the same time, black citizens found themselves losing economic ground to immigrants from Ireland and Eastern Europe.

By the early 20th century, migrating blacks from the south triggered the development of Harlem in Upper Manhattan, helping to create a well-defined community with churches, black-owned businesses and nightclubs that welcomed whites from other neighborhoods. For the first time, West Indians became a significant part of the area's population. But the 'Harlem Renaissance' – as captured in writings by Langston Hughes and in photographs by James VanDerZee – ended with the economic devastation of the Great Depression.

After WWII, the economic advancement of blacks again began to lag behind that of second- and third-generation white ethnic groups, but city officials did little to address the situation until riots broke out in Harlem in 1964. As in many US cities, lower-income black residents were stuck in ugly, decaying housing projects. By the 1970s, much of what was left of the black middle class had abandoned the city and followed earlier white residents in an exodus to the suburbs. In recent years, though, a new population of West African immigrants has started to bring life back to the heart of Harlem, with new small businesses opening up throughout the neighborhood.

Hispanics

About half of New York City's 1.8 million Hispanic residents are of Puerto Rican descent. They began migrating here from the island in significant numbers during the Depression and began displacing Italians in East Harlem. Throughout the 1960s, political activism by 'Nuyoricans' led to increased recognition of their contribution to city life and to the establishment of several important cultural institutions, including the Museo del Barrio near East Harlem.

Over the past 20 years, Latinos from many other countries have arrived in significant numbers. Immigrants from Ecuador and Colombia have created new communities in Queens, and the Washington Heights neighborhood in Manhattan is home to many former citizens of the Dominican Republic and El Salvador.

Jews

The first Jews, a group of 24 refugees fleeing persecution in Brazil, came to New York in 1654, when it was still a Dutch colony. Jews have been an important part of the city's population and politics ever since. Until the early 20th century, most of this population lived in Manhattan's Lower East Side, and the neighborhood still retains its traditional character, even though most New Yorkers of Jewish background now live elsewhere. In Brooklyn, the neighborhoods of Crown Heights and Williamsburg are still home to large numbers of Orthodox Jews, and an influx of immigrants from the Soviet Union during the '80s added to their numbers. Today New York's Jews make up about 12% of New York City's total population. They are the city's second-largest ethnic voting bloc, behind blacks, but are the most effective ethnic group politically because they vote in higher numbers.

Racial Tensions

Former mayor David Dinkins often spoke of New York City as a 'gorgeous mosaic' of differing peoples. But several well-publicized incidents have painted an uglier picture, largely because of a growing level of distrust between African Americans and other ethnic groups. In 1986, a black man confronted by a gang of white teens was beaten to death in Howard Beach, Brooklyn, leading city officials to promise a crackdown on so-called bias crimes or hate crimes.

Tensions between Jews and African Americans have resulted in two separate incidents that have rocked the city. When a black child was accidentally run over by a member of a Hasidic Jewish sect in Brooklyn's Crown Heights neighborhood during the summer of 1991, rumors quickly spread that the girl had been refused treatment by a Jewish ambulance crew. During several days of rioting that followed, an innocent Hasidic man was murdered by an angry mob.

More recent years have seen some devastating cases of police brutality or excessive force used against black New Yorkers. In one of the more publicized cases, four police officers shot an unarmed West African immigrant named Amadou Diallo a total of 19 times and expended 41 bullets in total. According to their court testimony, the officers first thought Diallo was reaching for a gun but later realized he had been reaching for his wallet, not a weapon. (The officers were acquitted by a jury of murder or misconduct, to general outrage, in February 2000.)

But despite these well-publicized tragedies, millions of New Yorkers live with each other and walk the streets together every day, usually without incident, and visitors who refuse to visit ethnic neighborhoods are, in their own way, giving in to irrational fears.

ARTS

Dance

Since the time Isadora Duncan (1877–1927) brought modern dance to the attention of New York audiences, the city has been home to most of the country's prominent companies and choreographers, including Martha Graham (1894–1991). Graham choreographed more than 140 dances and developed a new dance technique, still taught by her New York–based school, that emphasizes dramatic narrative.

The New York City Ballet was founded by Russian-born choreographer George Balanchine (1904–83) in 1948. The legendary talent combined traditional ballet and modern influences. Jerome Robbins (1918–1998), who took over from Balanchine in 1983, had previously collaborated with Leonard Bernstein on several of Broadway's biggest musicals, including *West Side Story* (1957).

Paul Taylor (born 1930) and Twyla Tharp (born 1942), two students of Martha Graham, borrow themes from popular culture. Taylor, who began with the Merce Cunningham company, heads his own group; Tharp is now associated with the American Ballet Theater.

Alvin Ailey (1931–89) set up his Alvin Ailey American Dance Theater in 1958, giving new prominence to African American dancers performing contemporary works. His most famous work is *Revelations* (1960), a dance suite set to gospel music. Mark Morris (born 1956) is a celebrated dancer and choreographer who formed his own dance group in 1988; the troupe performs original works, such as his reworking of *The Nutcracker* (called *The Hard Nut)* at the Brooklyn Academy of Music. The Dance Theater of Harlem, founded in Harlem by Arthur Mitchell in the late '60s, was the first major black classical company and appears regularly at Lincoln Center. Today, the Ailey, Graham and Taylor companies appear annually at City Center in Midtown, while Chelsea's Joyce Theater is the venue for the work of the Cunningham company and newer groups.

For more information, see the Dance section of the Entertainment chapter.

Music

Classical New York is home to some of the foremost classical music and operatic institutions in the world. Lincoln Center for the Performing Arts is the venue for such prestigious organizations as the New York Philharmonic Orchestra, the Metropolitan Opera Company and the New York City Opera. The century-old Carnegie Hall is the famous venue for solo and orchestral performances.

For years, New York attracted foreign-born composers and conductors, often because the city was home to some of the finest recording facilities in the world. Gustav Mahler (1860–1911) served as musical director of the New York Philharmonic in the last years of his life, and Arturo Toscanini (1867–1957) achieved great fame

Tin Pan Alley

A musical town, New York gave birth to most of the pop music industry during the first part of the 20th century. In the early days of pop, the composers and publishers of the music were usually more important figures than the performers. These famous tunesmiths worked together in offices on W 28th St between Broadway and Sixth Ave, a stretch dubbed 'Tin Pan Alley.' Here, they collaborated on a lot of faux ethnic music, along with light 'ragtime' jazz and sophisticated Broadway showstoppers.

In time, Tin Pan Alley became less of a geographic locale and more a state of mind, as people began to use the term for all popular music, no matter where it was created. The song factories diminished in power and influence with the emergence of individual stylists like Bing Crosby and Frank Sinatra, charismatic singers like Elvis Presley and rock and roll groups that wrote their own music (the Beatles being the most famous example). Still, Tin Pan Alley group writing lasted in one form or another into the late 1960s.

in the US as head of the Philharmonic and the NBC Orchestra.

Though born and educated in Massachusetts, Leonard Bernstein (1918–90) built his career in New York and became the first major American-born classical conductor. He achieved fame in 1943, when he stepped in for the ailing Bruno Walter at the last minute and did such an expert job conducting the New York Philharmonic that he became the subject of a front page article in the next day's *New York Times*. Later, Bernstein became musical director of the Philharmonic while making frequent forays into popular music, most notably with the stage musicals *On the Town*, *Candide* and *West Side Story*.

John Cage (1912–92) moved from his native Los Angeles to New York in the 1940s and became known as the leading avant-garde composer, using atonal structures and even silence in his famous works.

Jazz Ragtime, the progenitor of jazz, was widely popular in New York during the early 20th century, thanks to Scott Joplin (1868–1917), whose 'Maple Leaf Rag' is a classic example of the form, and to the young Irving Berlin (1888–1989), whose 'Alexander's Ragtime Band' illustrates his Tin Pan Alley brand of ragtime.

After cities like Kansas City and New Orleans gave way to New York as the US jazz capital in the 1940s, every performer of note (and thousands of wannabes) headed to Manhattan to be discovered. Jazz became mainstream, moving from clubs to orchestral spaces, thanks to the works of George Gershwin (1898–1937) and Duke Ellington (1899–1974). (Ellington's famous recording 'Take the A Train' grew out of the first line of instructions he gave to composer Billy Strayhorn on how to get to his Harlem apartment.)

In the '40s, trumpeter Dizzy Gillespie (1917–93) and saxophonist Charlie Parker (1920–55) ushered in bebop, which quickly gave way to the freer expressions of trumpeter Miles Davis (1926–91) and Sonny Rollins (born 1929). Many old speakeasies of the '20s – particularly those on 52nd St – became jazz clubs in the post-WWII era.

In the early 1960s, jazz was caught in a struggle between structuralists and those seeking unfettered free expression. By the late '70s, jazz had become an expressive

ANGUS OBORN

Tribute to Duke Ellington, Spanish Harlem

free-for-all, but a traditionalist movement has emerged in recent years, with trumpeter Wynton Marsalis and sax sensation Joshua Redman leading the way.

Today, Greenwich Village is still the site of many jazz clubs, including the 50-year-old Village Vanguard (see the Entertainment chapter), arguably the most famous jazz venue in the world. Each summer, the city hosts at least three major jazz festivals, and in 1996 Wynton Marsalis began the annual 'Jazz at Lincoln Center' program, bringing dozens of major contemporary artists to the cultural mecca.

Rock, Folk & Punk Most of the preeminent figures in US popular music (Bob Dylan, Jimi Hendrix) got their start elsewhere before heading to New York for validation and increased popularity. In fact, Alan Freed, the disc jockey credited with popularizing the term 'rock and roll,' was a

The New York Sound

In the 1970s, the music industry moved west, following the migrations of the film and television industry before it. But as the songwriting geniuses from Tin Pan Alley settled in a sunnier climate, their complacency was reflected in their music: the 'adult-orientated rock' that dominated the radio airwaves. Independent record labels that had made '60s protest music or other rock that captured the energy of the streets found they couldn't compete. And bebop jazz, which shook the city from the basements of Harlem through the clubs of 52nd St, died on both the commercial and creative fronts, as fusion jazz challenged its supremacy.

But Gotham music was not dead, or even sleeping. In the late '70s, a new generation of black and Puerto Rican New Yorkers began creating innovative street music called rap, which expressed such controversial themes as conflicts between blacks and whites, struggles between inner-city youth and police and rivalries among different street gangs. This gritty music gave rise to an urban subculture that became known as hip-hop, encompassing not only music but also fashion and graffiti art. Twenty years later, it's impossible to turn on a radio anywhere in the world and not hear music heavily influenced by the hip-hop sound generated in the New York streets of the '70s.

The hip-hop beat, the foundation of rap music, thumped to life around 1976 in the South Bronx, at the hands of a Bronx DJ known as Kool Herc. He's credited with discovering that playing two copies of the same record and repeating the 'breaks' over and over dramatically increased the dancing pleasure of his audience. (The break is the 'funkiest' snippet of a record, usually the point when percussion and bass meet up on a beat.) The so-called Grandmaster DJs of rap also began scratching LPs on turntables, creating a frenetic backdrop for the spoken-word lyrics that make up rap music.

When it started in the '70s, rap reacted against the upscale pretensions of disco, the most commercial music of the time. The Sugarhill Gang's 'Rapper's Delight' borrowed disco's perfect bass line from Chic's 'Good Times' to create the first international rap hit in 1979. And just as rappers tapped into mainstream music, mainstream bands soon began siphoning some energy from rap. The pop group Blondie was among the first to produce a crossover rap hit with 'Rapture,' which makes references to Bronx rappers Grandmaster Flash and Fab Five Freddie.

By the early '80s, technology forced a new wave of innovation in the hip-hop world, with disco drum machines and computer samplers gradually replacing record turntables and mixers. They've never been totally replaced, though – Funkmaster Flex still uses the 'wheels of steel' on his popular and influential weekly radio show.

The style of rap music also began to change in the '80s, as 'nu school' lyrical masterpieces exploded from the New York area. Some of the new stars included A Tribe Called Quest and De La Soul, both known for their gentler styles and the intelligent 'street poetry' in their songs. Public

Cleveland broadcaster who moved to New York to seek a bigger audience.

The Tin Pan Alley system of writers feeding songs to performers, which can be traced back to the early part of the 20th century, worked for the first wave of doo-wop and rock groups. But songwriters like Jerry Leiber and Mike Stoller ('Hound Dog' and 'Don't Be Cruel') and Carole King ('Be My Baby') eventually gave way to a new generation of singer-songwriters.

New York became the rock club capital of the world. By the '60s, performers like Jimi Hendrix were making waves in clubs like Cafe Wha?, while Dylan headed a group of singers based in the club Folk City. By the '70s, homegrown alternative rock groups such as the Ramones and the New York Dolls were appearing at the now-defunct Max's Kansas City.

Certainly, the most famous club of this era is CBGB, on the Bowery in the East

The New York Sound

Enemy, which some critics consider to be the greatest rap music group ever, also reinvigorated the genre during the '80s, using its hard-edged sound to express strong political views about race issues.

By the early '90s, 'gangsta' rap, a genre steeped in urban violence, had evolved into the most popular style of music in the hip-hop world. But the posturing of Los Angeles and New York 'gangsta crews' had deadly results, with the shooting deaths of the biggest hip-hop stars of the '90s, rivals Biggie Smalls and Tupac Shakur.

The subsequent decline of gangsta culture has led to the prominence of female performers such as Lil' Kim, who hails from Brooklyn, and Queen Latifah and Lauryn Hill, both of whom came out of the Newark, New Jersey, area. Some of their music expresses feminist themes or champions other socially conscious issues.

Queen Latifah

Today, there are a multitude of flourishing hip-hop clans outside New York, each with their own style and stars – but they can all trace their origins to the break masters in the South Bronx. In the city today, virtually every dance club's sound reflects this influence. See the Entertainment chapter for more information.

Village. Though its initials stand for 'Country, Bluegrass and Blues,' CBGB became known as ground zero for the '70s punk and alternative movements. The Talking Heads, the Police, the Dead Kennedys and Black Flag are among the many groups that have appeared there in the past 20 years.

Perhaps the most influential New York–based contemporary musician is Lou Reed (born 1943), one of the founders of the Velvet Underground. Reed's work with that group and his subsequent solo works ('Sweet Jane,' 'A Perfect Day') created an edgy, druggy, urban sound that's been echoed by dozens of bands worldwide. He now lives in the West Village with his companion, singer Laurie Anderson.

Theater

New York theater is, to a large extent, US theater. The first theater district was centered around the area now known as Herald Square. It was the site of the first Metropolitan Opera House and many musical theaters.

Vaudeville, the US version of British musical comedy, was largely performed in venues around Times Square, which is today's center of 'legitimate theater.' The first major theatrical impresario was Florenz Ziegfeld (1867–1932) who was best known for his 'Ziegfeld Follies,' featuring scantily clad female dancers. Performers like Buster Keaton, James Cagney, George Burns, the Marx Brothers and Al Jolson got their start in vaudeville, honing the talents that would make them famous in other media.

Alternative, experimental drama arose in New York City in the 1930s. The most prominent playwright of the era was Eugene O'Neill (1888–1953), whose works include *The Iceman Cometh* and the autobiographical *Long Day's Journey into Night*.

Today, Arthur Miller (born 1915) ranks as the most powerful living American playwright. Besides his Pulitzer Prize–winning *Death of a Salesman*, his famous works include *A View from the Bridge* (1955) and *The Crucible* (1953), which dramatized the Salem witch trials but indirectly commented on the anticommunist fervor of McCarthyism. Miller continues to produce new plays, but the decline of serious work on Broadway has meant that his most recent plays *(Broken Glass* and *The Ride Down Mount Morgan)* debuted in London before coming to the US stage.

Alternative theater has produced some of the most prestigious American playwrights of recent decades, some of whose works have also shown on Broadway. Sam Shepard (born 1943) is known for his thought-provoking plays, including *Buried Child*.

August Wilson (born 1945), the country's best-known black playwright, has found success on Broadway with *The Piano Lesson*, *Fences* and *Seven Guitars*, along with other works examining the African American experience. David Mamet (born 1947) has examined the seamier side of American life in plays like *Speed the Plow* and *American Buffalo*.

Neil Simon (born 1927), who got his start writing TV sketch comedy, is the modern playwright most closely associated with New York. His plays *The Odd Couple*, *Barefoot in the Park*, *Plaza Suite*, *Brighton Beach Memoirs* and *Biloxi Blues* have all been made into films. Though a Broadway theater has been named after him, Simon's last New York production, *London Suite*, actually opened in a smaller downtown theater.

Musicals have always been a mainstay of New York theater, and the Tin Pan Alley composers George Gershwin (1898–1937) and Cole Porter (1893–1964) produced many of the most enduring works, such as *Porgy & Bess* and *Kiss Me Kate*, respectively. Stephen Sondheim (born 1930) has written popular and experimental Broadway fare, including the lyrics for *West Side Story* and the music and words for *A Funny Thing Happened on the Way to the Forum* and *Sunday in the Park with George*.

Broadway and Times Square are currently experiencing a renaissance, thanks to big-dollar investment from companies like Disney, but this infusion of cash from corporations has led to some uninspired productions, including adaptations of movies such as *Beauty and the Beast*.

Recently, some Broadway productions have been trying to look more like off-

Broadway shows, with relatively austere sets and offbeat themes. These 'alternative' musicals include *Chicago* and *Rent*, both of which have become major Broadway hits. Still, though, many of the 'serious' plays in New York come from London.

Painting

When all is said and done, New York's place in art history looms largest as the home of many important collectors and gallery owners rather than as the inspirational center for artists. Nonetheless, it has long boasted an avant-garde art scene that periodically causes exciting controversies in the art world.

In 1913, for example, a young French painter named Marcel Duchamp (1887–1968) caused a sensation among the 300,000 people who attended the 1913 'Armory' show in New York (officially called the International Exhibition of Modern Art) and saw his *Nude Descending a Staircase*. Critics noted that the cubist painting didn't seem to portray a recognizable nude *or* a staircase. Duchamp responded that that was exactly the point, and thus the New York school of 'dada,' named after the French slang for hobbyhorse, began. Duchamp, fellow countryman Francis Picabia (1879–1953) and American Man Ray (1890–1976) led a dadaist group known for its antiwar attitudes and deconstructive art that sought to shock and offend. By the '20s, most of the dadaists had moved on, but the movement remained influential for the rest of the century.

In a more realist vein, the famous works of Edward Hopper (1882–1967) portray a New York of long nights and solitary citizens. *Night Hawks*, one of his signature works, focuses on late-night patrons at a coffee shop; it's displayed at the Art Institute in Chicago.

American art flourished after WWII with the emergence of a new school of painting called abstract expressionism, also called the New York School. Simply defined, it combined spontaneity of expression with abstract forms composed haphazardly. Abstract expressionism dominated world art until the mid-1980s, and two of its most famous exponents were Jackson Pollock (1912–56) and Willem de Kooning (1904–97). The Dutch painter Piet Mondrian (1872–1944) moved to New York in 1940 and used jazz music as his inspiration for a series of famous abstract works.

Beginning in the 1950s, modern art began to borrow images and themes from popular culture. At Andy Warhol's Factory studio in New York, the artist and his hangers-on commented on culture through many media. Warhol (1928–87) created the pop art movement, which encompassed mass-produced artworks, experimental films *(The Chelsea Girls)* and the monthly downtown magazine *Interview*. The '60s also saw the emergence of modernists Jasper Johns (born 1930) and Roy Lichtenstein (1923–97).

Andy Warhol – aren't the 15 minutes up yet?

In the '80s, Warhol's legacy of the artist as celebrity spawned a host of well-known painters and illustrators whose work, to many critics, is somewhat questionable. But several of the artists/hustlers have broken out from the SoHo gallery scene to become internationally known, among them Julian Schnabel, Kenny Scharf and the late Keith Haring, who began his career as an underground graffiti artist.

Sculpture

The city's museums are filled with many examples of fine sculpture. On the street, most of the statuary celebrates the past. The first major example of public outdoor art was a statue of King George III constructed in 1770 in Bowling Green; it was torn down six years later after the first reading of the Declaration of Independence.

Other public monuments have fared a bit more favorably. Among them are a statue to George Washington in Union Square (1856) and the Arch in Washington Square Park (1889), also dedicated to the first president, and the statue of Colonial patriot Nathan Hale (1890) at City Hall Park. The Mall in Central Park features bronze portrayals of famous artists and statesmen (1876 to 1908), including Beethoven, Shakespeare and Robert Burns. Madison Square Park holds a number of statues of Union Army Civil War heroes.

More-contemporary monuments can be found in the park at United Nations headquarters and all throughout ornate Rockefeller Center; these include Paul Manship's *Prometheus* (1934), overlooking the water fountain-skating rink, and Isamu Noguchi's *News* (1940), above the entrance of the Associated Press Building. Lincoln Center features Alexander Calder's *Le Guichet* (1963), at the New York Library for the Performing Arts, and Henry Moore's *Reclining Figure* (1965), in the reflecting pool in front of the Vivian Beaumont Theater.

Photography

Photography developed as an art form at the end of the 19th century thanks to the work and influence of Alfred Stieglitz (1864–1946), who produced a number of images of New York City.

In the 1920s and '30s, Man Ray (1890–1976) became a leading figure in modernism's move away from traditional art forms, as he experimented with new techniques and surreal images. But Ray moved from New York after his dada years and settled in Paris.

The city's role as a publishing center provided many opportunities for photographers, particularly with the addition of advertising agencies, fashion companies and news-gathering organizations. *Life* magazine was influential in the development of photojournalism, having spawned the famous Magnum photo agency. Among the most prominent photojournalists working in New York were the pioneering Margaret Bourke-White (1904–71), who was one of the first female photographers attached to the US armed forces, and Alfred Eisenstaedt (1898–1995), a portraitist and news photographer who took the famous image of a sailor kissing a nurse in Times Square at the end of WWII.

In more recent years, many photographers (including Richard Avedon, Herb Ritts and Annie Liebowitz) have become as famous for their commercial work as their more artistic endeavors. Others have forged careers with work that almost never reaches the general public. Prominent in this latter group are Nan Goldin, who charted the lives (and deaths) of her transvestite and junkie friends from the '70s to the present day, and Cindy Sherman, who specializes in conceptual series of photographs (such as those inspired by movie stills and crime scene photos).

Architecture

While many past treasures have been lost (like the much-lamented old Pennsylvania Station, which was demolished in the early 1960s), visitors to New York will nevertheless be able to explore the city's history in its architecture. Buildings all over New York are of interest to the student of architecture. The outer boroughs are filled with some of the oldest buildings in the United States, from the 17th-century John Bowne House in

Queens to the Williamsburg-like Richmond Town Restoration in Staten Island.

You'll discover grand architectural surprises in northern Manhattan, such as transplanted medieval monasteries at the Cloisters and the stunning yet little-visited Audubon Terrace, with its glowing, marble-faced Hispanic Society of America and the American Numismatic Society. Roosevelt Island features tumble-down Gothic ruins, and both Columbia University in Manhattan and Bronx Community College (New York University's former northern campus) boast imperial, beaux arts campuses that put other schools to shame.

Probably the city's largest collection of significant buildings can be spied in the Lower Manhattan, Greenwich Village and Midtown areas. These structures range from the 18th- and 19th-century bohemian haunts of the Village to Midtown prewar skyscrapers like the Chrysler building, and from the 19th-century cast-iron structures of SoHo to seminal modernist towers like the Seagram building. There are even groundbreaking new structures to be found. Just walk down 57th St east of 5th Ave and marvel at the just-opened LVMH Tower, with its crystal-faceted facade by Pulitzer Prize–winning architect Christian de Portzamparc.

Stanford White's New York

Many of New York's most impressive buildings were designed by Stanford White, the most talented and colorful architect of the Gilded Age. His firm (McKim, Mead and White) created many of New York City's beaux arts masterpieces, including the original Pennsylvania Station, built in 1911. Widely considered to be White's greatest creation, Penn Station was demolished in 1965 for a newer facility, over the protests of many prominent public figures, including modernist architect Philip Johnson.

RICHARD I'ANSON

Washington Square Arch

Once the elegant old train palace had been replaced by the ugly, inadequate and badly designed Penn Station/Madison Square Garden complex that now stands in Midtown Manhattan, public outcry forced the creation of the city's Landmarks Preservation Commission. Thanks to the laws protecting landmarks and to increased public awareness of the city's architectural treasures, other works by White – including the Player's Club on Gramercy Park, the Washington Square Arch and the Brooklyn Museum – will remain untouched by the wrecker's ball. In Chinatown, take note of the old **Bowery Savings Bank** building at 130 Bowery, designed in 1894 by White. The bank's Romanesque archway and vaulted gold-leaf interior are a quiet respite from the noisy fruit stands and traffic on the corner of Bowery and Grand St.

White himself met an ignominious end. A roué and spendthrift art collector, he was nearly bankrupt by 1905. He engaged in a wild affair with the young married socialite Evelyn Nesbit, and they often met for trysts in his apartment, located above an earlier version of Madison Square Garden. It was there, in the roof-garden restaurant, that White was shot and killed by Nesbit's jealous husband, Harry K Thaw. Subsequent revelations about the May-December romance during Thaw's trial permanently damaged White's reputation and led a jury to declare Thaw not guilty by reason of insanity.

SOCIETY & CONDUCT

Being 'on' may be the New York style, but there isn't any particular look you can adopt to fit in here – practically anything goes, unless you're looking to dine in a fine restaurant on the Upper East Side, where jacket and tie are required. Yet even the most confident tourist can be marked as an outsider in dozens of tiny ways – by actually looking up at the buildings you pass, crossing the street at a corner instead of jaywalking, or attempting to read the *New York Times* on a packed subway train without first folding it lengthwise and then in half.

RELIGION

New York City, often derided by 'religious' outsiders as some sort of modern-day Sodom, has more than 6000 places of worship – including Hindu and Buddhist temples and Jehovah's Witness kingdom halls.

Catholics are the single biggest religious group in New York City – about 44% of the population – and there are actually two dioceses here (one for Brooklyn and another for the rest of the city). Jews make up 12% of the population, as do Baptists. Methodists, Lutherans, Presbyterians and Episcopalians total a combined 10%. About 8% of the population classifies itself as agnostic or nonbelieving.

Muslims have been part of the city's religious landscape since the late 1950s and now number more than 500,000. Most adherents follow the Sunni Islam tradition. In 1991, a huge new mosque opened at 96th St and Third Ave – a monument to the city's fastest growing sect.

LANGUAGE

American English has borrowed words from the languages of successive waves of immigrants who made New York City their point of arrival. From the Germans came words like 'hoodlum'; from Yiddish-speaking Jews, words like 'schmuck' (fool); from the Irish, words like 'galore.'

While you will immediately recognize the elongated vowels of New York City dwellers, the local accent (especially in Manhattan) sounds like a much milder version of the 'Noo Yawk Tawk' popularized in film and TV. Older residents often have a peculiar cadence in their voices, pronouncing 'Broadway' and 'receipt' with a heavy emphasis on the *first* syllable. The New York accent grows stronger in the outer boroughs, provided the person you're speaking to was not born in another country!

The city's huge Hispanic population has led to the emergence of Spanish as a semi-official second language. But so far, a Spanish-English hybrid has not developed for popular use, though everyone knows that *bodega* is slang for a corner convenience store, a corruption of the word for wine cellar.

It's easier to identify common phrases used, or at least recognized, by most New Yorkers, though even this is tricky because rap music is changing English in profound (but uncharted) ways. The meaning of phrases even changes between neighborhoods: Asking for a 'regular' coffee in Midtown means you'll get it with milk and a bit of sugar. The same request at a Wall St area shop will lead the server to throw three heaping spoonfuls of the sweet stuff in the cup, because that's the way the hyper stockbrokers and lawyers like it served.

Facts for the Visitor

WHEN TO GO

New York is a year-round destination, so there isn't really an 'off-season' when local prices drop substantially. Winter bargains are sometimes available for airfares to the city, and many of the major hotels offer package deals for the slower months from January to mid-March.

If you want to base your decision solely on the weather, generally the nicest and most temperate time to visit is in mid-September to October, along with all of May and early June. Unfortunately, as these months are popular with tourists, hotel prices are scaled accordingly.

ORIENTATION

Most of Manhattan is easy to navigate, thanks to a street plan imposed by a city planning commission in 1811. The plan covered the area north of Houston St and featured a grid system of 14 named or numbered avenues running the north-south length of the island, crossed by east-west numbered streets. (If you intend to do a lot of walking, be aware that along the avenues, 20 blocks is approximately 1 mile.)

Because the grid system was established long before the advent of the automobile, modern Manhattan suffers from tremendous traffic congestion, giving rise to the term 'gridlock.' This street plan had at least one other unintended consequence: The narrow streets precluded the creation of grand avenues in the European tradition and discouraged the creation of buildings set back on large tracts of property. There was nowhere to go but up, and by the late 19th century Manhattan had a cluster of 'skyscrapers' – prominent, multistory office buildings.

Above Washington Square, Fifth Ave serves as the dividing line between the 'East Side' and the 'West Side.' Cross-street numbers begin there and grow higher toward each river, generally (but not exclusively) in 100-digit increments per block. Therefore, the Hard Rock Cafe, at 221 W 57th St, is slightly more than two blocks west of Fifth Ave.

Most New Yorkers give out addresses in shorthand by listing the cross street first and the avenue second (eg, 'we're at 33rd and Third'). If you are given an address on

KIM GRANT

an avenue – such as '1271 Sixth Ave' – be sure to ask for the nearest cross street to save time.

In the oldest part of New York City, from 14th St to the southern tip of Manhattan, travel becomes a bit trickier. Streets that perhaps began as cow paths or merchants' byways snake along in a haphazard manner, which is why it is possible today to stand at the corner of W 4th St and W 10th St in Greenwich Village.

Broadway, the only avenue to cut diagonally across the island, was originally a woodland path used by Native Americans; in some form or other, it runs from the tip of the island all the way to the state capital of Albany, 150 miles away. Today, Wall St stands at the place where the 17th-century Dutch residents of New Amsterdam constructed a wooden barrier at the town's northern border to ward off attacks from hostile natives.

MAPS

Lonely Planet publishes a pocket-size laminated map of New York City; it's available at all bookstores. You can also pick up downtown Manhattan maps for free in the lobby of any decent hotel. If you want to explore the city at large, buy a five-borough street atlas. Geographia and Hagstrom both publish paperback-size editions that sell for about $12.

Most subway stations in Manhattan have 'Passenger Information Centers' next to the token booth; these feature a wonderfully detailed map of the surrounding neighborhood, with all points of interests clearly marked. Taking a look before heading up the stairs may save you from getting lost.

You can buy maps at the Hagstrom Map and Travel Center (☎ 212-398-1222), 57 W 43rd St near Sixth Ave, and the Rand McNally Travel Store (☎ 212-758-7488), 150 E 52nd St between Lexington and Third, which ships globes and atlases worldwide. Both stores sell colorful wall maps of Manhattan made by the Identity Map Company for $30. Though not practical for walking the city, these detailed maps make a great souvenir of your trip.

TOURIST OFFICES

Local Tourist Offices

NYC & Company (also known as the Convention & Visitors Bureau) has opened its sleek new Information Center at 810 Seventh Ave at 53rd St in the Times Square area. You can pick up hundreds of brochures about cultural events here. The center's 24-hour phone line (☎ 212-397-8222, 800-692-8474 in the US) offers information and reservations for special events. (To speak directly with a multilingual counselor, call ☎ 212-484-1222.) The center is open 8:30 am to 6 pm weekdays and 9 am to 5 pm on weekends. You can also visit the Web site at www.nycvisit.com.

The Big Apple Greeters Program also offers special events information on its hotline (☎ 212-669-2896, fax 212-669-3685). The program's 500 volunteers welcome visitors to the city with free tours of lesser-known neighborhoods. These tours have been praised by many visitors. Some greeters are multilingual and can accommodate foreign tourists; others specialize in helping the disabled. You must make reservations in advance. The Web site (www.bigapplegreeter.org) has links in French, German and Spanish.

The New York State Travel Information Center (☎ 800-225-5697), 810 Seventh Ave at 53rd St, issues books that cover other areas upstate.

DOCUMENTS

Passports & Visas

Canadians must have proper proof of Canadian citizenship, such as a citizenship card with photo ID or a passport. Visitors from other countries must have a valid passport, and many visitors also require a US visa.

However, there is a reciprocal visa-waiver program in which citizens of certain countries may enter the USA for stays of 90 days or less with a passport but without first obtaining a US visa. Currently these countries are Andorra, Argentina, Australia, Austria, Belgium, Brunei, Denmark, Finland, France, Germany, Iceland, Ireland, Italy, Japan, Liechtenstein, Luxembourg, Monaco, the Netherlands, New Zealand,

Norway, San Marino, Slovenia, Spain, Sweden, Switzerland, and the UK. Under this program you must have a roundtrip ticket that is nonrefundable in the USA, and you will not be allowed to extend your stay beyond 90 days.

Other travelers will need to obtain a visa from a US consulate or embassy. In most countries, the process can be done by mail. To apply for a visa, your passport should be valid for at least six months longer than your intended stay in the USA, and you'll need to submit a recent photo (1½ inches square or 37mm x 37mm) with the application. Documents of financial stability and/or guarantees from a US resident are sometimes required, particularly for those from Third World countries.

Visa applicants may be required to 'demonstrate binding obligations' that will ensure their return to their countries. Because of this requirement, those planning to travel through other countries before arriving in the USA are generally better off applying for their US visa while they are still in their home country – rather than while they are traveling.

The most common visa is a Non-Immigrant Visitors Visa, which is available in two forms, B1 for business purposes and B2 for tourism or visiting friends and relatives. A visitor's visa is good for one or five years with multiple entries, and it specifically prohibits the visitor from taking paid employment in the USA. The validity period for US visitor visas depends on what country you're from. The length of time you'll be allowed to stay in the USA is ultimately determined by US immigration authorities at the port of entry. If you're coming to the USA to work or study, you will probably need a different type of visa, and the company or institution where you're going to work should make the arrangements. Allow six months in advance for processing the application.

Visa Extensions If you want, need or hope to stay in the USA beyond the date stamped on your passport, go to the local Immigration and Naturalization Service (INS) office, Information Branch, 3rd floor, 26 Federal Plaza near Worth St, *before* the stamped date to apply for an extension. Going *after* that date will usually lead to an uncomfortable conversation with an INS official who'll assume you want to work illegally. If you find yourself in that situation, it's a good idea to bring a US citizen with you to vouch for your character and to have some verification that you have enough currency to support yourself.

Travel Insurance

No matter how you're traveling, make sure you take out travel insurance. This should cover you not only for medical expenses and luggage theft or loss but also for cancellations or delays in your travel arrangements, and everyone should be covered for the worst possible case, such as an accident that requires hospital treatment and a flight home. Most policies also reimburse you if you lose your ticket. Coverage depends on your insurance and type of ticket, so ask both your insurer and your ticket-issuing agency to explain the finer points. When inquiring about insurance, make sure that the policy is for primary coverage and includes a 24-hour help line for emergencies.

Coverage usually costs between $80 and $150 for a 21-day trip, with surcharges for additional days running $3 to $5 extra for each day. Travel Guard (☎ 800-826-1300) is one of the better insurers available in the USA, offering comprehensive service. Access America (☎ 800-284-8300) offers similar options. The international student travel policies handled by STA Travel (www.statravel.com) are usually reasonably priced.

Buy travel insurance as early as possible. If you buy it the week before you fly, you may find, for instance, that you're not covered for delays to your flight caused by strikes or other industrial action that may have been in force before you took out the insurance.

After purchasing your insurance, make sure you keep a separate record of all your ticket details – or better still, a photocopy of it. Also make a copy of your policy, in case the original is lost.

Driver's License

You will need a driver's license and good driving record to rent a car. You may want to obtain an International Drivers Permit from your national automobile association before you leave for the USA.

Also, you should carry your license with you if you intend to drink or even enter a bar. By law, you must be 21 years of age to drink anywhere in the US, but in New York it's rather easy to buy alcohol without ID if you look old enough. Some bouncers at bars want to see a driver's license with a photo before they'll admit you – especially in the East Village, where young drinkers congregate. Bouncers often don't consider a passport adequate documentation. And remember: You can't win arguments with dim bouncers.

EMBASSIES & CONSULATES

US Embassies & Consulates

US diplomatic offices around the world include the following:

Australia (☎ 02-6214-5600), 21 Moonah Place, Yarralumla, ACT 2600

Canada (☎ 613-238-5335), 100 Wellington St, Ottawa, Ontario 1P 5T1

Denmark (☎ 3555-3144), Dag Hammarskjölds Allé 24, 2100 Copenhagen

France (☎ 01-43-12-22-22), 2 rue St Florentin, 75382 Paris

Germany (☎ 030-832-9233), Clayallee 170, 14195 Berlin

India (☎ 11-419-8000, fax 11-419-0017), Shanti Path, Chanakyapuri, 110021 New Delhi

Ireland (☎ 1-668-8777), 42 Elgin Rd, Ballsbridge, Dublin

Italy (☎ 06-46-741), Via Vittorio Veneto 119a, 00187 Rome

Japan (☎ 09-905-12122), 11-5 Nishitenma, 2-chome, Kita-ku, Osaka 530-8543

Netherlands (☎ 020-575-5309), Museumplein 19, 1071 DJ Amsterdam

New Zealand (☎ 9-303-2724), 4th floor General Building, 29 Shortland St, Auckland

Sweden (fax 8-660-5879), Dag Hammarskjölds Väg 31, Se-115 89 Stockholm

Switzerland (☎ 090-05-55154), Jubilaeumsstrasse 95, 3005 Berne

Thailand (☎ 2-205-4000), 95 Wireless Rd, Bangkok 10330

UK (☎ 020-7499-9000), 24 Grosvenor Square, London W1A 1AE

Consulates in New York City

The presence of the United Nations in New York City means that nearly every country in the world maintains diplomatic offices in Manhattan. Check the local yellow pages under Consulates for a complete listing. Some foreign consulates and consulate generals include the following:

Australia (☎ 212-351-6500), 150 E 42nd St, 34th floor, New York, NY 10017

Belgium (☎ 212-586-5110), 1330 Sixth Ave, New York, NY 10019

Brazil (☎ 917-777-7777), 1185 Sixth Ave, 21st floor, New York, NY 10036-2601

Canada (☎ 212-596-1628), 1251 Sixth Ave, New York, NY 10020-1175

France (☎ 212-606-3600), 934 Fifth Ave, New York, NY 10021

Germany (☎ 212-610-9700), 871 United Nations Plaza, New York, NY 10017

Ireland (☎ 212-319-2555), 345 Park Ave, 17th floor, New York, NY 10154-0037

Italy (☎ 212-737-9100), 690 Park Ave, New York, NY 10021

Netherlands (☎ 212-246-1429), 1 Rockefeller Plaza, 11th floor, New York, NY 10020

New Zealand (☎ 212-832-4038), 780 Third Ave, Suite 1904, New York, NY 10017

Spain (☎ 212-355-4080), 150 E 58th St, New York, NY 10155

UK (☎ 212-745-0200), 845 Third Ave, New York, NY 10022

Your Own Embassy It's important to realize what your own embassy – the embassy of the country of which you are a citizen – can and can't do to help you if you get into trouble. Generally speaking, it won't be much help in emergencies if the trouble you're in is remotely your own fault. Remember that you are bound by the laws of the country you are in. Your embassy will not be sympathetic if you end up in jail after committing a crime locally, even if such actions are legal in your own country.

In genuine emergencies, you might get some assistance, but only if other channels have been exhausted. If you need to get home urgently, a free ticket home is exceedingly unlikely – the embassy would expect you to have insurance. If all your money and documents are stolen, it might assist you with getting a new passport, but a loan for onward travel is out of the question.

Some embassies used to keep letters for travelers or have a small reading room with home newspapers, but these days most of the mail-holding services have been stopped and even newspapers tend to be out of date.

CUSTOMS

US customs allows each person over the age of 21 to bring 1 liter of liquor and 200 cigarettes duty-free into the USA. US citizens are allowed to import, duty-free, $400 worth of gifts from abroad, while non-US citizens are allowed to bring in $100 worth. If you're carrying more than $10,000 in US and foreign cash, traveler's checks, money orders and the like, you need to declare the excess amount. There is no legal restriction on the amount that may be imported, but undeclared sums in excess of $10,000 may be subject to investigation.

KIM GRANT

MONEY

Currency

The US dollar is divided into 100 cents (¢). Coins come in denominations of 1¢ (penny), 5¢ (nickel), 10¢ (dime), 25¢ (quarter) and the seldom seen 50¢ (half-dollar). Notes come in $1, $2, $5, $10, $20, $50 and $100 denominations (you'll come across $2 bills infrequently). There's also a $1 Susan B Anthony coin that the government tried unsuccessfully in the late '70s to bring into mass circulation; you may get them as change from ticket and stamp machines. Be aware that they look similar to quarters (which is why they failed to catch on with Americans). A new, gold-colored dollar coin, introduced in early 2000, has proven to be more popular than the Susan B Anthony dollar. A number of Americans have started to collect the new coin, which features a picture of Sacagawea, a Native American guide who led the explorers Lewis and Clark on their expedition through the western US.

In recent years, the US treasury has redesigned the $20, $50 and $100 bills to foil counterfeiters. The main visible distinction is that the portrait on each bill has been moved off-center. Most vendors are used to these bills by now, although you may encounter a few machines that still can't accept the 'new' $20 bill.

Exchange Rates

Exchange rates at press time were:

country	unit		dollar
Australia	A1$	=	$0.60
Canada	C$1	=	$0.70
Euro	€1	=	$0.95
France	FF10	=	$1.40
Germany	DM1	=	$0.50
Hong Kong	HK$1	=	$0.10
Japan	¥100	=	$0.90
New Zealand	NZ$1	=	$0.50
UK	£1	=	$1.50

Exchanging Money

Chase Manhattan Bank (☎ 212-552-2222), 1 Chase Manhattan Plaza (William St between Liberty and Pine Sts) in Lower Manhattan, offers a commission-free foreign-currency exchange service that's open 8 am to 3:30 pm weekdays. A Midtown branch, 349 Fifth Ave at 34th St, directly across the street from the Empire State Building, also offers foreign exchange during the same hours.

The main American Express office (☎ 212-421-8240), in the World Financial Center at West and Vesey Sts, has a reliable currency exchange service, but there are long lines in the afternoon. It's open 9 am to 5 pm weekdays. It has other offices at 111 Broadway (Map 5; ☎ 212-693-1100) and 420 Lexington Ave between E 43rd and 44th Sts (Map 7; ☎ 212-687-3700), among many others. Contact American Express at ☎ 800-221-7282 for more locations.

Thomas Cook offers currency exchange at eight locations in the city. The Times Square office (Map 8; ☎ 212-265-6049), 1590 Broadway at 48th St, is open 9 am to 7 pm Monday to Saturday and 9 am to 5 pm Sunday.

Chequepoint (Map 7; ☎ 212-750-2400), 22 Central Park South between Fifth and Sixth Aves, offers less favorable rates. The office is open 8 am to 8 pm daily.

Banks are normally open 9 am to 3 pm weekdays. Chase Manhattan's Chinatown branch, at the corner of Mott and Canal Sts, is open daily. Several other banks along Canal St also offer weekend hours.

Cash In New York, it's always wise to have some ready cash for purchasing food and trinkets from street vendors, not to mention subway tokens. Be aware, though, that some vendors and movie theater cashiers might balk at accepting bills in denominations of $50 or more, especially if they have to empty out their cash drawers making change for you. This policy is not strictly legal, but you won't get anywhere arguing about the law. Instead, keep $20 bills on hand for smaller purchases.

Traveler's Checks Traveler's checks offer protection from theft or loss. Checks issued by American Express and Thomas Cook (see Exchanging Money, earlier) are widely accepted, and both companies have efficient replacement policies.

Keeping a record of the check numbers and the checks you have used is vital when it comes to replacing lost checks. Keep this record in a separate place from the checks themselves.

You'll save yourself trouble and expense if you buy traveler's checks in US dollars. The savings you *might* make on exchange rates by carrying traveler's checks in a foreign currency don't make up for the hassle of exchanging them at banks and other facilities. Restaurants, hotels and most stores accept US-dollar traveler's checks as if they were cash, so if you're carrying traveler's checks in US dollars, the odds are you'll rarely have to use a bank or pay an exchange fee. Fast-food restaurants and smaller businesses may refuse traveler's checks, so ask at the outset of a meal or a purchase if you can use them.

Bring most of the checks in large denominations. It's only toward the end of a stay that you may want to change a small check to make sure you aren't left with too much local currency. Of course, traveler's checks are losing their popularity due to the explosion of ATMs (see below), and many visitors return home without using their entire supply.

ATMs Given the prevalence of automated teller machines (ATMs) in New York City, you can easily draw cash directly from a home bank account, provided that your bank is linked with the Cirrus or Plus ATM networks. ATM fees for foreign banks are usually about $3 to $5; foreign-currency exchange commissions range from $5 to $7. Most New York banks are linked by the NYCE (New York Cash Exchange) system, and you can use local bank cards interchangeably at ATMs.

Credit & Debit Cards Major credit cards are accepted at hotels, restaurants, gas stations, shops, and car rental agencies throughout the USA. In fact, you'll find it hard to perform certain transactions, such as renting a car or purchasing tickets to performances, without one.

Even if you dislike using credit cards and prefer to rely on traveler's checks and ATMs, it's a good idea to carry one for emergencies. If you're planning to rely primarily upon credit cards, it would be wise to have a Visa or MasterCard in your deck, since other cards aren't as widely accepted.

Places that accept Visa and MasterCard are also likely to accept debit cards. Unlike a credit card, a debit card deducts payment directly from the user's checking account. Instead of an interest rate, users are charged a minimal fee for the transaction. Be sure to check with your bank to confirm that your debit card will be accepted in other states or countries – debit cards from large commercial banks can often be used worldwide.

Carry copies of your credit card numbers separately from the cards. If you lose your credit cards or they get stolen, contact the company immediately. The following are toll-free numbers for the main credit card companies. Contact your bank if you lose your ATM card.

American Express	☎ 800-528-4800
Diners Club	☎ 800-234-6377
Discover	☎ 800-347-2683
MasterCard	☎ 800-826-2181
Visa	☎ 800-336-8472

International Transfers You can instruct your bank back home to send you a draft. Specify the city, bank and branch to which you want your money directed, or ask your home bank to tell you where a suitable one is, and make sure you get the details right. The procedure is easier if you've authorized someone back home to access your account.

Money sent by telegraphic transfer should reach you within a week; if it's coming by mail, allow at least two weeks. When it arrives, it will most likely be converted into local currency – you can take it as it is or buy traveler's checks.

You can also transfer money at the offices of American Express and Thomas Cook. See Exchanging Money, above, for the addresses of these companies' Manhattan branches.

Security

Most hotels and hostels provide safekeeping, so you can leave your money and jewelry there. Carry the money you'll need for each day somewhere inside your clothing (in a money belt, bra or socks) rather than in a handbag or an outside pocket. It helps to have money in several places, and don't venture around with an overstuffed

A Note on Prices

As any department store owner or Hollywood agent knows, if you have a hot commodity, you can always increase the price the public will pay for it. New York City, with its 30 million annual visitors, is certainly hot. Museums and tourist attractions are now in the habit of raising prices in $5 increments rather than by just a dollar or two at a time. Please factor in a few unpleasant price surprises in your budget, especially if you want to see a Broadway musical, where top prices have already reached $75 per seat.

If you're on a tight budget, when you go to museums, look closely for the word 'suggested' before the word 'admission.' Though you wouldn't know it by the forbidding guards posted at museum entrances, you're not required to pay admission at many New York museums (including the American Museum of Natural History and the Metropolitan Museum of Art). You can also call ahead to find out whether a museum has weekly 'pay as you wish/free admission' times, or pick up a copy of *Museums New York* (available free at most museum entrances), which offers discount admission coupons.

At meal times, you can still eat very cheaply in New York if you confine yourself to street vendors, pizza parlors and Asian noodle shops. And for those who come from countries with strong currencies, New York shopping still offers real opportunities for savings.

FACTS FOR THE VISITOR

wallet in your back pocket – it's the petty thief's dream. Remember that just using a simple safety pin to hold the zipper tags of a day pack together can help prevent theft of books and handbags.

Costs

All price levels are catered to in New York City. With the very significant exception of housing and hotels, it's possible to live pretty cheaply. Below are the average costs of consumer items:

Brewed coffee:	\$1.50
Bagel:	\$1
Beer:	\$5
Fruit:	50¢ to \$1
Pizza slice:	\$2
Soda:	\$1
Water:	75¢ to \$1.75
Local call:	25¢
Laundry:	\$3 a load at self-serve centers
Stamp:	33¢

Tipping

Tipping is expected in restaurants, bars and better hotels, as well as by taxi drivers, hairdressers and baggage carriers. In restaurants, wait staff are paid less than the minimum wage and rely upon tips to make a living. Tip at least 15% unless the service is terrible. Most New Yorkers tip about 20%, calculating the amount by doubling the 8.25% sales tax on a meal bill and rounding up a dollar or two. At bars, bartenders typically expect a \$1 tip for every drink they serve. Never tip in fast-food, take-out or buffet-style restaurants where you serve yourself. And beware of restaurants that don't itemize the tax separately on a bill – it's a way to get you to tip on the tax amount as well.

Taxi drivers expect 10%, and hairdressers get 15% if their service is satisfactory. Baggage carriers (skycaps in airports, bellhops in hotels) receive \$1 for the first bag and 50¢ for each additional bag. In 1st-class and luxury hotels, tipping can reach ludicrous proportions – doormen, bellboys and parking attendants all expect to be tipped at least \$1 for each service performed – including simply opening a taxi door for you. (Business travelers should tip the cleaning staff \$5 a day.) However, simply saying 'thank you' to an attendant who does something you could just as easily have done it yourself is OK.

Taxes & Refunds

Restaurants and retailers never include tax in their prices, so beware of ordering the \$4.99 lunch special when you only have \$5 in your pocket. New York State imposes a sales tax of 7% on goods, most services and prepared foods. New York City imposes an additional 1.25% tax, bringing the total surcharge to 8.25%. Several categories of so-called 'luxury items,' including rental cars and dry cleaning, carry an additional city surcharge of 5%, so you wind up paying an extra 13.25% for these services.

Hotel rooms in New York City are subject to a 13.25% tax, plus a flat \$2-per-night occupancy tax.

Believe it or not, that reflects a reduction in the previous hotel tax.

Since the US has no nationwide value added tax (VAT), there is no opportunity for foreign visitors to make 'tax-free' purchases. However, New York City has permanently suspended the sales tax on clothing items under $110, giving everyone a modest tax break.

POST & COMMUNICATIONS

Postal Rates

Rates for sending mail increase every few years. At the time of writing, rates for 1st-class mail within the USA are 33¢ for letters up to 1oz (22¢ for each additional ounce) and 20¢ for postcards.

International airmail rates (except to Canada and Mexico) are 60¢ for a half-ounce letter, $1 for a 1oz letter and 40¢ for each additional half-ounce. International postcard rates are 55¢. Letters to Canada are 48¢ for a half-ounce letter, 55¢ for a 1oz letter and 45¢ for a postcard. Letters to Mexico are 40¢ for a half-ounce letter, 46¢ for a 1oz letter and 40¢ for a postcard. Aerogrammes are 60¢.

The cost for parcels airmailed anywhere within the USA is $3.20 for 2lb or less, increasing by $1 per pound up to $6.50 for 5lb. For heavier items, rates differ according to the distance mailed. Books, periodicals and computer disks can be sent by a cheaper 4th-class rate.

Sending Mail

The general post office (☎ 212-967-8585), in the James A Foley Building, 380 W 33rd St at Eighth Ave (zip: 10001), is open 24 hours a day. Rockefeller Center's basement post office (☎ 212-265-3854), 610 Fifth Ave at 49th St (zip: 10020), is open 9:30 am to 5:30 pm weekdays.

The post office at Franklin D Roosevelt Station (☎ 212-330-5549), 909 Third Ave at 55th St (zip: 10022), is open for most postal business from 9 am to 8 pm weekdays.

Receiving Mail

It's almost vital to have a postal address arranged before arriving. Alternatively, the Mailboxes Etc stores that are scattered throughout the city offer post boxes for rent on a short- or long-term basis, as do the main branches of the US Post Office (see earlier).

General delivery *poste restante* mail is accepted at the main post office, provided it's marked 'General Delivery.' This method is not recommended or reliable, especially in the era of email and wire money transfers. The American Express offices at 420 Lexington Ave at E 42nd St, 374 Park Ave at 53rd St and 822 Lexington Ave at 63rd St offer a mail drop for cardholders.

Telephone

Phone numbers within the USA consist of a three-digit area code followed by a seven-digit local number. If you're calling locally, just dial the seven-digit number. If you're calling long distance, dial 1 + the three-digit area code + the seven-digit number. If you're calling New York from abroad, the international country code for the USA is '1.'

For local directory assistance, dial ☎ 411. For directory assistance outside your area code, dial ☎ 1 + the three-digit area code of the place you want to call + 555-1212. To find a number in Manhattan before you arrive, call ☎ 1 + 212 + 555-1212. (These requests are charged as one-minute long distance calls.)

In New York City, Manhattan phone numbers are in the 212 or 646 area code (although some businesses have a 917 area code), and the four outer boroughs are in the 718 zone. Dial carefully – the explosion of phone lines in Manhattan means that neglecting to add 718 to an outer-borough number will probably put you through to the wrong party in Manhattan.

All toll-free numbers are prefixed with an 800, 877 or 888 area code. Some toll-free numbers for local businesses or government offices only work within a limited region. But most toll-free phone numbers can be dialed from abroad – just be aware that you will be connected at regular long distance rates, which could become a costly option if the line you're dialing regularly puts customers on hold for extended periods.

Area Code Angst

For years, the prefix '212' marked all New Yorkers' telephone lines. The code was chosen back in the days of rotary phones because it was the fastest accessible combination to dial, perfectly in keeping with New York's fast lifestyle. (The same reasoning gave Los Angeles the '213' area code.)

In the '80s, the surge in telephone numbers in Manhattan led to the introduction of the '718' area code, which eventually was assigned for the four outer boroughs. But in the late '90s, the use of cell phones and faxes finally exhausted the 9.2 million phone numbers that can be assigned under any code.

At first, '917' was assigned to new business numbers and cell phones in Manhattan. But now the unthinkable has happened. New residences in Manhattan are being given phone numbers with a '646' area code. At the moment, few numbers have this area code, but 646 has already frightened the natives, who see it as something totally uncool. Perhaps Wall Street traders will find a way of creating a secondary market for numbers in the desirable '212' zone. Until then, newcomers must grin and bear it.

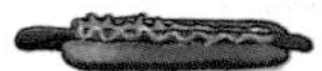

Long-distance rates vary depending on the destination and the telephone company you're using – call the operator (☎ 0) for rate information. Don't ask the operator to put your call through, however, because operator-assisted calls are much more expensive than direct-dial calls. Generally, the cheapest times to call (60% discount) are nights (11 pm to 8 am), all day Saturday and 8 am to 5 pm Sunday. A 35% discount applies from 5 to 11 pm Sunday to Friday. Daytime calls (8 am to 5 pm Monday to Friday) are full-price calls within the USA.

International Calls To make an international direct call, dial ☎ 011, then the country code, followed by the area code and the phone number. (To find the country code, check a local phone directory or dial ☎ 411 and ask for an international operator.) You may need to wait as long as 45 seconds for the ringing to start. International rates vary depending on the time of day and the destination. For example, the cheapest rates to London are available between 6 pm and 7 am, but if you're calling Sydney, the cheapest time is 3 am to 2 pm. Call the operator (☎ 0) for rates.

Hotel Phones Hotels (especially the more expensive ones) add a service charge of 50¢ to $1 for *every* call made from a room phone; they also levy hefty surcharges for long-distance calls. Public pay phones, which can be found in most lobbies, are always cheaper.

Pay Phones You can pump in quarters, use a phone credit card or make collect calls from pay phones. There are thousands of pay telephones on the New York City streets, but those maintained by Bell Atlantic are much more reliable than the others. On some pay phones in New York City, if you make a long-distance call with a credit card, you could end up with a whopping bill from an unscrupulous long-distance firm.

Phone directories are no longer provided at outdoor phone booths, so if you're unsure of a local address dial ☎ 411 (information) on a pay phone and ask for the location of the business. Tell the operator that you are looking for an address. If you don't indicate this, the operator will immediately call up a computer message with the telephone number only, forcing you to call the business and spend 25¢ to obtain information the phone company is supposed to provide gratis.

Phone Cards A new long distance alternative is phone debit cards, which allow purchasers to pay in advance, with access through a toll-free 800 number. In amounts of $5, $10, $20 and $50, these are available from Western Union, machines in some supermarkets, and some other sources.

There's a wide range of local and international phone cards. Lonely Planet's eKno

Communication Card is aimed specifically at independent travelers and provides budget international calls, a range of messaging services, free email and travel information – for local calls, you're usually better off with a local card. You can join online at www.ekno.lonelyplanet.com or by phone from New York City by dialing ☎ 800-707-0031. To use eKno from New York City once you have joined, dial ☎ 800-706-1333.

Check the eKno Web site for joining and access telephone numbers from other countries and updates on super budget local access numbers and new features.

When using phone credit cards in a public place, cover up the key pad to deter thieves from watching you punch in the numbers – they will memorize numbers and use your card to make phone calls to all corners of the earth. New York airports and the Port Authority Bus Terminal are notorious for this scam. Some newer pay phones (like those in Penn Station) provide shields at the telephone pad to prevent a stranger from viewing your number.

Fax

Kinko's offers 24-hour fax service in addition to its computer and photocopying services. (You can also have passport photographs taken at Kinko's.) The copy-store chain has many locations in Manhattan, including 16 E 52nd St between Fifth and Madison Aves (☎ 212-308-2679), and 24 E 12th St between Fifth Ave and University Place (☎ 212-924-0802). Check the yellow pages under Copying for the closest location of a Kinko's or equivalent service.

Email & Internet Access

The New York Public Library's main branch (☎ 212-930-0800), E 42nd St at Fifth Ave, offers free half-hour Internet access, though there may be a wait in the afternoons. At

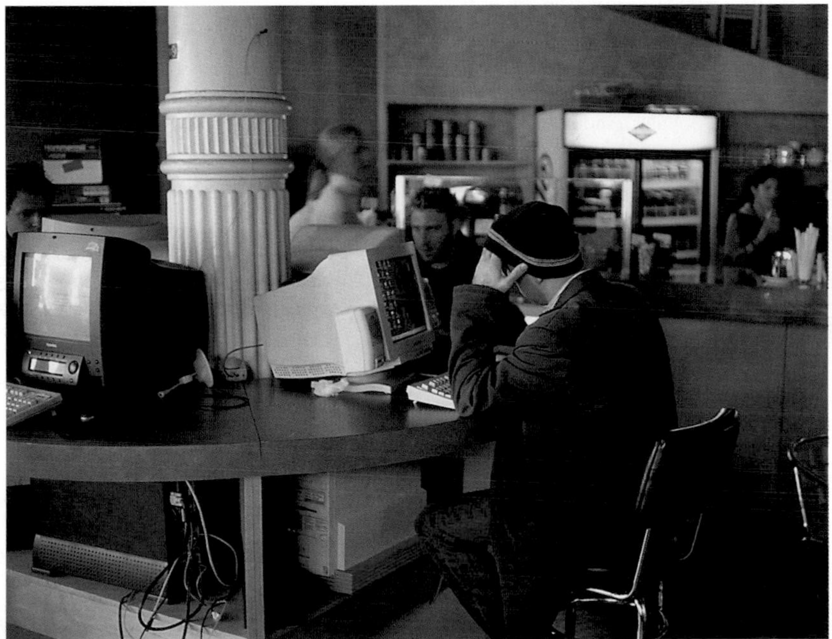

ANGUS OBORN

Checking email at an Internet cafe

several cyber cafes in the city, you can surf the net for an hourly fee, which ranges from $5 to $12. The Internet Cafe (☎ 212-614-0747), 82 E 3rd St between First and Second Aves in the East Village, is open 11 am to 2 am Monday to Saturday and 11 am to midnight Sunday. Also try Cyber Cafe (212-334-5140), 273 Lafayette St at Prince St in SoHo, or Cyberfeld's (☎ 212-647-8830), 20 E 13th St near Fifth Ave in Greenwich Village, where you can rent a computer until midnight.

INTERNET RESOURCES

The World Wide Web is a rich resource for travelers. You can research your trip, hunt down bargain airfares, book hotels, check on weather conditions and chat with locals and other travelers about the best places to visit (or avoid).

There's no better place to start your Web explorations than the Lonely Planet Web site (www.lonelyplanet.com). Here you'll find succinct summaries on traveling to most places on earth, postcards from other travelers and the Thorn Tree bulletin board, where you can ask questions before you go or dispense advice when you get back. You can also find travel news and updates for many of our most popular guidebooks, and the subWWWay section links you to the most useful travel resources elsewhere on the Web.

The following sites are particularly useful for finding out information about New York:

www.nycvisit.com The NYC & Company (Convention & Visitors Bureau) site offers general tourist information.

www.nytoday.com New York Today, run by the *New York Times*, features entertainment listings and an archive of reviews.

www.nytimes.com At the home site of the *New York Times*, you'll find a complete version of the daily paper, along with additional cyber content.

www.chowhound.com Chowhound, a *vox populi* site started by web restaurant reviewer Jim Leff, offers feedback for eateries at all income levels. If you live in New York, bookmark this one.

www.new-york-city-hotels.com This site offers discounts, last-minute room bookings and direct links to the hotels.

www.newyork.citysearch.com Visit City Search for a comprehensive roundup of city happenings.

www.nycsubway.org NYC Subway is an unofficial site detailing the transit system, with everything from practical information to historical trivia.

www.scenetrack.com Scenetrack features club and bar listings, with up-to-the-minute information on New York's nightlife.

BOOKS

Most books are published in different editions by different publishers in different countries. As a result, a book might be a hardcover rarity in one country but readily available in paperback in another. Fortunately, bookstores and libraries can search by title or author, so your local bookstore or library is the best place to advise you on the availability of the following recommendations.

To find the books listed below, you can also head to any large New York bookstore – it will have a special section dedicated to tomes about the city. For a list of bookstores, see the Shopping chapter, later in the book.

Lonely Planet

If you plan to go a little farther afield than New York City, pick up a copy of Lonely Planet's *New York, New Jersey & Pennsylvania*, which offers in-depth coverage of the region. For information on other US destinations, consult the *USA* guide.

History

Though it is a work of fiction rather than a straight history, Washington Irving's satirical *History of New York* (1809), published under the pseudonym of Dietrich Knickerbocker, includes glimpses of colonial-era New York. Those looking for a more historical perspective should seek out *Colonial New York* by historian Michael Kammen.

Irving Howe's *World of Our Fathers* offers a comprehensive look at the assimilation of Eastern European Jewish immigrants into late 19th-New York. It's a perfect book for anyone interested in the history of the East Village and Lower East Side.

Luc Sante has published two fine and colorful works dealing with the grittier aspects of early 20th century New York. *Low Life* examines the world of the tenements occu-

For the Bookworm

Thousands of novels are set in New York, and you've probably read a few already. The following nonfiction choices will stuff your head full of city trivia, except for the last one, which will stuff your stomach. All can be obtained in a large New York bookstore at discounted prices.

Writing New York (1998), edited by Phillip Lopate, offers the single best overview on the city's role in literature.

Gotham (1998), by Edwin G Burrows and Mike Wallace, is the one book you'll need to read about the city. A magisterial but lively work, the first volume covers the city's history from prehistoric times to the consolidation of the five boroughs in 1898. A second volume will chronicle greater New York City's first 100 years.

AIA Guide to New York City (2000), by Norval White, is a classic work that chronicles almost every significant building in the city. An updated version was published by the American Institute of Architects in 2000.

The Encyclopedia of New York City (1995), edited by Kenneth T Jackson, is a massive but entertaining array of facts and stories compiled by the distinguished Columbia University urban historian.

New York Cookbook (1992), by Molly O'Neill, is the ultimate New York nosh. The food columnist for the *New York Times* spent years asking New Yorkers both famous and obscure for their favorite recipes.

pied by immigrants, while *Evidence* is a picture book with an essay that focuses on the mayhem of this world, with old police crime-scene photos for illustrations.

The *WPA Guide to New York City*, published in 1939 as a Depression-era employment project for the city's writers (including John Cheever) and now back in print, offers a time-frozen look at a lost metropolis. This is a wonderful read for anyone who has lived in or explored the city in recent days.

Memoirs

The city has inspired and attracted more than its share of affectionate memories. E B White's essay *Here is New York* still stands today as an affectionate summary of fast-paced city life, though it was written in 1949. ('To bring New York up to date,' he writes, 'a man would have to be published with the speed of light.')

Kafka Was the Rage by Anatole Broyard, the late book reviewer for the *New York Times*, offers a bittersweet look at life in Greenwich Village just after WWII, a time also recalled by journalist Dan Wakefield in *New York in the '50s*.

Jack Kerouac's *Lonesome Traveler* focuses on his days in New York during the era of the Greenwich Village Beat writers and the publishing of Allen Ginsberg's *Howl and Other Poems* in 1956 amid great controversy. A year later, Kerouac published his most famous work, *On the Road* (1957); rumor has it that the book was written on a roll of teletype paper, in one sitting in the Chelsea Hotel.

The Andy Warhol Diaries (1990) is a bitchy and colorful account of the '70s nightclub culture by one of the most influential artists of the 20th century.

General

The publishing capital of the world has been featured in thousands of fictional books. Some of the following New York books have become classics in American literature.

O Henry, author of 'The Gift of the Magi' (1906), and F Scott Fitzgerald were distinctly New York writers whose short stories bring to life two distinctive social eras (the late 19th century and the Roaring '20s). Seek out Fitzgerald's *Tales of the Jazz Age* (1922), which includes 'The Diamond as Big as the Ritz,' and, of course, don't miss *The Great Gatsby* (1925).

Though largely an expatriate who lived in Europe for much of his life, American writer Henry James evokes New York upper-class life before the Civil War in the novel *Washington Square* (1881). The row houses that were then occupied by New York society still line the northern edge of Washington Square Park today.

James' contemporary Edith chronicles the Gilded Age of New York City in the Pulitzer Prize–winning *Age of Innocence* (1920) and in the collection *Old New York* (1924). Unfortunately, most of her New York – the original Metropolitan Opera House, the Metropolitan Museum of Art and the mansions of Fifth Ave's 'Millionaire's Row' – has disappeared or been altered beyond recognition.

JD Salinger's *Catcher in the Rye* (1951) has spoken to three generations of manic teenagers with its portrayal of the misadventures of Holden Caulfield. The novel's events culminate at the Museum of Natural History.

Of the many works by black artists set in New York, perhaps the most acclaimed is Ralph Ellison's *Invisible Man* (1952), a classic rumination on race and the USA.

EL Doctorow's works – including *Ragtime* (1975), *The Book of Daniel* (1971) and *World's Fair* (1985) – reflect on New York in its various eras, from turn-of-the-20th-century boomtown to Cold War ideological battleground. Mario Puzo's *The Godfather* (1969) describes the West Side's Hell's Kitchen neighborhood as it was in the years just after WWI.

Thomas Pynchon's debut novel *V* (1963) hops from the New York of the late 1950s to various points around the globe and illustrates the feverish attitudes of the young people who 'yo-yoed' their way through the city at the time.

Pynchon was the forerunner of those who ushered in a newer, more energetic style of writing in the '70s and '80s. Some authors adopted phantasmagoric or Gothic styles. Don DeLillo's *Great Jones Street* (1973) and Mark Helprin's *A Winter's Tale* (1983) are two prime examples of this disturbing new view of society. Paul Auster, who lives in the Park Slope section of Brooklyn, has won many followers abroad for his modern noir *New York Trilogy* (1990).

Jay McInerney was first blessed, then cursed by his association with the yuppified early '80s, occasioned by his blockbuster first novel *Bright Lights, Big City* (1984). Tom Wolfe's *Bonfire of the Vanities* (1987) followed that up, offering a comic portrait of a city out of control and noticeably split along racial lines. Tama Janowitz, author of *Slaves of New York*, covers much of the same ground and has enjoyed a life of literary celebrity.

For an overview of the city in literature, pick up Shaun O'Connell's *Remarkable, Unspeakable, New York* (1995), a look at how American writers have regarded the metropolis over two centuries.

FILMS

Just as it's nearly impossible to define the perfect New York book, there's almost no way to present a definitive list of films about the city. For years, New York movies were shot on Hollywood soundstages, although actors sometimes came to the city for a few days to shoot exteriors (a practice that continues to this day for TV shows such as *NYPD Blue*).

That began to change substantially in the '70s, when directors began striving for realism and equipment became more mobile, making location shooting a less expensive alternative to the studio. Today, it's common to see film production trucks on the streets of New York – though some lower-budget films try to pass off Canadian cities as New York (such as Jackie Chan's *Rumble in the Bronx*, which was shot in Vancouver). With a few noted exceptions, the following films were authentically set in New York and represent some sort of unique aspect of the city. They are all available on video.

On the Town (1949) stars Gene Kelly and Frank Sinatra as sailors on shore leave in

New York City. Since Sinatra was enjoying the height of his bobby-soxer popularity at the time of filming and was attracting crowds of spectators wherever he went, director Stanley Donen would 'steal' a shot by setting up the cameras and sending the actors out at the last minute. It didn't always work – which is why you can spot hundreds of onlookers as Sinatra and Kelly sing 'New York, New York' in Rockefeller Center.

The first major noir film to make use of the city streets was *Naked City* (1948), which was loosely based on the crime photos of the famous newspaper photographer named Weegee, who also inspired the Joe Pesci film *The Public Eye* (1992).

The best black-and-white film ever shot in New York is the gritty *Sweet Smell of Success* (1957), starring Burt Lancaster as a ruthless gossip columnist (a barely disguised Walter Winchell) and Tony Curtis as the desperate press agent he manipulates. The cinematography, by the legendary James Wong Howe, captures the city's '50s nightlife perfectly, revolving around a Midtown nightclub scene that has pretty much disappeared thanks to the building of skyscrapers.

West Side Story (1961) depicts love and gang rivalry in Hell's Kitchen and includes exterior shots of the tenements that were torn down to make way for the expansion of Lincoln Center.

A quintessential New York film, *The Taking of Pelham One, Two, Three* (1974) stars Walter Matthau as a beleaguered transit cop confronted with a subway hijacking. This cult classic, written by Peter Stone (the only writer to have won a Tony, an Oscar and an Emmy) includes a terrific twist in the last scene.

In recent years, foreign directors have come to New York to provide domestic audiences with a look at the city from an outsider's point of view. Wayne Wang's *Smoke* (1995) and *Blue in the Face* (1996) both star Harvey Keitel as a cigar-store owner in Brooklyn. In Ang Lee's bittersweet comedy *The Wedding Banquet* (1993), New York represents the land of sexual freedom for a Taiwanese gay man whose meddlesome parents arrive to supervise his 'marriage' to a woman.

In 1986, Spike Lee emerged as a major new New York filmmaker with *She's Gotta Have It* and followed it up with the controversial *Do The Right Thing* (1989), a film about racial tensions in Brooklyn. Since then, he's carved out a career that combines fine works like *Malcolm X* (1992) and *Clockers* (1995) with highly lucrative commercials for Nike. His 1999 feature *Summer of Sam* is a hard-driving portrayal of one of the city's worst years: the summer of 1977, when a serial killer stalked the city, a heat wave boiled citizens and a blackout inspired violent riots.

For more about New York films, see the boxed text 'Three New York Film Directors: Scorsese, Allen and Lumet.'

Spike

Three New York Film Directors: Scorsese, Allen and Lumet

Perhaps some of New York's recent history is best reflected in the cinema of the past 30 years. The following three filmmakers are among the most talented men ever to look through a camera.

Martin Scorsese This quirky, nervous and visionary director is celebrated for bringing the dark side of New York to life. Born in Queens in 1942, Scorsese grew up on Elizabeth St in Manhattan's Little Italy. After working as an editor on the documentary *Woodstock* (1970), he made *Mean Streets* (1973), a drama about Little Italy – actually shot in the Bronx – with Robert De Niro and Harvey Keitel. Both actors would become closely associated with Scorsese's films, starring together in *Taxi Driver* (1975), a critically acclaimed film about psychopaths in the East Village. De Niro won an Oscar for his performance in *Raging Bull* (1980), a brutal biography of boxer Jake La Motta; it became an instant classic.

In recent years, Scorsese has won praise for *Goodfellas* (1990), a true-life mob drama, and *The Age of Innocence* (1993), a detail-rich costume drama based on the Edith Wharton novel about 19th-century New York. Scorsese returned to New York's grittier underside in *Bringing Out The Dead* (1999), starring Nicholas Cage. Lately, Scorsese has led the fight to preserve American film heritage through the restoration of classic films.

Woody Allen This filmmaker equals Scorsese in prominence, but certainly Woody Allen has no equal among US filmmakers in enjoying so much control over his final product (though the younger Spike Lee is challenging Allen's position as all around *auteur)*. Allen, who writes, directs and often stars in his own films, turns out motion pictures the way others produce short stories – about one per year, with more than 30 so far.

Born Allen Stewart Konigsberg in 1935 in Brooklyn, he began writing gags for TV comedians and landed a job on Sid Caesar's legendary *Your Show of Shows* in the mid-1950s. He then graduated to stand-up comedy, perfecting the now-familiar persona of a sex-obsessed, intellectual 'nebbish' who nonetheless gets the girl in the end. He made his Hollywood debut as an actor and screenwriter in *What's New Pussycat?* (1965) and followed that up a year later with *What's Up Tiger Lily?*, in which he dubbed comic dialogue onto a Japanese James Bond–style spy movie. While he was writing and directing the purely comic *Take the Money and Run* (1969), *Bananas* (1971) and *Sleeper* (1972), among others, he also began writing feisty comic essays for the *New Yorker* and had a Broadway hit in *Play It Again, Sam*. The play, in which his loser character gets advice from the ghost of Humphrey Bogart, became a hit movie in 1972.

Three New York Film Directors: Scorsese, Allen and Lumet

But it was the classic *Annie Hall* (1975), one of the few comedies to ever win an Oscar for Best Picture, that forever established Allen's reputation as a comic artist. He followed it up with the serious drama *Interiors* (1978) and *Manhattan* (1979), an unabashed love letter to the city, beautifully shot in black and white.

His private and professional partnership with actress Mia Farrow produced a number of acclaimed films, including the Academy Award–winning *Hannah & Her Sisters* (1986). But Allen's affair with Soon-Yi Previn, Farrow's adopted daughter, led to a nasty breakup with Farrow in the early '90s.

Despite his controversial personal life, Allen still produces celebrated films that help actresses win Oscars. (Besides Farrow, his leading ladies have included Diane Keaton, Dianne Weist and Mira Sorvino). In recent years, he has released *Mighty Aphrodite* (1995), *Deconstructing Harry* (1997), *Celebrity* (1998), *Sweet & Lowdown* (1999) and *Everyone Says I Love You* (1996), a quirky musical comedy that features Goldie Hawn, Alan Alda and Allen himself crooning famous love songs in New York, Paris and Venice. In his spare time, Allen still plays clarinet in a traditional jazz band at Michael's Pub in Midtown most Monday nights.

Sidney Lumet Born in 1924, Sidney Lumet represents an older, more idealistic New York liberal sensibility, one formulated in the '50s, when he got his start directing live TV drama. Even when most directors went out to Hollywood, Lumet preferred to shoot many of his films in the city. His first feature was *12 Angry Men* (1957) with Henry Fonda, a reprise of one of the best live TV dramas.

He went on to direct *Serpico* (1974), a true-life story of a policeman who exposed widespread department corruption; *Dog Day Afternoon* (1975), another true-life about a bank robber (played by Al Pacino) who has a bizarre scheme to get his lover money for a sex-change operation; and *Network* (1976), a stinging satire that foreshadowed the '90s era of junk talk shows on TV. Lumet has also proven his versatility as a director with the baroque costume melodrama *Murder on the Orient Express* (1974), set entirely in Europe. In all, his films – which in later years have included *The Verdict* (1982), *Q&A* (1990, shot in Spanish Harlem), *Night Falls on Manhattan* (1997) and *Gloria* (1999) – have garnered more than 50 Academy Award nominations.

Lumet still holds extensive preshoot rehearsals for his actors in the East Village, in a large room in the Ukrainian National Home on Second Ave between 8th and 9th Sts. He has written a wonderful treatise on his craft called *Making Movies*, essential reading for film buffs.

NEWSPAPERS & MAGAZINES

Want a definition of 'information overload'? Walk into a well-stocked Manhattan newsstand. The world's major periodicals are all available in the city. Locally, it's hard to determine a single best source for listings – each periodical tends to emphasize a particular type of entertainment.

The New York Times (60¢, $2.50 Sunday) is still the nation's premier newspaper, with more foreign bureaus and reporters than any other publication in the world. Its Weekend section, published on Friday, is an invaluable guide to cultural events. The *Wall Street Journal* (75¢), published weekdays, is must reading for financial workers.

Every week in the *New Yorker* magazine, the 'Goings on about Town' section features an overview of major art, theater, cinema, dance and music events. The *Village Voice* (distributed free in Manhattan each Wednesday), is well known for its nightlife listings that cover the mainstream clubs and music venues. It's also the best-known source for fee-free rental apartments and roommate situations. *New York* magazine offers the same thorough listings for its restaurant-obsessed readers. The *New York Observer*, a weekly newspaper for people interested in local media and politics, strives for quirky listings, with notices about literary readings and parties.

Time Out New York, published on Wednesday, has the same format as its London cousin, with the most comprehensive listings of any publication. *Where New York* is the best free monthly guide to mainstream city events. Available at most hotels, it's more useful than two pocket-size rivals: the monthly *New York Quick Guide* and the weekly *City Guide*.

RADIO

The city boasts more than 100 radio stations, but most 'narrowcast' only one type of programming. This is particularly true on FM, where 'radio apartheid' exists and it's nearly impossible to receive hip-hop and rock on the same frequency unless you're listening to a college station. On FM, classical music lovers turn to WNYC (93.9) and WQXR (96.3), which includes reviews and news reports from its owner. WBGO (88.3) carries National Public Radio in the morning and commercial-free jazz the rest of the day. WNEW (102.7), one of the nation's pioneering rock stations, abandoned the format in 1999 in favor of male-oriented (ie, silly and smutty) talk slots. The best mixture of Top 40 pop and rock can be found on WHTZ (100.3). WBLS (107.5) is a premier spot for mainstream and light soul music, while WQHT (97.1) is known as 'Hot 97' for its hip-hop and rap programming. Those seeking the widest musical variety should listen to WKCR (89.9) and WFMU (90.1), fringe stations with eclectic programming.

On AM frequencies, talk and news rules. WCBS (880) and WINS (1010) carry news and weather updates and WNYC-AM (820) broadcasts National Public Radio programs. WABC (770) is a conservative pundit/radio shrink outlet. WOR (710), one of the nation's oldest stations, carries a calmer type of talk, and WFAN (660) is a 24-hour sports station. WQEW (1560) broadcasts big band music and crooner standards. Spanish speakers listen to WKDM (1380) and WADO (1280). WWRL (1660) is a talk station aimed at the city's black community.

TV

The flagship stations of all four major networks – NBC, CBS, ABC and FOX – are located in New York City and carry national prime-time fare in the evening.

Cable carries well-known networks like CNN, MTV and HBO. Channels dedicated to sports, culture, history and old movies are also available. News broadcasts from Britain, Ireland, France, Mexico, Greece, Korea, Japan and Germany also appear on different Manhattan cable channels between 7 and 11 pm. Cable also carries dozens of local amateur programs on the 'public access' channels. The most famous of them are essentially soft-core porn, carrying strip shows and ads for escort services. Because they are covered by the First Amendment, they are not pay-per-view, and most hotels will carry this regardless of whether their clientele want it or not.

PHOTOGRAPHY & VIDEO

Film & Equipment

Print film is widely available at supermarkets and discount drugstores (which offer the best prices). See the Shopping chapter for more on camera stores.

Drugstores are a good place to get your film cheaply processed. If you drop it off by noon, you can usually pick it up the next day. But if you want your pictures right away, you can find one-hour processing services in the yellow pages under Photo Processing. Be prepared to pay double the overnight cost.

Video Systems

The USA uses the NTSC color TV standard, which is not compatible with other standards (PAL or SECAM) used in Africa, Asia, Australia and Europe unless it is converted.

TIME

New York City is in the Eastern Standard Time (EST) zone – five hours behind Greenwich Mean Time, two hours ahead of Mountain Standard Time (including Denver, Colorado) and three hours ahead of Pacific Standard Time (San Francisco and Los Angeles, California). Almost all of the USA observes daylight-saving time: Clocks go forward one hour from the first Sunday in April to the last Saturday in October, when the clocks are turned back one hour. (It's easy to remember by the phrase 'spring ahead, fall back.')

ELECTRICITY

The USA uses 110V and 60 cycles, and plugs have two or three pins (two flat pins often with a round 'grounding' pin). Plugs with three pins don't fit into a two-hole socket, but adapters are available at hardware stores or drugstores.

WEIGHTS & MEASURES

Americans hate the metric system, and continue to resist it a full 25 years after it was supposed to be fully introduced.

Distances are in feet, yards and miles. Three feet equal 1 yard (.914m); 1760 yards, or 5280 feet, equal 1 mile. Dry weights are in ounces (oz), pounds (lb) and tons (16oz equal 1lb; 2000lb equal 1 ton), but liquid measures differ from dry measures. One pint equals 16 fluid oz; 2 pints equal 1 quart, a common measure for liquids like milk, which is also sold in half-gallons (2 quarts) and gallons (4 quarts). Gasoline is dispensed by the US gallon, which is about 20% less than the imperial gallon. Pints and quarts are also 20% less than imperial ones. There is a conversion chart on the inside back cover of this book.

LAUNDRY

Many New Yorkers live in apartments without laundry facilities, so most residential neighborhoods have an abundance of laundries. The Suds Cafe and Laundromat (☎ 212-741-2366), 141 W 10th St between Greenwich Ave and Waverly Place, has earned a reputation as a social scene. It's open 7 am to 10 pm daily.

Washing machines generally cost $1.50 for a 25-minute cycle; dryers are $1.50 for 30 minutes. (US washing machines run on far quicker cycles than their European counterparts.) Almost all laundries have change-making machines, so you won't have to visit a bank for quarters before doing laundry.

Many of these facilities also offer pick-up laundry services at a rate of about $1 per pound of clothing. Hotels charge very high prices for this service, so it's smart to look for an outside laundry.

TOILETS

New York is not friendly to the weak of bladder. The explosion in the homeless population in the 1970s led to the closure of subway bathrooms, and most facilities turn away nonpatrons from bathrooms.

The city has also quietly abandoned its planned program to introduce Paris-style public toilets in the city. It's possible to walk into a crowded bar or restaurant to use the bathroom if you're discreet and well dressed. The toilets at Saks Fifth Avenue, Macy's, Bloomingdale's and other major department stores are generally well-maintained (see the Shopping chapter for store locations).

LUGGAGE STORAGE

There are no public facilities that allow you to leave luggage at train stations or the airports (unless your bags have been delayed in flight, in which case the airline will hold onto them). All hotels will keep an eye on bags for guests, but do remember to take all items of value out beforehand – hotels will never assume responsibility for lost items.

HEALTH

You don't need any special immunization to visit the USA, and in New York your greatest health threat is heartburn from the wares sold by streetside food vendors.

Travel Insurance

Travel insurance may seem expensive – but it's nowhere near the cost of a medical emergency in the USA. Make sure that you purchase a policy, especially if you come from a country with a nationalized health program that doesn't extend beyond the country's borders. See Travel Insurance, earlier in this chapter, for details.

Medical Services

If you have a medical emergency, call ☎ 911 for assistance. All hospital emergency rooms are obligated to receive sick visitors whether they can pay or not. However, showing up without insurance or money will virtually guarantee a long wait unless you are in extremis. One of New York's largest hospitals is the New York University Medical Center (☎ 212-263-5550), 462 First Ave near 33rd St. For the location of the hospital nearest you, look in the yellow pages.

New York is practically bursting with 24-hour 'pharmacies,' which are really convenience stores with pharmaceutical counters. The main chains are Duane Reade and Rite Aid. The Duane Reade locations that have pharmacy facilities include the outlet on the corner of W 57th St and Broadway (☎ 212-541-9708), as well as Sixth Ave and Waverly Place (☎ 212-674-5357) near the W 4th St subway entrance.

For birth control and STD screening, women can go to Planned Parenthood (☎ 212-965-7000, 800-230-7526). Planned Parenthood has facilities in Manhattan at 26 Bleecker St near Mott St (☎ 212-965-7000), in Brooklyn at 44 Court St (☎ 212-965-7111) and in the Bronx at 349 E 149th St near Cortland St (☎ 212-965-7000 for appointments).

WOMEN TRAVELERS

In general, New York City is a pretty safe place for women travelers. Lesbian visitors will also feel safe and generally welcome in the city. If you are unsure which areas are considered unsafe, ask at your hotel or telephone the tourist office for advice. Given the almost historically low crime figures of the past few years, the subway needn't be shunned by solo female travelers, though it's wise to ride in the conductor's car (right in the middle of the train). If someone stares or acts in an annoying manner, simply move to another part of the car. You're far more likely to encounter obnoxious behavior on the street, where men may greet you with whistles and muttered 'compliments.' Any engagement amounts to encouragement – so simply walk on. If you're ever assaulted, call the police (☎ 911). The Violence Intervention Program can provide support and assistance; its bilingual hotline (☎ 212-360-5090) offers information in Spanish and English.

GAY & LESBIAN TRAVELERS

New York is one of the most gay-friendly cities on earth, and several neighborhoods – particularly Greenwich Village and Chelsea in Manhattan and Jackson Heights in Queens – are populated by many gays and lesbians.

The Gay and Lesbian Switchboard of NY Project (☎ 212-989-0999) and the Gay

& Lesbian National Hotline (☎ 888-843-4564) provide cultural and entertainment information, referrals and peer-counseling services. The hours for both are 6 pm to 10 pm weekdays and noon to 5 pm Saturday. Both share the same Web site (www.glnh.org).

The Lesbian and Gay Community Services Center (☎ 212-620-7310), 208 W 13th St between Seventh and Greenwich Aves, serves some 5000 people each week through its legal aid workshops and social events. The center also provides assistance to travelers and visitor information. A calendar of events at the center is available for those who stop in from 9 am to 11 pm daily. (The center is temporarily located at 1 Little W 12th St until the summer or fall of 2001.)

Gay Men's Health Crisis (☎ 212-367-1455, 800-243-7692) offers blood testing, health care for those with HIV and a wide range of counseling services.

The Anti-Violence Project (☎ 212-714-1184), 240 W 35th St, has a 24-hour hotline (☎ 212-714-1141).

For more information on gay life in the city, see the boxed text 'Gay & Lesbian New York' in the Facts about New York City chapter. Also, see the Gay & Lesbian Venues section in the Entertainment chapter.

DISABLED TRAVELERS

Federal laws guarantee that all government offices and facilities are available to the disabled. Most restaurant listings also note whether the location is wheelchair-accessible. For more information, contact the mayor's Office for People with Disabilities (☎ 212-788-2830).

SATH, the Society for the Advancement of Travel for the Handicapped (☎ 212-447-7284, sathtravel@aol.com) provides information to travelers with disabilities who are SATH members. For membership information, call or write SATH at 347 Fifth Ave, Suite 610, New York, NY 10016.

SENIOR TRAVELERS

Travelers who are 50 years old or older (particularly those over 65) can often avail themselves of reduced transit fares and discount rates on hotels, drug store prescriptions and museum admissions. New York restaurants don't generally offer age-specific discounts, but seniors are about the only class of person who can get a reduction in the $9.50 movie admission price.

Seniors over 65 with ID can obtain a free return-trip transfer slip when purchasing a token on the subway.

The country's most powerful elder organization is the American Association of Retired Persons (AARP; ☎ 800-424-3410), 601 E St NW, Washington, DC 20049. It's a good resource for travel bargains and information. A one-year membership for US residents costs $8.

NEW YORK CITY FOR CHILDREN

With its abundance of world-famous sites, tours and attractions, New York is an ideal place to bring children. You'll find three museums dedicated to children (the Children's Museum of Manhattan, the Brooklyn Chidren's Museum and the Staten Island Children's Museum) and many annual events that appeal to kids.

Kids will also love the Central Park Zoo (officially named the Central Park Wildlife Center) and the more elaborate Bronx Zoo. The Big Apple Circus visits Lincoln Center each winter, and the Ringling Bros and Barnum & Bailey Circus takes over Madison Square Garden every May and June.

See the boxed text 'What's a Kid To Do?' in the Things to See & Do chapter.

UNIVERSITIES

New York is home to many world-class private universities and fine public colleges, including Columbia, New York and Fordham Universities. There's also the New School for Social Research (which offers extensive evening adult classes), Cooper Union and the various colleges of the City University of New York (CUNY). These urban educational centers are not physically separated from the city – in fact, NYU's campus and dorm facilities are distributed throughout Greenwich Village. Columbia's main campus is on Broadway on Manhattan's Upper

ANGUS OBORN

The New York Public Library's majestic reading room

West Side. CUNY's City College campus at St Nicholas Terrace is significant for its neo-Gothic design and worth a visit.

LIBRARIES

The main branch of the New York Public Library (☎ 212-930-0800), Fifth Ave at 42nd St, is a significant architectural attraction and worth visiting if only to see the famous 3rd-floor reading room. Those looking for periodicals and book information will find fewer crowds at the Midtown Manhattan annex (☎ 212-340-0830), directly across the street, or at the Jefferson Market branch (☎ 212-243-4334), 425 Sixth Ave at W 10th St. For other branches, check the library's web site at www.nypl.org.

CULTURAL CENTERS

New York City's major cultural centers include:

Alliance Française (☎ 212-355-6100), 22 E 60th St between Park and Madison Aves

Asia Society (☎ 212-288-6400), 502 Park Ave at 59th St

Czech Center (☎ 212-288-0830), 1109 Madison Ave at 83rd St

Goethe Institute (☎ 212-439-8700), 1014 Fifth Ave between 82nd and 83rd Sts

Hispanic Society of America (☎ 212-926-2234), 613 Broadway at W 155th St in Audubon Terrace

Italian Cultural Institute (☎ 212-879-4242), 686 Park Ave

Japan House (☎ 212-832-1155), 333 E 47th St between First and Second Aves

Spanish Institute (☎ 212-628-0420), 684 Park Ave between 68th and 69th Sts

Swiss Institute (☎ 212-925-2035), 495 Broadway, 3rd floor, between Spring and Broome Sts in SoHo

DANGERS & ANNOYANCES

Beggars

When asked why he robbed banks, criminal Willie Sutton replied, 'That's where the money is!' The same philosophy prompts panhandlers to set up shop at subway entrances, banks, landmarks and street corners where tourists congregate. Requests for money come in dozens of forms, including appeals for a dubious support group ('I'm a member of the United Homeless Organization'), unsubtle appeals to tourist fear ('I don't want to hurt or rob anybody') or even guilt trips ('I know you won't help me because I'm black/poor/homeless...'). It's impossible to differentiate between those truly in need and someone on the hustle, and many tourists assuage their guilt by giving. But New Yorkers know that money handed out even to genuinely destitute beggars will likely go to support a drug or alcohol habit rather than toward a meal or a room for the night – in which case, it will certainly do nothing to change their condition.

It is the nature of life in New York that even some once-decent efforts to help panhandlers have been corrupted, such as the selling of *Street News*, a homeless publication. At least two subway beggars have taken to telling riders that the weather has prevented delivery of their copies or that they've nobly given their copies away to others. The upshot is that gullible listeners give these guys money anyway.

If you wish to give to a legitimate organization helping people in need, contact Citymeals-on-Wheels (☎ 212-687-1234), which reaches out to feed hundreds of hungry people each day.

Scams

A prominent scam that targets out-of-towners takes the form of a shoulder-shrugging appeal for help. This differs from outright panhandling in that the person asking for money makes no pretense of being impoverished. Instead, he or she approaches you with a sad story ('I just got locked out of my car and need money for a cab') and even promise to pay you back. Spare change isn't what these con artists are after – they are very persuasive in trying to get $5 or even $20 from you, and they'll never pay you back. When approached by anyone asking for money, remember that the person is asking a tourist for help because the police and most locals are wise to scams.

In another frequent scam, hustlers set up three-card monte games – where 'players' try to pick the red card out of three shuffled on the top of a cardboard box. This variation on the shell game is widely known to be a no-win scam. Yet enough people play along (or get their wallets lifted while watching the proceedings) to make it a common sight on downtown streets during the weekends.

Drugs

There is heavy drug activity in the far East Village in Alphabet City (Aves A, B, C and D), along Amsterdam Ave above 100th St and in Washington Heights near the George Washington Bridge bus stop. All three neighborhoods have the attendant dangers of such places. Expect to be approached by drug dealers if you wander into any of these places, and avoid walking through them with any amount of cash at night.

Prostitution

New York's strip joints are rather unspectacular (topless only) and either sleazy and cheap (in Midtown) or sleazy and expensive (near Wall St); they're not havens for prostitution. The city also contains sex clubs that cater to Japanese businessmen and pricey escort services that meet the demand for prostitution.

In recent years, police have cracked down on street prostitutes, and instead of being on the stroll on Eleventh Ave near the Lincoln Tunnel, the women ply their risky trade from vans. Elsewhere, prostitutes approach visiting businessmen in public places, such as the stretch of Sixth Ave near Central Park South, the Bull and Bear pub at the Waldorf-Astoria and the lobby of the Grand Hyatt Hotel, one of the most open spots in the city for the hotel sex trade (perhaps because the hotel hosts many visiting professional athletic teams).

Emergency

For police, fire and ambulance calls, dial ☎ 911 – it's a free call from any phone. For non-emergencies, call the police department at ☎ 212-374-5000 from 7:30 am to 6 pm Monday to Friday (this line will also direct you to the nearest station). All federal, state and city government offices appear in a special section in the white pages; the front

DAVE LEWIS

New York's finest (not Erik Estrada)

of every phone book also contains a complete list of community organizations.

Here are some useful numbers:

Alcoholics Anonymous	☎ 212-647-1680
Dept of Health's AIDS Hotline	☎ 212-447-8200
Dept of Consumer Affairs	☎ 212-487-4444
Gay & Lesbian National Hotline	☎ 212-989-0999
Crime Victims Services	☎ 212-577-7777
Legal Aid Society	☎ 212-577-3300

LEGAL MATTERS

If you're arrested, you're allowed to remain silent. There is no legal reason to speak to a police officer if you don't wish, but never walk away from an officer until given permission. All persons who are arrested are legally allowed (and given) the right to make one phone call. If you don't have a lawyer or family member to help you, call your consulate. The police will give you the number upon request.

In New York, police often ignore local laws against public drinking and even pot smoking in the park. But if you're arrested, the cops won't be swayed if you tell them that we told you they don't enforce the law! And the police department is making an effort to crack down on 'quality of life' infractions, so beware.

In 1998, the city briefly tried to stop the strong New York tradition of 'jaywalking' – that is, crossing the street in the middle of the block – but the experiment was largely a dud. There are foot-traffic barriers in parts of Midtown where tourists congregate, but beyond that it's open season.

BUSINESS HOURS

You can shop in New York for almost anything seven days a week, with some exceptions. Stores are generally open 10 am to 6 pm Monday to Saturday, with big department stores open late on Thursday nights. Sunday shopping hours tend to be from noon to 6 pm.

Bookstores and specialty shops often maintain regular night hours, and you'll find many 24-hour drug stores (Duane Reade, Rite Aid, Genovese) that sell pharmaceuticals and a variety of convenience items (toothpaste, candy, soft drinks and basic staples like milk and water).

In a barbaric holdover of the 'blue' laws, liquor stores are closed on Sunday throughout New York state. But you can buy beer at grocery stores after noon on Sunday.

Bakeries and clothing boutiques tend to be closed on Monday.

PUBLIC HOLIDAYS & SPECIAL EVENTS

Hardly a week goes by without a special event taking place in New York. In fact, some 50 officially recognized parades each year honor certain causes or ethnic groups. The city also hosts several hundred street fairs, most of which offer a rather unremarkable selection of fast food, house plants, athletic socks and cheap belts. You're bound to come across one as you stroll through town during the summer months.

Fifth Ave shuts down several times a year for the major parades, including the granddaddy of all ethnic celebrations, the St Patrick's Day Parade on March 17.

On national public holidays (many of which are celebrated on Mondays), banks, schools and government offices (including post offices) shut down, and public transportation, museums and other services operate on a Sunday schedule. If a national holiday falls on Saturday, it's typically observed on Friday; if it falls on Sunday, it's observed on the following Monday.

January

New Year's Day The first day of the year is a national holiday. (See December for information on New Year's Eve festivities.)

Three Kings Parade Every January 5, El Museo del Barrio (☎ 212-831-7272) sponsors this parade, in which thousands of schoolchildren – along with camels, donkeys and sheep – make their way up Fifth Ave to 116th St, the heart of Spanish Harlem.

Winter Antiques Show At this show (☎ 718-292-7392), held mid-month at the Armory (Park Ave at 67th St), dealers peddle $30,000 couches and $15,000 tea services. The crowd includes many celebrities and everyday strollers who couldn't possibly afford the prices.

Martin Luther King Jr Day On the third Monday of the month, this national holiday celebrates the birthday of the civil rights leader.

Chinese New Year The date of the lunar new year varies from late January to early February each year, but the fireworks crackle in Chinatown for days before and after the holiday. Call the Museum of Chinese in the Americas (☎ 212-619-4785) for information.

February

Black History Month The Martin Luther King Jr national holiday (see January) serves as the unofficial kickoff to February's monthlong celebration of African American history and culture. Call Harlem's Schomburg Center for Research in Black Culture (☎ 212-491-2200) for details.

Presidents' Day The third Monday of the month is a national holiday, celebrating the births of George Washington and Abraham Lincoln.

March

St Patrick's Day Parade For more than 200 years, the city's Irish population has honored their homeland's patron saint with this parade down Fifth Ave on March 17. In recent years, a gay Irish group has protested its exclusion from the parade with a demonstration at Fifth Ave and 42nd St.

Easter This Christian holiday falls on a Sunday in late March or April. A wild parade takes place along Fifth Ave in Midtown, as New Yorkers don their best Easter bonnets.

April

French Film Festival Held at a prominent Midtown theater each year, this film festival serves as a harbinger of cultural events to come in the spring and summer.

Antiques Fair At the East Side Armory on Lexington Ave, hundreds of dealers display antiques of all price levels for two weeks in April.

May

International Food Fair In mid-May, Ninth Ave between 42nd and 57th Sts literally teems with people eating ethnic fast food from stalls set up in the street.

Fleet Week Near the end of the month, thousands of sailors from many nations descend on New York for this annual convocation of naval ships and air rescue teams. Call the Intrepid Sea-Air-Space Museum (☎ 212-245-2533) for information.

Memorial Day The last Monday of the month is a national holiday honoring soldiers who died in past wars. It's also the unofficial start of summer.

Carnaval On Memorial Day weekend, Manhattan celebrates Hispanic cultures. Festivities take place on the Lower East Side, between Aves B and D.

June

Toyota Comedy Festival Comedians take to the stage of Carnegie Hall and at a host of clubs in early June. Call ☎ 212-247-7800 or ☎ 888-338-6968 for information.

Bell Atlantic Jazz Festival This early June festival is co-sponsored by the Knitting Factory night club. Call ☎ 212-219-3006 or visit www.jazfest.com for information.

JVC Jazz Festival Nearly all the major concert halls in town are jumping with the top names in jazz from mid- to late June. Call ☎ 212-501-1390 for information.

Museum Mile Festival On the second Tuesday in June, upper Fifth Ave is closed to traffic from 6 to 9 pm, and all nine museums in the area open their doors for free.

Buskers Festival A night of 'buskers' (street performers) highlights a series of free concerts and performances at the World Financial Center downtown. Call ☎ 212-945-0505 for details.

Celebrate Brooklyn This festival begins at the end of June, lasts the entire summer and includes concerts, Shakespearean plays and dance shows. Call ☎ 718-855-7882 or visit www.brooklynx.org for information.

Shakespeare in Central Park The Public Theater (☎ 212-539-8750) sponsors popular outdoor performances of the Bard's work from late June to September in Central Park's Delacorte Theater. In the past, Michelle Pfeiffer, Denzel Washington and other major stars have appeared in the free productions. The theater's Web site is at www.publictheater.org.

Lesbian and Gay Pride Week On the last weekend of June, a huge parade flows down Fifth Ave from Midtown to Greenwich Village. Dance parties take place on the Hudson River piers.

July

Independence Day On July 4, Macy's sponsors its annual fireworks spectacular in the East River. Independence Day is a national holiday.

Lincoln Center Events Lincoln Center hosts an astounding number of events throughout the summer, many of them free, including Lincoln Center Out-of-Doors (☎ 212-875-5108), the Mostly Mozart concert series (☎ 212-875-5103), and the Lincoln Center Festival (☎ 212-546-2656), a biennial event that brings many international actors, singers and acrobats to New York for the first time.

Central Park Summerstage This series of musical performances and author readings takes place near the park's bandshell in July and August. Call ☎ 212-360-2756 for information.

Classic Movies in Bryant Park On Mondays in July and August, the park next to the New York Public Library hosts a series of open-air film screenings.

Outdoor Concerts Also in July and August, the New York Philharmonic and the Metropolitan Opera perform under the stars in Central Park, with other performances in parks in all the boroughs. Call the Parks Department (☎ 212-360-3456, 888-697-2757) for information on all outdoor events.

August

Harlem Week Throughout the month, the city's premier black neighborhood celebrates with festivities that culminate in the Harlem Jazz & Music Fest. For information, call ☎ 212-862-4777.

Panasonic Village Jazz Festival In mid-August, a series of jazz performances takes place in intimate club settings, as well as outdoors in Greenwich Village.

September

Labor Day The first Monday of the month is a national holiday that honors American workers. It also marks the end of the summer tourist season.

US Open Tennis Tournament This world-class event takes place in Flushing Meadows in Queens annually. Attracting the top male and female tennis players, this two-week championship always includes matches on the Labor Day weekend. Call ☎ 888-673-6849 for information.

Fall Festival Also in Queens, this Fall Festival, sponsored by the Queens Council on the Arts (☎ 718-647-3377), starts after Labor Day and lasts until November. It features crafts and food.

Caribbean Day On Labor Day, more than one million people take part in a parade in Brooklyn, making this the single largest event of the year.

New York is Book Country Festival On a weekend in mid-September, publishers and rare book dealers set up shop along Fifth Ave between 53rd and 57th Sts.

New York Film Festival This major event in the film world takes place at Lincoln Center's Walter Reade Theater, beginning in late September. For information, call ☎ 212-875-5600.

October

Columbus Day The second Monday of the month is a national holiday.

Halloween Parade On October 31, this colorful and sometimes wild parade winds its way down Sixth Ave in Greenwich Village, ending in a street party on Christopher St.

November

New York Marathon As the weather cools, the New York Road Runners Club (☎ 212-860-4455) sponsors this annual 26-mile road race, in which some 25,000 runners travel through all five boroughs on the first weekend in November.

Thanksgiving Day On this national holiday, Macy's sponsors its famous parade, a big event with huge balloons and floats that travel down Broadway from W 72nd St to Herald Square.

December

Rockefeller Center Christmas Tree Lighting At 7 pm on the Tuesday after Thanksgiving, the big tree is plugged in. The event features celebrity performances and an appearance by the Radio City Music Hall Rockettes. Call ☎ 212-632-3975 for information.

Radio City Christmas Spectacular The high-kicking Rockettes are on display all month at the famous theater. Call ☎ 212-247-4777 for tickets.

Singing Christmas Tree Celebration At South Street Seaport, dozens of costumed carolers perform several times a day, beginning just after Thanksgiving. Call ☎ 212-732-7678 for information.

Christmas Day December 25 is a national holiday.

New Year's Eve In addition to the annual New Year's Eve festivities in Times Square, the city's celebration features a 5-mile midnight run in Central Park (☎ 212-860-4455), fireworks at the South Street Seaport (☎ 212-732-7678) and First Night, a day-long festival of alcohol-free family events, including ballroom dancing in Grand Central Terminal's main concourse. Events run from 11 am on December 31 to 1 am New Year's Day. Call ☎ 212-883-2476 for details.

ACTIVITIES

Gyms

Some consider the massive Chelsea Piers Complex (☎ 212-336-6000), at the western end of 23rd St on the Hudson River, to be the 'best gym complex in the world.' This huge facility includes a four-level driving range overlooking the river and an indoor ice-skating rink. A huge sports and fitness center contains a running track, swimming pool, workout center, sand for volleyball playing and a rock-climbing wall. A day pass costs $40. The complex is open 6 am to 11 pm weekdays, 7 am to 8 pm Saturday and 8 am to 8 pm Sunday.

Other gyms all over the city offer day rates of $15 to $25. Many advertise in the *Village Voice*. One well-located, no-frills, 'scene'-free gym to keep in mind is the Prescriptive Fitness Gym (☎ 212-307-7760), 250 W 54th St. You pay $20 a day to use its well-maintained machines.

All first-class hotels have at least a small room dedicated to fitness – call ahead or inquire when you reserve your room.

Running

The New York Road Runner's Club (NYRRC; ☎ 212-860-4455), 9 E 89th St, organizes weekend runs all over the city, as well as the annual New York Marathon (see Public Holidays & Special Events, earlier). For more information, visit the NYRRC booth at the Engineer's Gate entrance to Central Park at E 90th St.

You'll find several good spots for solo runs in Manhattan. The 6-mile loop road around Central Park offers runners a respite from city traffic, since it's closed to cars from 10 am to 3 pm and 7 to 10 pm weekdays and all weekend long. But if you don't want to jockey for space with rollerbladers and bikers, try the soft, 1.6-mile path around the Jacqueline Kennedy Onassis Reservoir. You can also jog on the runner's pathway that begins along West St and runs beside the Hudson River from 23rd St all the way to Battery Park City; it passes a very pleasant stretch of public park and offers great views of the Jersey shoreline and the Statue of Liberty. The Upper East Side boasts a path that runs along FDR Drive and the East River from 63rd St to about 115th St. If you're alone, it's not advisable to run farther north than 105th St since the path isn't well lit beyond that point.

Cycling

If you hit the city's pockmarked streets, use a trail bike with wide wheels. Always wear a helmet and be alert so you don't get 'doored' by a passenger exiting a taxi. The Five Borough Bicycle Club (☎ 212-932-2300 ext 115) sponsors free or low-cost weekend trips to the outskirts of the city. For more information, visit the club's office at Hostelling International-New York, 891 Amsterdam Ave at W 103rd St. The New York Cycle Club (☎ 212-828-5711) sponsors day trips and longer rides, and it offers printed guides to 65 of its members' favorite routes. Both of these organizations produce helpful newsletters.

Many places rent bicycles for the day, including Sixth Ave Bicycles (☎ 212-255-5100), 545 Sixth Ave, and Metro Bicycle (☎ 212-581-4500), 360 W 47th St at Ninth

ANGUS OBORN

Cycling through a New York autumn

Ave, among other locations. Frank's Bike Shop (☎ 212-533-6332), 533 Grand St, is an out-of-the-way shop in the Lower East Side with a helpful staff and very low prices.

In-Line Skating

Rollerblading is immensely popular in New York, and daredevil skaters with great bodies dart in and out of city traffic in warm weather. Central Park is the main place to show off your skills (or lack thereof); head to the mall that runs east of Sheep Meadow. You can also skate on Central Park Drive, which is off-limits to cars from 10 am to 3 pm and 7 to 10 pm weekdays and all weekend long. One warning, though: If you're a beginner, definitely avoid the wicked S-shaped curve near E 106th St and Lasker Pool.

If you're just starting out, rent a pair from the nearby Blades West (☎ 212-787-3911), 120 W 72nd St, for $16/27 a day weekdays/weekends, and then ask a volunteer at the W 72nd St park entrance to show you how to stop. If you take the plunge and buy, go to Paragon Athletic Goods (see the Sporting Goods section of the Shopping chapter).

Boating & Fishing

The city's western waterfront, now undergoing a renaissance, has turned greener, thanks to the addition of Hudson River Park in Lower Manhattan. Part of a long-term, 5-mile redevelopment project, the park already includes the Downtown Boathouse, just above Battery Park City, where you can take free kayaking lessons on weekends. Uptown, the 79th St Boathouse features a houseboat docking area and a nice restaurant, but few water sports activities are available for the visitor.

You can actually fish for striped bass on the piers overlooking the Hudson River, but the river's history of chemical contamination makes eating the fish inadvisable. For better fishing, head to City Island in the Bronx (see the Things to See & Do chapter). There, you'll find NY Sailing School (☎ 718-885-3103), 697 Bridge St, which runs sailing courses and rents boats during the summer months, as well as several boats offered for charter.

Getting There & Away

Served by three major airports, two train terminals and a massive bus depot, New York City is the most important transportation hub in the northeastern USA.

AIR

Airports

Most international flights land at John F Kennedy International Airport (JFK), just 15 miles from Midtown in southeastern Queens. La Guardia Airport, 8 miles from Midtown in northern Queens, serves mostly domestic flights, including air shuttles to Boston and Washington, DC.

Newark International Airport in New Jersey, 10 miles west of Manhattan, is the hub for Continental Airlines. Many major carriers use its new international arrivals terminal.

The Port Authority of New York & New Jersey operates all three airports and maintains a Web site with detailed information about each airport at www.panynj.gov.

For information about getting to/from the airports, see the Getting Around chapter.

JFK International Airport This airport serves 35 million passengers a year. It's sprawling and unpopular – and its crowded international arrivals terminal rivals the chaos of London's Heathrow Airport.

Airlines used to build showcase terminals at JFK, and thus the airport grew to its uncoordinated state with no coherent plan. While some of the original airlines (Eastern, Pan Am) have disappeared, the terminals remain, linked by the JFK Expressway and a free shuttle bus. American Airlines, British Airways, Delta and TWA have their own terminals; most other airlines use the crowded International Arrivals Building.

To find out if the airport is closed in bad weather, call the information line (☎ 718-244-4444), as individual airlines may be reluctant to give honest information about flight delays over the phone.

ANGUS OBORN

You're not in Kansas anymore.

Until the airport undergoes a much-needed renovation, set to be completed in 2005, it's best not to spend too much time there. JFK's Duty Free shops, like those in most US cities, are useless – you can get alcohol, electronics and clothes cheaper in town, so don't expect to embark on a last-minute purchasing spree for anything other than cigarettes.

La Guardia Airport If you're arriving or departing in the middle of the day, La Guardia Airport (☎ 718-533-3400) is a more convenient choice than JFK. US Airways and the Delta Shuttle have their own terminals; all other airlines use the Central Terminal Building in front of the parking garage.

La Guardia isn't equipped to accommodate wide-body jets, so cross-country or transatlantic flights can't land there. The airport mainly serves destinations in Canada and the northeastern USA.

Newark International Airport Newark International Airport (☎ 973-961-6000, www.newarkairport.com) is the best choice at the moment for foreign visitors, thanks to a new, well-organized international arrival terminal. This airport's advantages include a large immigration hall that speeds passport checks and a monorail system that links the terminals for quick transfers to domestic flights.

Moreover, flights to Newark are usually a bit cheaper because of the erroneous perception that the airport is less accessible than JFK. Most people who fly into Newark do have to endure a bus journey into Manhattan – but JFK arrivals are subject to similar delays. If you'd rather not face the potential gridlock of a bus ride into Manhattan, you can take a short shuttle bus ride to the PATH train, which travels from Newark's Penn Station into New York City. Call ☎ 800-234-7284 for more information.

By 2002, the airport plans to link its monorail system with New Jersey Transit trains; this should make for a speedy trip into Manhattan.

Warning

The information in this chapter is particularly vulnerable to change: Prices for international travel are volatile, routes are introduced and canceled, schedules change, special deals come and go, and rules and visa requirements are amended. Airlines and governments seem to take a perverse pleasure in making price structures and regulations as complicated as possible. You should check directly with the airline or a travel agent to make sure you understand how a fare (and ticket you may buy) works. In addition, the travel industry is highly competitive and there are many lurks and perks.

The upshot of this is that you should get opinions, quotes and advice from as many airlines and travel agents as possible before you part with your hard-earned cash. The details given in this chapter should be regarded as pointers and are not a substitute for your own careful, up-to-date research.

Departure Tax

All passengers bound for a foreign destination must pay a $6 airport departure tax, and all passengers entering the USA from abroad must pay a $6.50 North American Free Trade Agreement (NAFTA) tax. Most of the time, these taxes will be included in the purchase price of your airline ticket, and you won't have to worry about paying these fees at the airport.

Airline Offices

The following airlines have offices downtown or at the airports:

Aer Lingus (☎ 800-474-7424, www.aerlingus.ie), 509 Madison Ave

Aeromexico (☎ 212-754-2140, 800-237-6669, www.aeromexico.com), 37 W 57th St

Air Canada (☎ 212-869-8840, 800-776-3000, www.aircanada.ca), 15 W 50th St

Air France (☎ 212-830-4000, 800-321-4538, www.airfrance.fr), 120 W 56th St

American Airlines (☎ 800-433-7300, www.aa.com), 18 W 49th St

British Airways (☎ 800-247-9297, www.british-airways.com), 530 Fifth Ave

Continental Airlines (☎ 212-319-9494, www.continental.com), 100 E 42nd St

Delta Air Lines (☎ 800-221-1212, www.delta-air.com), 100 E 42nd St

Finnair (☎ 212-499-9000, 800-950-5000, www.finnair.com), 228 E 45th St

Japan Airlines (☎ 800-525-3663, www.jal.co.jp), JFK International Airport

Korean Air (☎ 800-438-5000, www.koreanair.com), 609 Fifth Ave

Olympic Airways (☎ 212-735-0200, www.olympic-airways.gr), 647 Fifth Ave

Philippine Airlines (☎ 800-435-9725, www.philippineair.com), JFK International Airport

Qantas Airways (☎ 800-227-4500, www.qantas.com.au), 712 Fifth Ave

Singapore Airlines (☎ 212-644-8801, 800-742-3333, www.singaporeair.com), 55 E 59th St

Swissair (☎ 800-221-4750, www.swissair.com), 608 Fifth Ave

TWA (☎ 800-893-5436, www.twa.com), 1 E 59th St

United Airlines (☎ 800-241-6522, www.ual.com), 100 E 42nd St

US Airways (☎ 800-428-4322, www.usairways.com), 101 Park Ave

Virgin Atlantic (☎ 800-862-8621, www.virgin.com)

Buying Tickets

The plane ticket will probably be the single most expensive item in your budget and buying it can be intimidating. Before you just walk into the nearest travel agent or airline office, do some research of the current market. Start looking early – some of the cheapest tickets and best deals must be bought months in advance, and some popular flights sell out early.

Note that high season in the USA is mid-June to mid-September (summer) and one week before and after Christmas. You'll find the best rates for travel to and in the USA from November through March.

If you're hunting for bargains, look at the travel sections of magazines like *Time Out* and *TNT* in the UK, the Sunday editions of newspapers like the *New York Times* and *Los Angeles Times* in the USA or the *Sydney Morning Herald* and *The Age* in Australia. Ads in these publications offer cheap fares, but don't be surprised if the discount tickets are sold out when you contact the agents. They deals are usually low-season fares on obscure airlines with conditions attached. Talk to other recent travelers if possible – they may be able to stop you from making some of the same old mistakes.

Call travel agents for deals. Council Travel (☎ 800-226-8624, www.counciltravel.com) and STA Travel (☎ 800-777-0112, www.statravel.com) offer some of the best rates, especially for students. Both agencies have offices in Manhattan. Council Travel offers reservation services at two locations: 148 W 4th St (☎ 212-254-2525) and 895 Amsterdam Ave (☎ 212-666-4177). STA Travel (☎ 212-627-3111) is at 10 Downing St near Sixth Ave. You might also try the main American Express office (☎ 212-421-8240), in the World Financial Center at West and Vesey Sts, which offers package deals.

Some travel agencies specialize in last-minute discount flights. Called 'consolidators,' they advertise in the Travel section of the Sunday *New York Times*, as well as the *Village Voice*. In Manhattan, try TFI Tours (☎ 212-736-1140), 34 W 32nd St.

Courier flights are another option for the budget traveler (see the 'Air Travel Glossary' boxed text). Given its importance as a cargo port, New York is the best place in the USA to arrange courier flights around the globe. Now Voyager (☎ 212-431-1616) books courier flights and last-minute domestic specials. It's best to call their busy office after business hours to hear a comprehensive voice menu of locations and conditions.

For courier flights to/from Asia, try East-West Express (☎ 516-536-2112); Central America, try Air Facility (☎ 718-712-1769); Europe, try Air Tech (☎ 212-219-7000). The magazine *Travel Unlimited*, PO Box 1058, Allston, MA 02134, publishes details of the cheapest airfares and courier possibilities.

Also, check out last-minute flight options on the Internet. The prominent online firm Priceline.com (www.priceline.com) offers cut-rate tickets; you name the price you're willing to pay and the date you want to leave, and the search engine matches you with an available airline seat. The catches: The flight is nonchangeable and nonrefundable, and your credit card will be billed right away, as soon as the service locates a flight to match your price. But some people report finding transatlantic flights for as little as $150 roundtrip even in high season. Other Web sites that offer discount airline tickets include www.cheaptickets.com and www.travelocity.com. Also, airline Web sites often list special deals available only through online purchases.

Outside the US, cheap tickets are available in two distinct categories: official and unofficial. Official tickets have a variety of names, including budget, advance-purchase, Apex and super-Apex. Unofficial tickets are simply discounted tickets that the airlines release through selected travel agents (not through airline offices).

If you're traveling from the UK, you'll probably find that the cheapest flights are advertised by obscure 'bucket shops' (see the 'Air Travel Glossary' boxed text). Many are honest and solvent, but there are a few rogues who'll take your money and disappear, to reopen elsewhere a month or two later under a new name. If you feel suspicious, don't give the agents all the money at once – leave a deposit of 20% or so and pay the balance on receiving the ticket. If they insist on cash in advance, go elsewhere. Once you have the ticket, phone the airline to confirm that you are booked on the flight.

No matter where you shop for your ticket, find out the fare, route, duration of the journey and any restrictions on the ticket. Fare levels change constantly, and some fares that include accommodations may be as cheap as roundtrip fares. Return (roundtrip) tickets usually work out cheaper than

Air Travel Glossary

Baggage Allowance This will be written on your ticket and usually includes one 20kg (44lb) item to go in the hold, plus one item of hand luggage.

Bucket Shops These are unbonded travel agencies that specialize in discounted airline tickets.

Bumped Just because you have a confirmed seat doesn't mean you're going to get on the plane (see Overbooking).

Cancellation Penalties If you have to cancel or change a discounted ticket, there are often heavy penalties involved; insurance sometimes protects you from these penalties. Some airlines impose penalties on regular tickets as well, particularly against 'no-show' passengers.

Check-In Airlines ask you to check in a certain time ahead of the flight departure (usually one to two hours on international flights). If you fail to check in on time and the flight is overbooked, the airline can cancel your booking and give your seat to somebody else.

Confirmation Having a ticket written out with the flight and date you want doesn't mean you have a seat until the agent has checked with the airline that your status is 'OK' or confirmed. Meanwhile you could just be 'on request.'

Courier Fares Businesses often need to send urgent documents or freight securely and quickly. Courier companies hire people to accompany the package through customs and, in return, offer a discount ticket that is sometimes a phenomenal bargain. In effect, what the companies do is ship their freight as your luggage on regular commercial flights. This is a legitimate operation, but there are two shortcomings – the short turnaround time of the ticket (usually not longer than a month) and the limitation on your luggage allowance. You may have to surrender all your allowance and take only carry-on luggage.

ITX An ITX, or 'independent inclusive tour excursion,' is often available on tickets to popular holiday destinations. Officially, it's a package deal combined with hotel accommodations, but many agents will sell you one of these for the flight only and give you phony hotel vouchers in the unlikely event that you're challenged at the airport.

Lost Tickets If you lose your airline ticket, an airline will usually treat it like a traveler's check and, after inquiries, issue you another one. Legally, however, an airline is entitled to treat it like cash; if you lose it, then it's gone forever. Take good care of your tickets.

MCO An MCO, or 'miscellaneous charge order,' is a voucher that looks like an airline ticket but carries no destination or date. It can be exchanged through any International Air Transport Association (IATA) airline for a ticket on a specific flight. It's a useful alternative to an onward ticket in those countries that demand one, and it's more flexible than an ordinary ticket if you're unsure of your route.

two one-way fares – often *much* cheaper. Ask about discounts, as airlines often offer competitive low-season, student and senior citizens fares.

Once you have your ticket, write down its number, together with the flight number and other details, and keep the information somewhere separate. If the ticket is lost or stolen, this will help you get a replacement.

Use the fares quoted in this book as a guide only. They are approximate and based on the rates advertised by travel agents and airlines at press time. Quoted airfares do not necessarily constitute a recommendation for the carrier.

Visit USA Passes Most US carriers offer special deals for non-US citizens who book abroad. These passes usually come in the form of coupons – you use one for each leg of your flight. Ask a travel agent about these offers.

Air Travel Glossary

No-Shows No-shows are passengers who fail to show up for their flight. Full-fare passengers who fail to turn up are sometimes entitled to travel on a later flight. Everyone else is penalized (see Cancellation Penalties).

On Request This is an unconfirmed booking for a flight.

Onward Tickets Many countries require that you have a ticket out of the country before you're allowed to enter. If you're unsure of your next move, the easiest solution is to buy the cheapest onward ticket to a neighboring country or a ticket from a reliable airline that can later be refunded if you do not use it.

Open Jaw Tickets On these roundtrip tickets, you fly out to one place but return from another. If available, these can save you backtracking to your arrival point.

Overbooking Airlines hate to fly with empty seats, and since every flight has some passengers who fail to show up, airlines often book more passengers than they have seats. Usually, excess passengers make up for the no-shows, but occasionally somebody gets bumped. Guess who it is most likely to be? The passengers who check in late.

Point-to-Point Tickets These discount tickets can be bought on some routes in return for passengers waiving their rights to a stopover.

Reconfirmation At least 72 hours prior to the departure time of an onward or return flight, you must contact the airline and 'reconfirm' that you intend to be on the flight. If you don't do this, the airline could delete your name from the passenger list and you could lose your seat.

Restrictions Discounted tickets often have various restrictions on them – such as advance payment, minimum and maximum periods you must be away (eg, a minimum of two weeks or a maximum of one year) and penalties for changing the tickets.

Round-the-World Tickets RTW tickets give you a limited period (usually a year) in which to circumnavigate the globe. You can go anywhere the carrying airlines go, as long as you don't backtrack. The number of stopovers, or the total number of separate flights, must be decided before you set off, and RTW tickets usually cost a bit more than a basic roundtrip flight.

Standby On this discounted ticket, you only fly if there is a seat free at the last moment. Standby fares are usually available only on domestic routes.

Travel Periods Ticket prices vary with the time of year – low (off-peak) season, high (peak) season, low-shoulder season or high-shoulder season. Usually, the fare depends on your outward flight – if you depart in the high season and return in the low season, you pay the high-season fare.

A typical Visit USA scheme is the one offered by Continental Airlines; this pass can be used with an international airline ticket from anywhere outside the USA except Canada and Mexico. You must have your trip planned in advance and complete your travels within 60 days of the first domestic flight in the USA or 81 days after arrival in the USA, whichever comes first. If you decide to change destinations once you're in the USA, you'll be penalized at least $50. During the high season, it costs around $500 for three coupons (minimum purchase; one coupon equals one flight). American Airlines offers a similar deal. See Airline Offices, earlier, for contact information.

Round-the-World Tickets Round-the-World (RTW) tickets that include travel within the USA are popular and can be bargains. Prices start at about UK£900, A$1800 or US$1500.

Official RTW tickets, usually put together by a combination of two airlines, permit you to fly anywhere you want on the airlines' route systems as long as you do not backtrack. Also, you usually must book the first sector in advance and pay normal cancellation penalties if you change your mind. Most airlines restrict the number of sectors that can be flown within the USA and Canada to four, and some airlines black out a few popular routes (like Honolulu to Tokyo), but otherwise you can usually enjoy as many stopovers as you like. In most cases, a 14-day advance purchase is required. After you purchase your ticket, you can change the dates without penalty and add or delete stops for $50 each. Tickets are usually valid for one year.

The majority of RTW tickets restrict you to just two airlines. For example, Qantas flies in conjunction with either American Airlines, British Airways, Delta Air Lines, Northwest Airlines, Canadian Airlines, Air France or KLM. Canadian Airlines links up with Philippine Airlines, KLM or South African Airways, among others. Continental Airlines flies with either Malaysia Airlines, Singapore Airlines or Thai Airways. The possibilities go on and on. Your best bet is to find a travel agent that advertises or specializes in RTW tickets. You can also see if your travel agent can create a de facto RTW pass using a combination of discounted tickets.

Travelers with Special Needs

If you have a special need – a broken leg, dietary restrictions, dependence on a wheelchair, responsibility for a baby, fear of flying – let the airline know as soon as possible so that it can make arrangements accordingly. Remind them when you reconfirm your booking (at least 72 hours before departure) and again when you check in at the airport. Before you buy your ticket, it may be worth phoning several airlines to find out how they handle your particular needs.

Airports and airlines can be surprisingly accommodating to passengers in wheelchairs, but they do need advance warning. Most international airports provide escorts from the check-in desk to the airplane if necessary, and most have ramps, lifts, accessible toilets and reachable phones. Aircraft toilets, on the other hand, are likely to present a problem; travelers should discuss this with the airline and, if necessary, with their doctor.

Guide dogs for the blind often have to travel in a specially pressurized baggage compartment with other animals, away from their owners, though smaller guide dogs may be admitted to the cabin. Guide dogs are not subject to quarantine as long as they have proof of being vaccinated against rabies.

Deaf travelers can ask for airport and in-flight announcements to be written down for them.

Children under two traditionally travel for 10% of the standard fare (or free, on some airlines), as long as they don't occupy a seat. (They don't get a baggage allowance either.) 'Skycots' should be provided by the airline if requested in advance; these can fit a child weighing up to about 22lb. Children between two and 12 usually occupy a seat for half to two-thirds of the full fare, and they do get a baggage allowance. Strollers can often be taken on as hand luggage.

Canada

The *Toronto Globe & Mail* and *Vancouver Sun* carry travel agents' ads; the magazine *Great Expeditions*, PO Box 8000-411, Abbotsford, BC V2S 6H1, is also useful. If you're looking for a reliable travel agency, try Travel CUTS, which has offices in all major cities.

Roundtrip fares to New York from Toronto start at around C$330 (US$200) on US Airways and Delta Air Lines. Fares from Montreal usually hover around C$300 (US$200), though you can sometimes find good deals for under US$200.

UK & Ireland

For special deals, check the ads in magazines like *Time Out* and *City Limits*, plus the Sunday papers and *Exchange & Mart*. Also check the free magazines widely available in London – start by looking outside the main railway stations.

Most British travel agents are registered with the Association of British Travel Agents (ABTA). If you've paid for your flight at an ABTA-registered agent who then goes out of business, ABTA will guarantee a refund or an alternative. Unregistered bucket shops are riskier but sometimes cheaper.

London is arguably the world's headquarters for bucket shops, which frequently place ads and can usually beat published airline fares. Two good, reliable agents for cheap tickets in the UK are Trailfinders (☎ 020-7937-5400), 194 Kensington High St, London W8 7RG, and STA Travel (☎ 020-7581-4132), 86 Old Brompton Rd, London SW7 3LQ. Trailfinders produces a lavishly illustrated brochure that includes airfare details.

In the winter, prices plummet on the crowded London-to-New York corridor – expect to get a roundtrip fare for about £250, though price wars can bring the fare all the way down to £150. In summer, the prices rise to £400 and above roundtrip. Virgin Atlantic offers a standard, roundtrip, weekday, high-season fare for £450 (US$680), but cheaper advance-purchase tickets are available.

Aer Lingus offers direct flights from Shannon and Dublin to New York City, but because competition on flights from London is fiercer, it sometimes costs less to fly to London first. The best fare you'll find from Ireland is about £300 (US$450).

The Globetrotters Club, BCM Roving, London WC1N 3XX, publishes a newsletter called *Globe* that covers obscure destinations and that contains ads for traveling companions.

Continental Europe

Though London is the travel-discount capital of Europe, several other cities offer a range of good deals, especially Amsterdam and Athens. Many travel agents in Europe have ties with STA Travel, where cheap tickets can be bought and STA Travel tickets can be altered free of charge (first change only). Council Travel also maintains partnerships with European travel agents.

In France, Council Travel works with Usit Connect, (☎ 1-43-29-69-50), 6 Rue de Vaugirard, 75006 Paris. In Germany, Council Travel's counterpart is Usit Campus, which has offices in Munich (☎ 89-38-838970), at Adalbert Strasse 32, and Frankfurt (☎ 69-97-128860), at Leipziger Strasse 1.

In the Netherlands, NBBS Reizen is a popular nationwide travel agency; it has offices in Amsterdam at Roken 38 (☎ 20-624-0989) and Leidestraat 53 (☎ 20-638-1736). In Athens, try International Student & Youth Travel Service (☎ 01-323-3767), Nikis 11.

Australia & New Zealand

In Australia and New Zealand, STA Travel and Flight Centres International are major dealers in cheap airfares; check the travel agents' ads in the yellow pages and call around. STA's main Australian office (☎ 9347-6911) is at 224 Faraday St, Carlton South, Melbourne, VIC 3053; its principal New Zealand office (☎ 0800-874-773, 309-0458) is at 10 High St in Auckland.

Qantas flies to Los Angeles from Sydney, Melbourne (via Sydney or Auckland) and Cairns (several times each week) with onward connections to New York City on a US carrier. United Airlines flies to San Francisco and Los Angeles from Sydney.

The cheapest tickets require a 21-day advance purchase, a minimum stay of seven days and a maximum stay of 30 days. Qantas flies from Melbourne or Sydney to New York (through Los Angeles) for a top price of A$2980 (US$1790) in the high season, but the usual standard, advance-purchase fare runs around A$2570 (US$1540). Sometimes, though, you can find fares for as low as A$1570 (US$900).

Flying with Air New Zealand can sometimes be cheaper. Both Qantas and Air New Zealand also offer tickets with longer stays or stopovers, but you'll pay extra. Full-time students can save on roundtrip fares to the USA with proper ID.

Asia

Hong Kong is the discount plane ticket capital of the region, but its bucket shops can be unreliable. Ask the advice of other travelers before buying a ticket. STA Travel has branches in Hong Kong, Tokyo, Singapore, Bangkok and Kuala Lumpur.

Many flights to the USA go via Honolulu. Those en route to the East Coast may stop in Anchorage, Alaska.

Japan Japan Airlines offers the only nonstop flight from Tokyo to New York City. Flights leave twice a day and start at ¥150,000 (US$1425), with some discounts at off-peak times. The airline also flies to the US West Coast and Dallas from Tokyo and to Honolulu from Osaka, Nagoya, Fukuoka and Sapporo.

United Airlines offers three flights a day to Honolulu from Tokyo, with connections to the West Coast cities of Los Angeles, San Francisco and Seattle. Northwest Airlines also offers daily flights to the West Coast from Tokyo.

Southeast Asia Numerous airlines fly to the USA from Southeast Asia; bucket shops in Bangkok and Singapore should be able to come up with the best deals. Tickets to the US West Coast often allow a free stopover in Honolulu.

Northwest Airlines flies to Honolulu from Hong Kong, Bangkok, Manila, Seoul and Singapore, with connections to the West Coast and East Coast. Korean Air and Philippine Airlines also offer flights from a number of Southeast Asian cities to Honolulu, with onward connections. But it's a long journey if you're going all the way to New York City.

Mexico & South America

Most flights from Mexico and Central and South America go via Miami, Houston or Los Angeles, but some fly directly to New York City. (LANChile Airlines offers this direct service.) Most countries' main carriers, including Aerolíneas Argentinas and LANChile, as well as US airlines like United and American, serve destinations in Mexico and South America.

Continental offers flights from about 20 cities in Mexico, Central and South America, including Lima, San José, Guatemala City, Cancún and Mérida, most of which arrive at Houston International Airport, with connections to the rest of the USA. Continental also operates daily nonstop flights from Mexico City to Newark International Airport. Flights from Mexico City to New York run around US$500; from Guatemala City, they run as high as US$800.

BUS

All suburban and long-distance buses leave and depart from the Port Authority Bus Terminal (☎ 212-564-8484), 41st St at Eighth Ave. Port Authority has been modernized and much improved in recent years. Though it's not as rough as its reputation, you can still be hassled by beggars asking for handouts or offering to carry bags for tips.

Greyhound (☎ 212-971-6300, 800-231-2222, www.greyhound.com) links New York with major cities across the country. Peter Pan Bus Lines (☎ 800-343-9999, www.peterpan-bus.com) runs buses to the nearest major cities, including a daily express to Boston for $35 one-way and $66 roundtrip.

Short Line (☎ 212-736-4700, www.shortlinebus.com) runs numerous buses to towns in northern New Jersey and upstate New York. New Jersey Transit buses (☎ 201-762-5100, www.njtransit.state.nj.us) serve the entire Garden State, with direct service to Atlantic City for $15 to $20 one-way.

Bus Passes

Greyhound's Ameripass is vital if you plan on doing a lot of bus traveling out of New York, as individual tickets will add up to far more than the pass price. It costs $209 for seven days of unlimited travel ($179 if bought abroad), $319 for 15 days and $429 for 30 days (these rates apply in any season). Children under 11 travel for half-price. Students and seniors travel at a small discount. You can get on and off at any Greyhound terminal.

The International Ameripass can be purchased at overseas travel agencies or from the Greyhound International Office (☎ 212-971-0492, fax 212-967-2239) at the subway level of the Port Authority Bus Terminal. It's open 8:30 am to 4:30 pm Monday to Thursday, 8:30 am to 4 pm Friday.

TRAIN

Pennsylvania Station (Penn Station), 33rd St between Seventh and Eighth Aves, is the departure point for all Amtrak trains (☎ 212-582-6875, 800-872-7245, www.amtrak.com), including the *Metroliner* service to Princeton, NJ, and Washington, DC. Note that the *Metroliner* is slightly faster than the *Northeast Direct* service to the same points, but the fare can be twice as high; the main advantage of the *Metroliner* is that you'll get a reserved seat. Basic service from New York to Washington, DC, costs around $65; a *Metroliner* ticket costs about $120. All fares vary based on the day of the week and the time you want to travel. Call Amtrak for information about special discount passes if you plan on traveling throughout the USA by train.

Long Island Rail Road (LIRR; ☎ 718-217-5477) serves several hundred thousand commuters each day, with service from Penn Station to points in Brooklyn, Queens and the suburbs of Long Island, including the resort areas. New Jersey Transit (☎ 973-762-5100) also operates trains from Penn Station, with service to the suburbs and the Jersey Shore.

The only train line that still departs from Grand Central Terminal, Park Ave at 42nd St, is the Metro-North Railroad (☎ 212-532-4900, www.mnr.org), which serves the northern city suburbs, Connecticut and the Hudson Valley.

TONY WHEELER

Grand Central's facade

CAR & MOTORCYCLE

It's a nightmare to have a car in New York, but getting there is easy. I-95, which runs from Maine to Florida, cuts east-to-west through the city as the Cross Bronx Expressway. Outside of New York City, I-95 continues south as the New Jersey Turnpike; north of the city, it becomes the Connecticut Turnpike. Via I-95, Boston is 194 miles to the north, Philadelphia, 104 miles to the south and Washington, DC, 235 miles south.

To reach the Long Island Expressway, take the Queens Midtown Tunnel out of Manhattan (a stretch of road often choked by traffic). Alternately, you can get out of town by taking the Grand Central Parkway (right off the Triborough Bridge), which cuts through Queens on its way to Long Island. Northern Blvd in Queens becomes Route 25A, which runs the northern length of Long Island.

Taking the Lincoln or Holland Tunnels out of town connects you with the New Jersey Turnpike, which runs roughly diagonally across the state to Philadelphia. The turnpike also connects to the Garden State Parkway (which travels to the Jersey Shore and Atlantic City). Leaving Manhattan by the Lincoln Tunnel also connects you (via Route 3) to the westbound I-80, which cuts through the middle of Pennsylvania. I-78, which goes to Harrisburg, PA, can be reached by taking the Holland Tunnel.

Highway speed limits in Connecticut and upstate New York are 65mph; in New Jersey, they remain 55mph.

HITCHHIKING

Hitchhiking has a bad reputation throughout the USA, and it is extremely rare to see anyone trying to thumb a ride, even at spots where it might be easy to do so (the entrance to the Lincoln Tunnel, for example). Generally, many Americans regard hitchhikers as potential homicidal maniacs or as easy prey. Because of this, Lonely Planet does not recommend it. Travelers who do try to hitchhike should understand that they are taking a small but serious risk. People who do choose to hitch will be safer if they travel in pairs and let someone know where they are planning to go.

BOAT

It's highly unusual for anyone to yacht their way into town, and those who do will find few ports ready to receive them – just an exclusive boat slip at the World Trade Center and a long term tie-up at the 79th St Boathouse on the Upper West Side. Manhattan, on the whole, does not welcome the temporary tie-up of recreational boats.

Visiting boaters should contact City Island Yacht (☎ 718-885-2300), a full-service marina on City Island off the mainland of the Bronx.

ORGANIZED TOURS

The well-known West Coast firm Green Tortoise Adventure Travel (☎ 415-956-7500, 800-867-8647, www.greentortoise.com), 494 Broadway, San Francisco, CA 94133, offers alternative bus transportation to New York, with stops at picturesque places along the way. The 10-day trip crosses the country on either southern or northern routes, depending on the seasonal weather, and costs about $300 for transportation, with an additional charge of about $81 for food. Lodging includes camping or sleeping on bunks on the bus. (Call ahead for information on current routes.) It isn't exactly luxury travel, but it's fun and a cheap way to see the country.

Getting Around

It's hard to exaggerate the problem of gridlock in Manhattan's streets. The entire center of the island's grid system is packed with cars during the day, and major avenues – primarily Lexington and Broadway – can be partially blocked by double-parked trucks making deliveries to stores. The subway is the fastest way to get between uptown and downtown points, and contrary to popular belief, taking the subway is statistically safer than walking the streets in broad daylight.

Like most New Yorkers, you should use the city buses exclusively to get to points located along the same avenue, when it's easy to calculate the amount of travel time by looking at the traffic. The best overall plan is to use the subway all day until about 9 pm, then use taxis at night.

TO/FROM THE AIRPORT

When departing for the airports in the middle of the day, allow at least one hour's travel time.

The Port Authority of New York and New Jersey's Air Ride Line (☎ 800-247-7433) offers comprehensive information on ground transportation to and from all three airports, as does the Web site www.panynj.gov.

No matter what airport you fly into, there are several advantages to using a car service for an airport journey. These hired cars are newer and larger than cabs, and you do not have to tip the driver. You can also order a pickup a day in advance and pay by credit card. If you ask for a 'price check' while ordering the taxi, the dispatcher can tell you the exact cost of the journey, which should run between $35 to $50, depending on your departure point and the airport destination.

Shared minivan shuttles deliver you door-to-door and can save you quite a bit of money, if you're willing to ride around while the driver drops off passengers all over town (some shuttles do promise to make no more than three stops, though). When you're ready to go back to the airport, taking the shuttle is a good alternative to hailing a taxi, especially if you're leaving town at rush hour. Gray Line (☎ 800-451-0455, www.graylinenewyork.com) runs from all three airports to most major hotels in Manhattan. SuperShuttle (☎ 212-315-3006, 800-258-3826) travels from the airports to hotels and residences. See the individual airport headings, below, for specific times, prices and locations for both services.

JFK Airport

Gray Line (☎ 800-451-0455, www.graylinenewyork.com) offers minivan shuttle service to hotels in Manhattan between 21st and 63rd Sts from all three New York area airports. The fare is $14 from JFK to the city and $19 from the city to the airport; the

RICHARD I'ANSON

roundtrip fare is $28. At the airport, the shuttle operates from 7 am to 11:30 pm, with hotel pickups from 5 am to 9 pm.

SuperShuttle (☎ 212-315-3006, 800-358-5826) serves hotels and residences in a wider area of Manhattan, from Battery Park at the tip of Lower Manhattan to 227th St. The fare is $14 to $22, depending on the pickup or drop-off location. SuperShuttle runs 24 hours a day.

New York Airport Service Express buses (☎ 718-875-8200) run to/from JFK every 15 to 30 minutes from 6 am to midnight daily. The fare is $13 one-way. Buses leave from several locations: Penn Station, 32nd St at Seventh Ave; Port Authority Bus Terminal, 42nd St at Eighth Ave (look for the Airport Bus Center); and Grand Central Terminal, Park Ave at 42nd St.

To reach JFK from Manhattan, you can also take the subway to the Howard Beach–JFK station on the A line (allow at least an hour) and then switch to a free yellow and blue bus at the long-term parking lot for a 15-minute ride to the terminals. (You have to haul your luggage up and over several flights of stairs at the Howard Beach terminal.)

The taxi fare is a flat rate of $30 from JFK to any location in Manhattan. (The fare is due to rise at least $2 in the near future, and you must pay for tolls, which could bring your bill to $35 without tip.) Be aware that this flat rate does *not* apply to trips out to the airport – you will pay for time spent in traffic.

The long-term parking lot at JFK costs $8 a day; short-term parking closer to the terminals costs $8 for four hours.

La Guardia Airport

Gray Line (☎ 800-451-0455) will take you to most major hotels in Manhattan. SuperShuttle (☎ 800-358-5826) offers door-to-door shuttle service throughout the city. The fare from La Guardia is $13 one-way on Gray Line, $13 to $17 on SuperShuttle. Roundtrip tickets are slightly cheaper. See the JFK Airport section for schedule information.

New York Airport Service Express buses (☎ 718-875-8200) run to/from La Guardia every 20 minutes from 6:40 am to 11:40 pm daily. The bus picks up and drops off passengers at three locations in Manhattan: Grand Central Terminal, Port Authority Bus Terminal and Penn Station. The one-way fare is $10.

The Delta Water Shuttle (☎ 800-221-1212), operated by Delta Air Lines, leaves frequently for La Guardia from three points in Manhattan: Pier 11 at South and Wall Sts, E 34th St on the East River and 62nd St. The trip takes 20 to 45 minutes, depending on where you board. The fare is $15 one-way, $25 roundtrip.

La Guardia is also accessible via public transportation. Ride the subway to the Roosevelt Ave-Jackson Heights or the 74th St-Broadway stops in Queens (two linked stations served by five lines). You then take the Q33 bus to the La Guardia main terminals or the Q47 bus to the Delta Shuttle's Marine Air Terminal. This journey takes well over an hour and costs two tokens ($3). In Upper Manhattan, you can also catch an M60 bus, which runs along the length of 125th St and heads directly to La Guardia; the fare is $1.50.

Taxis from La Guardia to Midtown cost $16 to $26 plus tolls.

Newark Airport

Gray Line (☎ 800-451-0455) and SuperShuttle (☎ 800-358-5826) offer shuttle service to many locations in Manhattan (though Gray Line only goes to hotels). Gray Line charges $14 one-way from the airport and $19 to the airport. SuperShuttle's prices range from $18 to $23 depending on where you're going. See the JFK Airport section, earlier in the chapter, for schedule information.

Olympia Airport Express (☎ 212-964-6233) buses travel to Newark from four points in Manhattan: Penn Station (5 am to 11 pm daily), Grand Central Terminal (5 am to 11 pm daily), Port Authority Bus Terminal (4:15 am to 2:45 am daily) and One World Trade Center, next to the Marriott Hotel (6:30 am to 8 pm weekdays, 7:30 am to 7:30 pm weekends). The fare is $11.

NJ Transit (☎ 973-762-5100) runs an Airlink Bus (No 302) from Newark International Airport to Newark's Penn Station (not to be confused with New York City's Penn Station); the fare is $4. At Newark's Penn Station, you can catch a PATH train to downtown Manhattan ($1.50). This may be the cheapest way to go, but if you have a few extra bucks, save yourself the hassle and take the Olympia bus.

A taxi to Manhattan costs $30 to $38, plus tolls. On the way back, you have to pay the metered rate (which could be over $50), plus tolls.

BUS

City buses operate 24 hours a day, generally along avenues in a south or north direction, and cross-town along the major thoroughfares (including 34th, 42nd and 57th Sts).

Buses that begin and end in a certain borough are prefixed accordingly: ie, M5 for Manhattan, B39 for Brooklyn, Q32 for Queens, Bx29 for Bronx.

Bus maps for each borough are available at subway and train stations, and each well-marked bus stop has Guide-a-Ride maps showing the stops for each bus and nearby landmarks. Remember that some 'Limited Stop' buses along major routes pull over only every 10 blocks or so at major cross streets. 'Express' buses are generally for outer borough commuters and should not be used for short trips; they cost about $5.

The regular bus fare is $1.50. You'll need exact change, a MetroCard or a token to board the bus, and if you plan on switching to a connecting route, you must ask for a transfer slip upon boarding.

Drivers will be happy to tell you if their bus stops near a specific site, but don't engage them in a conversation about directions unless you want to endure poisonous stares from the old-timers who prefer the bus to the subway. As a safety precaution, you can request to be dropped off at any location along a bus route from 10 pm to 5 am – even if it is not a designated bus stop.

Of course, if you attempt to ride the bus, you'll discover the same woes found in every other major city during bad weather: After a 25 minute wait for a bus, three will come along in a row.

For bus information, call ☎ 718-330-1234. Also see the boxed text 'Touring Manhattan on the Cheap – by Public Bus' in the Things to See & Do chapter.

TRAIN

New Jersey PATH (Port Authority Trans-Hudson; ☎ 800-234-7284) trains are part of a separate-fare system that runs down Sixth Ave, with stops at 34th, 23rd, 14th, 9th and Christopher Sts, en route to Hoboken, Jersey City and Newark. A second line runs from the World Trade Center to northern New Jersey. These reliable trains (called the 'Hudson Tubes' when they first opened) run every 15 minutes, and the fare is $1, payable in cash. Savvy New Yorkers know that the PATH offers easy transportation from Midtown to Greenwich Village for 50¢ less than the subway.

SUBWAY

As American humorist Calvin Trillin has noted, 'New Yorkers hate the idea of out of towners being able to find their way around the city,' speculating that is why the New York City Subway map is 'similar in design to spaghetti primavera.' But with a little attention to detail, you can figure out the 656-mile New York City subway system, used by four million people daily.

KIM GRANT

A Long Ride into the 21st Century

The city's subway system began in 1904 as a 9-mile privately operated line along Broadway between City Hall and W 145th St. Over the next 30 years, this Interborough Rapid Transit (IRT) line expanded service to the Bronx, Queens and Brooklyn and included several elevated lines called 'els.' Competition also came from the rival Brooklyn-Manhattan Transit company (BMT), and the city-owned Independent Line (IND) on Eighth Ave. The private companies basically collapsed during the Great Depression, and the city wound up owning all three lines – designed to *compete* with rather than augment each other – by 1940. To this day, many New Yorkers refer to the West Side 1, 2, 3 and 9 trains as the IRT line, and a few even use the designations BMT and IND for the rest of the system.

New York's subway system is older than those in many European cities, but even when it was relatively new, the system was considered 'drab and noisy' by the editors of the *WPA Guide to New York*, published in 1939. The book went on to describe a subway where 'intent and humorless hordes cover uptown and downtown platforms, choke narrow stairways, swamp change-booths, wrestle with closing train doors...and a few of the homeless use the subway as a flophouse.' But then, as now, 'the romance of the subways of New York may be found in their trajectories, and in the intricacy of their construction and operation.'

The problems and the physical plan of the subways are basically the same as they were when those words were written. Entryways are unprotected from the weather, and stairs tend to be icy, snowy or just plain wet, depending on the season. Stations are close to the surface of the street,

Although subway stations can be noisy and confusing (not to mention hot as the inner circle of hell in summer), you avoid them at your peril. The New York subway is the fastest and most reliable way to get around town, especially for trips totaling more than 20 blocks in north-south directions during the day. Taking a bus or a taxi guarantees that you'll hit traffic gridlock at places like Times Square and wind up arriving at your destination only after a long and frustrating ride.

Most major Manhattan attractions – especially those on the West Side and downtown – are easily accessible by several subway lines. Madison Square Garden, for example, is within four blocks walking distance of three subway stations on 34th St; these stations serve a total of 12 different lines.

Subway tokens, which allow you to ride the system for any distance, cost $1.50 and are available at booths near the turnstiles. The city is rapidly phasing these out in favor of MetroCards, which you can 'swipe' through the turnstile. The card also offers free transfers to city buses within 20 minutes of leaving a subway station. You can purchase MetroCards at token booths, at

A Long Ride into the 21st Century

and you can hear the noise and sense the smells of the avenue above. And platforms, supported by ugly steel beams, are too narrow, leading rush-hour crowds to back up the stairs at overcapacity stations like Rockefeller Center.

One reason there have been few major improvements was the short-sighted policy of artificially holding down the subway fare. For decades, politicians promised to 'keep the nickel fare,' and admission to the subway was a heavily subsidized 15¢ into the 1960s. (It was as low as 60¢ in 1980.) Meanwhile, the system was falling apart, and the building of a needed underground line to replace the razed Second Ave el was abandoned for lack of funds even though excavation had begun for the project. By the '80s, a consensus grew that the subways needed a major overhaul, but a multibillion-dollar infusion of federal, state and local funds only managed to stop the great decline in equipment and reliability, not to bring the system into the late 20th century.

Thanks to these belated improvements, trains are generally quieter, more reliable and free of graffiti. Ninety percent of them are air-conditioned – a glorious gift during a sweltering July or August heat wave. What's more, almost every token booth offers bus and subway maps and even pamphlets on such ludicrous subjects as 'Riding Escalators Safely.'

But in the technological sense, the New York City subway system is still back in the 19th century. The workers who monitor the trains still depend on bulb-studded maps, ledger books and visual train spotting to ferret out problems on the line. Radio communications are garbled and unreliable, and when a train is stuck or must be rerouted, engineers flip switches or pull knobs to move the rails. (The '70s thriller *The Taking of Pelham One, Two, Three* offers a good approximation of how engineers watch over the whole works.)

Somehow this creaky set of contraptions, which represented cutting-edge engineering in 1900, still works. But as one supervisor recently admitted to the *New York Times*, 'we can tell if a train is moving, but we can't say exactly where it is or how fast it is moving.' Now another multibillion-dollar program hopes to change that by dragging the subway into the 21st century – and not a moment too soon. The city is installing a computer-based system that will use hundreds of thousands of transponders on the track to gather information and avoid problems before they happen. Once the technology is installed fully (sometime in the 2010s), trains will be operated by remote control and without drivers, like the new systems already in place on line extensions in Paris, Washington and Barcelona.

automated machines in the stations or at convenience stores. A $15 card buys you 11 trip credits (ie, one free trip.) But the best deal is the weekly MetroCard, which costs $17. It offers unlimited travel on subways and buses for seven days.

Subway clerks sometimes seem to be irascible, since they barely slide your card through the booth slot and try to give you back as many singles as possible in change to avoid having a lot of dollar bills left to count at the end of their shift. But they are the single best source for information on how to get around.

The common mistake most visitors make (other than getting turned around and taking a train in the opposite direction) is boarding an express train only to see it blow by the local stop they desired. Pay attention to the subway map – local stops are shown with solid lines, and express stops are circles. (The back of this book contains official subway maps provided by the New York City Transit Authority.)

As for safety, standing in the middle of the platform will bring you to the conductor's car. The conductor can direct you through the system when he/she is not closing the doors of the train. Of course, it's not a good idea to leave a fat wallet bulging in your back pocket on a crowded subway, and day packs should be secured with a safety pin.

For subway schedules and other information, call ☎ 718-330-1234.

CAR

In New York, the cost, the traffic, and the high incidence of petty thievery more than offsets any convenience having a car may offer. The city adds to the problem with Byzantine street-cleaning rules that require you to move your car several times a week if you park on the street. Meanwhile, parking garages in Midtown are usually operated by the Kinney Corporation, whose near-monopoly in the garage industry means that parking a car will cost at least $30 a day during daylight hours.

You can find cheaper lots along West St in Chelsea, but even those $10 to $15 daily deals aren't a bargain after the city's phenomenal 18.25% parking tax is added. Using a hotel lot is no bargain either – Midtown hotels can charge $40 a day, even for their customers.

Rentals

Hopefully, there is a special section of hell reserved for the people who set car rental rates in New York. Though rental agencies advertise bargain rates for weekend or week-long rentals, these deals are almost *always* blacked out in New York or can only be obtained in conjunction with a purchased airline ticket.

If you want to rent for a few days, book through your travel agent before leaving home. Without a reservation, a rental will cost at least $70 for a midsize car, though you'll probably have to spend $95 or more a day. And that's before extra charges like the 13.25% tax.

The rental agencies will also try to sell you personal insurance coverage (about $15 a day), which you don't need if you have medical coverage, and a 'Collision Damage Waiver' or 'Liability Damage Waiver' (another $15), which covers the full value of the vehicle in case of an accident except those caused by acts of nature or fire. (Some credit cards cover collision insurance if you rent for 15 days or less and charge the full cost of rental to your card.)

Agencies also add a $5 daily fee for each additional driver in the car. In all, you're talking about $100 a day – plus the option to prepay for a tank of gas to avoid filling up before you return; this costs $20, but it's worth it, due to the high price of gasoline in the city.

With costs running well over $300 for a three-day weekend rental, you may be better off renting a car on a weekly basis to save money in the long run. It used to be possible to play agencies against each other or to rent cars at a cheaper rate at the airport, but the companies have gotten wise to just about any money-saving move and have blocked them by bureaucratic rules or with the statement that 'agreements can be revised or discontinued without prior notice,' printed on coupons and airline tickets. That about covers any possibility that you'll beat them at this game.

ANGUS OBORN

If you don't find the above discouraging...then you must be on an expense account.

To rent a car, you must have a valid driver's license and present a major credit card. In March 1997, the New York state supreme court ruled that the nationwide policy of restricting rentals to drivers who are at least 25 years old was discriminatory. Though the major companies now must offer cars to teens, they are allowed to charge a higher rate and will no doubt make it prohibitively expensive for college-age consumers to take advantage of their new rights.

Call the agencies' toll free numbers to inquire about office locations in the New York area.

Avis	☎ 800-331-1212
Budget	☎ 800-527-0700
Dollar	☎ 800-800-4000
Hertz	☎ 800-654-3131
Thrifty	☎ 800-367-2277

TAXI

Taxi drivers may be the butt of jokes, but most New York cabs are clean and, compared to those in most international destinations, pretty cheap.

Taxis cost $2 for the initial charge, plus 30¢ for every additional quarter-mile and 20¢ a minute while stuck in traffic. There's an additional 50¢ surcharge for rides after 8 pm. Tampered meters turn over every 20 seconds or so while the cab is stopped in traffic or at a light, and if you notice it happening, don't hesitate to ask if it is 'running too fast.' If the driver apologizes a bit too energetically, you've probably busted him and can negotiate a lower fare than the meter. Tips are expected to run 10% to 15%, with a minimum of 50¢. If you feel ripped off, ask for a receipt and note the driver's license number. The city's Taxi and Limousine Commission (☎ 212-302-8294) is particularly aggressive, and the threat of a complaint puts the fear of god into some cabbies.

For hauls that will last 50 blocks or more, it's a good idea to instruct the driver to take a road well away from Midtown traffic. Suggest the West Side Highway or Eleventh Ave if you hail a taxi west of Broadway; on the East Side, the best choice may be Second Ave (heading downtown) or First Ave (uptown), since you can hit a string of green lights in either direction.

It's very important to note that taxis are obligated to take you anywhere you want to go within the five boroughs, as well as to Newark International Airport (though you must pay tolls each way). During rush hours, taxi drivers often brazenly refuse fares from airport-bound customers (particularly during bad weather) because they can pick up easier fares in town. *Do not* ask permission to get into the cab if you're going to the airports, and do not negotiate a higher price for the job above the metered fare. If the cabbie refuses your business, threaten to report his/her license number to the Taxi and Limousine Commission. Even if this is an empty threat, the cab driver will take it seriously enough to relent.

Under no circumstances should you take an unlicensed taxi – these are by and large rip-off merchants who target tourists, usually at the airport arrival terminals, and even if you do manage to save some money by taking one of these, you face a greater risk of becoming the victim of a crime or a traffic accident.

One cab cliché does hold: Only about one in five cab drivers actually thanks you for the tip, no matter how generous.

Checkered History

For some 60 years, the tank-like Checker Cab was the toughest warrior on New York City's hard streets and appeared in many movies (including, appropriately enough, Martin Scorsese's *Taxi Driver)*. The cabs sat higher off the street, making for a smoother ride, and offered a roomy interior and lift-up extra seats. Although checker cabs made up half the city's taxi fleet in the early 1970s, the Kalamazoo, Michigan, company that made them eventually went out of business, a victim of increased gas prices and regulations on pollution. By the early '90s, only 10 checkers were left in Manhattan. In July 1999, Earl Johnson, the very last checker cab driver, went into retirement and took his 1978 taxi off the streets. Johnson's cab, which he called Janie after an old girlfriend, went on the auction block at tony Sotheby's, and nostalgic bidders were undeterred by the fact that the taxi clocked up 994,050 miles and cost just $8000 new. The car, which the auction house described as having 'traditional New York exterior yellow livery with checker boarding' and 'interior black Naugahyde in good condition with one small repaired scratch to the upper portion of the back seat' – went to a private bidder for $134,500.

KIM GRANT

New taxis playing 'checkers'

BOAT

In the late 19th century, hundreds of ferries operated on New York's rivers, but most disappeared after several East Side bridges opened. Now New Yorkers are rediscovering the convenience of ferries. New York Waterway (☎ 800-533-3779, www.nywaterway.com) operates several routes, including one up the Hudson River Valley and another from Midtown to Yankee Stadium in the Bronx. Its main ferry route runs between Hoboken's Erie Lackawanna Train Terminal and the World Financial Center in Lower Manhattan. Ferries leave every 20 minutes at peak times. The trip takes about eight minutes and costs $2 each way.

New York Waterway also offers substantial services for tourists, including Hudson River cruises, trips to the New Jersey and Long Island beaches (a good way to avoid traffic), as well as tours of riverside restaurants. Call for more information.

One of the most popular boat rides in New York is the free Staten Island ferry (☎ 718-815-2628). For details, see the Staten Island section of the Things to See & Do chapter.

In the summer of 1997, the New York Water Taxi company (☎ 212-681-8111) began running its ferries from various points along the Hudson and East Rivers. Call for information.

BICYCLE

There are some US towns where you can leave your bike unattended and even unlocked – but New York is not one of them. The hassles of bike ownership may have contributed to the move toward in-line skaters, since thieves can pick bike locks with the greatest of ease and an expensive new bike can vaporize within minutes of being left on the street. But if you're determined to ride, use a banged-up bike that no one would really want, and lock it up anyway.

But bicycle theft may be the least of your worries, compared to the fear for your life. Only bicyclists with a death wish would try to navigate the crazy streets of New York. You'll be a lot safer if you use the subway or taxis to get around and bike only in traffic-free areas set aside for outdoor activities. For information on recreational bicycling in New York, see Activities in the Facts for the Visitor chapter.

WALKING

The best way to get around – especially in Manhattan – is by using your own two feet. Pick a subway destination near a set of major attractions (W 4th St, 34th St, Rockefeller Center, Canal St) and head out from there. Manhattan's Midtown grid pattern and prominent north-south avenues make it difficult to get badly lost. And don't be shy about asking for directions if you find yourself confused.

The Things to See & Do chapter divides New York City into neighborhoods and offers some suggestions for self-guided walking tours.

ORGANIZED TOURS

Bus Tours

Gray Line (☎ 212-397-2620, 800-669-0051) offers more than 29 different tours of the city from its main bus terminal at Eighth Ave and 54th St, including a hop-on, hop-off loop of Manhattan. Tours range from $25 to $68 for adults, $16 to $48 for children. Although these tours can offer a good overview of the city, there's always the chance that you may end up with a nonnative guide who knows far less about the city than some of the passengers.

New York Apple Tours (☎ 800-876-9868), 53rd St at Broadway next to the Ameritana Hotel, offers tours on rumbling old London double-decker buses that sometimes break down in mid-tour. In 2000, the company faced criminal charges for a fatal accident, so ride at your own risk. Two days of unlimited travel on the buses cost $40 for adults, $25 for children.

Boat Tours

More than one million people a year take the three-hour, 35-mile Full Island Circle Line cruise (☎ 212-563-3200, www.circleline.com), which leaves from Pier 83 at 42nd St on the Hudson River, from March to December. This is *the* tour to take, provided the weather is good and you can enjoy the waterside breezes on an outside deck. The quality of the narration depends on the enthusiasm of the guide; be sure to sit well away from the narrator if you'd like to avoid the inevitable 'where are you from?' banter. Tickets cost $24 for adults, $19 for seniors, $12 for children.

In the summer, Circle Line also runs Seaport Music Cruises (☎ 212-630-8888), which last about three hours. You can sway to blues on Tuesday night, enjoy some fine jazz on Thursday and shake your booty at a DJ dance party on Wednesday, Friday and Saturday. Prices range from $20 to $40.

World Yacht (☎ 212-563-3347, www.worldyacht.com) offers well-regarded culinary cruises around Manhattan year-round; these leave from Pier 81 at W 41st St. Reservations and proper dress are required, and tickets range from $42 for a two-hour brunch to $79 for a three-hour dinner.

The ferry company New York Waterway also offers some organized tours. See the Boat section, earlier in the chapter, for more information.

KIM GRANT

Walking Tours

Many companies and organizations conduct urban treks, and their phone lines offer detailed information on the latest schedules. Big Onion Walking Tours (☎ 212-439-1090), established by two Columbia University history doctoral candidates, specializes in ethnic New York and offers an annual Christmas Day tour of the Jewish Lower East Side. Walks cost $10 for adults, $7 for seniors and students.

New York City Food Tours (☎ 732-636-4650) offers $20 walking and tasting tours of SoHo and Greenwich Village food shops; the price includes samples of the fare.

Greenwich Village Literary Pub Crawl (☎ 212-613-5796) offers a 2½-hour tour of pubs where famous literati drank themselves to death – from Ernest Hemingway to Dylan Thomas. Tours cost $12, and reservations are highly recommended.

To take some of the city's most comprehensive walking tours, contact the 92nd Street Y (☎ 212-996-1100, www.92ndsty.org), the city's main Jewish cultural center. This group offers more than 45 one-day tours that range from a visit to the Bukharian community to a tea at Gracie Mansion. Tours range from $15 to $40, and you must make reservations in advance or pay a $5 onsite registration charge.

Radical Walking Tours (☎ 718-492-0069) offers 15 tours through radical political history. You can visit Black Panther landmarks in Harlem or learn about Stonewall in Greenwich Village.

Adventures on a Shoestring (☎ 212-265-2663) charges $5 (the price has stayed the same for more than 30 years) for tours of historic houses, ethnic neighborhoods, and other places of interest. Howard Goldberg, the founder/director/docent, will give your money's worth.

New York Talks and Walks (☎ 888-377-4455, www.newyorktalksandwalks.com) features 20 historical tours, including 'Lincoln's New York.' Prices run around $12 for adults, $6 for children.

The Municipal Art Society (MAS; ☎ 212-935-3960) leads an array of weekly tours that focus on architecture, including a Grand Central Terminal tour that begins at 12:30 pm each Wednesday. Other tour themes include Indoor New York: The Stylish '50s, which visits interiors designed by IM Pei, Frank Lloyd Wright and Isamu Noguchi. Prices are usually $10 for adults, $8 for seniors and students. (MAS walks are listed each week in the 'Spare Times' section of the Friday *New York Times*.

For information on walking tours in Harlem, see the boxed text 'To Tour or Not to Tour' in the Things to See & Do chapter.

Helicopter Tours

If you have some money to blow try a helicopter tour. Liberty Helicopter Tours (☎ 212-967-4550) offers bird's eye views of the city. Tours depart from two locations: W 30th St at Twelfth Ave in Midtown and Pier 6, on the East River near Whitehall St in Lower Manhattan. Tickets cost $59 to $187 depending on the length of the tour (5 to 15 minutes). Gray Line (☎ 212-397-2600) also offers tours that depart on the half hour from the heliport at E 34th St and First Ave. All rides are ten minutes long and cost $83 on a weekday, $104 on a weekend.

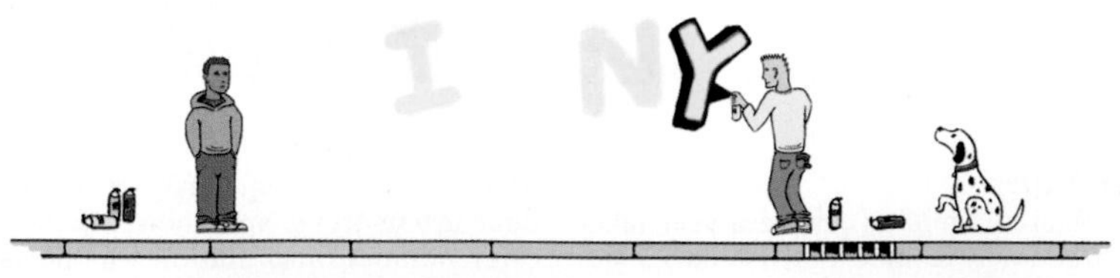

Things to See & Do

Manhattan

For most visitors, Manhattan (population 1,487,536) *is* New York City. Even the residents of the outer boroughs refer to it as 'the city,' a tacit acknowledgment of the island's primacy. But it's important to remember that the Bronx, Brooklyn, Queens and Staten Island each have their own attractions. Only visitors who include at least one excursion out of Manhattan are truly taking advantage of what the entire city has to offer.

The following sections cover Manhattan neighborhood by neighborhood from the island's southern tip to the north. While the neighborhoods have no official borders (and most are something of a state of mind), the extents run generally as follows.

Lower Manhattan encompasses the area below Chambers St to Battery Park, including the Civic Center and Financial District. Tribeca, the 'Triangle Below Canal St,' is bordered by Canal St in the north, West St in the west, Chambers St in the south and Broadway in the east. To the east of Tribeca, Chinatown runs from Centre St east to the Manhattan Bridge, with Canal St and Chambers St as its northern and southern borders. Nearby Little Italy starts north of Canal St and stretches from Broadway to the Bowery.

East of the Bowery, the Lower East Side begins; it ends at the East River. Houston St marks the northern boundary. Between Houston St and 14th St to the north, Greenwich Village and the East Village cut a large swath through the middle of the city. The Village proper surrounds Washington Square Park, where Fifth Ave begins.

North of the Village, Chelsea stretches from 14th to 23rd Sts, west of Sixth Ave. The area to the east of Sixth Ave includes the smaller neighborhoods of Union Square, Gramercy Park and the Flatiron District.

Midtown generally refers to the largely commercial district from 23rd St north to 59th St, an area that includes Rockefeller Center, Times Square, the Broadway theater district, major hotels, Grand Central Terminal and the Port Authority Bus Terminal. The Upper East Side and Upper West Side include the areas above 59th St on either side of Central Park.

Harlem begins above Central Park and runs from 111th St to 150th St, between Frederick Douglass Blvd in the west and the East River in the east. Hamilton Heights begins above Harlem and gives way to Washington Heights above W 145th St.

Significant neighborhoods in the outer boroughs include Brooklyn Heights, Park Slope, Williamsburg and Brighton Beach in Brooklyn; Arthur Ave, Riverdale and City Island in the Bronx; and Astoria, Jackson Heights, Forest Hills and Flushing Meadows in Queens.

For information on orienting yourself in Manhattan, see Orientation in the Facts for the Visitor chapter. The back of this book contains full maps for all of the neighborhoods in Manhattan, as well as some in the outer boroughs.

Highlights

- Yes, that spectacular skyline is the one you've seen in all those movies
- The astounding array of cultures on the streets
- The unparalleled cultural offerings: world-class museums, spectacular theatrical events and concerts of every kind
- New York's 18,000-odd restaurants – a foodie's paradise offering every cuisine, often at bargain prices
- Shopping, shopping and more shopping

LOWER MANHATTAN (Map 5)

The home of Wall St, Lower Manhattan is famous as the world's financial capital, but what many don't know is that this area of urban canyons is an unrivaled museum of

Naming Neighborhoods

There's no method to the names that New Yorkers have given their neighborhoods. They can be purely geographical (the Lower East Side), ethnically descriptive (Chinatown) or just plain scary (Hell's Kitchen, which takes its name from a slum area dominated by Irish gangs in the 19th century).

Tribeca, an abbreviation for the area called 'Triangle Below Canal St,' has passed into popular use. As has the nickname SoHo, which describes the area south of Houston St (no relation to London's Soho, which was named after a fox hunting call). Nolita, a new coinage, designates the area just north of Little Italy.

The city's early Dutch occupation has left its mark on some street and neighborhood names. Harlem, for example, takes its name from Haarlem, a town in the Netherlands.

Some neighborhoods have long outgrown their designations. Few residents of Chelsea know their area was named after an 18th-century farm owned by a British army officer. Turtle Bay, a fashionable enclave surrounding the United Nations on the East Side of Manhattan, took its name from a riverside cove that was drained in 1868.

architecture. Along these cramped and circuitous side streets and the grand avenue of Broadway you'll find Federal homes, Greek revival temples, Gothic churches, Renaissance palazzos and one of the finest collections of early 20th-century skyscrapers.

After the Dutch bought Manhattan from local Indians in the early 17th century, they protected their newfound home with a fort and erected a wood-and-mud wall to keep out hostile Indians as well as the British. While no Dutch buildings from this period have survived, the paths and lanes mapped out by the engineer Cryn Fredericksz in 1625 have since restrained and influenced every architect who ventured to build here.

Likewise, little lasts from more than 100 years of British rule. Indeed, seven years of British military occupation during the Revolutionary War and major fires in 1776 and 1778 ruthlessly altered the face of the city. By the end of the war, a quarter of the settled area – more than 1000 shops and homes – lay in burnt decay. Only one building survives as an example of that era: St Paul's Chapel (see Lower Manhattan Walking Tour), which private citizens saved from the flames. The other buildings of note in this area date from the late 18th to early 20th centuries.

ANGUS OBORN

ANGUS OBORN

Lower Manhattan

It is essential to explore this area on a weekday, since it revolves around the Monday-to-Friday activities of business, politics and the law. Expect this walk to take anywhere from three hours to a whole day, depending on how often you stop for attractions. It's a good idea to get an early start, between 9 and 10 am, to avoid fellow travelers and midday crowds.

Lower Manhattan is served by 15 subway lines and nearly 20 stations, but for the purposes of this tour, it's best to take the 4, 5 or 6 subway trains to Brooklyn Bridge-City Hall, where the tour begins.

Start at **City Hall**, near the pedestrian approach to the Brooklyn Bridge (for details on visiting City Hall, see the separate heading, later in the chapter). Directly behind City Hall stands **Tweed Courthouse**, an inadvertent monument to late 19th-century municipal corruption. An estimated $10 million of the $14 million budget for this 1872 city courthouse wound up being embezzled by William Magear 'Boss' Tweed, the ruthless leader of the Democratic Party's Tammany Hall organization. At one point, Tweed's gang was stealing about $1 million a month from the city treasury. The subsequent scandal over the building's cost toppled Tweed from power – but left an architecturally significant site with an impressive central hall.

Nearby, at the intersection of Chambers and Centre Sts, sits the former **Surrogate's Court**, a 1914 structure with an interior that deliberately imitates the beaux arts style of Charles Garnier's Paris Opera House. The building is now home to New York City's official archival collection.

If you stroll north on Centre St, you'll reach **Foley Square**, a complex of city, state and federal courthouses. The **US Courthouse**, 40 Centre St, plays host to high-profile organized crime trials. One block north, the **New York County Courthouse** serves as home to the state supreme court. Check out the lawyers holding noisy impromptu negotiations in its huge, bustling rotunda.

LOWER MANHATTAN WALKING TOUR

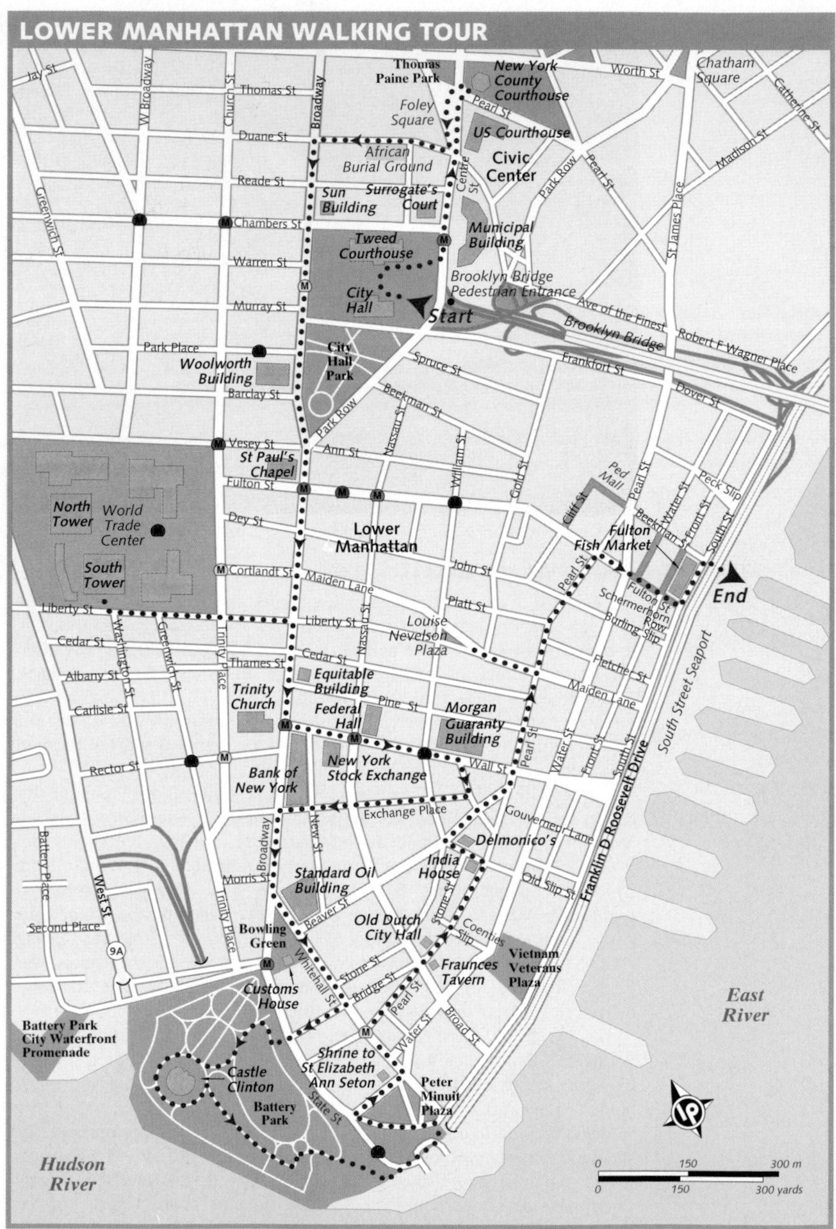

Heading west on Duane St (directly in front of the US Courthouse) brings you to the **African Burial Ground**, a cemetery for the city's early black residents. It was unearthed in the late '80s and declared a national historic site. Many of the bodies discovered were those of slaves wearing British uniforms – soldiers who were promised their freedom for fighting for the loyalists during the Revolutionary War.

Turn left on Broadway and proceed two blocks to the **Sun Building**, at the corner of Chambers St. The *New York Sun* – one of many newspapers located in this area during the early 20th century – no longer exists, but its clock remains, promising that the publication 'shines for all.'

Continuing down Broadway, you'll pass the City Hall complex again (from the other side this time) and come to the **Woolworth Building**, 233 Broadway. When completed in 1913, it was the world's tallest building (792 feet, 60 stories). Frank Woolworth, head of the famous discount store chain, reputedly paid the $15 million cost of the building with nickels and dimes. The lobby of this so-called Cathedral of Commerce includes a gargoyle of Woolworth counting his change.

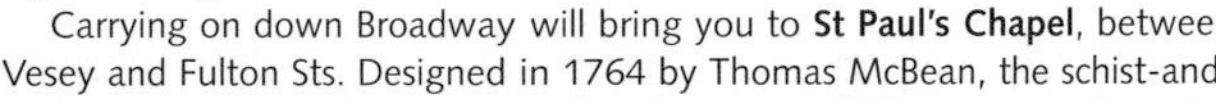

Carrying on down Broadway will bring you to **St Paul's Chapel**, between Vesey and Fulton Sts. Designed in 1764 by Thomas McBean, the schist-and-brownstone chapel is one of the greatest Georgian structures ever built in the country and the last remaining colonial building in the area. When New York served as the nation's capital, President George Washington attended services in the chapel's airy interior, with its fluted Corinthian columns and Waterford chandeliers. His personal pew is still on display. Noon music recitals take place every Monday and Thursday.

Three blocks down, a right turn on Liberty St leads to the **World Trade Center** (see separate heading, later). On clear days, the South Tower's 107th floor observatory affords unbeatable views of the city and beyond.

Head back to Broadway, turn left and continue down the corridor to the 41-story **Equitable Building**, between Cedar and Pine Sts. When it opened just before WWI,

TOM SMALLMAN

Below: Woolworth Building, the tallest building in the world in its time

ANGUS OBORN

Right: St Paul's Chapel

its sheer unapologetic bulk changed the shape of Manhattan – and world architecture – forever. At 1.2 million sq feet, it ranked as the largest office building on the planet. Its size created such an uproar that four years after its opening New York enacted the nation's first zoning laws requiring building setbacks.

A block farther down Broadway, you'll come upon **Trinity Church** (see separate heading, later), one of the city's oldest surviving religious landmarks. When British-born Richard Upjohn built the brownstone church in 1846, its buttresses, finials and octagonal spire made it the tallest and most richly decorated building in the city.

Wall St, which begins directly across from Trinity Church, stands at the site where early Dutch settlers constructed a northern barrier to protect New Amsterdam from attacks by Native Americans and the British. Today, it is the metaphorical home of US commerce. Check out the blazing red-and-gold art deco lobby inside the **Bank of New York**, 1 Wall St, which serves as a distinctive monument to money. The **New York Stock Exchange** (see separate heading, later), the metaphorical center of Wall St, officially stands at 8 Broad St.

Across Wall St from the Stock Exchange, you'll see **Federal Hall**, the finest surviving example of classical architecture in Lower Manhattan. Designed by the influential architects Ithiel Town and Alexander Jackson Davis, the 1842 building is truly a temple to purity, with its hefty Doric porticos, two-story rotunda, circular colonnade and paneled dome. (For details on visiting Federal Hall, see separate heading, later.)

A block past Federal Hall, at 60 Wall St, stands the 1988 Morgan Guaranty Building, whose sleek, modern design symbolizes the financial successes of the '80s. From here, turn right down Hanover St and make the next right on Exchange Place, which leads back to Broadway; turn left there. As Broadway veers east and becomes Whitehall St, note the **Standard Oil Building**, 26 Broadway. One of many early monuments to capitalism that line the Broadway

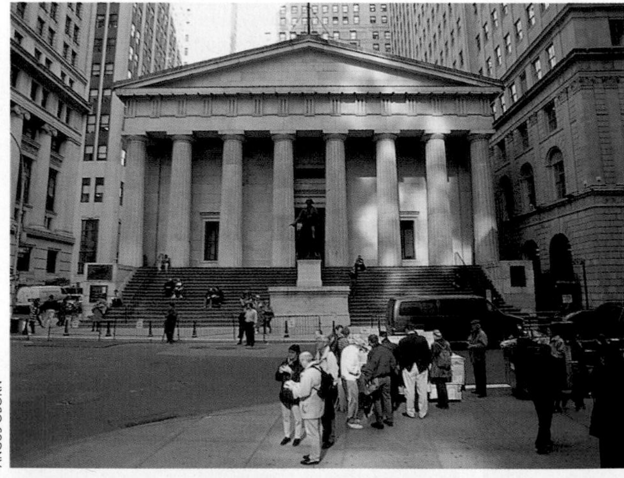

ANGUS OBORN

Left: Federal Hall's classical stylings

ANGUS OBORN

corridor from St Paul's Chapel down to Battery Park, this curved edifice was built in 1922 by John D Rockefeller. Its 2nd floor houses the Museum of American Financial History (☎ 212-908-4519), which is open 10 am to 4 pm Tuesday to Saturday.

Continue down Whitehall St, past Bowling Green (the city's first public park), and you'll come upon the **Customs House**, completed in 1907. Architect Cass Gilbert's vast seven-story limestone building melds art and architecture in a tribute to the grandeur of trade. Walls, doors, ceilings and floors are festooned with marine ornamentation, such as shells, sails, sea creatures and sea signs. Dormers are the prows of galleons, and the glorious elliptical rotunda is a 135-foot-long room encircled by Reginald Marsh's murals (added in 1937), portraying everything from the great explorers of America to Greta Garbo at an impromptu dockside press conference. It is simply one of the most sumptuous beaux arts buildings ever built. Today, the Customs House functions as the **National Museum of the American Indian** (see separate heading, later). Just north of the museum is a bronze statue of a raging bull, the symbol of a healthy stock market.

Turn right down Bridge St, which leads directly to Battery Park and **Castle Clinton**, a fortification built in 1811 to protect Manhattan from the British. Originally located 300 yards offshore before landfill engulfed it, the imposing fortress with 8-foot-thick walls and a rusticated gate once brimmed with 28 guns set in the embrasures. Its guns were never fired in anger, though, and in the 1820s the government decommissioned the fort and turned it into Castle

Above: Battery Park, baby

Garden, a concert hall–resort that is said to have hosted up to 6000 people beneath a domed roof. Since then, it has also served as an immigration station and aquarium. Today, the castle is literally just a shell of its former self – there's no roof on the building anymore, but it houses the ticket office for the Statue of Liberty ferry.

By circling the castle and then continuing southeast, you'll exit Battery Park at **Peter Minuit Plaza**, reputedly the sight of the purchase of Manhattan for the equivalent of $24.

Turn right on State St and proceed to the **Shrine to St Elizabeth Ann Seton**, dedicated to America's first Roman Catholic saint. Lone survivor of a series of graceful row houses that once hugged the shoreline (before landfill arrived), this delicate Georgian home dates from 1793. A Federal-style western wing was added in 1806, reputedly by John McComb, the first major New York–born architect. This section of the structure is enlivened with a curved porch and a double colonnade of attenuated Doric and Ionic columns supposedly made from recycled ship masts. Such an unusual building material apparently suited the so-called 'Peep-o'-Day Boys' – merchants who began each morning by walking out onto their porches and anxiously gazing through their telescopes to see if their far-flung cargo ships were approaching the port.

Tucked just behind this building is **New York Unearthed**, a rather interesting little exhibit of historical items discovered by archaeologists and construction workers over the years. It's open noon to 6 pm weekdays.

Make a left on Whitehall St and a right on Pearl St. Heading east up Pearl St will lead you to the historical block at Coenties Slip, a Dutch docking station that became a street as landfill extended the city further south. Near here, you can see the archeological site of the **old Dutch City Hall**, just across the street from the **Fraunces Tavern**. The current tavern is a 1907 renovation of the place where Washington gave his farewell address to Continental Army officers in 1783.

Continuing up Pearl St, you'll pass the **India House**, 1 Hanover Square, a former bank building that's now an exclusive and somewhat secretive businessmen's club. At the India House, make a left on Old Slip St. A short block later, at the corner of Beaver St (a name indicative of the trading activities of colonial New York) stands **Delmonico's**, part of the chain of famous restaurants that created the American notion of 'dining out' in the 19th century. This 1891 structure includes a marble portico supposedly bought in Pompeii; the storied restaurant is now a microbrewery and steak house.

Make a right on Beaver St and bear left on Pearl St when Beaver St ends. Walk three more blocks and turn left at Maiden Lane to take a brief detour to **Louise Nevelson Plaza**. Here, in a somewhat incongruous business setting, a series of seven sculptures by the famous Russian-American artist stand where Maiden Lane meets William and Liberty Sts.

Head back to Pearl St, turn left and proceed several blocks to Fulton St. Here, make a right turn toward the Hudson River, the **Fulton Fish Market** (the city's wholesale seafood distribution point) and the **South Street Seaport** (see separate heading, later). Try to arrive as night falls so you can watch the Brooklyn and Manhattan bridges light up for the evening. The sight is worth the money you'll pay for a drink at a bar or cafe with a good view. Alternatively, you can cross the bridge and look at Manhattan from the Brooklyn Heights Promenade or from Fulton Landing near the River Cafe (see the Brooklyn Heights Walking Tour, later in this chapter).

City Hall

City Hall (☎ 212-788-6871), along Park Row near the entrance to the Brooklyn Bridge, has been home to New York's government since 1812. In keeping with the half-baked civic planning that has often plagued big New York projects, officials neglected to finish the building's northern side in marble, betting that the city would not expand uptown. The mistake was finally rectified in 1954, completing a structure that architectural critic Ada Louise Huxtable has called a 'symbol of taste, excellence and quality not always matched by the policies inside.'

Inside, the highlights include the spot where Abraham Lincoln's coffin sat for a brief time in 1865, as the assassinated president's remains made their way from Washington, DC, to Springfield, Illinois. (Walk to the top of the staircase on the 2nd floor to view the historic site.) The Governor's Room, a reception area where the mayor entertains important guests, contains 12 portraits of the founding fathers by John Trumbull, George Washington's old writing table and other examples of Federal furniture, plus the remnants of a flag flown at the first president's 1789 inaugural ceremony. If you peek into the City Council chambers, you might see the lawmakers deliberating over the renaming of a city street in someone's honor – an activity that accounts for about 40% of all the bills passed by the 51-member body.

City Hall's steps are a popular site for demonstrations and press conferences by politicians, including the mayor. Don't be discouraged by the phalanx of security personnel – the building is open to the public from 10 am to 4 pm weekdays. Ⓜ 4, 5, 6 to Brooklyn Bridge-City Hall; J, M, Z to Chambers St.

World Trade Center

The massive twin towers of the World Trade Center (WTC; ☎ 212-323-2340, www.wtc-top.com) rise 1350 feet above the ground, over a square at the corner of Church and Vesey Sts. This towering complex houses more than 350 different businesses employing 50,000 people. Built at a cost of $700 million between 1966 and 1973, the sleek WTC has never stirred people's hearts in the same manner as the Empire State Building. But the project did change

What's a Kid to Do?

It's hard to narrow down the many choices for kids, but here are a few good picks for the pint-size traveler. We're assuming you've already put the Statue of Liberty, the Empire State Building and the Children's Museum of Manhattan on the 'to do' list. For more details on all of the following, see the individual headings elsewhere in this chapter.

Central Park Horse-drawn carriages, rollerbladers, a children's zoo and a famous carousel are just some of the reasons to spend an afternoon in New York's most famous open space.

Rockefeller Center at Christmas Families can ice skate in the shadow of the center's huge Christmas tree, then take in the Radio City Music Hall Christmas show, a pricey spectacular.

Rose Center for Earth & Space The American Museum of Natural History's fabulous new planetarium is an up-to-the-minute facility for the would-be space explorer. Teenagers tend to like the nighttime laser rock shows.

Bronx Zoo Visiting the oldest wildlife facility in the USA makes a journey to the Bronx worth it. But if you don't want to go that far with kids in tow, take in the smaller and much more manageable Central Park Zoo, right in Manhattan.

Circle Line A classic New York delight, this boat trip around Manhattan is a perfect way to cool off on a hot summer day.

the city in a profound way: The one million cubic yards of rock and dirt unearthed for its foundation became the landfill on which the 24-acre Battery Park City development was built.

The twin towers attract daredevils: George Willig used mountain-climbing equipment to scale the side of one building, and circus performer Philippe Petit claimed he was able to use a crossbow to run a tightrope across both buildings and put on a show a quarter-mile above the ground without anyone stopping him. The observation deck has also attracted two parachutists who have gotten away with jumping off the building and landing in Battery Park.

The WTC's array of federal and state government offices have also made it a tempting target for terrorists, a few of whom set off a truck bomb in the underground parking garage on February 26, 1993, killing six people. A discreet memorial to those who perished in the blast is located on the WTC plaza.

The **Commodities Exchange Center** (☎ 212-938-2025), on the 9th floor of 4 World Trade Center, no longer offers views of its trading floor. For a close-up view of commerce, you'll have to stroll through the shopping plaza on the subway level underneath the buildings; it holds the dubious distinction of being the first indoor mall to open in New York City.

Most visitors don't come here for the shopping, though. They come for the fabulous view. On a clear day, you can see for more than 55 miles from the lofty 107th floor of the South Tower. The most courageous visitors can also buy a ticket for the open-air observation platform, where you can look down from 110 stories.

The ticket booth for the WTC observation decks is open 9:30 am to 11:30 pm daily from June to August and 9:30 am to 9:30 pm daily the rest of the year. Admission is $13/9.50/6.50 for adults/seniors/children.

If you'd like to linger over the view, you can always shell out the big bucks for drinks or dinner at the Windows on the World restaurant (see the Places to Eat chapter). Ⓜ 1, 9 to Cortlandt St.

World Financial Center This complex (☎ 212-945-0505, www.worldfinancialcenter.com), on West and Vesey Sts across from the WTC, stands on the landfill created by the excavation for the WTC's foundation. A group of four office towers surrounds the **Winter Garden**, a glass atrium and ostentatious centerpiece that hosts free concerts during the summer and exclusive black-tie events year-round. During good weather, it's pleasant to walk, run or bike down the mile-long esplanade that runs from the Battery Park City apartments past the World Financial Center to the tip of Manhattan; when it's rainy, you can pass an hour in the shopping area and art gallery located next to the Winter Garden.

Trinity Church

This former Anglican parish (☎ 212-602-0872, www.trinitywallstreet.org), at the corner of Broadway and Wall St, was founded by King William III in 1697 and once presided over several constituent chapels, including the still-existent St Paul's Chapel, at the corner of Fulton St and Broadway. Its huge land holdings in Lower Manhattan made it the wealthiest and most influential church throughout the 18th century.

The current Trinity Church is the third structure on the site. Designed by English architect Richard Upjohn, this 1846 building helped to launch the picturesque neo-Gothic movement in America. At the time of its construction, its 280-foot bell tower made it the tallest building in New York City before the advent of skyscrapers.

The long, dark interior of the church includes a beautiful stained glass window over the altar. Trinity, like other Anglican churches in America, became part of the Episcopal faith following US independence from Britain. A pamphlet describing the parish's history is available for a small donation.

The church is open to visitors from 9 am to 4 pm weekdays, 10 am to 3:45 pm Saturday, and 1 to 3:45 pm Sunday, except during lunchtime services. Trinity also hosts midday music concerts during the week. Call ☎ 212-602-0747 for a schedule. Ⓜ 2, 3, 4, 5 to Wall St; I, R to Rector St; A, C, E to Chambers St.

THINGS TO SEE & DO

New York Stock Exchange

Though 'Wall St' is the widely recognized metaphor for US capitalism, the world's best-known stock exchange (☎ 212-656-5167, www.nyse.com) is actually around the corner at 8 Broad St, behind a portentous facade reminiscent of a Roman temple. A visitor's gallery overlooks the frenetic trading floor and includes an exhibit describing the exchange's history. The modern business of the exchange isn't explained very well, however, and not much is made of the famous 1929 stock market crash or the threat to the exchange now posed by electronic trading, which makes the trading floor virtually irrelevant.

Tickets, which admit spectators to the visitor's gallery every 45 minutes throughout the day, are usually snapped up by noon. If you're lucky, you'll receive a ticket for the time period that includes the end of trading at 4 pm, when a retiring broker or other financial worthy does the honors of bringing the business day to a close by ringing a bell. Cheers ring out if the market closes on a high note; groans and oaths abound on a down day.

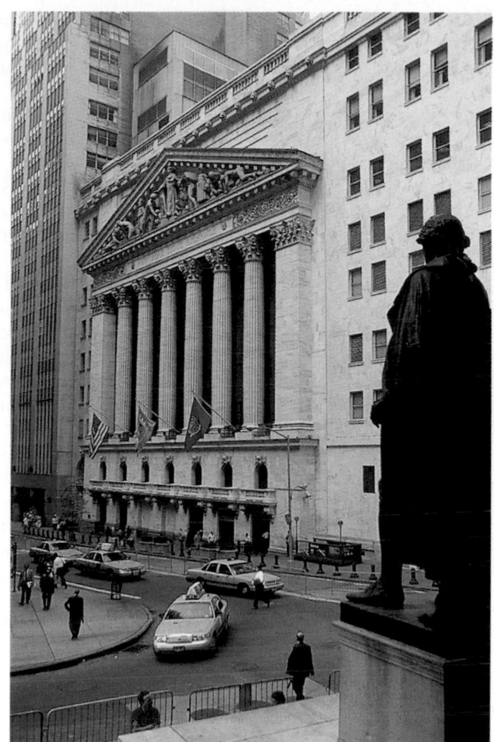

ANGUS OBORN

New York Stock Exchange

To get a ticket, go to the booth at 20 Broad St; it's open 9:15 am to 4 pm weekdays. While you're waiting in line, you'll see dozens of brokers dressed in color-coordinated trading jackets popping out of the NYSE for a quick cigarette or hot dog. Ⓜ 4, 5 to Wall St.

Federal Hall

Distinguished by a huge statue of George Washington, Federal Hall (☎ 212-825-6888, www.nps.gov/feha), 26 Wall St, stands on the site of New York's original City Hall, where the first US Congress convened and Washington took the oath of office as the first US chief executive. After that structure's demolition in the early 19th century, this Greek Revival building gradually arose in its place between 1834 and 1842. Considered to be one of the best examples of classical architecture in the country, it served as the US Customs House until 1862. Today, the building contains a small museum dedicated to post-colonial New York. It's open 9 am to 5 pm weekdays. Free guided tours of the building leave every hour on the half hour from 12:30 to 3:30 pm.

Federal Hall serves as the starting point for four self-guided Heritage Trail walking tours that explore the area's history in greater detail. A free Heritage Trails map, which details the 42 cast-iron site markers explaining downtown history, is available in the lobby. Ⓜ 2, 3, 4, 5 to Wall St; J, M, Z to Broad St.

National Museum of the American Indian

This museum (☎ 212-668-6624, www.si.edu/nmai), an affiliate of the Smithsonian Institution, abandoned its uptown spot at 155th St in 1994 and moved to the former US Customs House on Bowling Green. The beaux arts monument to commerce was built to collect federal duties imposed on foreign goods in the days before income tax; it is a grand but somewhat incongruous space for the USA's leading museum on Native American art, established by oil heir George Gustav Heye in 1916. The facility's information center can be found in the former collection office, with computer banks located next to old wrought-iron teller booths.

The galleries are on the 2nd floor, beyond a vast rotunda featuring statues of famous navigators and murals celebrating shipping history. This museum does little to explain the history of Native Americans but instead concentrates its attention on Native American culture, boasting a million-item collection of crafts and everyday objects. Computer touch-screens feature insights into Native life and beliefs, and working artists often offer explanations of their techniques. You'll find Native American jewelry for sale in the gift shop.

Although a similar museum being constructed in Washington, DC, threatens to overshadow this facility, it's still worth a look (and you can't beat the free admission). It's open 10 am to 5 pm daily. Ⓜ 4, 5 to Bowling Green.

Museum of Jewish Heritage

This new facility (☎ 212-786-0820), 18 First Place in Battery Park City, explores all aspects of Jewish New York, from immigration to assimilation. Recent exhibitions include a holographic history of the museum's establishment and a display of Jewish-owned art that was stolen by the Nazis and eventually returned to the surviving family members. Audio tours of the museum are available for $5. You'll also find a plaza that serves as New York City's Holocaust Memorial just outside the museum.

The museum is open 9 am to 5 pm Sunday to Wednesday and Friday, 9 am to 8 pm Thursday (closed Saturday). The museum closes at 3 pm on Friday during the off season. Admission is $7 for adults, $5 for students and seniors. Ⓜ 1, 2, 3, 9 to Rector St.

Statue of Liberty

The most enduring symbol of New York City – and indeed, the New World, in general – can trace its origins to a Parisian dinner party in 1865. There, a group of intellectuals opposed to the government of Napoleon III gathered in the house of political activist Edouard René Lefebvre de Laboulaye to discuss ways to promote French Republicanism. That notion of building a monument honoring the American conception of political freedom intrigued sculptor Frédéric-Auguste Bartholdi, a fellow dinner guest, and he dedicated most of the next 20 years to turning the dream into a reality.

Laboulaye and Bartholdi decided that the structure should wind up in the USA, and the latter traveled to New York in 1871 to choose a site for the work he had modeled on the Colossus of Rhodes. Soon afterward, the pair created a lottery to cover the $250,000 cost of construction of the statue, which included a metal skeleton by railway engineer Alexandre Gustave Eiffel, who later became world famous for his eponymous Parisian tower. In the USA, meanwhile, a campaign by the *New York World* newspaper beat the drums for the project.

In 1883, poet Emma Lazarus published a poem called 'The New Colossus' as part of a fund-raising campaign for a statue pedestal. Her words have long since been associated with the monument: 'Give me your tired, your poor, / Your huddled masses yearning to breathe free, / The wretched refuse of your teeming shore, / Send these, the homeless, tempest-tost to me, / I lift my lamp beside the golden door!' (Ironically, these famous words were added to the base only in 1901, 17 years after the poet's death.)

On October 28, 1886, the 151-foot *Liberty Enlightening the World* was finally unveiled in New York harbor in front of President Grover Cleveland and a multitude of tooting ships.

By the 1980s, a restoration of the statue was in order, and more than $100 million was spent to shore up Miss Liberty for her centennial. The rotting copper skin required substantial work, and workers installed a new gold-plated torch, the third in the statue's history. The older stained-glass torch is now on display just inside the entrance to the staircase, near a fine museum that describes the statue's history and its restoration. The exhibition also shows how the statue has been exploited for commercial purposes.

Speaking of which, the Circle Line ferry company (☎ 212-269-5755, www.circleline.com) has made more than a few dollars shuttling visitors to the statue and back. Well over four million people a year ride the boats to the Statue of Liberty and Ellis Island (see separate heading, later), while millions more take the boat ride just for the spectacular view of Manhattan (which surpasses the view from the statue itself), but they pass on climbing the 354 steps to the statue's crown, the equivalent of ascending a 22-story building. (No one is allowed onto the statue's torch balcony.)

Although the ferry ride lasts only 15 minutes, a trip to both the Statue of Liberty and Ellis Island is an all-day affair. In the summer, you may wait up to an hour to embark on an 800-person ferry, only to be confronted by a three-hour trek to the crown, followed by a bottleneck getting off the island. Circle Line strongly advises visitors who show up at noon or later that they will *not* be able to get to the statue's crown.

Though there is no charge to get off at Liberty Island, the ferries cost $7 for adults, $6 for seniors, $3 for children. They depart from Battery Park (Ⓜ South Ferry; Bowling Green) every 30 minutes from 9 am to 5 pm, with boats leaving as early as 8 am during the summer. The boats run daily except Christmas. You'll find the ticket office in Castle Clinton, the fort built in 1811 to defend Manhattan from the British (Ⓜ 1, 9 to South Ferry; 4, 5 to Bowling Green).

KIM GRANT

If the crowds are too much, why not try the nearby Staten Island ferry? It doesn't take you to the statue but provides a great view of it and downtown Manhattan – best of all, it's free! (See the Staten Island section, later in this chapter, for details.)

Ellis Island

Ferries to the Statue of Liberty make a second stop at Ellis Island, New York's main immigration station from 1892 until 1954. More than 15 million people passed through here before the island was abandoned. Barely visible further up the slip from the boat docks are the rotting remains of *Ellis Island*, a passenger ferry that sank in 1968 after years of neglect.

A $160 million restoration has turned the impressive red-brick main building into an **Immigration Museum**, where a series of galleries explore the history of the island. The exhibitions begin at the Baggage Room, and continue on to 2nd-story rooms where medical inspections took place and foreign currency was exchanged.

At all points, the exhibits emphasize that, contrary to popular myth, most of the shipborne immigrants were processed within eight hours and that conditions were generally clean and safe. The 338-foot long Registry Room includes a beautiful vaulted tile ceiling made by immigrants from Spain. But walking though the registry today – described as 'light and airy' in the museum literature – surely can't compare to days when the same room housed a line of 5000 confused and tired people waiting to be interviewed by overworked immigration officers and inspected by doctors.

You can take a 50-minute audio tour of the facility for $6. But for an even more affecting take on history, pick up one of the phones in each display area and listen to the recorded memories of real Ellis Island immigrants, taped in the 1980s.

If that's not enough for you, go to see *Ellis Island Stories*, a 30-minute play about the experience of arriving at Ellis Island. The show (☎ 212-883-1986 ext 742) plays five times daily on the half hour from 10:30 am to 3:30 pm. Admission is $3 for adults and $2.50 for seniors and children over 14.

A 30-minute film on the immigrant experience is also worth checking out, as is the exhibition on the influx of immigrants just before WWI.

Circle Line ferries run to Ellis Island daily. The fare is $7 for adults, $6 for seniors, $3 for children. For ticket and schedule information, see Statue of Liberty, earlier.

Fraunces Tavern Museum

Fraunces Tavern Museum (☎ 212-425-1778), 54 Pearl St, sits on a block of historic structures that, along with nearby Stone St and the South Street Seaport, comprise the final examples of colonial-era New York that remain largely intact – the buildings here can be traced to the early 18th century.

On this site stood the Queen's Head Tavern, owned by Samuel Fraunces, who changed the name to Fraunces Tavern after US victory in the Revolutionary War. It was in the 2nd-floor dining room on December 4, 1783, that George Washington bade farewell to the officers of the Continental Army after the British relinquished control of New York City. In the 19th century, the tavern closed and the building fell into disuse. It was also

TONY WHEELER

Millions of immigrants passed through Ellis Island's halls.

THINGS TO SEE & DO

Ellis Island, *New Jersey*?

After several years of dispute with New York, in 1998 a special adjudicator appointed by the Supreme Court ruled that Ellis Island was largely the territory of the state of New Jersey, given that most of the original landmass of Ellis Island was augmented by landfill from New Jersey. But the victor in this fight won more than bragging rights for the 27½-acre tourist spot – it got to collect tax revenues from the sale of items in the Ellis Island gift shop.

Since winning the court case, New Jersey officials have launched an ambitious $300 million program to restore the island's buildings, many of which are in a desperately derelict state. Initially, $10 million will help to shore up the decaying hospital buildings. The remainder will be used to build a Public Health Learning Center, a Center for Immigrant Experience, and an International Conference Hall, the first such facility to be built on publicly owned land. All this should be in the works when you visit; it's scheduled to be finished in 2008.

damaged during several massive fires that swept through old downtown areas and destroyed most colonial buildings and nearly all structures built by the Dutch. In 1904, the Sons of the Revolution historical society bought the building and returned it to an approximation of its colonial-era look – an act believed to be the first major attempt at historic preservation in the USA.

The museum sits over a restaurant that closed in 1999 following a lease dispute; it may reopen soon under new management. The museum remains open 10 am to 4:45 pm weekdays, noon to 4 pm Saturday. Admission is $2.50 for adults, $1 for seniors, students and children.

Just across the street from the tavern are the excavated remains of the old Dutch **Stadt Huys**, which served as New Amsterdam's administrative center, courthouse and jail from 1641 until the peaceful British takeover in 1664. This building, destroyed in 1699, was originally on the city's waterfront until landfill added a few more blocks to southern Manhattan. Ⓜ 4, 5 to Bowling Green; 2, 3 to Wall St.

Federal Reserve Bank

The only reason to visit the Federal Reserve Bank (☎ 212-720-6130), 31 Liberty St near Nassau St, is to see the facility's high-security vault, located 80 feet below ground. More than 10,000 tons of gold reserves reside here. You'll only see a small part of that fortune, but you'll learn a lot about the US Federal Reserve System on the informative tour. You can also browse through an exhibit of coins and counterfeit currency. While the Fed recommends tour reservations, it's likely that you can sign up for a tour when you show up at the bank. Ⓜ J, M, Z to Fulton St-Broadway Nassau.

South Street Seaport

This 11-block enclave of shops and historic sights (☎ 212-732-7678, www.southstseaport.org) combines the best and worst in historic preservation – and, despite its shortcomings, manages to attract more than 12 million visitors each year. Pier 17, beyond the elevated FDR Drive, is a waterfront development project that's home to a number of shops and overpriced restaurants. But the area also contains a number of genuinely significant 18th- and 19th-century buildings that once surrounded this old East River ferry port, which fell into disuse upon the building of the Brooklyn Bridge and the establishment of deepwater piers on the Hudson River.

Schermerhorn Row, a block of old warehouses bordered by Fulton, Front and South Sts, contains novelty shops, seafood restaurants and a pub. Across the street, the **Fulton Market Building**, built in 1983 to reflect the red-brick style of its older neighbors, is nothing more than a glorified fast-food court and shopping arcade.

The **South Street Seaport Museum** (☎ 212-748-8600) offers a glimpse of the seaport's history and a survey of the world's great ocean liners in its permanent exhibits. The museum operates several interesting sights in the area, including three galleries, an antique printing shop, a children's center, a maritime crafts center and historic ships. These are open 10 am to 6 pm daily (until 8 pm Thursday) from April to September, 10 am to 5 pm daily except Tuesday from October to March. Admission to the collection of buildings is $6 for adults, $5 for seniors, $4 for students and $3 for children.

Museum Bargains

Several New York attractions have borrowed the all-in-one pass concept from Paris and now offer visitors a solid bargain in the **CityPass** (www.citypass.net). Good for nine days, the pass covers admission to the **American Museum of Natural History**, the **World Trade Center** observation deck, the **Empire State Building** observatory, the **Guggenheim Museum**, the **Intrepid Sea-Air-Space Museum** and the **Museum of Modern Art**.

The pass costs $32 for adults, $21.75 for seniors and $24 for children ages 12 to 17. That might sound steep, but if you paid full price at all of these attractions, it would cost you twice as much as the CityPass. You can purchase passes at any of these six attractions or order them online.

Just south of Pier 17 stands a group of tall-masted sailing vessels, including the *Peking*, the *Wavertree*, the *Pioneer* and the lightship *Ambrose*. You can take a close look at all of them with the price of admission to the museum.

Pier 17 is home to the **Fulton Fish Market**, where most of the city's restaurants get their fresh seafood. The market is a perfect example of how this area maintains

KIM GRANT

Fishmongers at Fulton Fish Market

its old character while still catering to tourists. The fishmongers go about their workaday business while spectators watch the nightly goings-on from midnight until 8 am. Meanwhile, intrigue continues to swirl around the facility, which many suspect an organized crime family manages. A federal and city government crackdown on corruption led to months of labor unrest and a suspicious 1995 fire that destroyed part of the market. Ⓜ 2, 3, 4, 5, J, M, Z to Fulton St.

Harbor Tours A booth on Pier 16 sells tickets for an hour-long riverboat excursion aboard the Circle Line's Seaport Liberty Cruises (☎ 212-630-8888, www.circleline.com). Tours, which highlight Manhattan's maritime history, run at least four times a day from April to the end of November; they cost $12 to $25. Evening music cruises are also offered. Pioneer Sail (☎ 212-748-8590) offers sailing trips on the East River, as well as sunset tours.

New York Waterway (☎ 800-533-3779) operates 45-minute cruises that depart from Pier 17 and also offers direct water-taxi service to New York Yankees and New York Mets baseball games during the summer.

Brooklyn Bridge

When the world's first steel suspension bridge opened in 1883, the 1596-foot span between its two support towers was the longest in history. Today, the Brooklyn Bridge continues to dazzle as a magnificent example of fine urban design. Many regard it as the most beautiful bridge in the world.

Plans for an East River suspension bridge were drawn up by the Prussian-born engineer John Roebling, who was knocked off a pier by a ferry in Fulton Landing in June 1869; he died of tetanus poisoning before construction of the bridge began. His son Washington Roebling supervised construction of the bridge, which lasted 14 years and managed to survive budget overruns and the deaths of 20 workers. The younger Roebling himself suffered from the bends while helping to excavate the riverbed for the bridge's western tower and remained bedridden for much of the project. There

ANGUS OBORN

was one final tragedy to come in June 1883, when the bridge opened to pedestrian traffic: Someone in the crowd shouted, perhaps as a joke, that the bridge was collapsing into the river, setting off a mad rush in which 12 people were trampled to death.

There's no fear of collapse today, as the bridge enters its second century, following an extensive renovation in the early 1980s. The pedestrian walkway that begins just east of City Hall affords a wonderful view of Lower Manhattan, and you can stop at observation points under both stone support towers and view brass panorama histories of the waterfront. Once you reach the Brooklyn side (about a 20-minute trek), you can bear left and walk to Cadman Plaza West to a park that will bring you to Middagh St, which runs east to west in the heart of Brooklyn Heights. Bearing right brings you to Brooklyn's downtown area, which includes the ornate Brooklyn Borough Hall and the Brooklyn Heights Promenade (see the Brooklyn Heights Walking Tour, later in this chapter). Ⓜ 4, 5, 6 to Brooklyn Bridge-City Hall.

TRIBECA (Map 6)

This neighborhood of old warehouses, loft apartments and funky restaurants derives its name from its geographical location: the 'TRIangle BElow CAnal' St, an area roughly bordered by Broadway to the east and Chambers St to the south. Though not as touristy or architecturally significant as

SoHo, its northern neighbor, Tribeca features a fair number of 'scene' restaurants and bars, along with actor Robert De Niro's Tribeca Films production company.

Most of the warehouses, which retain long truck-loading platforms covered by metal awnings, make great apartment spaces. As such, the neighborhood is not yet overrun with boutiques and chain stores, which have driven some art galleries and plenty of well-heeled residents out of SoHo. Tribeca is now well-known as the neighborhood where the late John F Kennedy Jr resided. In winter, it's not unusual to spot a star like Harvey Keitel or Robert De Niro hanging out at a local restaurant like the Tribeca Grill, which DeNiro owns. (In the summer, the celebs head for the Hamptons and cooler beachfront locales.)

Harrison St

Built between 1804 and 1828, the eight townhouses on the block of Harrison St immediately west of Greenwich St constitute the largest collection of Federal architecture left in the city. But they were not always neighbors: Six of them once stood two blocks away, on a stretch of Washington St that no longer exists. In the early 1970s, that area was the site of Washington Market, a wholesale fruit and vegetable equivalent of the Fulton Fish Market (see the Lower Manhattan section). But the development of the waterfront (which resulted in the construction of Manhattan Community College and the unattractive concrete apartment complex that now looms over the townhouses) meant that the market had to move uptown and the historic row houses needed a new home. Only the buildings at 31 and 33 Harrison St remain where they were originally constructed. Ⓜ 1, 9 to Franklin St.

Clocktower Gallery

The PS1 Contemporary Art Center (718-784-2084, www.ps1.org), 108 Leonard St at Broadway, runs a free art space and studios known as the Clocktower Gallery. It is little-known to most visitors and sits at the top of the ornate old headquarters of the New York Life Insurance Company. (The building now houses the headquarters of the New York City Probation Department and the Public Health and Hospitals Corporation.) To get to the gallery, take the elevator to the 12th floor (which is as far as it goes) and walk up the clearly marked staircase to the tower, on the 13th floor.

The art studios here belong to artists who've been sponsored by the Institute for Contemporary Art, which funds the gallery. You can see their works in progress during the gallery's opening hours: noon to 6 pm Thursday to Saturday.

If you're planning to be in the neighborhood when the gallery is closed but the weather is clear, take the elevator up to the tower anyway. You can look down Broadway or enjoy an uptown panorama through dirty windows; walk to the right of the gallery entrance and look out through the northern face of the building. Ⓜ 1, 9 to Franklin St.

CHINATOWN & LITTLE ITALY (Map 6)

You'll find two of Manhattan's most famous ethnic enclaves – Chinatown and Little Italy – just north of the Civic Center and the financial district; Chinatown sprawls largely south of Canal St, east of Centre St to the Manhattan Bridge, although it's been steadily creeping farther east into the Lower East Side and north into Little Italy, which is a narrow sliver extending north of Canal St.

About 130,000 Chinese-speakers live in Chinatown, a community with its own unique rhythms and traditions. For example, some banks along Canal St keep Sunday hours, and Chinatown newsstands sell no fewer than six Chinese newspapers. Throughout the '90s, Chinatown has attracted a growing number of Vietnamese immigrants, who have set up their own shops and opened incredibly cheap restaurants here.

In contrast, Little Italy has lost a lot of its ethnic character in the last half of the 20th century. The area began as a strong Italian neighborhood (film director Martin Scorsese grew up on Elizabeth St), but in the mid-20th century, Little Italy suffered a large exodus, as many residents moved to the Cobble Hill section of Brooklyn and the city's suburbs. For that reason, few cultural sites remain, and most people come to Little Italy only to eat, even though you can find dozens of good Italian restaurants at all price levels elsewhere.

A few blocks east and west of Mulberry St, on Lafayette and Elizabeth Sts, Little Italy begins to take on a more cosmopolitan character, as SoHo-style shops, cafes and restaurants overflow into the area. This area is now known as Nolita (for 'North of Little Italy') or NoHo (for 'North of Houston St,' where it extends into the East Village). It's essential to walk the streets immediately east of Broadway below Houston St to experience the flavor of this redeveloped neighborhood. Of course, the development only threatens to erode the historic Italian character of Little Italy further. Who would have believed 30 years ago that this would be the site of several *French* cafes? Ⓜ J, M, N, R, Z, 6 to Canal St.

Night Court as Entertainment

If you find the 'Disneyfied' streets of New York disappointingly clean and safe, why not take an offbeat look at the city's dark underside by spending a few hours in Night Court? It's already popular with some more adventurous tourists.

State law dictates that anyone arrested in New York must be arraigned – that is, formally charged with the crime – within 24 hours of his or her arrest. So the city that never sleeps maintains an all-day schedule of court cases in the Criminal Courts Building, a forbidding structure at 100 Centre St near Chinatown. The evening shift runs from 5:30 pm to 1 am, with a parade of sad cases passing before a judge in two courtrooms in the fortress-like building. The accused plead guilty or not guilty and usually are set free on bail until the trial begins.

As all pretrial hearings must be open to the public, several benches are available for observers, who are free to come and go during breaks in the proceedings. It's a perfect way to research a crime novel – or simply see another side of life. But if you dare to attend the overnight shift, remember that there's no sleeping in the courtroom!

ROBERT REID

Chinatown & Little Italy

Start your tour on Canal St near Broadway. Walk south for one block to **Cortlandt Alley**, a perfectly preserved three-block enclave of gloomy old factories and warehouses that Hollywood loves to use as a backdrop in movies – it's worth a quick exploration. Head back up to Canal St and continue southeast toward Chinatown. West of Lafayette St, before Chinatown begins, Canal St maintains a decidedly seedy character, with an assortment of hardware and electrical supply stores and an array of street vendors selling phony designer clothing and bootleg videos of films still playing in theaters. If you buy anything off a street-seller, make sure it's something you can wear or check out on the spot – a hat, a book or a leather jacket.

The Chinese shopping district begins east of Baxter St, with several stands selling fresh fish and exotic produce, including guavas and durians, the infamously smelly fruit banned from the subways of Singapore. Once you cross Mott St, you'll find yourself on a strip full of Asian restaurants.

Turn right onto Mott St. The **Eastern States Buddhist Temple**, in a storefront at 64B Mott St, is a busy shrine with dozens of golden and porcelain Buddhas on display. You can buy a fortune and watch the devout make offerings.

Continue south on Mott St and turn right on Bayard St. At the corner of Mulberry St, you'll come to the **Museum of Chinese in the Americas** (☎ 212-619-4785, www.moca-nyc.org), on the 2nd floor of a former public school building. The museum offers walking tours, sponsors workshops on making paper lanterns and other crafts and hosts exhibits on the experiences of Chinese people who have immigrated to North and South America. It's open noon to 5 pm Tuesday to Saturday. The suggested donation is $3 for adults, $1 for seniors and students.

ROBERT REID

Top: Selling durians – a lonely business

Left: Along Mott St

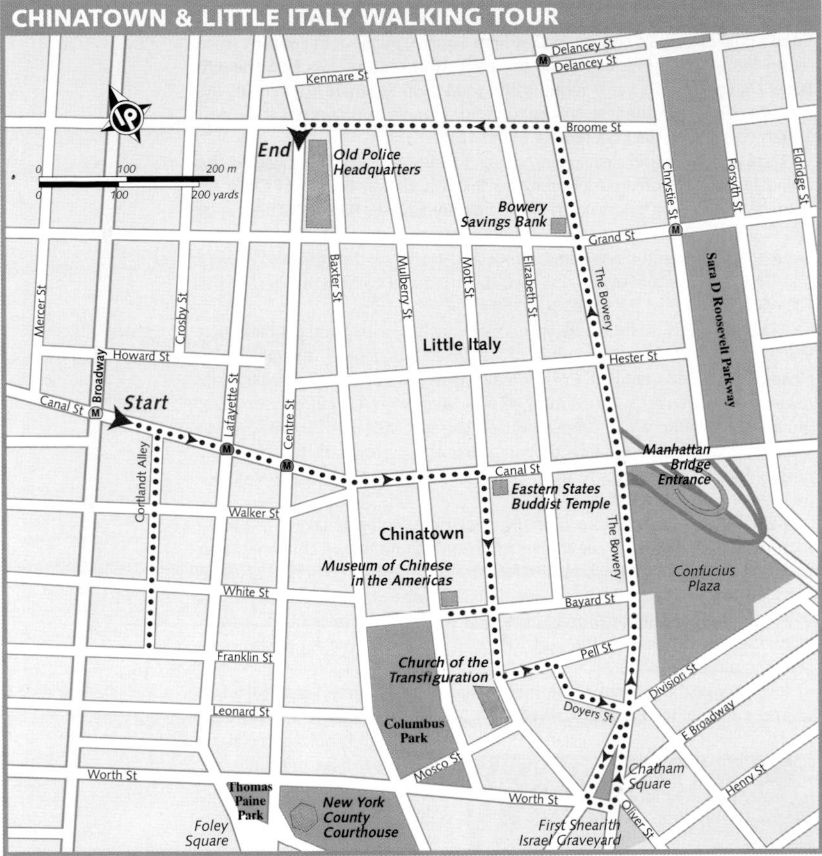

Backtrack on Bayard St to Mott St and turn right. In another block, you'll reach the **Church of the Transfiguration**, 29 Mott St at Pell St. This building began as an Episcopal church in 1801, but the Roman Catholic Church purchased it 50 years later to meet the needs of what was then an Irish and Italian neighborhood. (In the 1890s, the ascendant and spiteful Irish church leaders forced Italian patrons to worship in the basement.) The church got its first Chinese pastor in the 1970s and today holds services in Chinese.

Turn left on Pell St (an old road named for a butcher who plied his trade here in the colonial period), then bear right on Doyers St. Chinatown began in this small enclave in the 1870s, when Chinese railway workers, fed up with racial discrimination in the American West, moved to New York City in large numbers. During Chinese New Year celebrations in late January and early February, papier-mâché dragons snake their way around this corner to the sounds of firecrackers shooing away evil spirits.

At the end of Doyers St, you'll come upon two examples of the neighborhood's previous ethnic history. At **Chatham Square**, public auctions took place to sell the goods of Irish debtors in the early 19th century. The **First Shearith Israel Graveyard** (150 yards south of the square on St James Place) holds the remains of early Portuguese and Spanish immigrants and ranks as the oldest Jewish cemetery in the USA (dating to the 1680s).

Turning around and heading north up the Bowery will bring you to the grand but pollution-marred entrance to the Manhattan Bridge, at Canal St. From here, walk two blocks north to the **Bowery Savings Bank**, 130 Bowery at Grand St. The bank's Romanesque archway and vaulted gold-leaf interior offer a quiet respite from the noisy fruit stands and traffic on the corner of Bowery and Grand St. Stanford White, the most talented and colorful architect of the Gilded Age, designed the building in 1894.

Continue north on the Bowery one block to Broome St and turn left. In a little over four blocks, at the corner of Centre St, you'll reach the **Old Police Headquarters**, 240 Centre St. Completed in 1909, this building overwhelms its neighbors and serves as an example of poor planning. A hundred years ago, public officials in New York often approved the construction of European-style monuments without providing proper setback space or park land to allow passers-by to fully appreciate their grandeur. In 1988, the elegant structure became an apartment building.

Although the walking tour officially ends here, you can take in a couple more Little Italy sights by continuing north on Centre St, which merges into Lafayette St, for a few more blocks to Houston St. Near the corner of Lafayette and Houston Sts sits the **Puck Building**, 295 Lafayette St, home of the turn-of-the-century American humor magazine. The stunning red-brick building, with its two gold-leaf statues of the portly Puck, is a popular spot for wedding receptions and film shoots.

If you turn right on Houston St, then turn right again on Mulberry St, you'll soon come to **Old St Patrick's Cathedral** (☎ 212-226-8075), 263 Mulberry St. Although it looks a little bland (thanks to a fire that destroyed much of its exterior), the structure served as the city's first Roman Catholic cathedral from 1809–78, when its more famous successor was built uptown on Fifth Ave. You can catch a glimpse of its damaged Georgian interior only during weekend services: Saturday at 5 pm and Sunday at 9:30 am and 12:30 pm. The cathedral hosted the public memorial mass for John F Kennedy Jr, who lived nearby, after his death in 1999.

To return to Chinatown, head south on Mulberry St, the heart of traditional Little Italy.

ANGUS OBORN

Left: Puck Building

LOWER EAST SIDE (Map 6)

In the early 20th century, half a million Jews from eastern Europe streamed into the Lower East Side, and today it remains one of the most desirable entry-level neighborhoods in the city, although it attracts a different crowd these days. On Saturday nights, grunge rockers, dance club addicts and underage drinkers pack the streets, hopping among the no-name bars and late-night lounges that populate the four-block area on and around Ludlow St, which runs south from Houston St.

Architecturally, this storied old tenement area still retains its hardscrabble character, with block after block of crumbling buildings. You can still see why the early residents lamented that 'the sun was embarrassed to shine' on their benighted neighborhood.

But like Little Italy, the Lower East Side has lost much of its traditional ethnic flavor. Only a small Jewish community and a handful of traditional businesses remain. Today, the people living behind the crumbling doorways of the contemporary Lower East Side are usually young twentysomethings living in their first city apartment or long-term residents holding onto a rent-controlled place. Also, a growing Latino community has spilled over on the Lower East Side's northern border, and the Chinese have been moving into the area south of Delancey St.

With its array of restaurants and nightlife, the Lower East Side now ranks as one of New York City's hottest neighborhoods. Over the next few years, you'll be able to visit this area repeatedly and marvel at the number of new cafes, eateries and late night bars here. What you probably won't be able to do is find an apartment in the neighborhood, unless money is no object.

Orchard St

Bargain hunters congregate in the Orchard St Bargain District, a market area that spreads across Orchard, Ludlow and Essex Sts above Delancey St, which runs east to west. When the Lower East Side was still a largely Jewish neighborhood, Eastern European merchants set up pushcarts to sell their wares here.

KIM GRANT

Bargain shopping on Orchard Street

Today, the 300-odd shops in this modern-day bazaar sell sporting goods, leather belts, hats and a wide array of off-brand 'designer fashions.' While the businesses are not exclusively owned by Orthodox Jews, they still close early on Friday afternoon and remain shuttered Saturday in observance of the Sabbath. There's an unspoken rule that shop owners should offer their first customer of the day a discount – usually 10% – for good luck, so it helps to arrive at 10 am if you're serious about buying something. Offering to pay in cash may also attract a discount.

You won't find much for sale in the Lower East Side that you couldn't pick up elsewhere in the city, with the exception of kosher food products. You can buy kosher wine at Schapiro's Wines (☎ 212-674-4404), 126 Rivington St. This winery, which is closed on Saturday, offers a tour of its facilities each Sunday (call ahead for information). You can pick up unleavened bread at Streit's Matzoh Company (☎ 212-475-7000), 150 Rivington St; potato knishes at Yonah Shimmel Bakery (☎ 212-477-2858), 137 E Houston St; and sweet and sour pickles directly out of the wooden barrels at Essex Pickles, 25 Essex St. Ⓜ F to Delancey St; J, M, Z to Essex St.

Lower East Side Tenement Museum

This museum (☎ 212-431-0233, www.tenement.org), 90 Orchard St at Broome St, puts the neighborhood's heartbreaking heritage on display in a reconstructed tenement. The museum's visitor center shows a video about the difficult life endured by the people who once lived in the surrounding buildings, which often did not have running water or electricity. The visitor center, which includes a gift shop, is open 11 am to 5 pm Tuesday through Sunday. Museum visits are available only as part of scheduled tours, so call ahead for the tour schedules.

Across the street, the museum has recreated a turn-of-the-20th-century tenement owned by Lucas Glockner, a German-born tailor. This building, in which an estimated 10,000 people lived over 72 years, is accessible only by guided tour. The tours leave at 1, 1:30, 2, 2:30, 3 and 4 pm Tuesday through Friday and every half hour from 11 am to 4:30 pm on the weekend. Tickets to the museum, which include the tenement tour, are $9 for adults, $7 for seniors and students.

On weekends, the museum also offers an interactive tour in which kids can try on period clothes; this tour leaves on the hour from noon to 3 pm and costs $8 for adults, $6 for seniors and students. From April to December, the staff also leads walking tours of the neighborhood at 1 and 2:30 pm on weekends ($9 for adults, $7 for seniors and students). Ⓜ F to Delancey St; J, M, Z to Essex St.

Synagogues

Four hundred Orthodox synagogues once thrived here in the early 20th century, but few remain today. The **First Roumanian-American Congregation** (☎ 212-673-2835), 89 Rivington St at Orchard St, features a wonderfully ornate wooden sanctuary that can hold 1800 of the faithful, but membership has dwindled. Ⓜ F to Delancey St; J, M, Z to Essex St.

The landmark **Eldridge St Synagogue** (☎ 212-219-0888), 12 Eldridge St between Canal and Division Sts east of the Bowery, is another struggling place of worship in an area that is now completely part of Chinatown. This Moorish-style synagogue faces one of the oldest surviving blocks of tenements in New York City. Ⓜ B, D, Q to Grand St.

SOHO (Map 6)

Not named after its London counterpart, this hip and trendy neighborhood takes its name from its geographical placement (SOuth of HOuston St). The rectangular area extends as far down as Canal St and runs from Broadway west to West St.

When you're in the area, make sure that you pronounce Houston St as '**how**-ston.' No one can definitively explain the unusual pronunciation, though it's assumed that a man named William Houstoun, who lived in the area, pronounced his surname in that manner. (Somewhere along the line the second 'u' in the spelling of the street was dropped.)

SoHo is filled with block after block of cast-iron industrial buildings that date to the period just after the Civil War, when the area was the city's leading commercial district. These multistory buildings housed linen, ribbon and clothing factories, which often featured showcase galleries on the street level. But the area fell into disfavor as retail businesses relocated uptown and manufacturing concerns moved out of the city. By the 1950s, the huge lofts and cheap rents attracted artists and other members of the avant-garde. Their political lobbying not only saved the neighborhood from destruction but assured that a 26-block area was declared a legally protected historic district in 1973. Thanks to this inadvertent urban renewal, today SoHo contains some of the city's best art galleries, clothing stores and boutiques.

As you walk through SoHo, stop to look up at the buildings – many still have elaborately decorated flourishes that have been obscured or destroyed on the street level. Some of the preserved structures here include the **Singer Building**, 561-563 Broadway between Prince and Spring Sts, an attractive iron and brick structure that used to be the main warehouse for the famous sewing machine company.

At 521-523 Broadway between Spring and Broome Sts, above the fabric store and gourmet food shop, you can view what's left of the marble-faced **St Nicholas Hotel**, the 1000-room luxury hotel that was *the* place to stay when it opened in 1854. The hotel, which closed in 1880, also served as the headquarters of Abraham Lincoln's War Department during the Civil War.

Built in 1857, the **Haughwout Building**, 488 Broadway at Broome St, was the first building to use the exotic steam elevator developed by Elisha Otis. Today this former headquarters of the EV Haughwout crockery company houses the Staples office supply store.

It's preferable to visit SoHo on a weekday morning, when the neighborhood is populated largely by the people who work in the galleries and assorted offices. True to the 'downtown' cliches, these office workers invariably dress in sleek black outfits and

The Gallery Scene: Been There, Done That

In 1996, art dealer Mary Boone, who launched the careers of Julian Schnabel, David Salle and Jean-Michel Basquiat, shocked the cultural elite by moving her gallery from SoHo to 745 Fifth Ave. Boone, a pioneer in mixing art and commerce in the 1980s, claimed that the 'energy and focus of art has shifted uptown.' But skeptics blamed her move on her distaste for the cafes and shops that have sprung up in SoHo, attracting crowds of tourists interested in looking at – but not buying – expensive art.

Boone immediately set a trend that's been followed by Paula Cooper and Jay Gorney, who both moved their galleries north to Chelsea in recent years. But even if some of the contemporary heavyweights have moved on, a number of galleries still populate the streets of SoHo. These include the **Ward-Nasse Gallery** (☎ 212-925-6951), 178 Prince St at Thompson St, which specializes in yet-to-be-discovered artists, and the **Howard Greenberg Gallery** (☎ 212-334-0010), 120 Wooster St at Prince St, which features photography. For information on current exhibits, pick up the free monthly *NY/SOHO* map in one of the downtown galleries or scan the 'Goings on about Town' section in the *New Yorker* or the entertainment section of the Sunday *New York Times*. On the Internet, go to www.artseensoho.com.

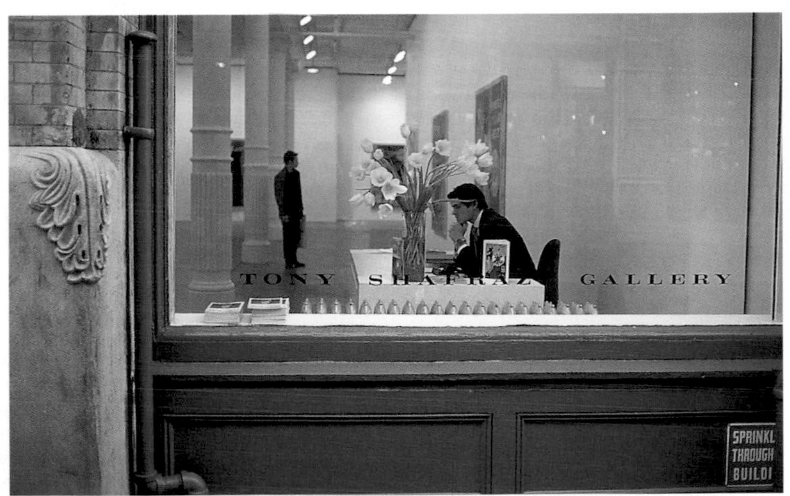

ANGUS OBORN

'Sorry, just browsing.'

spread their aloof, cooler-than-thou atmosphere throughout the neighborhood. On weekends, West Broadway (a separate street from Broadway) becomes a sea of suede, and it and nearby Prince St attract hordes of tourists and street artists selling homemade jewelry and paintings in defiance of the laws requiring a city license to sell such wares.

Museum for African Art

This facility (☎ 212-966-1313, www.africanart.org), 593 Broadway at Houston St, is the city's only space dedicated solely to the works of African artists, and its collection reflects a heavy concentration on tribal crafts, musical instruments and depictions of spirituality. The interior was designed by Maya Lin, the young architect who first found fame for her stunning Vietnam Memorial in Washington, DC. The museum is open 10:30 am to 5:30 pm Tuesday to Friday, noon to 6 pm Saturday and Sunday. Admission is $5 for adults, $2.50 for seniors, students and children. It's free for everyone on Sunday. Ⓜ B, D, F, Q to Broadway-Lafayette St; N, R to Prince St.

New Museum of Contemporary Art

This museum (☎ 212-219-1222, www.newmuseum.org), 583 Broadway between Houston and Prince Sts, at the vanguard of the contemporary SoHo scene, offers exposure to sculptures, painting, installations and other international artworks that are less than 10 years old, meaning that you'll encounter artists you might not already know. The museum is open noon to 6 pm Wednesday and Sunday, noon to 8 pm Thursday to Saturday (closed Monday and Tuesday). Admission is $6 for adults, $3 for artists, students and seniors, with free entry for those under 18 and for everyone on Thursday evening. There's never a charge to browse the interactive exhibits in the 1st-floor drop-in space, where you can sit down and read for awhile. Ⓜ B, D, F, Q to Broadway-Lafayette St; N, R to Prince St.

Guggenheim SoHo

When the Solomon R Guggenheim Museum's downtown branch (☎ 212-423-3500, www.guggenheim.org), 575 Broadway at Prince St, opened in the early '90s, it reinforced SoHo's reputation as the center of the American art scene. Although its initial exhibitions left the impression that this branch intended to showcase art by living artists in the middle of their careers, recently it's taken a turn toward displaying works from the uptown Guggenheim's permanent collection. A recent exhibition featured Andy Warhol's *Last Supper*, a series of works inspired by the da Vinci masterpiece and the last art created by the famous pop artist before his death in 1987.

The Guggenheim SoHo is open 11 am to 6 pm Thursday to Monday (closed Tuesday and Wednesday). Admission is free. Ⓜ N, R to Prince St; B, D, F, Q to Broadway-Lafayette St.

New York City Fire Museum

The New York City Fire Museum (☎ 212-691-1303), 278 Spring St near Varick St, occupies a grand old firehouse dating back to 1904. Inside, you'll find a well-maintained collection of gold horse-drawn fire-fighting carriages along with modern-day red fire engines. Exhibits explain the development of the New York City fire-fighting system, which began with the 'bucket brigades.' All the colorful heavy equipment and the museum's particularly friendly staff make this a great place to bring children, even though they're not allowed to hop on any of the engines.

The museum is open 10 am to 4 pm Tuesday to Sunday; the suggested admission is $4 for adults, $1 for children. Ⓜ 1, 9 to Houston St; C, E to Spring St.

GREENWICH VILLAGE (Map 6)

Roughly bordered by 14th St in the north and Houston St in the south, 'the Village' runs from Lafayette St all the way west to the Hudson River. Once a symbol for all things outlandish and bohemian, this storied and popular neighborhood looks considerably less edgy now than it has in the past. Today, some sophisticated clubs and restaurants line the streets, alongside fashionable brownstones. But the student culture at New York

University (NYU), which owns most of the property around Washington Square Park, keeps things lively and always a bit offbeat. In the area south of Washington Square Park (including Bleecker St, all the way west to Seventh Ave), you'll find an eclectic and crowded collection of cafes, shops and restaurants; beyond Seventh Ave is the West Village, a pleasant neighborhood of winding streets and townhouses.

Greenwich Village began as a trading port for Native Americans, who took advantage of the area's easy access to the shores of what is now Hoboken, New Jersey, just across the Hudson River. Later, Dutch settlers established a number of tobacco plantations, and their English successors named the peaceful wooded area Greenwich Village. As the city began to develop a large servant class, Greenwich Village became New York's most prominent black neighborhood until many of those residents moved to Harlem in search of better housing just before the 1920s.

Its reputation as a creative enclave can be traced back to at least the early 1900s, when artists and writers moved in, and by the '40s the neighborhood became known as a gathering place for gays. In the '50s, the Village's coffeehouses, bars and jazz clubs attracted scores of bohemians, including the Beat poets, who adopted the neighborhood as their East Coast headquarters and listened to bebop and poetry throughout the Village. The area became an important incubator of American literature. Poet Allen Ginsberg lived here most of his life, and novelist Norman Mailer helped to found the influential *Village Voice* newspaper.

In the '60s, the neighborhood's rebellious spirit led to the birth of today's gay rights movement (see the boxed text 'Gay & Lesbian New York' in the Facts about New York City chapter). Today, many still think of Christopher St as the center of gay life in New York, even though the gay community has been shifting to Chelsea in recent years. Crowds of gay men and lesbians continue to make pilgrimages to the Village in June for the annual Lesbian and Gay Pride Parade (see the Public Holidays & Special Events section of the Facts for the Visitor chapter).

RICK GERHARTER

George Segal sculpture *Gay Liberation*, Sheridan Square

Greenwich Village

RICHARD I'ANSON

Plenty of companies offer guided walking tours of this famous neighborhood, some focusing only on certain aspects of history, others providing a general overview of Greenwich Village – but they all come at a price. Here's one you can do for free that should take about 90 minutes.

The best place to start any tour of the Village is the arch at **Washington Square Park** (see separate heading, later), Fifth Ave at Waverly Place. Head south through the park to **Judson Memorial Church**, which graces the park's southern border. This yellow-brick Baptist church honors Adoniram Judson, an American missionary who served in Burma in the early 19th century. Designed by Stanford White, the National Historic Site features stained-glass windows by muralist John La Farge, who was born near the park, and a marble frontage by Augustus Saint-Gaudens.

This page: Chess sets and a busy Greenwich Village street corner

As you exit the park, walk down Thompson St, past a series of chess shops where Village denizens meet to play the game for $1.50 an hour. At the intersection of Thompson and Bleecker Sts (Bleecker being the main east-west thoroughfare in Greenwich Village), look up at the southwest corner to see the old sign for the legendary jazz club the Village Gate, which relocated to Midtown a few years back.

Turn right on Bleecker St and head west for two blocks, which will bring you to two old coffeehouses associated with New York's '50s beatnik culture: **Le Figaro**, 184 Bleecker St, which still features a weekend jazz brunch, and **Caffe Borgia**, 185 Bleecker St. You're better off just taking a look around Bleecker St and then turning right on MacDougal St, where you'll find a great cup of cappuccino at **Caffe Reggio**, 119 MacDougal St, which still retains some old-world character, thanks to its dark walls and massive trademark espresso machine.

Double back half a block on MacDougal St to the corner of Minetta Lane, where you'll find **Minetta Tavern**, an old Village hangout. This decent Italian restaurant is a great place to linger over a beer or glass of wine while you admire old photos of the '50s-era celebrities who used to hang

MICHAEL S CLARK

out here. On the opposite side of Minetta Lane, you'll see **Cafe Wha?**, a legendary old club where Jimi Hendrix once played. (Its 'in' days are long past.)

KIM GRANT

Walk down Minetta Lane and turn left onto Minetta St. Here, you'll pass a block of 18th-century slums that have been transformed into very desirable row houses. The old Minetta Brook still runs under some of the houses.

Cross Sixth Ave, bear right and walk up Bleecker St, past a three-block stretch full of record stores, leather shops, restaurants and great Italian pastry shops. Turn left onto Seventh Ave, walk half a block and make a quick right onto quiet Commerce St, then proceed one block to Bedford St. At the corner of Commerce and Bedford Sts, you'll be standing just a few yards from 75½ Bedford St, a quirky 9½-foot-wide house where poet Edna St Vincent Millay lived from 1923–24. (Cary Grant, John Barrymore and Margaret Mead also lived here at different times.) Right next door, at 77 Bedford St, stands what is possibly the oldest house in the Village, a red-brick residence that was built in 1799.

Turn around and continue up Bedford St past Commerce St again. A short block beyond Commerce St, you might want to detour for a moment up Barrow St to check out the ivy-covered **Federal row houses** at Nos 49 and 51, and then have a look at the block of six perfectly preserved handsome red-brick residences on the west side of the street.

Head back to Bedford St; just beyond the corner of Bedford and Barrow Sts, you'll come to a spare wooden door at 86 Bedford St – this is **Chumley's**, a former speakeasy run by Lee Chumley, a socialist who welcomed many writers to his place in the late '20s. The bar's address is said to have inspired the slang phrase '86 it' – a shorthand imperative to get rid of something; this expression may have been whispered to patrons drinking alcohol right before a prohibition-era police raid began.

A wonderful old horse stable from 1894 survives at 95 Bedford St, just past Chumley's. Before continuing farther on Bedford, take a look down **Grove St** – a curved stretch of row houses that's been featured in several movies, including Woody Allen's *Annie Hall*. Back on Bedford St, note the early 19th-century home called **Twin Peaks** at No 102; it got its name from the dual mock-Tudor tops that were added in the 1920s. The 1843 Greek Revival residence at 113 Bedford St used to belong to a local saloon keeper. (Other buildings in this neighborhood sport detailed plaques noting who built them.) Bedford St ends at raucous Christopher St, the spiritual center of gay life in the Village.

Right: No ordinary joe at Caffe Reggio.

Turn left on Christopher St and walk one block to Hudson St. At this stage, if it's a fine day, you might want to turn left and take a small detour down

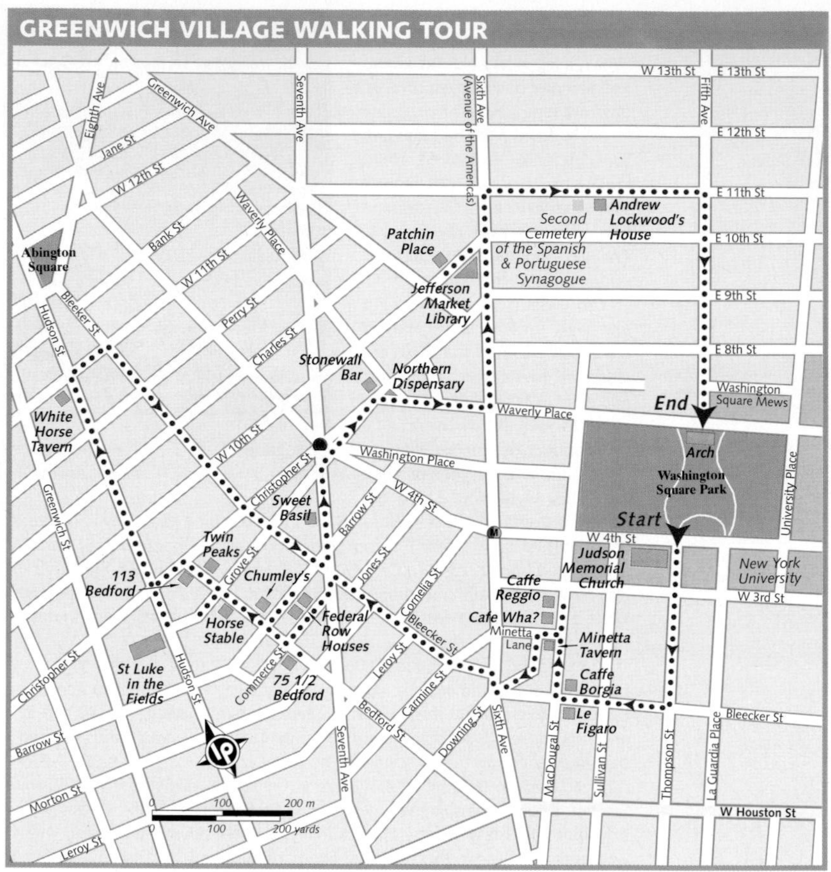

Hudson St to check out the gardens at **St Luke in the Fields**, an Episcopal church and school. On weekends, the church holds rummage sales in the garden. Or you can take a break entirely by turning right on Hudson St and heading four blocks north to the storied **White Horse Tavern**, on W 11th St, where you can enjoy a drink and a burger.

Turn right on W 11 th St and walk one block to Bleecker St, where you should turn right and proceed several blocks, past tony clothing and knick-knack shops. At the corner of Bleecker and Seventh Ave, you'll see the jazz club **Sweet Basil** on the left (see the Jazz & Blues section of the Entertainment chapter).

Head north one block on Seventh Ave to Grove St, where a right turn will lead you to **Stonewall Place**, site of the 1969 gay rebellion (see the boxed text 'Gay & Lesbian New York' in the Facts about New York City chapter). The **Stonewall Bar** lies on the north side of Christopher St.

From Grove St, turn right on Waverly Place and look for the oddly shaped **Northern Dispensary**, 165 Waverly Place. (The three-sided dispensary marks New York's strangest intersection: the corner of Waverly Place and Waverly Place!) Built in 1831 to combat a cholera epidemic sweeping through this neighborhood, the dispensary was New York's oldest public health facility until 1989, when it closed. This prime spot has often been pegged for redevelopment, but nothing has happened yet.

Continue to Sixth Ave and turn left. Walk two blocks to the red-brick **Jefferson Market Library**. The library's gardens are sometimes open to the public on weekends. Just behind the library on W 10th St is **Patchin Place**, an enclosed courtyard block of flats where journalist John Reed (chronicler of the Soviet revolution) and poet EE Cummings once lived.

Double back to Sixth Ave, walk a block to W 11th St and head east. On the right, you'll find the tiny **Second Cemetery of the Spanish & Portuguese Synagogue**, which was used from 1805 to 1829. Continue along W 11th St and you'll pass by a series of traditional row houses, including builder **Andrew Lockwood's House**, 60 W 11th St, constructed in 1842 on a lot that was originally part of the larger Wouter Van Twiller farm in the Dutch colonial era.

Turn right on Fifth Ave, and you'll be heading directly back toward the arch in Washington Square Park. These last few apartment blocks on and around Fifth Ave abound with the offices of psychologists, and some claim that this area boasts the greatest concentration of shrinks in the entire world. Before you reach the end of Fifth Ave, wander up **Washington Square Mews**, a quiet, cobblestone street with old stables that now house NYU facilities.

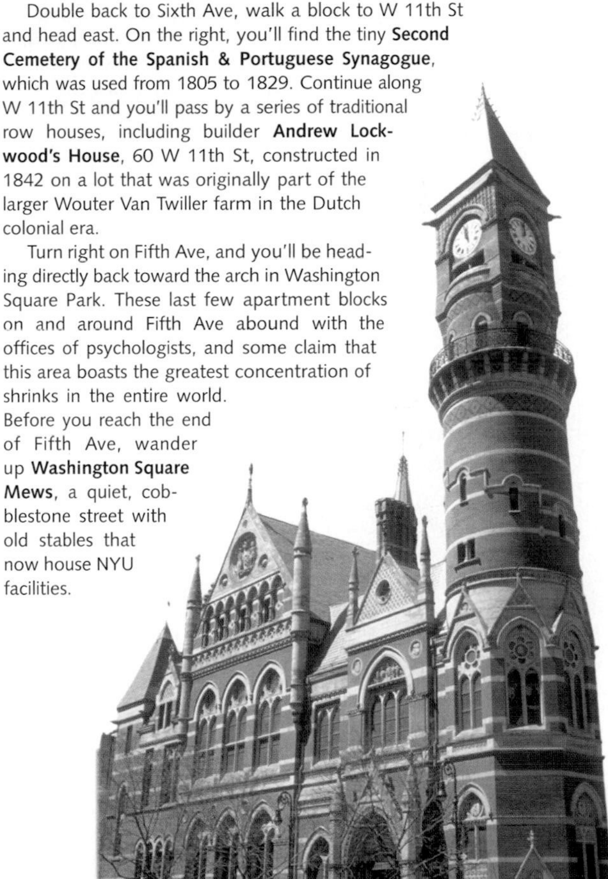

KIMBERLY GRANT

Right: Jefferson Market Library

Washington Square Park

Washington Square Park, like many public spaces in the city, began as a potter's field – a burial ground for the penniless. Its status as a cemetery protected it from development. It also served as the site of public executions; when French statesman Marquis de Lafayette visited in 1824, several petty criminals were hung in his honor. The magnificent old tree near the northwestern corner of the park bears a plaque memorializing it as the 'Hangman's Elm,' though no one is quite sure if it was actually used for executions.

Pay particular attention to the Stanford White **Arch**, originally designed in wood to celebrate the centennial of George Washington's inauguration in 1889. The arch proved so popular that it was replaced in stone six years later and adorned with statues of the general in war and peace (the latter work is by A Stirling Calder, the father of artist Alexander Calder).

KIM GRANT

The mellow scene at Washington Square Park

In 1916, artist Marcel Duchamp climbed to the top of the arch by its internal stairway and declared the park the 'Free and Independent Republic of Washington Square.' These days, the anarchy takes place on the ground level, as comedians and buskers use the park's permanently dry fountain as a performance space. The fountain was once used as a turnaround for the Fifth Ave buses that ran under the arch.

Judson Memorial Church graces the park's south border. For more on the church, see the Greenwich Village Walking Tour, above.

One block east of the park, at 245 Greene St, sits the building where the Triangle Shirtwaist Fire took place on March 25, 1911. This sweatshop had locked its doors to prevent the young seamstresses from taking unauthorized breaks. The inferno killed 146 young women, many of whom had jumped to their deaths from the upper floors because the fire department's ladders did not extend to the top floors of the 10-story building. Every year on March 25, the New York Fire Department holds a solemn ceremony in memory of the city's most deadly factory fire.

The row of townhouses at Washington Square North inspired *Washington Square*, Henry James' novel about late 19th-century social mores, though James did not live here as is popularly assumed. Ⓜ A, B, C, D, E, F, Q to W 4th St.

Forbes Galleries

The Forbes Galleries (☎ 212-206-5549), 60-62 Fifth Ave at 12th St, house curios from the personal collection of the late publishing magnate Malcolm Forbes. The eclectic mix of objects on display include Fabergé eggs, ship models, autographs, tin soldiers and art deco wood panels. Walking through here, you get the sense that the wily Forbes might have opened these galleries to the public as a way of giving his impulse purchases a tax-deductible status.

The Forbes Galleries are open 10 am to 4 pm Tuesday, Wednesday, Friday and Saturday. It's free to visit. Ⓜ F to 14th St.

Greenwich Village Rock Landmarks

In addition to checking out Cafe Wha?, on the corner of MacDougal St and Minetta Lane, rock and roll fans will want to take note of 161 W 4th St, where Bob Dylan once lived and found inspiration for the song 'Positively 4th St.' He often performed (and reputedly smoked his first joint) at Gerdes Folk City, which originally stood at 11 W 4th St. Folk City moved to 130 W 3rd St in 1969 and closed in 1986, though its neon sign remains half-lit above the building. Jimi Hendrix lived and recorded at the Electric Lady Studios, 52 W 8th St at Sixth Ave. The brown brick building recently became a shoe store.

EAST VILLAGE (Map 6)

Life is a bit different in the East Village, a neighborhood that extends from 14th St south to E Houston St and from the East River west to Lafayette St (although the Bowery, one block east of Lafayette St, serves as the semi-official dividing line between Greenwich Village and the adjacent East Village).

While the East Village takes its name from Greenwich Village, the two neighborhoods don't have much in common historically. Large farmland estates once stretched over this area, but urban development ate up the acreage in the late 19th century, as New York became more industrial and extended northward from Lower Manhattan. By the early 20th century, this region was considered the northern section of the Lower East Side, a poorer cousin to Greenwich Village. But it has certainly come into its own during the '90s. The East Village has been essentially gentrified, and the once dangerous **Alphabet City** – which includes Aves A, B, C and D – has seen tenements turned into pricey housing.

The best way to explore the East Village is by simply walking up or down First, Second or Third Aves between 14th and Houston Sts. On this 15-minute walk, you'll see burgeoning businesses everywhere. The buildings that line both sides of the avenue house laundries, bars, coffee shops, Eastern European meat stores, pharmacies and restaurants that'll take you on a culinary world tour – you can find virtually every type of cuisine here, including Italian, Polish, Indian, Lebanese, Japanese and Thai. On E 9th St just east of Second Ave, a cluster of boutiques sell all-natural products, antiques, new furniture and vintage clothing (see the Shopping chapter). There are also a number of herbal medicine stores nearby.

Astor Place

This square is named after the Astor family, who built an early New York fortune on beaver trading and lived on **Colonnade Row**, 429-434 Lafayette St, just south of the square (on E 8th St between Third and Fourth Aves). Four out of the original nine marble-faced Greek Revival residences on Lafayette St still exist, but they are entombed beneath a layer of black soot. Across the street, in the public library built by John Jacob Astor, stands the **Joseph Papp Public Theater**, 425 Lafayette St. When it went up in 1848, this building cost $500,000, a then-phenomenal sum. The Public is now one of the city's most important cultural centers and presents the famous Shakespeare in Central Park (see Theater in the Entertainment chapter).

Astor Place itself is dominated by the large brownstone **Cooper Union**, the public college founded by glue millionaire Peter Cooper in 1859. Just after its completion, Abraham Lincoln gave his 'Right Makes Might' speech condemning slavery in the Union's Great Hall. The fringed lectern he used still exists, but the auditorium is only open to the public for special events.

Right across the square, you'll see a symbol of the real change happening in this now-gentrified neighborhood – the city's first K Mart, which opened in 1996. The following year, Irish rock band U2 kicked off its Rock Mart tour here, and despite initial protest from the neighborhood, the store seems to have won residents over with its bargain prices. Ⓜ 6 to Astor Place.

Grace Church

This Gothic Revival Episcopal church, two blocks north of Astor Place on E 10th St, was made of marble quarried by prisoners at Sing Sing, the state penitentiary in the upstate town of Ossining. After years of neglect, Grace Church has recently been cleaned up, and its floodlit white marble makes for a strangely elegant nighttime sight in this neighborhood of dance clubs, record stores and pizza parlors. James Renwick designed the church, and many also credit him with creating **Renwick Triangle**, a movie-set-perfect group of brownstone Italianate houses one block to the east at 112-128 E 10th St. You can't enter these houses, but if you stand outside, you can imagine you're standing in the New York City of the 1880s. Ⓜ 6 to Astor Place.

ANGUS OBORN

St Mark's-in-the-Bowery

St Mark's-in-the-Bowery

The Episcopal church St Mark's-in-the-Bowery (☎ 212-674-6377), Second Ave at E 10th St, stands on the site of the farm, or *bouwerie*, owned by Dutch Governor Peter Stuyvesant, whose crypt lies under the grounds. The 1799 church, damaged by fire in 1978, has been restored. You can enjoy an interior view of its abstract stained-glass windows when the church is open to the public, from 10 am to 6 pm weekdays. On some nights, it also hosts occasional folk music performances or small literary readings. Ⓜ 6 to Astor Place; L to Third Ave.

Old Merchant's House Museum

Not much remains of the neighborhood that existed here before the tenement boom, but this museum (☎ 212-777-1089), 29 E 4th St between Lafayette and the Bowery, is a remarkably well-preserved example of how the business class lived. The 1831 house once belonged to drug importer Seabury Tredwell, and because Tredwell's youngest daughter Gertrude lived here until her death in 1933, its original furnishings were still intact when it began life as a museum three years later. The forlorn and abandoned building just past the empty lot was also owned by the Tredwell family, but not much has been done with it.

The Old Merchant's House Museum is open 1 to 5 pm Thursday to Monday. Admission is $5 for adults, $3 for seniors and students. Ⓜ 6 to Bleecker St.

10th St Baths

The waning of Eastern European traditions on the Lower East Side led to the closure of many old bath houses in Manhattan, and the AIDS crisis prevented their continuation as gay gathering places. But these historic old Russian & Turkish Steam Baths (☎ 212-674-9250), 268 E 10th St between First Ave and Ave A, still remain. Here, you can get a Russian-style oak-leaf massage followed by a plunge in an ice-cold bath, provided your heart can stand the strain. There's also a small cafe on the premises.

The 10th St Baths are open 9 am to 10 pm weekdays, 7:30 am to 10 pm weekends. The baths are co-ed daily except 9 am to 2 pm Wednesday (women only) and 7:30 am to 2 pm Saturday (men only). General admission is $20, with massage rates starting at $45 an hour. Ⓜ 6 to Astor Place.

CHELSEA (Map 7)

North of Greenwich Village, Chelsea extends from 14th St north to 23rd St and Broadway west to the Hudson River. Once the dry goods and retail center during the city's Gilded Age in the late 19th century, the neighborhood drew well-heeled shoppers to its many emporia, which have since been turned into office buildings. Closer to the Hudson River, you can still find plenty of old warehouses. At the heart of the neighborhood, on Eighth Ave, numerous cafes, shops, gyms, restaurants and bars have sprung up in recent years, and a big chunk of the gay community has moved from Greenwich Village, its traditional home, to Chelsea.

The prime sight on noisy 23rd St is the **Chelsea Hotel**, a red-brick hotel with ornate iron balconies and no fewer than seven plaques declaring it a literary landmark. Even before Sid Vicious murdered his girlfriend here, the hotel became famous as a literary hangout for the likes of Mark Twain, Thomas Wolfe, Dylan Thomas and Arthur Miller. Jack Kerouac allegedly typed his best-known book, *On the Road*, on a single roll of teletype paper during one marathon session at the Chelsea. Ⓜ 1, 9, A, C, E to 23rd St.

The **Chelsea Piers** complex (☎ 212-336-6000, www.chelseapiers.com), on the Hudson River at the end of 23rd St, caters to sporting types of all stripes – you can set out to hit a bucket of golf balls at the four-level driving range, then change your mind and ice skate in the complex's indoor skating rink instead, or even rent in-line skates to cruise along the Hudson River waterfront down to the Battery. Though the Piers complex is somewhat cut off by the busy West Side Hwy, its wide array of attractions brings in the crowds. Also located here are the Chelsea Studios, where the TV series *Law & Order* is shot. Ⓜ 1, 9, A, C, E to 23rd St.

UNION SQUARE (Map 7)

This square, at the convergence of 14th St and Broadway, originally served as one of New York City's first uptown business districts, and throughout the mid-19th century it offered a convenient site for many workers' rallies and political protests – hence its name. By the 1960s, this area had become something of a depressed part of town and a hangout for junkies. But the '90s heralded a big revival, helped along by the arrival of the Greenmarket farmers' market, held in the square from 8 am to 4 pm on Wednesday, Friday and Saturday throughout the year. Today, Union Square hops with nighttime activity; its plethora of bars, microbreweries and restaurants makes it one of the most popular places in the city to hang out in the evenings. Ⓜ 4, 5, 6, L, N, R to 14th St-Union Square.

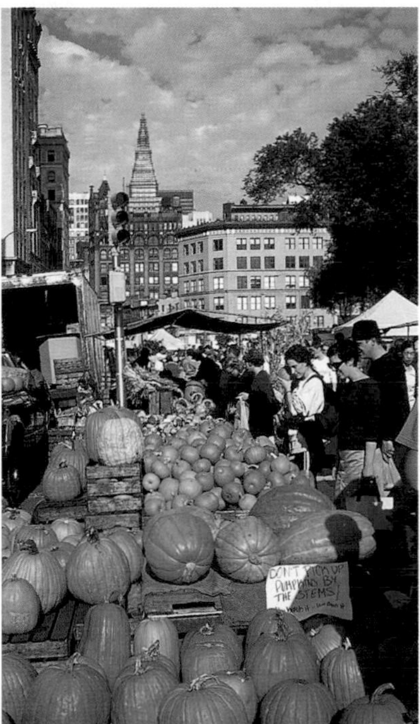

ANGUS OBORN

Future jack-o'-lanterns in Union Square

THINGS TO SEE & DO

Touring Manhattan on the Cheap – by Public Bus

If you're interested in a guided bus tour of Manhattan, see the Organized Tours section of the Getting Around chapter. But if you'd rather not spend the money (or listen to the prattle of a tour guide), why not take a self-guided loop tour of Manhattan on the city buses? You can hop on and off as often you like to see the sights and even return by way of the subway down Broadway. If you do go this route, though, make sure you start in the morning, because traffic can turn this two-hour journey into a frustrating three-hour crawl.

For more details on most of the sights mentioned here, see the Chelsea, Midtown, Upper West Side and Washington Heights sections in this chapter.

Catch the uptown-bound M5 bus anywhere along Sixth Ave above Houston St (where the bus route begins). Be sure to board a 'Limited Stop' bus, which picks up passengers at several clearly marked spots, including W 3rd St and Sixth Ave, and then stops only at major cross streets (14th St, 23rd St, etc), since you're taking the bus far uptown. Buses do not take dollar bills, so pay the $1.50 fare with a token, a MetroCard or exact change and ask for a transfer just in case you want to visit the Cloisters by switching to the M4 bus.

As the M5 continues up Sixth Ave, it travels first through **Chelsea**, past Ladies' Mile, where fashionable women shopped for millinery and china in the late 19th century. Today, the old ornate buildings between 14th and 23rd Sts have been taken over by modern superstores (Staples, Bed Bath & Beyond, Barnes & Noble, etc).

The bus continues past **Herald Square** and Macy's department store and, to the right, the western edge of Bryant Park, located behind the main New York Public Library. In another six blocks, you'll travel by **Rockefeller Center**, which includes the GE building and **Radio City Music Hall**, on your right at 50th St.

Turning left at 59th St, the bus skirts the southern end of Central Park before turning uptown at **Columbus Circle**. This circle, with the statue of Christopher Columbus (built in 1892) as its centerpiece, is the closest thing New York has to a grand traffic circle in the European tradition. But the 1969 construction of the huge Gulf Western Building, north of the circle between Central Park West and Broadway, pretty much destroyed the European aesthetic here. Developer Donald

Touring Manhattan on the Cheap – by Public Bus

Trump has since refashioned the ugly black-and-white office tower into a more muted brown glass luxury apartment building and hotel.

As the bus continues up Broadway, you'll soon see **Lincoln Center** to your left between 62nd and 65th Sts. The white marble complex houses the Metropolitan Opera, New York Philharmonic and the Juilliard School of Music. Ten blocks later, the bus turns left and heads over to Riverside Drive, upper Manhattan's westernmost street, which is lined with block after block of well-kept apartment buildings. As the bus turns north, you'll see a statue of Eleanor Roosevelt that was dedicated in 1996 by Hillary Rodham Clinton.

Riverside Park looks downright elegant in beautiful weather, with its sloping hills and view of the cliffs of northern New Jersey. (In the '60s, Riverside Park was known as a wind-swept gathering place for drug users, but now the new nuisances in the park aren't criminals but dog owners who let their pets run wild.) The park contains a number of monuments, including the 1902 **Soldiers' and Sailors' Monument** that honors those who served in the Civil War. At 89th St, turn to your left to note the monument's grand campanile. There's also a statue of Joan of Arc at 93rd St.

When the bus returns to Broadway at 120th St, you may be tempted to hop off the bus and explore. **Grant's Tomb** sits just a few hundred yards above you, at 122nd St and Riverside Drive. To the right of Grant's Tomb, you'll find the magnificent **Riverside Church**, with its grand organ and bell tower observation deck.

After 125th St – the southern end of Harlem – the neighborhood abruptly shifts from a middle-class college culture (Columbia University stretches along Broadway from 114th to 121st Sts) to a working-class Hispanic area, with blocks of *bodegas*, variety stores and fruit stands.

At 155th St, you'll reach **Audubon Terrace**, which sits on the west side of the street. The former home of naturalist John James Audubon now contains two under-appreciated museums: the American Numismatic Society and the Hispanic Society of America.

Provided you haven't hopped off the bus for any extended period of time, you can use your transfer on Broadway to take the M4 bus farther uptown. Like the M5, the M4 runs along Broadway until W 168th St, when it continues on Fort Washington Ave to the **Cloisters** in Fort Tryon Park. Since it opened in the 1930s, this spectacular museum has housed the Metropolitan Museum of Art's collection of medieval art, including parts of several medieval European monasteries. Nearby, on Broadway at 204th St, the 1783 **Dyckman House** is the last Dutch farmhouse to survive in Manhattan, although it's no longer sitting on a 28-acre farm.

If you took time out to see anything on the way, you'll want to take the subway back, using the A, 1 or 9 trains depending on your location. To continue sightseeing from the bus, take the M4 back downtown; it travels south along Fort Washington Ave, then Broadway, cutting across to Fifth Ave at Central Park North (110th St) and continuing down to Midtown. (This will mean a separate fare.) The bus will pass the **Museo del Barrio**, the **Museum of the City of New York**, the **Guggenheim Museum** and the **Metropolitan Museum of Art** (see these attractions in the Upper East Side and Harlem sections for further details).

The M4 then passes by Rockefeller Center's eastern edge and St Patrick's Cathedral. By this point, you're bound to be caught in traffic or just fed up with the bus, so hop off by the time it reaches the Empire State Building, on 34th St at Fifth Ave.

FLATIRON DISTRICT (Map 7)

This neighborhood takes its name from the **Flatiron Building**, at the intersection of Broadway, Fifth Ave and 23rd St. Built in 1902, the Flatiron Building (famously featured in a haunting 1905 photograph by Edward Steichen) dominated this plaza when the district contained the city's prime stretch of retail and entertainment establishments. The Flatiron ranked as the world's tallest building until 1909, when it was overtaken by the nearby **Metropolitan Life Tower**, 24th St at Madison Ave, which includes an impressive clock tower and golden top. Just above the Flatiron Building is **Madison Square Park**, which defined the northern reaches of Manhattan until the city's population exploded just after the Civil War.

ANGUS OBORN

Flatiron Building

The area of Fifth Ave just south of Madison Square used to be known as **Ladies' Mile**, back when stores such as B Altman's and Lord & Taylor catered to women shoppers in the late 19th century. Modern-day zoning laws have welcomed retail stores back to nearby Sixth Ave between 14th and 23rd Sts, although today's businesses are mostly chain stores (Staples, Old Navy and Barnes & Noble). The late 19th-century building that once housed the Hugh O'Neill dry goods store, at 655 Sixth Ave at 20th St, is one of the few cast-iron palaces that have yet to be taken over by a big store. But it has been cleaned up, and its flood-lit Corinthian columns look quite dramatic at night.

For a 10-block radius, the Flatiron District, loaded with loft buildings and boutiques, does a good imitation of SoHo without the European pretensions and crowds. Ⓜ 6, N, R to 23rd St.

GRAMERCY PARK (Map 7)

Gramercy Park is one of New York's loveliest spaces, the kind of garden area commonly found throughout Paris and other European cities. Unfortunately, when developers began to transform the surrounding marsh into a city neighborhood in 1830, admission to the park was restricted to residents. The tradition still holds, and mere mortals must peer through iron gates at the foliage.

Two other exclusive institutions are located here, both worth noting for their architecture. The **National Arts Club** (☎ 212-475-3424), 15 Gramercy Park South, boasts a beautiful vaulted stained-glass ceiling above its wooden bar. Calvert Vaux, one of the men behind the creation of Central Park, designed the building. The club holds art exhibitions (ranging from sculpture to photography) that are sometimes open to the public from 1 to 5 pm. Ⓜ 6 to 23rd St.

The **Players Club**, 16 Gramercy Park South, is an actors' hangout created in 1888 by Shakespearean actor Edwin Booth (brother of Lincoln assassin John Wilkes

Booth) and designed by Stanford White. It's not open to the public. Ⓜ 6 to 23rd St.

Fortunately, you can get inside **Pete's Tavern** (☎ 212-473-7676), 129 E 18th St at Irving Place, the spot patronized by the short story writer O Henry, who is said to have written his beloved Christmas story 'The Gift of the Magi' in a front booth. The author probably didn't eat the free popcorn at Pete's, but it tastes as if it were made in his day. You can order a decent burger and beer here or find the same fare by walking a block away to the equally popular **Old Town Bar and Grill** (☎ 212-529-6732), 45 E 18th St between Broadway and Park Ave, a wood-paneled 1892 pub. Ⓜ 6 to 23rd St.

Theodore Roosevelt's Birthplace

This National Historic Site (☎ 212-260-1616, www.nps.gov/thrb), 28 E 20th St between Park Ave and Broadway, is a bit of a cheat, since the house where the 26th president was born was demolished in his lifetime. His relatives re-created the house and joined it with another family residence next door. If you are interested in Roosevelt's extraordinary life, which has been somewhat overshadowed by the enduring legacy of his younger cousin Franklin, plan to visit here, especially if you don't have the time to see his summer home in Long Island's Oyster Bay (see the Excursions chapter). The museum is open 9 am to 5 pm Wednesday through Sunday, with house tours offered on the hour until 4 pm. Admission is $2 for adults, free for children. Ⓜ 6, N, R to 23rd St.

MIDTOWN (Map 7)

You'll wind up spending a great deal of time in New York's teeming Midtown area, home to many of the city's most popular attractions. Very few people live in the center of Manhattan, with most apartment houses located east of Third Ave and west of Eighth Ave. Midtown isn't the most dangerous part of town, but as in any similar district in cities around the world, you should be particularly savvy in this area, since you'll meet up with some of the city's most aggressive panhandlers.

Hell's Kitchen

For years, the far West Side of Midtown was a working-class district of tenements and food warehouses known as Hell's Kitchen, a neighborhood that attracted predominately Italian and Irish immigrants. Hollywood films have often romanticized the district's rough-and-tumble character, but by the 1960s, the local population of junkies and prostitutes had made it a foreboding place that few cared to enter, including a lot of movie directors.

Although the East Side on Lexington and Third Aves exploded with new office buildings, companies shied away from the West Side. In 1989, the construction of the World Wide Plaza building, W 50th St and Eighth Ave, was supposed to make a big difference. (The complex took over the site of the 1930s-era Madison Square Garden, which had been a parking lot in the interregnum.) Yet throughout the mid-'90s, Hell's Kitchen, and especially W 49th St, hardly changed. Eighth and Ninth Aves between 35th and 50th Sts still contain a fair share of wholesale food stores (not exactly big tourist attractions), and few buildings rise more than eight stories above the street.

But the economic boom of the late '90s seriously changed Hell's Kitchen. A perfect

ANGUS OBORN

Midtown lets out some steam.

THINGS TO SEE & DO

link between the Upper West Side and Chelsea, the neighborhood started exploding with nightspots and restaurants, as chefs eyed the large quantities of fresh food from nearby wholesalers. Moreover, many tourists began to filter into the neighborhood after glimpsing it on the David Letterman *Late Show*, a late-night talk show taped at the Ed Sullivan Theater, on Broadway between 53rd and 54th Sts. Culturally, there's not much here – but it's a great place to grab a meal away from the more crowded streets around Rockefeller Center or to start your day with a hearty plate of pancakes at a typical New York City diner.

Intrepid Sea-Air-Space Museum

At the western edge of Midtown, the Intrepid Sea-Air-Space Museum (☎ 212-245-2533, www.intrepidmuseum.org) sits on an aircraft carrier on the waterfront at W 46th St. The flight deck of the USS *Intrepid*, which served in WWII and Vietnam, features several fighter planes, and the pier area contains the Growler guided-missile submarine, an Apollo space capsule and Vietnam-era tanks, along with the 900-foot destroyer *Edson*. The Intrepid is the nexus for the **Fleet Week** celebrations each May, when thousands of the world's sailors descend on Manhattan (see Public Holidays & Special Events in the Facts for the Visitor chapter).

The museum is open 10 am to 4 pm weekdays, 10 am to 5 pm weekends. (Call ahead to confirm hours, as they do change seasonally.) Admission is $12 for adults, $9 for seniors, veterans and students, $2 to $9 for children ages two to 17. You can also use your CityPass here; see the boxed text 'Museum Bargains,' earlier in this chapter, for more information. Ⓜ A, C, E to 42nd St.

Herald Square

This crowded convergence of Broadway, Sixth Ave and 34th St is best known as the home of **Macy's** department store, which for years has inaccurately claimed to be the world's largest department store. (That title probably belongs to the massive GUM in Moscow.) The busy square doesn't offer much in the way of cultural landmarks or even shopping opportunities. Two indoor malls south of Macy's on Sixth Ave contain a boring array of shops. Ⓜ B, D, F, N, Q, R to 34th St-Herald Square.

Garment District

The Garment District, where most of New York's fashion firms have their design offices, stands to the west of Herald Square, on Seventh Ave from 34th St to Times Square. During workdays, the side streets are packed with delivery trucks picking up racks of clothing. Broadway between 23rd St and Herald Square is called the **Accessories District** because of the many ribbon and button shops that serve the city's fashion industry. A number of stores on 36th and 37th Sts immediately west of Seventh Ave sell so-called designer clothing at wholesale prices. Ⓜ B, D, F, N, Q, R to 34th St-Herald Square.

Little Korea

If Herald Square bores you, head to nearby Little Korea, a small enclave of Korean-owned shops that stretches from 31st to 36th Sts between Broadway and Fifth Ave. Over the past few years, this little neighborhood has seen an explosion of restaurants serving Korean fare, with authentic Korean barbecue available around the clock at many of the all-night spots on 32nd St. Ⓜ B, D, F, N, Q, R to 34th St-Herald Square.

Empire State Building

New York's original skyline symbol (☎ 212-736-3100), Fifth Ave at 34th St, is a limestone classic built in just 410 days during the depths of the Depression at a cost of $41 million. Located on the site of the original Waldorf-Astoria Hotel, the 102-story, 1454-foot Empire State Building opened in 1931 and immediately became the most exclusive business address in the city. The famous antenna was originally meant to be a mooring mast for zeppelins, but the Hindenberg disaster put a stop to that plan. One airship accidentally met up with the building: A B25 crashed into the 79th floor on a foggy day in July 1945, killing 14 people.

ANGUS OBORN

The Empire State Building: a New York icon seen in a different light

Since 1976, the building's top 30 floors have been floodlit in seasonal and holiday colors (eg, green for St Patrick's Day in March, red and green for Christmas, pink for Gay Pride weekend in June). This tradition has been copied by many other skyscrapers, including those with ornate golden tops around Union Square, lending elegance to the night sky.

If you'd like to look down on the city from the building's 102nd floor, be prepared to stand in line for an elevator on the concourse level and then (possibly) to wait in another line at the top. Getting there very early or very late will help you avoid these delays. Once you reach the top, you can stay as long as you like. Coin-operated telescopes offer an up-close glimpse of the city, and diagrams map out the major sights. Don't bother with the other exhibits on the concourse level; they attract attention only because of their proximity to the ticket office.

The Empire State Building's observatories on the 86th and 102nd floors are open 9:30 am to midnight daily, with the last tickets sold at 11:25 pm. Admission is $7 for adults, $4 for seniors and children. You can also use your CityPass here; see the boxed text 'Museum Bargains,' earlier in this chapter, for more information. Ⓜ B, D, F, N, Q, R to 34th St-Herald Square.

Pierpont Morgan Library

The Pierpont Morgan Library (☎ 212-685-0008, www.morganlibrary.org), 29 E 36th St near Madison Ave, is part of the 45-room mansion owned by steel magnate JP Morgan. This formerly private collection features cold temperatures (the better for the Morgan's manuscripts, tapestries and books), a study filled with Italian renaissance artwork, a marble rotunda and a three-tiered East Room main library. Morgan spared little expense in his pursuit of ancient works of knowledge or art: The collection includes no fewer than three Gutenberg Bibles.

Although the Morgan Library has long had a stuffy reputation, its curator has livened things up with a year-round program of lectures and concerts in the Garden Court. This lovely glass-enclosed space also contains a cafe and bookstore. The Morgan is open 10:30 am to 5 pm Tuesday to Thursday, 10:30 am to 8 pm Friday, 10:30 am to 6 pm Saturday, noon to 6 pm Sunday. Admission is $7 for adults, $5 for seniors and students, free for children. Ⓜ 6 to 33 rd St.

New York Public Library

The monumental New York Public Library (☎ 212-930-0800, www.nypl.org), 42nd St at Fifth Ave, offers a glimpse of life during the grand Gilded Age, when major industrialists poured immense sums of money into public works projects such as this elaborate beaux arts building. When it was dedicated in 1911, New York's flagship library ranked as the largest marble structure ever attempted in the USA, with a vast 3rd-floor reading room designed to hold 500 people.

Today, this building, now called the Humanities and Social Sciences Library, is one of the best free attractions in the city. On a rainy day, hide away with a book in the airy reading room and admire the original Tiffany lamps, or stroll through the hallway display galleries, which contain precious manuscripts by just about every author of note in the English language. If you don't have a chance to go inside, be sure to stop for a look at the library's trademark stone lions, which flank the entrance.

The library is open 10 am to 6 pm Monday and Thursday to Saturday, 11 am to 7:30 pm Tuesday and Wednesday.

Located just behind the library, **Bryant Park** offers a pleasant break in the middle of a day of a sightseeing, especially if you can find a seat on one of the park's marble benches or folding chairs. Once overrun by drug dealers, the impressively restored park has become a popular sunbathing site. In summer, Bryant Park hosts a free outdoor movie festival (☎ 212-983-4142) on Monday evening. Ⓜ B, D, F, Q to 42nd St; 7 to Fifth Ave.

Grand Central Terminal

One of New York's grandest public spaces has seen better days – an ugly car ramp now mars its Romanesque south facade – but its interior remains as impressive as ever. Now restored, Grand Central Terminal (also called Grand Central Station), 42nd St at Park Ave, recalls the romance of train travel back when people set off on cross-country journeys here.

Today, Grand Central's underground electric tracks only serve commuter trains en route to the northern suburbs and Connecticut. But the beaux arts architecture still merits a special trip. The building offers a number of prime vantage points. A nice bar on the western balcony overlooks the concourse, with its gleaming brass clock and passenger information center. You can also stand atop the new marble staircase at the eastern end of the concourse, which mirrors its partner on the western end, and take in the sparkling starlight painted on the terminal's vaulted ceiling.

The lower levels of the terminal now contain a lively mix of shops and restaurants, including the **Oyster Bar**, a famous seafood restaurant that's quite noisy thanks to its tile ceiling.

The Municipal Art Society (☎ 212-935-3960) leads walks through Grand Central every Wednesday at 12:30 pm; the suggested donation is $6. During the hour-long tour, you'll cross a glass catwalk high above the concourse and learn some of the building's secrets – for example, the ceiling constellation was mistakenly laid out in a 'god's eye view,' with the stars displayed from above rather than below. Tours meet at the visitor information booth in the middle of the terminal. Ⓜ S, 4, 5, 6, 7 to Grand Central-42nd St.

Chrysler Building

The 1048-foot Chrysler Building, just across from Grand Central Terminal at Lexington Ave and 42nd St, briefly reigned as the tallest structure in the world until superseded by the Empire State Building a few months later. An art deco masterpiece designed by William Van Allen in 1930, the building celebrates car culture with gargoyles that resemble hood ornaments (barely visible from the ground). The 200-foot steel spire, constructed in secret, was raised through the false roof as a surprise crowning touch – which came as quite a shock to a competing architect who was hoping that his new Wall St building would turn out to be New York's tallest skyscraper of the time (it wasn't).

Nestled at the top is the Cloud Club, a businessmen's club that closed years ago, and a private apartment built for Walter Chrysler, head of the company. For a long time, developers have been planning to convert part of the building into a hotel, but so far they haven't made any progress.

Although the Chrysler Building has no restaurant or observation deck, you can go inside to admire the elaborate elevators and the 1st floor's ceiling mural, depicting the promise of industry. Ⓜ S, 4, 5, 6, 7 to Grand Central-42nd St.

United Nations

The UN headquarters (☎ 212-963-4440/8687), whose visitors' entrance is at First Ave and 46th St, is technically located on international territory overlooking the East River.

Created in 1945 by an international conference in San Francisco, the body of world leaders known as the United Nations met for two years in Flushing Meadows-Corona Park in Queens before the Rockefeller family donated $8.5 million for the purchase of land in Manhattan. Appropriately enough, a large international committee of architects designed this complex. For years, various nations have complained about the UN's spendthrift ways, but you won't find much evidence of these free-spending habits at headquarters. The buildings have a dated, late-1950s feel, with a lot of Norwegian wood, and the carpeting is woefully worn.

On a tour of the facility, you'll see the **General Assembly**, where the annual autumn convocation of member nations takes place; the **Security Council Chamber**, where crisis hearings are held year-round; and the **Economic and Social Council Chamber**. A park south of the complex includes Henry Moore's *Reclining Figure* and several other sculptures with a peace theme.

It's open 9:15 am to 4:45 pm daily from March to December and 9:15 am to 4:45 pm weekdays in January and February. English-language tours of the complex leave every 45 minutes; there are also limited tours in several other languages. Admission is $7.50 for adults, $6 for seniors, $5 for students and $4 for children; children under five are not admitted. Ⓜ S, 4, 5, 6, 7 to Grand Central-42nd St.

KIM GRANT

Chrysler Building's distinctive spire

Sutton Place

Sutton Place encompasses several blocks of European-style luxury apartments that run parallel to First Ave from 54th to 59th Sts. The dead-end streets, which have pleasant benches that look out on the East River, served as the setting for Diane Keaton and Woody Allen's first date in the movie *Manhattan*. Under the 59th St Bridge (also known as the Queensboro Bridge), you'll see Sir Terence Conran's Bridgemarket, a collection of food stalls and restaurants in the arches of the bridge.

At one time, Third Ave was the site of an elevated train line that cast shadows on the old speakeasies and middle-class businesses. Thanks to the destruction of the 'el' and a subsequent building boom, Third Ave now consists of large office and apartment blocks almost exclusively. (One remnant from the early days is PJ Clarke's, an old bar from the

1890s, at the corner of Third Ave and 55th St.) Second Ave, however, has lagged behind in this development and still retains much of its old character – you'll see dozens of look-alike Irish bars and moderately priced restaurants.

Rockefeller Center

Built during the height of the Great Depression in the 1930s, the 22-acre Rockefeller Center complex (☎ 212-632-3975), which stretches from 48th to 51st Sts between Fifth and Sixth Aves, gave jobs to 70,000 workers over nine years – plus, it created a new pastime for 'sidewalk supervisors,' passers-by who peered through holes cut into the fence around the site. By the time all the crews had finished their jobs, the 19-building center had turned into one of the country's most attractive projects.

But a controversy over artwork tainted the completion of Rockefeller Center. A mural painted by Mexican artist Diego Rivera in the lobby of the 70-story RCA Building (now the GE Building) was rejected by the Rockefeller family because it featured the face of Lenin. The fresco was covered during the opening ceremony and was later destroyed. Its replacement features the more acceptable figure of Abraham Lincoln.

In 1989, a Japanese consortium bought a controlling interest in Rockefeller Center, triggering lamentations in the press about the selling of American icons to foreigners, as if the buildings were in danger of being relocated to Tokyo. (The Japanese holding company actually went broke when real estate values plummeted.)

But the center's money travails have not seemed to result in a lack of exterior maintenance. Take special note of the tile work above the Sixth Ave entrance to the GE Building, the three flood-lit cameos along the side of Radio City Music Hall and the back-lit gilt and stained-glass entrance to the East River Savings Bank Building at 41 Rockefeller Plaza, immediately to the north of the skating rink/outdoor garden cafe.

Perhaps the best-known feature of Rockefeller Center is its huge Christmas tree, which overlooks the skating rink during the holiday season. (This tradition dates back to the '30s, when construction workers set up a small Christmas tree on the site.) The annual lighting of the Rockefeller Center Christmas tree on the Tuesday after Thanksgiving attracts thousands of visitors to the area and semi-officially kicks off the city's holiday season. Ⓜ B, D, F, Q to 47th-50th Sts/Rockefeller Center.

Radio City Music Hall This 6000-seat art deco movie palace (☎ 212-247-4777, www.radiocity.com), 51st at Sixth Ave, had its interior declared a protected landmark. It has reopened after extensive renovation work to restore the velvet seats and furnishings back to the exact state they were in when the building opened in 1932. (Even the smoking rooms and toilets are elegant at the 'Showplace of the Nation.') Concerts here sell out quickly, and tickets to the annual Christmas pageant featuring the hokey-but-enjoyable Rockette dancers now run up to $70. You can see the interior by taking a tour; these leave every half hour from 10 am to 5 pm Monday to Saturday and 11 am to 5 pm Sunday. These cost $15

TONY WHEELER

Gliding across the ice at Rockefeller Center

for adults, $9 for children. Tickets are sold on a first come, first served basis. Ⓜ B, D, F, Q to 47th-50th Sts/Rockefeller Center.

NBC Studios The NBC television network (☎ 212-664-3700, www.nbc.com) has its headquarters in the 70-story GE Building, which looms over the Rockefeller Center ice-skating rink (a cafe in the summer months). The *Today* show broadcasts live from 7 to 9 am daily from a glass-enclosed street-level studio near the fountain.

Tours of the NBC studios leave from the lobby of the GE Building; they're offered from 8:30 am to 5:30 pm Monday to Saturday, 9:30 am to 4:30 pm Sunday, with extended hours during the holiday season in November and December. Tours cost $17.50 for adults, $15 for children six to 16; children under six are not permitted. Ⓜ B, D, F, Q to 47th-50th Sts/Rockefeller Center.

St Patrick's Cathedral

St Patrick's Cathedral (☎ 212-753-2261), just across from Rockefeller Center at 50th St and Fifth Ave, is the main place of worship for the 2.2 million Roman Catholics in the New York archdiocese (although it can only seat 2400 of them).

The cathedral, built at a cost of nearly $2 million during the Civil War, originally didn't include the two front spires; these were added in 1888. Despite its French Gothic style, the well-lit St Patrick's isn't as gloomy as its Old World counterparts, and the new TV monitors in restricted-view seats testify to the church's determination to stake out a place in the modern world.

When services aren't taking place, you're free to wander around inside. After you enter, walk by the eight small shrines along the side of the cathedral, past the main altar, to the quiet **Lady Chapel**, dedicated to the Virgin Mary. From here, you can see the handsome stained-glass **Rose Window** above the 7000-pipe church organ. A basement crypt behind the altar contains the coffins of every New York cardinal.

Unfortunately, St Patrick's is not a place for restful contemplation during the day because of the constant buzz from visitors.

ANGUS OBORN

It's also a regular site of protest by gays who feel excluded by the church hierarchy. Since 1933, the exclusion of Irish gays from the St Patrick's Day Parade (an event not sponsored by the Catholic Church per se, but identified with Catholic traditionalists) has triggered protests near the cathedral every year in March.

The cathedral is open 6 am to 9 pm daily. Frequent masses take place on the weekend, and New York's archbishop presides over the service at 10:15 am Sunday. Ⓜ B, D, F, Q to 47th-50th Sts/Rockefeller Center.

Fifth Ave

Immortalized in both film and popular song, Fifth Ave first developed a reputation as a high-class area in the early 20th century, when a series of mansions on the avenue's uptown portion became known as Millionaire's Row. Today, the avenue's Midtown stretch still boasts high-end shops and hotels, including the garish **Plaza Hotel** at Grand Army Plaza overlooking the corner of Central Park and Fifth Ave. The huge institution really doesn't have much of a grand lobby, but it is worth a walk through just to say you've been there. The fountain in front of the hotel, which features a statue of the Roman goddess Diana and faces the southeastern entrance to Central Park, is a good spot for a rest and a bit of lunch – provided you're not downwind from the horse-drawn carriages that line 59th St during the summer months.

Most of the heirs of the millionaires who built mansions on Fifth Ave above 59th St either sold them for demolition or converted them to the cultural institutions that make up Museum Mile (see the Upper East Side section). The **Villard Houses**, actually located on Madison Ave behind St Patrick's Cathedral, are surviving examples of these grand homes. Financier Henry Villard built the six four-story townhouses in 1881; they were eventually owned by the Catholic Church and then sold to become part of the 1000-room Mayfair hotel and the famous restaurant La Cirque 2000.

While a number of the more exclusive boutiques have migrated to Madison Ave (see the Shopping chapter), several still line Fifth Ave above 50th St, including Liz Claiborne, Henri Bendel, and Tiffany's. On 57th St nearby, you can shop at Burberry's, Hermès and Charivari, among several other designer boutiques.

Museum of Television & Radio

This couch potato's paradise (☎ 212-621-6800, www.mtr.org), 25 W 52nd St between Fifth and Sixth Aves, contains a collection of more than 50,000 American TV and radio programs, all available from the museum's computer catalog with the click of a mouse. It's a great place to hang out when it's raining or when you're simply fed up with walking. Nearly everybody checks out their favorite childhood TV programs and watches them on the museum's 90 consoles, but the radio listening room is an unexpected pleasure. Your entry fee entitles you to two hours of uninterrupted viewing enjoyment. The museum is open noon to 6 pm Tuesday to Sunday (until 8 pm on Thursday). Admission is $6 for adults, $4 for students and seniors, $3 for children. Ⓜ E, F to Fifth Ave.

Museum of Modern Art

The Museum of Modern Art (☎ 212-708-9400, www.moma.org), 11 W 53rd St between Fifth and Sixth Aves, known as MoMA, boasts an impressive collection of art that you can take in on a single day, unlike the vast array of objects at the Metropolitan Museum of Art. You won't get lost here, at least not yet – though the museum is currently expanding into an adjacent building and plans to double its exhibition space by 2005.

ANGUS OBORN

A starry night at the MoMA

The first-rate works in its sculpture and painting galleries include Van Gogh's *Starry Night*, Matisse's *Dance 1* and a number of pieces by Picasso. A quiet stand-alone gallery displays Monet's paneled *Water Lilies*. At least once a year, MoMA puts on an important exhibit of a single major artist's work – past retrospectives have focused on Piet Mondrian, Picasso's portraiture and American painter Jasper Johns.

The museum places a special emphasis on photography and film, two areas of visual expression that get short shrift at the larger Metropolitan Museum of Art. MoMA's two basement theaters feature daily film screenings, and an Academy Award, bestowed on the museum's film department in 1978, is on permanent display, along with an impressive collection of film posters.

If you're pressed for time or simply undecided where to go, it's a good idea to rent the audio tour of the museum narrated by chief curator Kirk Varnedoe; it's a cell phone that you can program to get more information about specific works of interest.

In July and August, the Abby Aldrich Rockefeller Sculpture Garden here hosts a series of concerts.

The museum is one of the few major cultural institutions in New York City that is open on Monday (it's closed on Wednesday instead). It's open 10:30 am to 5:45 pm Saturday to Tuesday and Thursday, 10:30 am to 8:15 pm Friday. Admission is $10 for adults, $6.50 for seniors and students, free for children under 16. The museum offers pay-what-you-can admission on Friday after 4:30 pm. You can also use your CityPass here; see the boxed text 'Museum Bargains,' earlier in this chapter, for more information. Ⓜ E, F to Fifth Ave.

American Craft Museum

Directly across the street from MoMA, the American Craft Museum (☎ 212-956-3535), 40 W 53rd St between Fifth and Sixth Aves, displays innovative and traditional crafts in a spectacularly well-designed and airy space. The museum is currently hosting a 10-year series of exhibitions that examine American craft making, and you can view examples of works from the eight identifiable periods of artisanship. The museum also exhibits 77 examples of traditional craftmaking from the White House.

It's open 10 am to 6 pm Tuesday to Sunday (until 8 pm on Thursday). Admission is $5 for adults, $2.50 for seniors, free for children. Ⓜ E, F to Fifth Ave.

Newseum New York

This museum (☎ 212-317-7503, www.newseum.org), 580 Madison Ave between 56th and 57th Sts, can't fail to attract news junkies. Established by the Gannett newspaper publishing group, it primarily features photojournalism exhibitions and displays that examine the media's coverage of particular events and issues, but it also hosts debates on current affairs. The museum is open 10 am to 5:30 pm Monday through Saturday. Admission is free. Ⓜ N, R to Fifth Ave.

Times Square (Map 8)

Now in the midst of a major renaissance, Times Square can once again trumpet its reputation as the 'Crossroads of the World.' Smack in the middle of Midtown Manhattan, this area around the intersection of Broadway and Seventh Ave has long been synonymous with gaudy billboards and glittery marquees – before the advent of TV, advertisers went after the largest audience possible by beaming their messages into the center of New York.

Once called Long Acre Square, the area took its present name from the famous newspaper that is still located there – the *New York Times*. Also dubbed the 'Great White Way' after its bright lights, Times Square dimmed quite a bit in the 1960s, as once-proud movie palaces that had previously shown first-run films turned into 'triple X' porn theaters. But in recent years, the city has changed the area's fortunes by offering big tax breaks for businesses that relocated here. Today, the square draws 27 million annual visitors, who spend something over $12 billion in Midtown.

The combination of color, zipping message boards and (at last count) six massive color TV screens make for quite a sight these days. Televisions networks like MTV and ABC have opened studios in Times Square, and major companies have created such commercial showcases as the Virgin Megastore and the Official All Star Café.

RICHARD I'ANSON

The blinding lights of Times Square

THINGS TO SEE & DO

Several media conglomerates – among them German publisher Bertelsmann, Reuters and the US magazine group Condé Nast – have built headquarters in and around the square recently, and the storied *New York Times* is moving to a new skyscraper here.

Times Square also continues to serve as the center of New York theater, with dozens of Broadway and off-Broadway theaters located in an area that stretches from 41st to 54th Sts, between Sixth and Ninth Aves. See the Entertainment chapter for more information.

Up to a million people gather in Times Square every New Year's Eve to see a brightly lit ball descend from the roof of One Times Square at midnight. While this event garners international coverage, it lasts just 90 seconds.

Times Square Visitor's Center The Times Square Visitor's Center (☎ 212-869-1890, www.timessquarebid.org), 1560 Broadway between 46th and 47th Sts, sits right in the middle of the famous crossroads of Broadway and Seventh Ave. More than one million visitors annually stop in to use the center's ATMs, video guides to the city and computer terminals that offer free access to the Internet. The center also offers free walking tours of the neighborhood every Friday at noon. It's open 8 am to 8 pm daily. Ⓜ 1, 2, 3, 7, 9, N, R, S to 42nd St-Times Square.

UPPER WEST SIDE (Map 9)

The Upper West Side begins as Broadway emerges from Midtown at Columbus Circle and ends at the southern border of Harlem, around 125th St. A number of mid-range to

THINGS TO SEE & DO

How to Be a Face in the Crowd

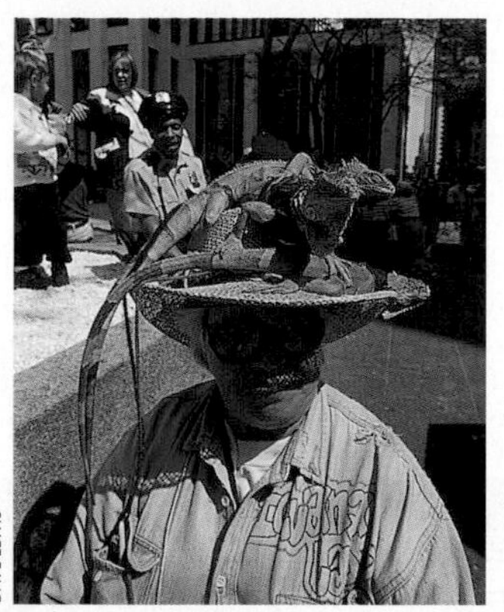

DAVE LEWIS

It's not hard to wave to the folks at home on television, because New York has become a popular backdrop for network morning shows from 7 am to 9 am Monday to Friday. The NBC *Today* show started it all with a windowed studio in Rockefeller Center. ABC then unveiled a *Good Morning America* studio that overlooks Times Square at Broadway and W 44th St. CBS's *The Early Show* followed suit with a ground-level studio in the General Motors Building on Fifth Ave across from the Plaza Hotel. MTV's US network overlooks Times Square, and the David Letterman *Late Show* features man-in-the-street gags near the Ed Sullivan Theater, on Broadway near 53rd St.

If you'd rather sit in the studio audience of a TV show, you might be able to obtain free standby tickets on the same day as a show's taping (the advance tickets are usually snapped up months ahead by people who write to the shows). NBC (☎ 212-664-3056) distributes tickets from its offices at 30 Rockefeller Plaza on 49th St. Line up for *The Rosie O'Donnell Show* at 7:30 am, *Late Night with Conan O'Brien* at 9 am Tuesday to Friday and *Saturday Night Live* at 9:15 am on Saturday. For standby tickets to one of New York's most popular morning shows, *Live with Regis and Kathie Lee*, go to the show's studio at 67th St and Columbus Ave by 8 am on weekdays. CBS sometimes offers standby tickets for the *Late Show*; call the network's standby ticket line (☎ 212-247-6497) at 11 am. But don't get your hopes up, as the show's staff typically overbook the theater. If you do get a ticket, take something warm to wear to the taping – the studios are freezing.

top-end hotels lie along Central Park South, and many celebrities live in the massive apartment buildings that line Central Park West all the way up to 96th St.

Lincoln Center

The Lincoln Center complex (☎ 212-546-2656, www.lincolncenter.org), at Columbus Ave and Broadway, includes seven large performance spaces built in the 1960s; these replaced a group of tenements that were the real-life inspiration for the musical *West Side Story*. During the day, Lincoln Center presents a clean, if architecturally uninspired, face to the world, but at night the chandeliered interiors look simply beautiful from across Columbus Ave.

If you're at all interested in high culture, Lincoln Center is a must-see, since it contains the **Metropolitan Opera House**, adorned by two colorful lobby tapestries by Marc Chagall; the **New York State Theater**, home of both the New York City Ballet and the New York City Opera, the low-cost and more daring alternative to the Met. The New York Philharmonic holds its season in **Avery Fisher Hall**.

The Lincoln Center Theater company performs at the 1000-seat **Vivian Beaumont Theater**, which also contains the smaller and more intimate **Mitzi Newhouse Theater**. To the right of the theaters stands the **New York Public Library for the Performing Arts**, which houses the city's largest collection of recorded sound, video and books on film and theater.

The Juilliard School of Music, attached to the complex by a walkway over W 65th St, includes **Alice Tully Hall**, home to the Chamber Music Society of Lincoln Center, and the **Walter Reade Theater**, the city's most comfortable film-revival space and the major screening site of the New York Film Festival, held every September.

Daily tours of the complex explore at least three of the theaters, though just which ones you see depends on production schedules. It's a good idea to call ahead for a space (☎ 212-875-5350). Tours leave from the Tour Desk on the concourse level at 10:30 am and 12:30, 2:30 and 4:30 pm daily. They cost $9.50 for adults, $8 for students and seniors, $4.75 for children. Ⓜ 1, 9 to 66th St-Lincoln Center.

New-York Historical Society

As the antiquated, hyphenated name implies, the New-York Historical Society (☎ 212-873-3400, www.nyhistory.org), 2 W 77th St at Central Park West, is the city's oldest museum, founded in 1804 to preserve artifacts of history and culture. It was also New York's only public art museum until the founding of the Metropolitan Museum of Art in the late 19th century.

The New-York Historical Society museum has suffered severe financial problems in recent years, and to further compound its woes, most city visitors don't even notice it on their way to its neighbor institution, the American Museum of Natural History. But it is well worth a visit, since taking in its quirky permanent collection is a bit like traipsing through New York City's attic. The works on display include John James Audubon's original watercolors for his *Birds of America* survey.

It's open noon to 5 pm Tuesday to Sunday. The suggested donation is $5 for adults, $3 for seniors and students. Ⓜ B, C to 81st St.

American Museum of Natural History

Founded in 1869, this museum (☎ 212-769-5100, www.amnh.org), Central Park West at 79th St, began with a mastodon's tooth and a few thousand beetles; today, its collection includes more than 30 million artifacts. It's most famous for its three large dinosaur halls, which reopened several years ago after a significant renovation and now feature the latest knowledge on how these behemoths behaved. Knowledgeable guides roam the dinosaur halls ready to answer questions, and the 'please touch' displays allow kids to handle the skullcap of a pachycephulasaurus, a plant-eating dinosaur that roamed the earth 65 million years ago, among other items.

Other treasures in the permanent collection include the enormous (fake) blue whale that hangs from the ceiling above the

ANGUS OBORN

Hall of Ocean Life. Newer exhibitions, such as the Hall of Biodiversity, feature a strong ecological slant, with a video display about the earth's important habitats.

While some of the mammal halls still contain plenty of gloomy stuffed animal displays (in the Victorian style), the museum has aggressively updated its facilities in recent years. The giant new **Rose Center for Earth & Space** benefits from the latest technology, with state-of-the-art star shows at the Hayden Planetarium. Lasers and other special effects re-create the birth of the universe at the Big Bang Theater. The museum also has an IMAX theater.

The museum is open 10 am to 5:45 pm Sunday to Thursday and 10 am to 8:45 pm Friday and Saturday. Suggested admission (meaning that you can pay less) is $10 for adults, $7.50 for seniors and students, $6 for children. You can also use your CityPass here; see the boxed text 'Museum Bargains,' earlier in this chapter, for more information. Ⓜ B, C to 81st St; 1, 9 to 79th St.

Children's Museum of Manhattan

This museum (☎ 212-721-1234, www.cmom.org), 212 W 83rd St near Amsterdam Ave, features discovery centers for toddlers and a postmodern Media Center where technologically savvy kids can work in a TV studio. The museum also runs craft workshops on weekends.

Both Brooklyn and Staten Island have affiliated children's museums. See the appropriate sections for more information.

The Children's Museum of Manhattan is open 10 am to 5 pm Wednesday to Sunday. Admission is $6 for adults and children over age one, $3 for seniors. Ⓜ 1, 9 to 86th St; B, C to 81st St.

Cathedral of St John the Divine

The massive Cathedral of St John the Divine (☎ 212-316-7540), Amsterdam Ave at 112th St, is the largest place of worship in the USA – and it's not done yet. When it's completed, the 601-foot long Episcopal cathedral should rank as the third-largest church in the world (after St Peter's Basilica in Rome and the newly built Our Lady at Yamoussoukro in the Ivory Coast).

But it's unlikely that St John's will be finished in your lifetime, even though its cornerstone was laid in 1892. Work has yet to begin on the stone tower on the left side of the west front or on the crossing tower above the pulpit. In 1978, the Episcopal Diocese of New York began training local young people in stone cutting, and their work can be seen in the courtyard to the south of the church, behind the sundial. Other features shown on the church's cutaway floor plan near the front entrance, such as a Greek amphitheater, remain wistful visions of the distant future.

Still, the cathedral is a flourishing place of worship and community activity, as well as the site of holiday concerts, lectures and memorial services for famous New Yorkers. There's even a Poet's Corner just to the left of the front entrance – though, unlike Westminster Abbey, no one is actually buried here. You should also check out the altar designed and built by the late artist Keith Haring, a popular figure in the '80s art world.

The cathedral is open 8 am to 6 pm Monday to Saturday and 8 am to 8 pm on Sunday. Ⓜ 1, 9 to Cathedral Parkway.

Columbia University

When Columbia University (☎ 212-854-1754), Broadway between 114th and 121st Sts, and the affiliated Barnard College began, their founders chose a spot far removed from the downtown bustle. Today, the city has definitely enveloped and moved beyond Columbia's gated campus. But the school's main courtyard, with its statue *Alma Mater* perched on the steps of the Low Library, is still a quiet place to enjoy the sun and read a book. Hamilton Hall, in the southeast corner of the main square, was the famous site of a student takeover in 1968, and since then it's seen periodic protests and pretty wild student parties.

The surrounding neighborhood is filled with inexpensive restaurants, good bookstores and cafes. The ordinary lunch spot **Tom's Restaurant** (☎ 212-864-6137), 2880 Broadway at W 112th St, also called Tom's Diner, got a lot of attention when Suzanne Vega sang about sipping coffee at its window – and the exterior appeared nearly every week on TV as the hangout for the crowd on *Seinfeld*.

If you'd like to eavesdrop on the crisis-driven student conversations while waiting for your espresso, try one of the many cafes, including the landmark **Hungarian Pastry Shop** (☎ 212-866-4230), 1030 Amsterdam Ave near W 111th St. The **West End** (☎ 212-662-8830), 2911 Broadway between W 113th and 114th Sts, is no longer a breeding ground for intellectuals as it was in Beat poet Allen Ginsberg's day, but you can still find inexpensive food and decent jazz there on weekend nights. Ⓜ 1, 9 to 116th St-Columbia University.

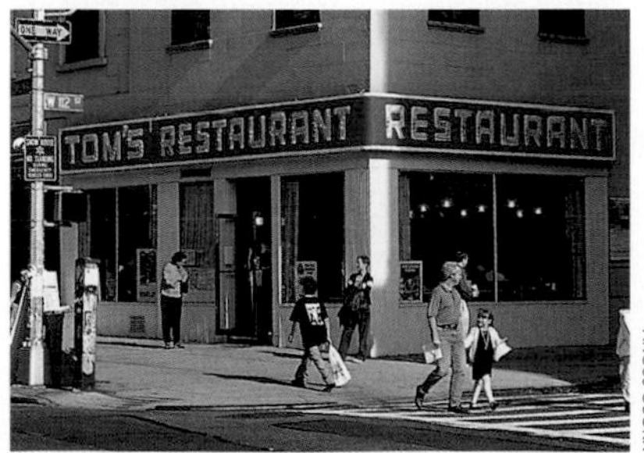

ANGUS OBORN

As seen on TV

Riverside Church

Built by the Rockefeller family in 1930, Riverside Church (☎ 212-870-6700), 490 Riverside Drive at W 120th St, is a gothic marvel overlooking the Hudson River. In good weather, you can climb 355 feet above the ground to the observation deck ($2). The church rings its 74 carillon bells, the largest grouping in the world, every Sunday at noon and 3 pm.

It's open 9 am to 4 pm daily, with interdenominational services at 10:45 am on Sunday. Ⓜ 1, 9 to 116th St-Columbia University.

General US Grant National Memorial

Popularly known as Grant's Tomb (☎ 212-666-1640), Riverside Drive at W 122nd St, this landmark monument holds the remains of Civil War hero and president Ulysses S Grant and his wife, Julia. Completed in 1897 – 12 years after Grant's death – the granite structure cost $600,000 and is the largest mausoleum in the country. The building languished as a graffiti-marred mess for years until the general's relatives shamed the National Park Service into cleaning it up by threatening to move his body somewhere else.

It's open 9 am to 4:30 pm Wednesday to Sunday. Admission is free. Ⓜ 1, 9 to 116th St-Columbia University.

CENTRAL PARK (Map 9)

This 843-acre rectangular park (☎ 212-360-3444, www.centralparknyc.org), right in the middle of Manhattan, offers an oasis in the midst of the urban bustle, and on warm weekends joggers, in-line skaters, musicians and tourists pack the green lawns and meandering, wooded paths. (You can find some quieter areas above 72nd St, where the crowds recede and the flowers and trees come to the fore.) Its sometimes scary reputation as a dark and menacing place (especially for women runners) hasn't frightened many off, and today it ranks as one of the safest parts of the city.

Created in the 1860s and '70s by Frederick Law Olmstead and Calvert Vaux on the marshy northern fringe of the city, the immense park proved to be popular even in its planning stages: The wealthy hoped to have a place for carriage rides, while social reformers believed the park would lure working-class men out of the saloons. Over the years, the park has survived the trampling of rock fans and hippies at mass 'be-ins,' the bad publicity generated by occasional assaults within its confines and even an overzealous park commissioner with a fondness for new parking lots. Today, it's still one of the city's most popular attractions and carries on its tradition as the 'people's park,' attracting throngs of New Yorkers with outdoor concerts and the famous annual Shakespeare in Central Park productions (see Public Holidays & Special Events in the Facts for the Visitor chapter).

Many people come to the park for sheer recreational pleasure; unlike the streets of downtown Manhattan, Central Park Drive, a 6-mile loop road, contains a lane for bicyclists, skaters and runners. Automobile traffic can only pass through the park in a few places, mainly on unobtrusive transverses that dip below ground level. Central Park Drive closes to traffic altogether from 10 am to 3 pm and 7 to 10 pm weekdays and all weekend long, which should offer your ears a break from the ubiquitous honking horns in Manhattan.

A good stroll through the park begins on the west side at the Columbus Circle entrance. Walk through the **Merchants' Gate** up to **Sheep Meadow**, a wide green expanse that attracts sunbathers and Frisbee players. If you turn right, a pathway will lead you along the south side of the meadow to the enclosed **Carousel**, which boasts some of the largest hand-carved horses in the country.

Continue past the Carousel along the 65th St pathway to the **Dairy**, overlooking the Wollman Rink. The Dairy houses the

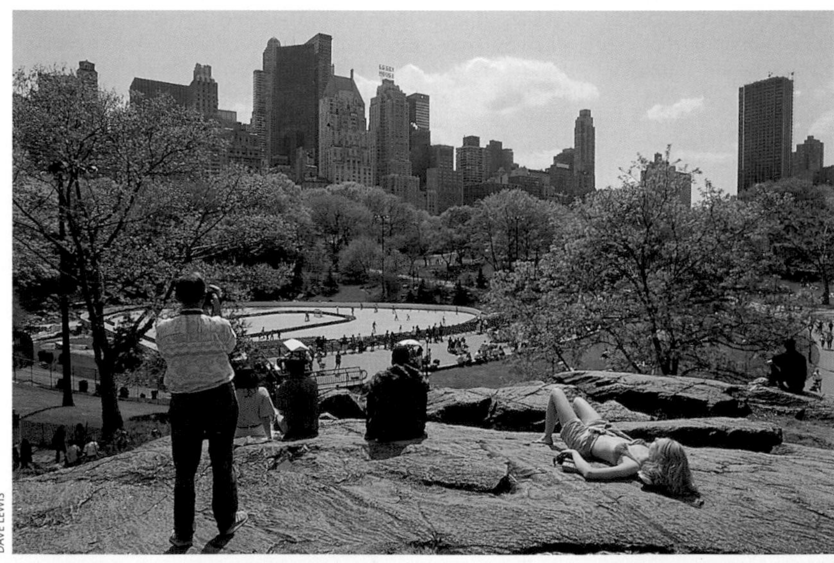

DAVE LEWIS

park's visitor center, where you can pick up maps and information about park activities. It's open 11 am to 5 pm daily (11 am to 4 pm in winter).

Across East Drive from the Dairy, you'll find the **Central Park Wildlife Center** (☎ 212-861-6030), a small zoo built in the 1930s but renovated in the 1980s in order to increase the comfort of the animals. Zoo residents include a lazy polar bear and several seals, whose frequent feedings delight the visiting children. The zoo is open 10 am to 5 pm weekdays, 10:30 am to 5:30 pm weekends from April to October; in the winter, it's open 10 am to 4:30 pm daily. Admission is $3.50 for adults, $1.25 for seniors, 50¢ for children ages three to 12. Admission to the zoo includes entry to the smaller **Tisch Children's Zoo**, a petting center for toddlers; it's right across 65th St from the main zoo.

After the zoo, walk north on the path that parallels East Drive, cross the 65th St Transverse to a group of statues (including Christopher Columbus and William Shakespeare) that marks the beginning of **The Mall**, an elegant walkway lined on both sides by a collection of 150 American elms. These trees, which have not suffered from the Dutch elm disease that destroyed most of the country's elms, are believed to be the largest surviving stand in the country.

At the north end of the mall, you'll come to a band shell. Behind that, on the far side of the 72nd Transverse, lies **Bethesda Fountain**, a hippie hangout in the '60s; the fountain, with its *Angel of Waters* sculpture at the center, has since been restored.

Continue on the path to the west of the fountain until you reach **Bow Bridge**. You can cross the bridge to the **Ramble**, a lush wooden expanse that serves as both a gay pickup area and a meeting place for dog owners of all sexual persuasions.

If you manage to emerge from the Ramble's rambling paths without being hopelessly turned around, continue north to the 79th St Transverse. Right across the transverse, you'll find the 19th-century **Belvedere Castle** and the **Delacorte Theater**, where the Joseph Papp Public Theater holds

RICK GERHARTER

free, extremely popular Shakespeare productions each summer.

Immediately beyond the theater is the appropriately named **Great Lawn**, where occasional free concerts take place, along with annual open-air performances by the New York Philharmonic and Metropolitan Opera in June and July. In recent years, the Great Lawn has undergone a much needed reseeding, although it still closes to 'rest' in the winter. The New York Philharmonic has returned to the Great Lawn, but the occasional rock and pop concerts that attract 75,000 people have been banished to the rougher **North Meadow** above 97th St.

If you walk to the north end of the Great Lawn and cross the 86th St Transverse, you'll come upon the **Jacqueline Kennedy Onassis Reservoir**, named for the former first lady who regularly used the track here. A soft, 1.6-mile cinder path encircles the reservoir and draws a continual parade of runners. The New York Road Runners Club (☎ 212-860-4455), which sponsors regular runs through the park, operates an information booth near the reservoir entrance at E 90th St and West Drive.

To wrap up the walking tour, head south on West Drive to the W 72nd St park entrance and **Strawberry Fields**, the 3-acre landscape dedicated to the memory of John Lennon; it contains plants from more than 100 nations. This spot was frequently visited by the former Beatle, who resided in the massive Dakota apartment building across the street, where he was shot to death on December 8, 1980.

For more information on outdoor activities in Central Park, see the Activities section of the Facts for the Visitor chapter.

Carriage Rides When Central Park was first created, wealthy New Yorkers got their wish: a quiet place for carriage rides. Some traditions never die – although today a true New Yorker probably wouldn't be caught dead in a horse-drawn carriage. But tourists love them, despite the expense and the less-than-pleasant smell in the summer. Carriages line up along 59th St (Central Park South) and cost $40 for a half hour ($10 for every 15 minutes thereafter). Drivers expect a tip on top of that charge. Ⓜ 1, 9, A, B, C, D, E to 59th St-Columbus Circle.

UPPER EAST SIDE (Map 9)

The Upper East Side is home to New York's greatest concentration of cultural centers – many refer to Fifth Ave above 57th St as Museum Mile. The neighborhood includes many of the city's most exclusive hotels and residential blocks. The side streets from Fifth Ave east to Third Ave between 57th and 86th Sts feature some stunning townhouses and brownstones, and walking through this area at nightfall offers voyeurs the chance to peer inside the grand libraries and living rooms in these homes.

Temple Emanu-El

Temple Emanu-El (☎ 212-744-1400, www.emanuelnyc.org), 1 E 65th St at Fifth Ave, is the world's largest reformed Jewish synagogue. Stop by for a look at its notable Byzantine and Near-Eastern architecture. It's open to the general public from 10 am to 5 pm daily (it closes at 4 pm on Friday). Ⓜ N, R to Fifth Ave.

Frick Collection

The Frick Collection (☎ 212-288-0700, www.frick.org), 1 E 70th St at Fifth Ave, sits in a 1914 mansion built by businessman Henry Clay Frick, one of the many such residences that made up 'millionaire's row.' Most of these mansions proved too expensive for succeeding generations and were eventually destroyed, but the wily and very wealthy Frick, a Pittsburgh steel magnate, established a trust to open his private art collection as a museum.

It's a shame that the 2nd floor of the residence is not open for viewing, though the 12 rooms on the ground floor are grand enough. The Frick's Oval Room is graced by Jean-Antoine Houdon's stunning figure *Diana the Huntress*; the intimate museum also displays works by Titian, Vermeer, Bellini, and portraits by Gilbert Stuart, Sir Joshua Reynolds, Thomas Gainsborough and John Constable. An audio tour that's included in the price of admission helps visitors to appreciate the art more fully; with the 'ArtPhone,' you can dial up information on paintings and sculptures of your choosing.

The Frick is open 10 am to 6 pm Tuesday to Saturday and 1 to 6 pm Sunday. Admission is $7 for adults, $5 for students and seniors. Children under 10 are not permitted. Ⓜ 6 to 68th St.

Whitney Museum of American Art

The brutalist structure that houses this museum (☎ 212-570-3600, 570-3676, www.echonyc.com/~whitney), 945 Madison Ave at 75th St, makes no secret of the institution's mission to provoke. Bauhaus architect Marcel Breur designed the rock-like edifice, a notable contrast to the classical style of the Metropolitan Museum of Art and a fitting setting for the Whitney's collection of cutting-edge American art. In recent years, high-profile exhibitions at the Museum of Modern Art and the Brooklyn Museum of Art have overshadowed the Whitney's efforts to display innovative work, but it continues to stage its famous Biennial (scheduled for 2000 and 2002), an ambitious survey of contemporary art that rarely fails to generate controversy.

Established in the 1930s by Gertrude Vanderbilt Whitney, who began a Greenwich Village salon for prominent artists, the collection features works by Edward Hopper, Jasper Johns, Georgia O'Keeffe, Jackson Pollock and Mark Rothko. Recent major exhibits included a retrospective of dadaist art and a survey of 20th-century American art trends.

The Whitney is open 11 am to 6 pm Tuesday and Wednesday, 1 to 9 pm Thursday and 11 am to 6 pm Friday to Sunday. Admission is $10 for adults, $8 for seniors and students, free for children. Admission is free from 6 to 8 pm on the first Thursday of each month. Ⓜ 6 to 77th St.

The Whitney also has smaller exhibits at its branch in the Philip Morris Building, 120 Park Ave, across the street from Grand Central Terminal. It's open 11 am to 6 pm daily (until 7:30 pm Thursday). Admission to this museum is free.

Metropolitan Museum of Art

With more than five million visitors each year, the Metropolitan Museum of Art (☎ 212-879-5500, www.metmuseum.org), Fifth Ave at 82nd St, ranks as New York's most popular single-site tourist attraction, and it boasts one of the richest coffers in the arts world. The Met, as it's called, is virtually a self-contained cultural city-state, with two million individual objects in its collection and an annual budget of over $120 million. And, as the saying goes, the rich get richer – in 1999, the Museum received a donated collection (worth $300 million) of modern masterpieces, including works by Picasso and Matisse.

Once inside the **Great Hall**, pick up a floor plan and head to the ticket booths, where you will find a list of exhibits closed for the day along with a lineup of special museum talks. The Met presents more than 30 special exhibitions and installations each year, and clearly marked floor plans show you how to get to them. It's best to target exactly what you want to see and head there first, before culture and crowd fatigue sets in (usually after two hours). Then you can put the floor plan away and get lost trying to get back to the main hall. It's a virtual certainty that you'll stumble across something interesting along the way.

To the right of the Great Hall, an information desk offers guidance in several languages (these change depending on the volunteers) and audio tours of the special exhibits ($7 to $10). The Met also offers free guided walking tours of museum highlights and specific galleries. Check the calendar, given away at the information desk, for the specific schedule. For a self-guided walking tour, see below.

KIM GRANT

Chillin' at the Met

If you can't stand crowds, definitely don't come to the museum on a rainy Sunday afternoon in summer. But during horrible winter weather, you might find the 17-acre museum nearly deserted in the evening.

The Met is open 9:30 am to 5:30 pm Tuesday to Thursday and Sunday, 9:30 am to 9 pm Friday and Saturday. Suggested admission is $10 for adults, $5 for seniors and students, free for children. (You may pay as little as a penny to enter.) Ⓜ 4, 5, 6 to 86th St.

Walking Tour – Permanent Galleries

If you don't want to see anything in particular, then make a loop of the 1st floor before heading to the 2nd-floor painting galleries. Entering the Egyptian art section in the north wing, you'll pass the tomb of Pernebi (circa 2415 BC), as well as several mummies and incredibly well-preserved wall paintings before you come to the **Temple of Dendur**. The temple, threatened with submersion during the building of the Aswan Dam, found a home in New York under this glass enclosure – if you look closely at its walls, you can see the graffiti etched by European visitors to the site in the 1820s. (The accompanying history makes plain that the temple was a gift to the USA in exchange for building a permanent space for it.) This room often hosts museum fundraisers and corporate Christmas events.

If you exit the gallery through the door behind the temple, you'll probably experience culture shock when you see the Met's collection of **baseball cards**, including the rarest and most expensive card in existence: a 1909 Honus Wagner worth some $200,000. Continue on to the left to arrive at the **American Wing** of furniture and architecture, with a quiet, enclosed garden space that serves as a respite from Met hordes. Several stained-glass works by Louis Comfort Tiffany frame the garden, as does an entire two-story facade of the Branch Bank of the US, preserved when the building was destroyed downtown in the early 20th century.

After exiting through the far door of the American Wing, you'll pass through dark galleries dedicated to **medieval art**. Turn right and walk across the European decorative arts section to the pyramid-like addition that houses the Robert Lehman Collection of **impressionist and modern art**, featuring several works by Renoir (including *Young Girl Bathing)*, Georges Seurat and Pierre Bonnard. An unexpected bonus in this gallery is the rear terra-cotta facade of the original 1880 Met building, now completely encased by later additions and standing mutely on view as its own piece of architectural art.

Continue on through the European decorative arts section and turn left into the Rockefeller Collection of **Africa and Pacific Island** arts, heading toward Fifth Ave. At the museum cafe (at the far end of the Rockefeller collection), turn left and wander through the **Greek and Roman art** section. The museum has recently restored much of its Greek and Roman work, including the 2nd-floor Cypriot Gallery, which contains some of the finest pieces outside of Cyprus.

Elsewhere on the 2nd floor, you'll see the Met's famous collection of **European paintings**, located in some of the museum's oldest galleries, beyond colonnaded entryways. The exhibition features works by every artist of note, including self-portraits by Rembrandt and Van Gogh and *Portrait of Juan de Parej* by Velazquez. An entire suite of rooms focuses on impressionist and post-impressionist art. The new collection of modern masters is housed on this level, as well as the photographs recently purchased by the Met.

Solomon R Guggenheim Museum

A big sculpture all by itself, Frank Lloyd Wright's sweeping spiral building almost overshadows the collection of 20th-century art housed in the Solomon R Guggenheim Museum (☎ 212-423-3500, www.guggenheim.org), 1071 Fifth Ave between 88th and 89th Sts. Because of its unusual design, the building generated plenty of controversy during its construction in the 1950s, but today it's a distinctive landmark that architects fiddle with at their peril. An unpopular 1993 renovation added an adjoining 10-story tower that many complained made the museum look like a toilet.

Inside the Guggenheim, you can view some of the museum's 5000 permanent works (plus changing exhibitions) on a winding path that coincides with Wright's coiled design. The Guggenheim's collection includes pieces by Picasso, Chagall, Pollock and Kandinsky. In 1976, Justin Thannhauser's major donation of impressionist and modern works added paintings by Monet, Van Gogh and Degas. In 1993, the Robert Mapplethorpe Foundation gave 200 photographs to the museum, spurring curators to devote the 4th floor of the tower to photography exhibitions.

The museum is open 9 am to 6 pm Sunday to Wednesday, 9 am to 8 pm Friday and

Saturday. Admission is $12 for adults, $7 for seniors, free for children. You can pay what you wish from 6 to 8 pm on Friday. You can also use your CityPass here; see the boxed text 'Museum Bargains,' earlier in this chapter, for more information. Ⓜ 4, 5, 6 to 86th St.

National Academy of Design

Founded by painter-inventor Samuel Morse, the National Academy of Design (☎ 212-369-4880), 1083 Fifth Ave at 89th St, includes a permanent collection of paintings and sculptures housed in a beaux arts mansion designed by Ogden Codman, who also designed the Breakers mansion in Newport, Rhode Island. The building's grand features include a marble foyer and spiral staircase.

The museum is open from noon to 5 pm Wednesday, Thursday, Saturday and Sunday, 10 am to 6 pm Friday. Admission is $8 for adults, $4.50 for seniors and students, free for children. You can pay what you wish from 5 to 6 pm on Friday. Ⓜ 4, 5, 6 to 86th St.

Cooper-Hewitt National Museum of Design

The Cooper-Hewitt National Museum of Design (☎ 212-849-8400, www.si.edu/ndm), 2 E 91st St at Fifth Ave, sits in the 64-room mansion built by billionaire Andrew Carnegie in 1901 in a spot then-removed from the downtown bustle. Within 20 years, the country surroundings that Carnegie sought disappeared as other wealthy men followed his lead and built palaces around him.

Part of the Smithsonian Institution in Washington, this museum is a must for anyone interested in architecture, engineering, jewelry or textiles. Exhibitions have examined everything from advertising campaigns to household-item design. Even if none of this grabs you, the museum's garden is still worth a visit.

The museum is open 10 am to 9 pm Tuesday, 10 am to 5 pm Wednesday to Saturday, noon to 5 pm Sunday. Admission is $8 for adults, $5 for seniors and students, free for children. There is no admission charge from 5 to 9 pm Tuesday. Ⓜ 4, 5, 6 to 86th St.

ANGUS OBORN

The Guggenheim's dizzying spiral

Jewish Museum

The Jewish Museum (☎ 212-423-3200), 1109 Fifth Ave between 92nd and 93rd Sts, primarily features artwork that examines 4000 years of Jewish ceremony and culture. The building, a 1908 banker's mansion, houses more than 30,000 items of Judaica. It underwent a substantial expansion in 2000.

It's open 11 am to 5:45 pm Sunday to Thursday (until 8 pm Tuesday). Admission is $8 for adults, $5.50 for students and seniors, free for children. Everyone gets in free from 5 to 8 pm Tuesday. Ⓜ 6 to 96th St.

International Center of Photography

The ICP (☎ 212-860-1777), 1130 Fifth Ave between 94th and 95th Sts, remains the city's most important showcase for major photographers. Its past exhibitions have included work by Henri Cartier-Bresson, Man Ray, Matthew Brady and Robert Capa and explored such diverse themes as seascapes in contemporary photography and the impact of AIDS.

It's open 10 am to 5 pm Tuesday to Thursday, 10 am to 8 pm Friday and 10 am to 6 pm Saturday and Sunday. Admission is $6 for adults, $4 for seniors and students, $1 for children. You can pay what you wish from 6 to 8 pm Friday. Ⓜ 6 to 96th St.

At press time, the ICP's smaller gallery in Midtown (☎ 212-768-4682), 1133 Sixth Ave near 43rd St, was closed for renovations, but it's scheduled to reopen in the fall of 2000. Call for information.

Museum of the City of New York

The Museum of the City of New York (☎ 212-534-1672, www.mcny.org), 1220 Fifth Ave at 103rd St, not only lacks a coherent plan for its displays, but it also tends to duplicate the function of the older New-York Historical Society across town (see the Upper West Side section). Consequently, both institutions – overshadowed by their many world-class neighbors – attract relatively few visitors and have suffered financially.

Nevertheless, the Museum of the City of New York has expanded its facility and now offers a lot of Internet-based historical resources. The notable 2nd-floor gallery includes entire rooms from demolished homes of New York grandees, an exhibition dedicated to Broadway musicals and a collection of antique doll houses, teddy bears and toys.

The museum is open 10 am to 5 pm Wednesday to Saturday and noon to 5 pm Sunday. The suggested donation is $7 for adults, $4 for seniors, students and children, or $12 for an entire family. Ⓜ 6 to 103rd St.

Mount Vernon Hotel Museum and Garden

This 1799 carriage house, formerly known as the Abigail Adams Smith Museum (☎ 212-838-6878), 421 E 61st St between First and York Aves, once belonged to a large riverside estate owned by the daughter of John Adams, the second US president. In the early part of the 19th century, it became the Mount Vernon Hotel. Historic re-creations of tea parties and balls now take place here. It's open noon to 4 pm weekdays, 1 to 5 pm Sunday; admission is $4 for adults, $3 for seniors and students, free for children. Ⓜ 4, 5, 6 to 59th St.

Carl Shurtz Park

Beginning at 63rd St and York Ave, a jogger's path runs parallel to FDR Drive along the East River all the way up to the E 80s, where it becomes Carl Shurtz Park, a favorite spot for seniors and women with babies in strollers. **Gracie Mansion** (☎ 212-570-4751), the 1799 country residence where New York's mayors now live, presides over the end of the park at E 89th St. It's only open for public viewing on Wednesday from late March to mid-November, and you must call to reserve a tour slot. Tours take place Wednesday at 10 and 11 am and 1 and 2 pm. Ⓜ 4, 5, 6 to 86th St.

Roosevelt Island

New York's most planned neighborhood sits on a tiny island no wider than a football field in the East River between Manhattan and Queens. Once known as Blackwell's Island after the farming family that lived here, the island was purchased by the city in 1828 and became the location of several public hospitals and an insane asylum. In the 1970s, the state of New York built apartments for 10,000 people along the island's only street. The planned area along the cobblestone roadway resembles an Olympic Village or, as some less kindly put it, a college dorm.

Most visitors take the three-minute aerial tramway over to the island, admire the stunning view of the East Side of Manhattan framed by the 59th St Bridge, then head straight back. But it's worth spending an hour or so on the island during good weather, if only to enjoy the quiet and the flat roadway and paths; the island makes a great spot for both running and picnicking.

The Roosevelt Island tramway station (☎ 212-832-4543) is located at 59th St and Second Ave. Trips leave every 15 minutes on the quarter hour from 6 am to 2 am daily (to 3:30 am Friday and Saturday); the fare is $1.50. Roosevelt Island also has its own subway station; from Manhattan, take the Q train during the day and the B train on nights and weekends. Just make sure that the train you board lists '21st St-Queensbridge' as its final destination.

HARLEM (Map 10)

The setting for a major cultural renaissance in the 1920s, New York's best-known African American neighborhood now finds itself in the midst of another transition. After suffering through decades of economic depression, Harlem has begun to thrive again in the '90s, partly due to a large influx of West African immigrants and partly due to the tourist revenues generated by the many Japanese and European visitors who are eager to learn about Harlem's significant history. But the tour buses here give off an unseemly vibe – much like an urban safari undertaken by people too fearful to move about on foot.

Despite Harlem's past reputation as a crime-ridden no-man's-land, today the area shouldn't cause you to exercise any more caution than you would in any other New York neighborhood. Perhaps even less, since the former troubles have led the city to step up the police presence in Harlem. City officials have also aggressively promoted Harlem to developers, and the plan seems to be working: The new **Harlem USA** entertainment and retail complex (☎ 212-316-2500), 300 West 125th St, opened in 2000. It features a dance club, 12-screen cinema, a rooftop skating rink and a Disney store.

Those in search of true Harlem-style entertainment, though, go to the famous Apollo Theater (see heading, later), which continues to host its popular amateur night on Wednesday. Plenty of fine amateur singing performances also go on at the neighborhood's Sunday morning church services, which feature rousing gospel choirs (see Church Services, later). No matter what you decide to do while you're in Harlem, don't forget to stop in for some soul food at one of the spots on Malcolm X Blvd (Lenox Ave).

VERONICA GARBUTT

All ready for church in Harlem

THINGS TO SEE & DO

To Tour or Not to Tour

Harlem has become a very popular destination for foreign visitors who want to see the neighborhood but don't wish to walk its streets. As a consequence, bus companies have been doing big business on guided tours to the neighborhood. But it's worth checking the true cost of the service. One operator offers a $70 trip to amateur night at the Apollo, with dinner at an unspecified soul food restaurant. Taking the subway yourself ($3 roundtrip), picking up a ticket at the Apollo box office (prices range from $7 to $20) and finding your own restaurant ($15 or less) represents a huge savings for those on a budget. Moreover, Harlem residents tend to give a better welcome to street-bound visitors than those who gawk at the neighborhood from the ersatz safety of a double-decker bus.

Nevertheless, if you'd like some local insight into the neighborhood, a tour may be worth your money. Harlem Spirituals (☎ 212-757-0425, www.harlemspirituals.com) offers several black heritage excursions for $15 to $75. Harlem, Your Way! (☎ 212-690-1687, 800-382-9363, www.harlemyourway.com) offers tours for $25 to $55. Musical Feast of Harlem (☎ 212-222-6059) offers Sunday morning tours of gospel services in local churches, with prices starting at $55 for adults, including lunch.

For walking tours, contact Urban Explorations (☎ 718-721-5254). Big Onion Walking Tours (☎ 212-439-1090, www.bigonion.com) offers a very informative tour of historic Harlem for $10 to $12.

First-time visitors will probably be surprised to discover that Harlem is but one express subway stop away from the Columbus Circle-59th St station. The trip on the A and D trains takes just five minutes, and both stop just one block from the Apollo Theater and two blocks from Malcolm X Blvd (Lenox Ave). The 2 and 3 trains from the West Side stop at 116th St, the site of the Harlem open-air market, and at 125th St.

Orientation As you explore Harlem, you should note that the major avenues have been renamed in honor of prominent African Americans, but many locals still call the streets by their original names, making getting around a little confusing. Eighth Ave (Central Park West) is Frederick Douglass Blvd. Seventh Ave is Adam Clayton Powell Jr Blvd, named for the controversial preacher who served in Congress during the 1960s. Lenox Ave has been renamed for the Muslim activist Malcolm X. 125th St, the main avenue and site of many businesses, is also known as Martin Luther King Jr Blvd.

KIM GRANT

Take the A train.

Apollo Theater

The Apollo Theater (☎ 212-531-5305), 253 W 125th St at Frederick Douglass Blvd, has been Harlem's leading space for political rallies and concerts since 1914. Virtually every major black artist of note in the '30s and '40s performed there, including Duke Ellington and Charlie Parker. After a brief desultory spell as a movie theater and several years of darkness, the Apollo was bought in 1983 and revived as a live venue. It still holds its famous weekly amateur night – 'where stars are born and legends are made' – Wednesday at 7:30 pm. Watching the crowd call for the 'executioner' to yank hapless performers from the stage is often the most entertaining part of amateur night. On other nights, the Apollo hosts performances by established artists like Whitney Houston and comedian Chris Rock. Ⓜ A, B, C, D to 125th St.

Striver's Row

While you're in Harlem, check out Striver's Row, also known as the St Nicholas Historic District, just east of St Nicholas Park on W 138th and 139th Sts between Adam Clayton Powell Jr and Frederick Douglass Blvds. These row houses and apartments, many of which were designed by Stanford White's firm in the 1890s, were much prized. When whites moved out of the neighborhood, Harlem's black elite occupied the buildings, thus giving the area its colloquial name. This is one of the most visited blocks in Harlem – so try to be a little discreet, since the locals (modern-day Harlem elite) are a bit sick of all the tourists. Streetside plaques explain more of the area's history. Check out the alleyway signs advising visitors to 'walk their horses.' Ⓜ B, C to 135th St.

Studio Museum in Harlem

The Studio Museum in Harlem (☎ 212-864-4500), 144 W 125th St close to Adam Clayton Powell Jr Blvd, has displayed the crafts and culture of African Americans for nearly 30 years and provides working spaces to promising young artists. Its photography collection includes works by James

VanDerZee, the master photographer who chronicled the Harlem Renaissance of the '20s and '30s.

It's open noon to 6 pm Wednesday and Thursday, noon to 8 pm Friday and 1 to 6 pm Saturday and Sunday. Admission is $5 for adults, $3 for seniors and students, $1 for children. Metro: 2, 3 to 125th St.

Schomburg Center for Research in Black Culture

The nation's largest collection of documents, rare books and photographs resides at the Schomburg Center for Research in Black Culture (☎ 212-491-2200), 515 Malcolm X Blvd (Lenox Ave) near W 125th St. Arthur Schomburg, a Puerto Rican native with a white father and black mother, started gathering works on black history during the early 20th century while becoming active in the movements for civil rights and Puerto Rican independence. His collection was puchased by the Carnegie Foundation and eventually expanded and stored in this branch of the New York Public Library. The Schomburg Center also contains a theater where lectures and concerts are regularly held.

It's open noon to 7:45 pm Monday to Wednesday and 10 am to 5:45 pm Thursday to Saturday. The center's gallery spaces are also open 1 to 5 pm Sunday. Admission is free. Ⓜ 2, 3 to 125th St.

Church Services

Some of the churches in Harlem have cut deals with tour bus operators, and their services are packed with visitors who attempt to take pictures during the services or even leave early. It's probably better to go on your own to a place that welcomes visitors but not tour groups.

Founded by an Ethiopian businessman, the **Abyssinian Baptist Church** (☎ 212-862-7474), 132 W 138th St (now Odell Clark Place) near Adam Clayton Powell Jr Blvd, began as a downtown institution but moved north to Harlem in 1923, mirroring the migration of the city's black population. Its charismatic pastor, Calvin O Butts, is an important community activist whose support is sought by politicians of all parties. The church has a superb choir and holds services every Sunday at 9 and 11 am. Ⓜ 2, 3 to 135th St.

The **Canaan Baptist Church** (☎ 212-866-0301), 132 W 116th St near St Nicholas Ave, may be Harlem's friendliest church. It's a good idea to show up a bit early and introduce yourself to the parishioners before the 10:45 am service on Sunday (10 am from July to September). Ⓜ B, C, 2, 3 to 116th St.

Harlem Market

Vendors at the semi-enclosed Harlem Market, near the intersection of W 116th St and Malcolm X Blvd (Lenox Ave), do a brisk business selling tribal masks, oils, traditional clothing and assorted African bric-a-brac. You can also get cheap clothing, leather goods, music cassettes and bootleg videos of films still in first-run theaters.

Most of the vendors at the market used to sell their wares from tables set up along 125th St, but in 1995, amid great controversy, they were forced to move to this open-air site after

retailers complained about their presence. The market is operated by the **Malcolm Shabazz Mosque**, the former pulpit of Muslim orator Malcolm X.

The market is open 10 am to 5 pm daily. Ⓜ 2, 3 to 116th St.

Spanish Harlem

East of Harlem, Spanish Harlem extends from Fifth Ave to the East River, above 96th St. This former Italian neighborhood now contains one of the biggest Latino communities in the city. Here, you'll find **La Marqueta**, a colorful, ad-hoc collection of produce stalls on Park Ave above 110th St.

El Museo del Barrio Located in a bland office block, El Museo del Barrio (☎ 212-831-7272), 1230 Fifth Ave between 105th and 106th Sts, began in 1969 as a celebration of Puerto Rican art and culture and has since expanded its brief holdings to include the folk art of Latin America and Spain. Its galleries now feature pre-Columbian artifacts and a collection of more than 300 *santos*, hand-carved wooden saints in the Spanish Catholic tradition. Temporary exhibits feature the work of local artists who live in Spanish Harlem.

Every January 5, as part of its Christmas festivities, the museum holds a **Three Kings Parade**, in which hundreds of schoolchildren, along with camels, donkeys and sheep, make their way up Fifth Ave to 116th St, the heart of the neighborhood.

El Museo del Barrio is the best starting point for any exploration of Spanish Harlem. It's open 11 am to 5 pm Wednesday to Sunday (until 7 pm Thursday in summer). Admission is $4 for adults, $2 for seniors and students, free for children. Ⓜ 6 to 103rd St.

Italian Harlem

East Harlem was predominantly a working-class Italian neighborhood at the beginning of the 20th century, and some traces of this heritage have lasted into the 21st century, with Italian restaurants still present in Harlem. See the Places to Eat chapter for more information.

WASHINGTON HEIGHTS

Near the northern tip of Manhattan (above 145th St), Washington Heights takes its name from the first US president, who set up a Continental Army fort here during the Revolutionary War. An isolated rural spot until the end of the 19th century, Washington Heights is today an unremarkable neighborhood full of large apartment buildings. A few grand homes here and there hint at the early residents' aspirations, but Washington Heights never became the sophisticated area that some New Yorkers envisioned. In the last decade, the neighborhood has taken on an increasingly Latino flavor, with thousands of new immigrants from the Dominican Republic settling here.

Most visitors to Washington Heights come to see the handful of museums, particularly the Cloisters in Fort Tryon Park, a beautiful spot in warm weather. Free shuttle buses run between the area's museums from 11 am to 5 pm. (Call any one of the following museums to find out the schedule.)

Audubon Terrace

Naturalist John James Audubon once lived in Audubon Terrace, Broadway at 155th St, which now houses three little-known and free museums. Ⓜ 1 to 157th St.

The **American Numismatic Society** (☎ 212-234-3130) owns a large permanent collection of coins, medals and paper money. It's open 9 am to 4:30 pm Tuesday to Saturday and 1 to 4 pm Sunday. Admission is free.

The **Hispanic Society of America** (☎ 212-926-2234) displays Spanish and Portuguese furniture and artifacts, including significant artworks by El Greco. The courtyard features some nice statues. Few people make the journey up here – guards often outnumber visitors, and they'll have to accompany you upstairs to turn on the lights for the 2nd floor gallery. It's open 10 am to 4:30 pm Tuesday to Saturday and 1 to 4 pm Sunday. Admission is free.

The **American Academy and Institute of Arts and Letters** (☎ 212-368-5900) opens its bronze doors to the public several times a year for temporary exhibitions; call ahead for the schedule. Admission is free.

Five Secret Pleasures (One for Each Borough)

- **City Island in the Bronx** Thirteen miles from Midtown, this incongruous New England–style enclave offers opportunities for fishing and watersports.
- **Strand Bookstore** At this downtown institution (the best bookstore in the world), you might find that obscure out-of-print paperback – or a cut-rate copy of a current bestseller.
- **Jacques Marchais Center of Tibetan Art** This quirky Staten Island museum is worth the ferry trip on a sunny summer day.
- **Brighton Beach** A little bit of old mother Russia lives right in the middle of Brooklyn.
- **Panorama of New York City** See the incredibly detailed miniature city at the Queens Museum of Art in Flushing.

Morris-Jumel Mansion

Built in 1765, the columned Morris-Jumel Mansion (☎ 212-923-8008), 65 Jumel Terrace at 160th St east of St Nicholas Ave, served as George Washington's Continental Army headquarters. After the war, it returned to its former function as the summer residence of a wealthy local family. A designated landmark, the mansion's interior contains many of the original furnishings, including a 2nd-floor bed that reputedly belonged to Napoleon. Some believe that the ghost of Eliza Jumel, the woman who lived here until her death in 1865, still moves about the place.

It's open 10 am to 4 pm Wednesday to Sunday. Admission is $3 for adults, $2 for seniors, students and children 10 and older; admission is free for younger children. Ⓜ C to 163rd St-Amsterdam Ave.

The Cloisters

Simply put, the Cloisters (☎ 212-923-3700, www.metmuseum.org), in Fort Tryon Park, is one of the most peaceful places in the city to visit on a sunny summer day. Built in the 1930s, the museum incorporates fragments of old French and Spanish monasteries and houses the Metropolitan Museum of Art's collection of medieval frescos, tapestries and paintings. In the summer, the best time to visit, concerts take place on the grounds, and more than 250 varieties of medieval flowers and herbs are on view. The museum and the surrounding gardens in Fort Tryon Park are particularly popular with European visitors.

The museum is open 9:30 am to 4:45 pm Tuesday to Sunday from November to February, 9:30 am to 5:15 pm Tuesday to Sunday the rest of the year. The suggested admission is $10 for adults, $5 for seniors and students, free for children. Ⓜ A to Dyckman St.

Dyckman House Museum

Built in 1784 on a 28-acre farm, the Dyckman House (☎ 212-304-9422), 4881 Broadway, is the lone Dutch farmhouse to survive in Manhattan. Excavations of the property have turned up valuable clues about colonial life, and the museum includes period rooms and furniture, decorative arts, a half acre of formal gardens and an exhibit on the neighborhood's history.

It's open 11 am to 4 pm Tuesday to Sunday. Admission is free, although donations are welcome (and needed for funding).

To get to the Dyckman House take the subway to the 207th St station and walk one block south – many people mistakenly get off one stop too soon at Dyckman St. Ⓜ A to 207th St.

Outer Boroughs

THE BRONX

The Bronx – a geographic area with a curious article before its name, like the Hague and the Yucatán – takes its name from the Bronck family, Dutch farmers who owned a huge tract of property in the area. They in turn gave their name to Bronck's River, which led to the derivation used today.

The Bronx, once a forest-like respite from the rest of the city but now home to 1.2 million people, has long been a metaphor for urban decay – many know it only as the poverty-plagued and crime-ridden borough that gave birth to the disenfranchised voices of American rap music (see boxed text 'The New York Sound' in the Facts about New York City chapter). But even the southwestern part of the Bronx – the area unofficially referred to as the South Bronx – doesn't quite live up to its reputation, thanks to a 10-year, multibillion dollar program to build low-income housing.

Although some sections of the lower Bronx, including Morrisania, still contain a fair share of abandoned buildings, the northern reaches of the borough feature thriving areas like Fieldston, a community of Tudor homes occupied by some of the city's richest residents. The Bronx also boasts the quiet and isolated fishing community of City Island, as well as the 2764-acre Pelham Bay Park, the city's largest.

The only borough of New York City that's part of the US mainland, the Bronx begins northeast of Manhattan (across the Harlem River) and extends into upstate New York. The northern part of the borough gives way to the leafy suburbs of Westchester County.

The Bronx Tourism Council (☎ 718-590-3518, www.ilovethebronx.com) offers a visitor's guide to the borough and keeps track of community events. The Bronx County Historical Society (☎ 718-881-8900) sponsors weekend walking tours of various sites. Call for details.

Yankee Stadium

The Yankees like to call their legendary ballpark 'the most famous stadium since the Roman Coliseum.' Yankee Stadium (☎ 718-293-6000, www.yankees.com), E 161st St and River Ave, hosts 81 home games for the New York Yankees throughout the summer (see the boxed text 'The New York Yankees: Team of the Century'). Gates open 90 minutes before night games on weekdays (or two hours before on weekends), and if you have some extra time before the first pitch, you can always visit left field's **Monument Park**, where plaques commemorate such baseball greats as Babe Ruth, Lou Gehrig, Mickey Mantle and Joe DiMaggio. The park closes 45 minutes before the game begins.

You can also visit the dugout, the press room and the locker room during a guided tour of the ballpark (☎ 718-579-4531 for reservations). The hour-long tours take place 10 am to 4 pm weekdays and 10 am to noon Saturday when the team is on the road, or 10 am to noon Monday to Friday when the team's at home. Tours cost $8 for adults, $4 for seniors and children. An expanded tour that also includes a short film costs $15 for adults, $10 for children.

Across the street from the stadium stand several bustling memorabilia shops and restaurants. **Stan's Sports Bar** gets particularly raucous when the Yankees play their rival, the Boston Red Sox.

Game tickets cost $15 to $42.50, with distant bleacher seats priced at $8 (but avoid these on hot days, since there is no shade). Ⓜ 4, D to Yankee Stadium.

Bronx Museum of the Arts

If you're taking in a ballgame, you might want to make a slight detour to this museum (☎ 718-681-6000), 1040 Grand Concourse at 165th St. (The Grand Concourse, the Borough's largest avenue, is three blocks to the east of Yankee Stadium.) The museum often shows the work of young city artists. It's open 3 to 9 pm Wednesday, 10 am to 5 pm Thursday and Friday, noon to 6 pm Saturday and Sunday. Admission is $3 for adults, $2 for students and seniors; it's free on Wednesday. Ⓜ B, D, 4 to 161st St-Yankee Stadium; D to 167th St.

Hall of Fame for Great Americans

One of New York's most neglected sites is the Hall of Fame for Great Americans at Bronx Community College (☎ 718-289-5100) in University Heights, 183rd St at Sedgwick Ave. This outdoor colonnade, which overlooks the Hudson River and features the

The New York Yankees: Team of the Century

No team has loomed larger in American baseball history than the New York Yankees. The 'Bronx Bombers' are arguably the most famous sports team in the world, and millions recognize their team symbol, an interlocking 'NY' on a navy blue hat. You can find folks sporting Yankees caps in cities as diverse as London, Beijing, Sydney and Cairo. Even the Yankees' ballpark has become famous; it's hosted a number of heavyweight title fights, a famous National Football League championship match and masses celebrated by two Popes (Pope Paul VI and John Paul II).

ANGUS OBORN

The Yankees' dynasty began in 1920, when the team picked up a pitcher named George Herman 'Babe' Ruth from the Boston Red Sox. Ruth's spectacular home-run hitting drew huge crowds, and he helped the Yankees win their first American League pennant in 1921 and their first World Series in 1923. When it was built in 1923, Yankee Stadium earned the nickname the 'House that Ruth Built' because it was partly designed to suit his hitting style and to fit the many fans who came just to see him.

In 1927, Babe Ruth hit 60 homers, which remained a record for a single season until 1961. His career total of 714 home runs (659 for the Yankees) wasn't surpassed until Hank Aaron beat it in 1974.

This baseball team had a talent for attracting one major star after another from the 1920s to the '60s. Lou Gehrig, Joe DiMaggio and Mickey Mantle became popular cultural icons even to people who didn't follow baseball. Although the Yankees finally experienced a fallow period in the '80s, the team came roaring back at the end of the century, capturing three World Series victories from 1996 to 1999 and setting several records in the process. In 1999, the Yankees handily won a 25th World Series title, marking the team as the most successful baseball club of all time.

busts of more than 100 notables, originally belonged to New York University, whose main campus resided here until the early 1970s. When NYU abandoned the site, the local community college took it over.

The Hall of Fame languished in disrepair until a $3 million restoration spiffed things up in the mid-1980s. For years, the 620-foot-long hall contained the bust of but one woman, suffragette Susan B Anthony, but now it also includes American Red Cross founder Clara Barton, astronomer Maria Mitchell and writer Harriet Beecher Stowe, among other women. The men on display include George Washington, Ben Franklin and Alexander Graham Bell.

The neighborhood is rather out of the way, so if you visit the Hall of Fame, do so during the day, preferably when the college is in session. It's open 10 am to 5 pm daily. Admission is free. Ⓜ 4 to 183rd St.

New York Botanical Garden

The 250-acre New York Botanical Garden (☎ 718-817-8700, www.nybg.org) features several beautiful gardens and the restored Victorian **Enid A Haupt Conservatory**, a grand iron and glass edifice. You can also stroll through an outdoor **rose garden**, just next to the conservatory, and a **rock garden** with a multitiered waterfall.

The garden is open from 10 am to 6 pm Tuesday to Sunday (10 am to 4 pm from November through March), with the same hours on Monday holidays. Admission is $3 for adults, $2 for seniors and students, $1 for children.

Metro-North trains (☎ 212-532-4900) leave hourly from Grand Central Terminal and stop right at the garden; the fare is $3.50 each way. You can also take the subway to the Bedford Park Blvd station and walk east down the hill seven blocks to the gate. Ⓜ B, D to Bedford Park Blvd.

Bronx Zoo

The Bronx Zoo (☎ 718-367-1010), also known by its more politically correct title 'Bronx Wildlife Conservation Society,' attracts more than two million visitors annually. Nearly 5000 animals live at the 265-acre facility, all in comfortable, naturalistic settings. It's best to visit the zoo in warm weather, since many of the outdoor rides close during the winter months and the animals retreat into shelter areas – which means that you'll be stuck touring the older buildings, where the reptiles and birds reside.

To see the usual array of lions, tigers and bears, take the Bengali Express, a 25-minute narrated monorail journey through the Wild Asia areas; it operates from May to October and costs $2. The large Jungle World indoor exhibit, open year-round, recreates the Asian tropics with 100 different species of animal and tropical plants. You'll either be delighted or terrified by the World of Darkness, where bats hover nearly unseen (but not unsmelled).

The zoo is open 10 am to 5 pm weekdays and 10 am to 5:30 pm weekends in summer, or 10 am to 4:30 pm daily in winter (but there are extended evening hours between Thanksgiving and New Year's). Admission varies by season and ranges from $4 to $9 for adults, $2 to $5 for seniors and children over two. General admission is free on Wednesday.

Liberty Lines Express (☎ 718-652-8400) charges $7 for a bus ride to the Bronx Zoo from Manhattan; buses pick up passengers along Madison Ave (at 26th, 47th, 54th, 63rd, 69th, and 84th Sts). You can also drive to the zoo via the Bronx River Parkway. Ⓜ 2, 5 to Pelham Parkway.

Arthur Ave

Just south of Fordham University is the Belmont section of the Bronx, the most authentic Italian neighborhood in the city. You can soak up true Italian American culture while your stomach absorbs plenty of olive oil and wine (see the Places to Eat chapter).

Belmont is the perfect place to stock up on Italian provisions, including live chickens at the Arthur Ave Poultry Market, 2356 Arthur Ave, and Teitel Brothers Wholesalers (☎ 718-733-9400), on the corner of 186th St and Arthur Ave. The Arthur Ave Retail Market, 2344 Arthur Ave, contains indoor food stalls, including Mike & Sons, a cheese shop with heartbreakingly good aged parmesan and prosciutto. Cosenza's fresh fish store, 2354 Arthur Ave, sells clams on the half-shell to pedestrians from a small table on the street, while clerks at the Calabria Pork Store (☎ 718-367-5145), 2338 Arthur Ave, offer free samples of hot and sweet homemade sausages that age on racks along the ceiling.

The **Belmont Italian American Playhouse** (☎ 718-364-4700), 2384 Arthur Ave, is the neighborhood's most lively performance spot. Its season of new theatrical works runs from April to December, and local authors and musicians perform year-round.

To reach Arthur Ave, take the Metro-North train (or the subway) from Grand Central to Fordham Rd and walk east 11 blocks; turn right at Arthur Ave and continue south for three blocks. Ⓜ B, D to Fordham Rd.

City Island

Surely the oddest neighborhood in the Bronx is City Island, a 1½-mile-long fishing community 15 miles from Midtown. Its numerous boat slips and three yacht clubs make City Island the place to go if you're interested in diving, sailing or fishing in Long Island Sound. Perhaps the strangest thing about this self-contained little spot, cut off from the rest of the Bronx by Pelham Bay Park, is the virtual absence of any New York accent in the locals' speech – in fact, their inflections betray a New England influence.

You'll find all of City Island's shops and its 20-odd seafood restaurants along City Island Ave, which runs the length of the island. On the short side streets, attractive clapboard houses overlook the surrounding water.

Most activities on City Island revolve around the sea. If you're interested in fishing or sailing, head to the island's western side, home to all the main marinas. NY Sailing School (☎ 718-885-3103), 697 Bridge St, runs sailing courses and rents boats during the summer. Boats offering early-morning trips include the *Riptide III* (☎ 718-885-0236) and *Daybreak II* (☎ 718-409-9765). (These boats also embark on nighttime bluefish trips during the summer.) Fishing trips cost about $45 per person.

To reach City Island, take the subway (line 6) to its terminus at Pelham Bay Park, then get on the Bx29 bus, which runs directly to City Island Ave. You can also take an express bus from Madison Ave in Midtown (it stops every four blocks or so on Madison Ave, beginning at E 24th St) directly to City Island; the fare is $6 each way.

BROOKLYN (Maps 11 & 12)

This is the only outer borough that gives Manhattan a run for its money when it comes to attracting both tourists and hip young residents. For years, a sign on the eastern side of the Brooklyn Bridge welcomed visitors to the 'fourth-largest city in America.' The sign has been replaced by one with a less separatist sentiment, but Brooklyn's pride – and right to claim big city status – still remains (it is home to 2.3 million people). The borough even boasts that 'one out of every seven famous people' in America was born in Brooklyn!

Brooklyn, officially called Kings County, derives its name from *breucklen*, the Dutch word for marshland. For most of its 350-year history, Brooklyn was a collection of farming villages, and its citizens joined greater New York City with great reluctance. Even after the 1898 consolidation, the borough remained independent in spirit: Citizens enjoyed Prospect Park (Brooklyn's own version of Central Park), followed the fortunes of the Brooklyn Dodgers baseball team and sun-worshipped at the ritzy resort hotels on Coney Island. But much of Brooklyn's separate city pretensions ended in the late 1950s, when the Dodgers moved to the West Coast and many of the borough's residents began relocating to the suburbs. Today, newer immigrants from the Caribbean, Eastern Europe and the former Soviet Union live in Brooklyn's inner neighborhoods, while Manhattan professionals have snapped up the old carriage houses and brownstones in the eastern part of the borough.

Information

BRIC/Brooklyn Information & Culture (☎ 718-855-7882, www.brooklynx.org), 647 Fulton St on the 2nd floor, issues a free calendar of events called *Meet Me in Brooklyn*. You can pick up a copy at all Brooklyn cultural institutions. BRIC also has maps and other tourist information. *Brooklyn Bridge*, a monthly magazine available in shops and newsstands throughout the borough, offers a more extensive list of happenings. A number of free neighborhood newspapers also cover local events.

Brooklyn Heights Walking Tour

This neighborhood of brownstones and mansions near the mouth of the East River developed as a ferry departure point for Lower Manhattan in the early 19th century. If you walk along its promenade, you'll get a stunning view of Manhattan's skyscrapers, framed at the bottom by the far less impressive metal storage warehouses along the waterfront.

If you're particularly energetic, you can begin this walking tour all the way back in Lower Manhattan, at the entrance to the Brooklyn Bridge. After a 20-minute walk across the bridge, bear right on the bridge's pedestrian walkway, which will bring you south along Adams St to Joralemon St, only a few feet from the beginning of this tour.

Start at the landmark 1848 beaux arts **Brooklyn Borough Hall**, 209 Joralemon St near Court St. Borough Hall is open weekdays during business hours; a free tour of the historic facility takes place at 1 pm every Tuesday. On the tour, you'll see the massive central rotunda, marble entrance hall and beaux arts–style courtroom.

Bear right on Court St and walk two blocks to Montague St, the main avenue for cafes and bars. Before heading left on Montague St, you might want to take a brief detour north one block to the parallel Pierrepont St (pronounced **pier**-pont), site of the **Brooklyn Historical Society** (☎ 718-624-0890, 254-9830 for walking tours, www.brooklynhistory.org), 128 Pierrepont St. This research library also features a museum dedicated to borough history and a fine terra-cotta auditorium that's a national landmark. When the museum is open, you can browse through the society's digitized collection of 31,000 photographs and prints on computers in the 2nd-floor library. It's open noon to 5 pm Tuesday to Saturday.

Head back down to Montague St and proceed several blocks to the waterfront promenade at the end of the street. From here, you can turn right and continue north on Columbia Heights to **Fulton Landing**, the old ferry dock at the base of the Brooklyn Bridge. Most Manhattan-bound ferries departed from here before the bridge loomed overhead, beginning in 1883. Now classical music concerts take place on a barge nearby, and it's a perfect spot to watch the sun set beyond Manhattan.

Turn around and start back the way you came on Columbia Heights, but bear left on Middagh St. Note the old wooden frame houses around the intersection of Middagh and Henry Sts prior to turning right on Henry St and continuing uphill to **Atlantic Ave**, the busy thoroughfare that contains several Middle Eastern spice shops and an array of restaurants. The wholesale broker Sahadi Importing Co (☎ 718-624-4550), 187-189 Atlantic Ave, sells its dried fruits and nuts all over the country, and it's worth stopping in to pick up some tasty snacks or simply to enjoy the exotic smells and atmosphere. It's open until 7 pm Monday to Saturday.

From Henry St, turn left on Atlantic Ave and walk two blocks to Court St. Turn right to reach the Italian enclave of **Cobble Hill**. Mostly a commercial district, Court St features a good mix of pastry shops, convenience stores and cafes, with brownstone residences on the surrounding streets. (See the Places to Eat chapter for more about the restaurants here.)

ANGUS OBORN

Walk south on Court St for 11 blocks, making sure to stop in at the fine Bookcourt Book Shop (☎ 718-875-3677), 163 Court St. At Carroll St, turn right and walk west one block to Clinton St, where you'll find the red-brick Greek Revival **Rankin residence** on the southwest corner. Now a funeral home, this 1840 mansion was once the only house on a large farm with a view of New York Harbor. It sits today in the middle of the **Carroll Gardens Historic District**, a remarkably well-preserved neighborhood of brick and brownstone houses that date from the mid- to late 19th century, most with small fenced front yards.

Head back to busy Atlantic Ave on Clinton St, where it should be easy to see why some call Brooklyn the 'Borough of Churches' – you'll pass at least half a dozen on your walk around the neighborhood.

New York Transit Museum

Appropriately enough, the transit museum (☎ 718-243-8601), at the corner of Boerum Place and Schermerhorn St, resides in a decommissioned subway station from the 1930s. Its exhibits include an impressive collection of subway cars from the transit system's first 100 years; most have their original ads still intact. Keep an eye out for the silver car used in the 1995 film *Money Train*, along with the model R-1, the vintage that inspired Duke Ellington's *Take the A Train*. You'll also see the 1947 R-11 model, which featured 'germicidal' lighting designed to sterilize tunnel air; this model was discontinued amid fears that the lights would also sterilize subway conductors and trainmen.

These relics from days gone by set the tone for the whole museum, whose lack of modern, interactive exhibits means that it's been in serious need of an update for some time – a perfect metaphor for the subway system's needs, too. At press time, the museum was finally scheduled to undergo a major renovation, due to begin in the fall of 2000. Call for information about the temporary closure of the museum.

The museum's hours are 10 am to 4 pm Tuesday to Friday, noon to 5 pm Saturday and Sunday. Admission is $3 for adults, $1.50 for seniors and students. Ⓜ A, C, F to Jay St-Borough Hall.

Brooklyn Academy of Music

The oldest concert center in the USA, the Brooklyn Academy of Music (BAM; ☎ 718-636-4100, www.bam.org), 30 Lafayette Ave between Ashland Place and St Felix St, has hosted such notable events as Enrico Caruso's final performance. Today, it continues to feature first-rate arts programs, including performances by visiting opera companies from around the world and the residents Mark Morris dance troupe. The complex contains the **Majestic Theater**, the **Brooklyn Opera House** and the new **Rose Cinema** (☎ 718-623-2770), the first outer-borough movie house dedicated to independent and foreign films.

You can take public transportation to BAM (which is easily accessible) or reserve a spot on the BAMbus, which leaves from the Philip Morris Building, 120 Park Ave at E 42nd St in Manhattan, an hour before most performances; on the return trip, it makes numerous Manhattan stops. The fare is $10 roundtrip ($8 for students). For reservations, contact BAM at least 24 hours in advance. Ⓜ 2, 3, 4, 5, D, Q to Atlantic Ave.

Prospect Park

Created in 1866 by the same landscaping duo that designed Central Park, this 526-acre masterwork by Frederick Law Olmsted and Calvert Vaux may be their greatest achievement. Though less crowded than its more famous Manhattan sister space, Prospect Park (☎ 718-965-8951, www.prospectpark.org) offers many of the same activities along its broad meadows, including **ice skating** at the Kate Wollman Rink (☎ 718-287-6431), which is open daily from October to early March. Admission is $4 for adults, $2 for seniors and children, with skate rental for $3.50.

Kids should enjoy the **Lefferts Homestead Children's Historic House Museum** (☎ 718-965-6505), which is open 1 to 4 pm Thursday and Friday and 1 to 5 pm Saturday and Sunday from April to November, and a small **zoo** (☎ 718-399-7339), which is open 10 am to 5 pm daily with an admission charge of $2.50 for adults, 50¢ for children. For information on other activities, including park walks, carousel rides and art exhibitions, visit the boathouse or call the events hotline (☎ 718-965-8999).

Grand Army Plaza stands at the northwest entrance to the park, at the intersection of Eastern Parkway and Flatbush Ave. Its 80-foot **Soldiers' and Sailors' Monument**, constructed in 1892, commemorates the Union Army's triumph during the Civil War. In the summer, a gallery in the arch displays work by local artists, and the observation deck just below the bronze chariot offers a view of the park. At press time, though, the arch was closed for repairs. Call for information.

New York City's only structure honoring President John F Kennedy stands in a small fountain park just to the north of the Grand Army arch. The immense art deco **Brooklyn Public Library** faces the arch on its south side.

On Saturday and Sunday year-round, a free hourly trolley service makes a loop from Prospect Park to points of interest around the Brooklyn Museum of Art, including the park zoo and ice rink, the botanical garden, and the Brooklyn library. Ask at the museum's information desk (see Brooklyn Museum of Art, later). Ⓜ 2, 3 to Grand Army Plaza; F to 15th St-Prospect Park.

Park Slope

This rectangular-shaped residential neighborhood sits immediately west of Prospect Park, and most of its shops and restaurants lie along the 18 blocks of Seventh Ave between the two subway stations at 9th St and at Park Place. Novelist Paul Auster and essayist Ian Frazier live in this neighborhood, so don't be surprised to find a literary atmosphere here. Bookshops within easy walking distance include Community Bookstore (☎ 718-783-3075), 143 7th Ave at Carroll St, which puts on readings by noted authors on a regular basis. This smaller bookstore has a cafe, which it added in an attempt to keep its customers after mega-chain Barnes & Noble invaded the neighborhood some years ago.

Park Slope is a pleasant place to have lunch or dinner or just linger over coffee. Local celebrities like to frequent the coffee shop-cum-literary hangout Ozzie's (☎ 718-398-6695), 57 7th Ave near Lincoln Place, one of several cafes along the street. Ⓜ D, Q to 7th Ave; F to 7th Ave-Park Slope.

ANGUS OBORN

Brooklyn Public Library

Eastern Parkway

Named after the six-lane boulevard that runs along the north end of Prospect Park, this area used to be one of the most exclusive neighborhoods in Brooklyn. Today, it encompasses both Prospect Heights and Crown Heights, home to the Lubavitch sect of Orthodox Jews and a large Caribbean community. Major ethnic tensions have divided the two groups in the not-too-distant past, but you'll find it safe to explore the shops and restaurants along Washington Ave, which runs in front of the Brooklyn Museum of Art.

Brooklyn Museum of Art Were it located anywhere else, the Brooklyn Museum of Art (☎ 718-638-5000, www.brooklynart.org), 200 Eastern Parkway near Washington Ave, would be considered a premier arts institution. Even though it's overshadowed by the Met in Manhattan, this museum is very much worth a visit. It's never really crowded, even on Sunday, and you can take up an entire day exploring its collection and visiting the nearby Botanic Garden and Brooklyn Children's Museum.

The museum received a lot of publicity in 1999, when it sponsored an exhibition of young British artists, including Chris Ofili, who uses elephant dung in his paintings. Mayor Giuliani himself attacked Ofili's portrait of the Virgin Mary, giving the exhibition (and the mayor) a lot of exposure in the press.

For those turned off by cutting-edge art, the museum showcases plenty of more traditional exhibits as well. The permanent galleries feature African, Islamic and Asian art, with colorful Egyptian cartonnages (mummy casings) and funerary figurines on display in the modern 3rd-floor galleries. The 4th floor, which overlooks a tiled court crowned by a skylight, contains period rooms, including a reconstruction of the Jan Schenck House, a 17th-century Dutch settlement in Brooklyn. On the 5th floor, the colonial portraiture on display includes a famous Gilbert Stuart painting of Washington in which the general looks particularly uncomfortable wearing his false teeth. You'll also find a collection of 58 Auguste Rodin sculptures nearby.

The Brooklyn Museum of Art is open 10 am to 5 pm Wednesday to Friday, 11 am to 6 pm Saturday (11 am to 11 pm on the first Saturday of the month) and 11 am to 6 pm Sunday. Suggested admission is $4 for adults, $2 for seniors and students, free for children. Ⓜ 2, 3 to Eastern Parkway-Brooklyn Museum.

Brooklyn Botanic Garden The 52-acre botanical garden (☎ 718-623-7200), 1000 Washington Ave near Eastern Parkway, features more than 12,000 different plants in its 15 gardens. The fanciful Celebrity Path with slate steps honors famous Brooklynites, and the Fragrance Garden makes for a wonderful walk. Unfortunately, a few years ago someone made off with several of the Steinhardt Conservatory's bonsai trees, a few of which were 250 years old or more.

The botanic garden is open 8 am to 6 pm Tuesday to Friday and 10 am to 6 pm on weekends and holidays from April to September. Winter hours are 8 am to 4:30 pm Tuesday to Friday, 10 am to 4:30 pm on weekends and holidays. Admission is $5 for adults, $2 for seniors and children. Ⓜ 2, 3 to Eastern Parkway-Brooklyn Museum.

Brooklyn Children's Museum The Brooklyn Children's Museum (☎ 718-735-4400), 145 Brooklyn Ave at St Marks Ave, emphasizes art, music and ethnic culture. Founded in 1899, this century-old institution features a world playground that celebrates different cultures and a greenhouse designed to teach kids about environmental preservation. Each June, the museum holds a balloon festival of custom-made balloons from around the world. It also hosts frequent cultural events. It's open 2 to 5 pm weekdays and noon to 5 pm weekends. The suggested donation is $3. Ⓜ 3 to Kingston Ave.

Coney Island

Now somewhat desolate and unattractive, Coney Island once thrived as a bustling showplace where sweating city dwellers came to enjoy the fun house and bumper-car rides in the Dreamland amusement park before WWI. Coney Island's storied Cyclone roller coaster still manages to attract crowds in summer, but tourists desert the area after Labor Day, when the coaster closes. In fall and winter, the New York Aquarium here and Brighton Beach nearby still make Coney Island worth the 60-minute subway trip from Manhattan.

As you emerge from the colorfully decrepit subway station, you'll see a 24-hour coffee shop right in the middle of the station. Hard-bitten patrons sit at a countertop hunched over their meals, oblivious to the festive yellow walls, while the smells of sausages, hot dogs, home fries and other greasy delights assault your nose. If none of this tempts you, pass through the doors to Surf Ave, where Russian residents pick up odd tools and electronic equipment at **flea market** stalls along the street.

Not far from here is the **Coney Island Sideshow** (☎ 718-372-5159), 1208 Surf Ave, a small museum and freak show where you can see snake charmers, tattooed ladies and sword-swallowers for a $5 admission charge. The sideshow is open 2 pm to midnight Friday and Saturday from Easter to Labor Day.

Nathan's, the city's prototypical fast-food stand, has stood at the same Surf Ave site

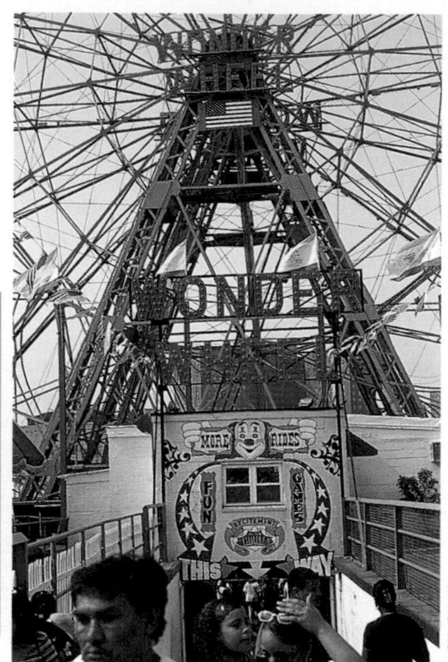

JENNIFER STEFFEY

Thrills and chills at Coney Island

for more than 75 years and still sells its famous hot dogs ($2.50) from 8 am to 4 am daily.

Along the Boardwalk, you'll see two relics of Coney Island's past glory: the bright red parachute jump, moved here from the 1939 World's Fair in Queens, and the ivy-covered **Thunderbolt** roller coaster, which operated from 1925 to 1983; it's older than the more famous Cyclone in the Astroland Amusement Park, just up the boardwalk. Ⓜ B, D, N, F to Stillwell Ave-Coney Island.

New York Aquarium The New York Aquarium (☎ 718-265-3400), along the Coney Island boardwalk, has received a fancy new name: the Aquarium for Wildlife Conservation. But its manageable scale still makes it a perfect place for young children. At the touch pool, kids can handle starfish and other small forms of sea life, and the small amphitheater features Sea World–style dolphin shows several times daily. Most kids love viewing whales and seals from the outside railing overlooking their tanks or from the observation windows that afford views of the animals' underwater habitats. You can spend the better part of a day at the aquarium viewing its 10,000 specimens of sea life.

It's open 10 am to 6 pm daily; the last ticket is sold at 4:15 pm weekdays, 4:45 pm weekends. Admission is $9.75 for adults, $6 for seniors and children. Ⓜ F, D to W 8th St-NY Aquarium.

Brighton Beach

There's more than a little bit of Russia to be found in Brighton Beach, just a five-minute walk north on the boardwalk from the New York Aquarium. Home to the largest group of Russian emigrés in the USA, this community features a full array of Russian shops, bakeries and restaurants along Brighton Beach Ave, which runs parallel to the boardwalk just one block from the beach.

Although police have uncovered money laundering schemes run by the Russian mafia in Brighton Beach, you don't have to worry about crime on the street – just about the only criminal behavior you'll observe are the *babushkas* selling illegal prescription medicine Moscow-style on the street corner.

This community is so close-knit that a non-Russian speaker will stick out like a sore thumb, but the shopkeepers are friendly to outsiders, a category that includes Brooklynites from any other neighborhood. Ⓜ D, Q to Brighton Beach.

Williamsburg

This neighborhood, located just over the namesake Williamsburg Bridge in northern Brooklyn, contains a large Orthodox Jewish community – a living embodiment of what Manhattan's Lower East Side was in the early 20th century. But the windswept northern area of Williamsburg features a much more diverse population. A large population of Central European immigrants, mostly from Poland, has lived in the north a long time, but in recent years, this aging community has welcomed new, younger neighbors – aspiring artists and writers who are taking advantage of the cheap rents and large loft spaces. The two distinct communities coexist quite peacefully. On sunny Sunday afternoons, Polish senior citizens hang out on just about every other doorstep, exchanging greetings in their native language after church services, while paint-splattered younger folks gather in the local bars for brunch, beer and cigarettes.

Though the local press has noted Williamsburg's growing popularity with the cutting-edge art crowd, art galleries have not yet invaded the neighborhood, nor have rents risen to Manhattan levels (though apartments are still shockingly expensive here compared to those in other cities). A college campus atmosphere prevails along Bedford St, where locals looking for apartment shares post signs on mini 'democracy walls' and musicians advertise for band mates.

Though Williamsburg does not have much to offer culturally as yet, it's only a five-minute subway trip from Manhattan's Union Square, and it's worth seeing in good weather: You can grab a good meal here and admire the sunset view of Manhattan from Kent Ave along the waterfront. Ⓜ L to Bedford Ave.

Brooklyn Brewery Since 1988, the Brooklyn Brewery has made its award-winning Brooklyn Lager under contract at breweries outside of the borough. But the beer 'came home' to Brooklyn in 1996 with the opening of a microbrewery in Williamsburg (☎ 718-486-7422), 79 N 11th St. Housed in a series of buildings that once made up the Hecla Ironworks factory (the firm that made the structural supports for the Waldorf-Astoria Hotel), the brewery has become a Williamsburg institution.

In the tasting room, you'll find a display of historical beer bottles and monthly specials. Happy hour takes place every Friday between 6 and 10 pm, and many nights of the week feature live entertainment. On Saturday, the brewery offers free tours, which include a free tasting, from noon to 4:30 pm. Call ahead during summer to find out if the tours have been booked.

QUEENS (Maps 13 & 14)

Manhattan has the fame. Brooklyn has the pride. The Bronx has the attitude. Staten Island, the temperament of the put-upon. Where does that leave Queens, a borough of boring, low-slung row houses and a transitional zone between Manhattan urban and Long Island suburban? Despite all architectural appearances, though, New York's largest borough (282 sq miles) ranks as the most diverse spot in the USA. The area's cheap rents and proximity to the airports has long made Queens attractive to the newest New Yorkers, immigrants from all over the world.

A strange phenomenon has happened over the years – most of the newer immigrant groups have augmented, rather than replaced, those already in Queens. More than 100 minority groups now live here, and the borough's population exceeds two million.

The Queens Council on the Arts operates a 24-hour hotline (☎ 718-291-2787) on community cultural events; in keeping with the multicultural demographics of the borough, it provides information in English, Spanish, Korean and Chinese.

Astoria

Named after millionaire fur merchant John Jacob Astor, the area of eastern Queens known as Astoria began as a mid-19th century ferry depot, but it soon developed into a neighborhood of factories, including the Steinway piano company, which still operates here and which you can visit (see the boxed text 'Artisans at Work'). German and Italian craftsmen helped to settle Astoria, but Greek immigrants replaced them in the years following WWII.

Today, the brick-and-concrete apartment blocks and two-story wooden homes that make up this largely working-class, residential neighborhood house the largest Greek community in the USA, as well as a smattering of Eastern European immigrants. Ⓜ N to Broadway; R to Steinway St.

American Museum of the Moving Image The American Museum of the Moving Image (☎ 718-784-0077, www.ammi.org),

35th Ave at 36th St, stands right in the middle of the **Kaufman Astoria Studios** complex. A number of movies and TV shows have been shot at this 75-year-old film production center, including the Marx Brothers' *Coconuts*, *Glengarry Glen Ross* and television's *Cosby Show*.

Unfortunately, the studios are not open to the public, but this museum does a good job of showing the mastery behind filmmaking. Galleries display the makeup and costumes from films like *The Exorcist*, as well as sets from the 1987 movie *The Glass Menagerie*, directed by Paul Newman, and the popular TV series *Seinfeld* (fans will appreciate such artifacts as Jerry's infamous 'puffy shirt').

The museum also holds interesting film retrospectives year-round, with several movies screened daily in a small theater built by conceptual artist Red Grooms, who was inspired by the Egyptian-themed movie palaces of the '30s. If you decide to take the short 15-minute subway ride out to Queens, go when there's an interesting film on the schedule – and end your day with a Greek meal on Broadway.

The museum is open noon to 5 pm Tuesday to Friday, 11 am to 6 pm on weekends. Admission is $8.50 for adults, $5.50 for seniors and students, $4.50 for children. Ⓜ R to Steinway St.

Artisans at Work

You can view two very different examples of skilled craftsmanship in Astoria. The **Byzantion Woodworking Company** (☎ 718-932-2960), 37-20 Astoria Blvd, doesn't offer tours, but you can drop by from Monday to Saturday to see artisans at work carving elaborate Greek Orthodox religious items for clients in the USA and Canada.

The **Steinway Piano Company** (☎ 718-721-2600 ext 164), 19th Ave at 38th St, has been making world-class pianos in Queens for more than 100 years. Steinway produces the leading concert piano and displays its instruments in a showroom near Carnegie Hall, across the street from Planet Hollywood. The factory in Astoria offers free 90-minute tours of its facility every Thursday. It's vital to call ahead to reserve a place, since the tours are often booked by school groups months in advance. Ⓜ N to Ditmar Blvd.

Isamu Noguchi Garden Museum Tucked away among the East River warehouses in Long Island City, the cinder-block Isamu Noguchi Garden Museum (☎ 718-721-1932), 32-37 Vernon Blvd, stands on the site of a studio designed by the Japanese-American sculptor, who died in 1988, three years after the museum opened. The 12 galleries and garden contain more than 300 examples of his work.

It's open 10 am to 5 pm Wednesday to Friday, 11 am to 6 pm on Saturday and Sunday from April to October, and a tour of all the galleries takes place at 2 pm. Admission is $4 for adults, $2 for students and seniors.

Just two blocks north, where Broadway meets Vernon Blvd, you'll find the **Socrates Sculpture Park** (☎ 718-956-1819), a free, year-round, open-air public space on a former illegal waste dump overlooking the East River. The local artists' work on display, including the five wind chimes along the shoreline, have a stark industrial look to them, in keeping with the park's location right next to a steel company. It's open from 10 am to dusk; admission is free. Ⓜ N to Broadway.

Flushing Meadows-Corona Park & Shea Stadium

A big attraction for sports fans, Flushing Meadows-Corona Park includes both **Shea Stadium**, the ballpark of the New York Mets (see Spectator Sports in the Entertainment chapter), and the **USTA National Tennis Center**, home of the premier US Open tournament every fall (see Public Holidays & Special Events in the Facts for the Visitor chapter). The spectacular 1939 and 1964 World's Fairs also took place here.

The center of the park is dominated by the distinctive, 380-ton **Unisphere** globe, built for the 1964 fair by US Steel. A few of the old buildings constructed for the fair are

Ride on the International Express

The phrase 'National Historic Trail' may bring to mind the Oregon Trail or the Trail of Tears – probably not the No 7 subway line, which cuts through the heart of Queens and is known as the International Express. But the US government has designated it as just that, since the burgundy-colored subway trains pass through the longtime immigrant neighborhoods of Woodside, Jackson Heights and Corona in the middle of Queens.

These areas, with their cheap rents and direct subway connection to Midtown Manhattan, have attracted an international array of residents. Recent arrivals hail from Ireland, Uruguay, Panama, Korea, China and many other countries.

While the view from the train won't impress you (you'll see a bland landscape of two-story brick buildings punctuated by wooden houses), if you look closer, a plethora of cheap, tasty ethnic restaurants await you (see the Places to Eat chapter for more information).

In Manhattan, board the No 7 subway at Grand Central Terminal or Times Square and disembark at the following stations to explore the blocks nearby. If you're headed for Woodside, home to one of the city's oldest Irish neighborhoods, get off at 46th St-Bliss St, 52nd St-Lincoln Ave or 61st-Woodside. To visit Jackson Heights, get off at 74th St-Broadway (where you'll find Filipino, Korean and Indian communities) or 82nd St-Jackson Heights (if you're looking for some South American spots). The Junction Blvd station marks the dividing line between Jackson Heights and Corona; here, several Latino subcultures exist side by side, including Cuban and Dominican communities. In Corona (disembark at 103rd St-Corona Plaza), you'll find a large group of Mexicans, as well as Muslims from Pakistan and India.

You won't get lost if you keep Roosevelt Ave, which runs directly under the elevated train tracks for the final third of the line, as a reference point. The journey from Manhattan to the very end of the line at Main St-Flushing takes about 35 minutes.

The Queens Council on the Arts offers information on the sites along the International Express. Call ☎ 718-647-3377 or send $1 for postage to the organization at 7901 Park Lane South, Woodhaven, NY 11421. You can also stop by and pick up a guide for free at the council's main office, which also offers other cultural information.

still in use, though Philip Johnson's New York State Pavilion is a mess: rusty, overgrown with weeds and closed to the public. Ⓜ 7 to 111th St or Willets Point-Shea Stadium.

New York Hall of Science This former World's Fair pavilion (☎ 718-699-0005), which resembles a Stalin-era concrete block, houses a children's museum dedicated to technology. It stands next to an outdoor park with a few early space-age rockets.

It's open 9:30 am to 2 pm Monday to Wednesday, 9:30 am to 5 pm Thursday to Sunday; in the summer months, it stays open until 5 pm on Tuesday and Wednesday. Admission is $7.50 for adults, $5 for children. Ⓜ 7 to 111th St.

Queens Museum of Art The former New York City building from the 1939 World's Fair has been completely renovated and turned into the Queens Museum of Art (☎ 718-592-5555, www.queensmuse.org), which contains displays dedicated to both fairs held in the park. The building also hosted the first sessions of the UN before the body moved into its permanent quarters on Manhattan's East Side; a gallery here explains the history of those early peacemaking meetings.

The major attraction here is the **Panorama of New York City**. This 9335-sq-foot model of the metropolis debuted at the 1964 World's Fair, where visitors marveled at its details, reproduced at a scale of 1200:1.

In 1994, the panorama was cut up into 273 sections and updated to include all of the significant new additions to the local skyline. Today, it's a stunning sight, with more than 835,000 tiny buildings. A glass-bottom observation deck encircles the panorama, and every 15 minutes a mock sunset takes place, prompting thousands of tiny lights to flicker across the diorama.

The museum is open 10 am to 5 pm Tuesday to Friday and noon to 5 pm Saturday and Sunday. Admission is $5 for adults, $2.50 for seniors and children. Ⓜ 7 to 111th St.

Flushing

It's hard to imagine that this bustling neighborhood once served as a secret meeting place for 17th-century Quakers determined to circumvent Dutch Governor Peter Stuyvesant's religious intolerance by hiding away in the woods. The former country village was also the site of the first commercial nursery in the USA; George Washington visited it soon after his inauguration as president.

Despite these auspicious beginnings, Flushing eventually became an urban eyesore, home to a huge commercial ash heap (mentioned in F Scott Fitzgerald's *The Great Gatsby)* and a number of junkyards often noted by travelers to Long Island. Before the World's Fair of 1939, city officials turned this area into parkland again, but much of the neighborhood contains wall-to-wall discount shops, 24-hour coffee shops and municipal offices.

In the 1980s, Flushing attracted a huge influx of Korean and Chinese immigrants. At some spots, with most of the signs printed in Korean, you might think you're in a residential neighborhood in Seoul. While some of the older residents have resented the incursion of new Asian immigrants, Flushing has not suffered from any outward tensions between the various communities.

Flushing's attractions (besides those in the Walking Tour, later) include the **Flushing Council on Culture & the Arts** (☎ 718-463-7700), 137-35 Northern Blvd, which houses a contemporary art museum and historical gallery. Built in 1864, this Romanesque Revival building also hosts a year-round series of jazz and classical concerts. The museum is open 10 am to 5 pm weekdays and noon to 5 pm weekends. Admission is $3 for adults, $2 for seniors and students, $1 for children.

The 40-acre **Queens Botanical Gardens** (☎ 718-886-3800), 43-50 Main St, includes a variety of flora not native to the area. It's open 8 am to 4:30 pm Tuesday to Sunday (and on national holidays that fall on Monday); from April to October, hours are 8 am to 6 pm Tuesday to Friday and 8 am to 7 pm weekends. Admission is free. On weekends, a trolley runs between the botanical garden and Flushing Meadows-Corona Park.

Flushing's center is located at the corner of Roosevelt Ave, which runs east-west, and Main St, which runs north-south; these two streets meet right at the subway exit. Ⓜ 7 to Main St-Flushing.

Flushing Walking Tour If you're exiting the subway station, walk three blocks east on Roosevelt Ave, then turn left on Parsons Blvd and proceed two blocks north to 37th Ave. Make a left to find the **Queens Historical Society** (☎ 718-939-0647), 143-35 37th Ave, in the Kingsland Homestead, a wooden 1765 estate house just beyond Margaret Carmen Green.

The historical society offers maps of Freedom Mile, listing 19 places of religious significance, and brochures published in English, Korean, Spanish and Chinese. The tour is a bit of a cheat, since some of the sites are merely the former locations of important places that no longer exist. But you can still see the oldest residence in Queens: the 1661 **John Bowne House**, which stands today at 37-01 Bowne St, just steps away from the Kingsland Homestead. Quakers once met in the house.

If you turn around and take a 10-minute walk south on Bowne St (passing Roosevelt Ave again), you'll come to what must be Flushing's most exotic sight: the **Hindu Temple Society of North America** (☎ 718-460-8484), 45-57 Bowne St. The temple, complete with carved elephant-headed gods, was designed and built in India and reconstructed here in 1977. You'll have to take your shoes off before you enter the 2nd floor of the temple, where you can observe devotees offering coconut milk to the deity Maha Vallabha Ganapati. The temple, which is open 8 am to 9 pm, holds daily services, and, at the side of the building, a cafe serves yogurt drinks and light fare.

In late August, the temple holds a festival to the god Ganesh that lasts nearly two weeks and features visiting performers from India and a parade through Flushing.

When you leave the temple, you should turn right on Holly Ave, then right again on Kissena Blvd, which will eventually bring you back to Main St.

STATEN ISLAND

Residents of the 'forgotten borough' of Staten Island have long entertained thoughts of secession from greater New York City. Its tiny population of 378,977 – largely white, middle-class and politically Republican – has historically had little clout in predominately Democratic New York City. Most politicians have made little secret of their disdain for this suburban tract of land close to the New Jersey shoreline. What's worse, the borough is home to the city's largest garbage dump – a fact snickered about in Manhattan and deeply resented on Staten Island. (The dump is scheduled to be closed permanently by 2001.) And the gray, dirty waterfront near the ferry terminal doesn't help the borough's image.

Staten Island grew when railway magnate Cornelius Vanderbilt established a ferry service between the island and the port of New York in the 19th century. For more than 100 years, Staten Island remained a quiet outpost for the wealthy, who built large estates among the verdant farmlands. But large-scale development finally got underway in the 1960s, after the construction of the Verrazano Narrows Bridge forged a land link with the rest of New York City. Even still, most New Yorkers view the borough only as the destination of a pleasantly breezy ferry ride on a hellish summer day or as the starting point of the New York City Marathon. Of course, there's more to Staten Island than just that, and it's worth a day trip.

The Staten Island Chamber of Commerce (☎ 718-727-1900), at 130 Bay St near Vistory Blvd, provides information on cultural events and attractions. Pick up a copy of the *Staten Island Advance* for coverage of local news and events.

Eighteen bus routes converge on the St George Ferry Terminal in Staten Island; from there, you can pick up buses to all the major sites. The buses leave within minutes of the ferry's arrival.

Staten Island Ferry

One of New York's best bargains, the free ferry (☎ 718-815-2628) takes 70,000 passengers each day on the 25-minute, 6-mile journey from Lower Manhattan to Staten Island. The roundtrip fare to Manhattan used to be 50¢, but since Staten Island votes Republican, Mayor Giuliani (a Republican himself) abolished the fee.

If you're eager to avoid the crowds and the expense of a boat trip to the Statue of Liberty and Ellis Island, try this. You'll pass

ANGUS OBORN

The view from the Staten Island ferry

THINGS TO SEE & DO

within a half mile of both attractions on the way out to Staten Island, and the view of Manhattan and Brooklyn Heights is breathtaking. It's best to pack up a lunch or snack before heading out to the ferry, since the boat itself sells dreadful food and Lower Manhattan's South Ferry Terminal, an outdated facility that's been slated for replacement within a few years, doesn't have a decent place to eat.

The ferry operates on the half hour, 24 hours each day, and only the most brutal weather will keep the ferries in their slips. Ferries carrying cars operate from early morning until 11:30 pm and charge $3 per vehicle each way; call to confirm schedules. Bicycles are free. In Manhattan, you'll find the ferry terminal at the bottom of Whitehall St, just east of Battery Park.

Snug Harbor Cultural Center

The Snug Harbor Cultural Center (☎ 718-448-2500), 1000 Richmond Terrace, sits on the site of an old retirement complex built between 1831 and 1917 for about 1000 sailors. The group of five buildings just inside the north gate features some of the finest small-scale Greek Revival architecture left in the USA. The Great Hall and the Veterans Memorial Chapel nearby both have impressive interiors.

In 1976, the city took control of the rundown 83-acre site, which overlooks the oil tankers and container ships docking in New Jersey, and restored it as a complex for the borough's cultural institutions. You can easily spend a day exploring these three attractions: the **Staten Island Botanical Garden** (☎ 718-273-8200); the **Staten Island Children's Museum** (☎ 718-273-2060), which specializes in science and nature exhibits and is open noon to 5 pm Tuesday to Sunday (admission $4); and the **Newhouse Center for Contemporary Art** (no phone), which is open noon to 5 pm Wednesday to Sunday. A free tour of the 28 landmark buildings on the site leaves from the visitor center at 2 pm every Saturday and Sunday.

You can reach the Snug Harbor Cultural Center by taking the S40 bus 2 miles west from the ferry terminal.

Jacques Marchais Center of Tibetan Art

Home to the largest collection of Tibetan art outside China, the Jacques Marchais Center (☎ 718-987-3500), 338 Lighthouse Ave, was built by art dealer Edna Koblentz, who collected the artworks under an alias that did not betray her gender. The center opened to the public in 1947, a year before her death.

The unusual objects on display include a number of golden sculptures and religious objects made from human bone. Just about the only authentic thing missing from the center, built in the style of a Tibetan temple, is the smell of yak butter. In the early part of October, the museum holds its annual weekend-long Tibetan cultural festival among the stone Buddhas in the outdoor garden.

The Marchais Center is open 1 to 5 pm Wednesday to Friday from December to March and 1 to 5 pm Wednesday to Sunday from April to November, with concerts and demonstrations at 2 pm Sunday. Admission is $3 for adults, $2.50 for seniors and students and $1 for children. The Sunday afternoon events cost an additional $3.

To get to the center, take the S74 bus along Richmond Rd for 30 minutes and ask the driver to let you off at Lighthouse Ave. The museum sits at the top of a hill.

Wright Residence

There's a bonus in store for those who make the trek out to the Jacques Marchais Center. Just across Lighthouse Ave from the museum sits the only private home that famed architect Frank Lloyd Wright ever built in New York City. Look for the low-slung, cliff-side residence at 48 Manor Court, constructed in 1959. Don't knock on the door, though – people still live here.

Historic Richmond Town

The village of Richmond (☎ 718-351-1611) once served as the county seat of Staten Island, and 11 original buildings still stand in what is now a borough preservation project maintained by the Staten Island Historical Society. Historic Richmond Town includes the 300-year-old redwood **Voorlezer's House**, which is believed to be the oldest surviving school building in the country. In the 1960s, other historic structures were moved here from around the island in an ambitious attempt to protect local history.

Visit historic Richmond Town in warm weather, when you can enjoy the surrounding landscape along Richmond Creek. During the summer season, volunteers dressed in period garb roam the grounds and describe 17th-century rural colonial life.

Begin your exploration of the 100-acre site at the village courthouse, which serves as a visitor center. Every hour, a guide conducts tours beginning at the courthouse. You'll find a historical museum in the former county clerk's office.

Richmond Town is open year-round 1 to 5 pm Wednesday to Sunday, with extended hours in July and August. Admission is $4 for adults, $2.50 for children over five.

You can reach the center by taking the S74 bus from the ferry to Richmond Ave and St Patrick's Place, a journey of about 35 minutes.

Greenbelt Nature Walks

The 2500-acre Greenbelt environmental preserve (☎ 718-667-2165) in the middle of Staten Island encompasses several parks with five different ecosystems, including swamp areas and freshwater wetlands. It's one of New York City's unexplored nature treasures, offering some spectacular walks not far from the bustle of downtown Manhattan. The 28 miles of trails should suit both casual walkers and aggressive hikers. Birdwatchers can track 60 different species of birds here.

The **High Rock Park** section of the Greenbelt includes six trails through hardwood forest, as well as three gardens. To get there, take the S74 bus from the ferry to Rockland Ave, walk up Rockland and bear right at Nevada Ave to the park entrance.

The **William T Davis Wildlife Refuge** once housed the wells that gave Staten Islanders their drinking water; today, it's a sanctuary for migrating birds and the site of the Greenbelt Native Plant Center. To reach the refuge walking trails, take the S62 or S92 buses from the ferry along Victory Blvd to Travis Ave.

Places to Stay

Although New York City already contains more than 70,000 hotel rooms, it can barely keep up with its continued and growing popularity as a tourist destination. With visitor numbers running at 30 million a year, more than 70% of the city's hotels fill up every day year-round.

Hotel Discounts

To accommodate the hordes of tourists who encounter problems booking inexpensive hotel rooms, NYC & Company (the New York Convention & Visitors Bureau) has set up a special hotline (☎ 800-692-8474, fax 212-245-5943); call to request a free city guide that offers rooms at 100 hotels for $125 and up.

As in airline travel, consolidators have moved into the hotel market to snap up unsold rooms at the last minute and sell them at a discount. If you use one of these services, make sure you ask where the room is in the hotel – booking at the last minute may mean that you'll get a room no one else wants. As with airline consolidators, you must pay in advance, though in many cases, if you cancel the reservation at least 24 hours ahead you'll receive a refund.

Quickbook (☎ 800-789-9887, www.quickbook.com) offers up to 60% discounts on rooms at moderately priced Midtown hotels (including many of those listed in this book); the phone lines are open 9 am to 7 pm.

The Hotel Reservations Network (☎ 800-964-6835, www.hoteldiscount.com) handles accommodations in 20 US cities. When booked through the network, rooms in nearly 100 Manhattan hotels cost as little as $80 a night.

Accommodations Express (☎ 800-906-4685, www.accommodationsexpress.com) offers smaller discounts – around 15% – but handles a larger number of rooms in every price category. Operators answer the phones from 7 am to 11 pm daily.

PLACES TO STAY

The laws of supply and demand mean that New York City hotel rooms don't come cheap. Indeed, the average room costs a whopping $245 a day, compared to the US average of $80 a night. If you come from a part of the world where a decent, clean room runs about $50, you're in for a shock, since $50 here won't buy you much more than a night in a flophouse.

The bottom line: A decent hotel room costs $150 or more a night. If you want to find a good, cheap place to stay in New York City, then make a friend who lives here. Failing that, you must plan this part of your trip very carefully. Keep in mind that two long-distance phone calls could turn out to be the smartest money you spent on your vacation; first, call to make a reservation as far in advance as possible, then call again to confirm the booking just before you arrive. If you do come to New York on the fly and with a limited budget, select a few inexpensive choices and go in person well before noon on the day you want to stay.

Beware of relatively inexpensive hotels that ask you to pay for your full stay in advance. That usually means that customers tend to flee the place after a night or two, and the payment policy could be a ploy to keep you there. Insist on paying only for the first night; that way, you can always leave early without losing money.

Rates quoted in this book do not include city taxes, which are a steep 13.25% plus a $2-per-night room charge. Prices fluctuate depending on the season.

HOSTELS

For more information on a number of the hostels listed here (among others), visit the Web site www.hostels.com, which features links to the hostels' own sites.

Chelsea (Map 7)

A party atmosphere prevails at the ***Chelsea International Hostel*** *(☎ 212-647-0010, fax 727-7289, 251 W 20th St)*, between Seventh and Eighth Aves, where free pizza parties take place on Wednesday night. Beds cost $25 in the bunk rooms, which sleep four to six, and private rooms are $60. Amenities include communal kitchens and laundry facilities. You must present a passport when you check in (but you don't have to be a foreigner to stay here). For more information, visit the Web site www.chelseahostel.com. Ⓜ 1, 9 to 18th St; F to 23rd St.

The quieter ***Chelsea Center Hostel*** (*☎ 212-643-0214, 313 W 29th St*), near Eighth Ave, charges $27 for its 22 beds. Ⓜ 1, 9 to 28th St; A, C, E to 34th St-Penn Station.

When you step inside the ***Gershwin Hotel*** (*☎ 212-545-8000, 7 E 27th St*), near Fifth Ave, you may think you've walked into a performance space. Just four blocks north of the Flatiron Building, this increasingly popular spot (half youth hostel, half hotel) features a funky lobby that's a shrine to Andy Warhol. In many ways, it's more bohemian in character than the far more famous (and pricey) Chelsea Hotel (see Hotels, later), and it's becoming a favorite hangout spot for young travelers who are staying in hostels and hotels elsewhere in the city. Reservations are a must. Dorm beds cost $35; private rooms start at $95. You can reserve a bed online at www.gershwinhostel.com. Ⓜ 6 to 28th St.

Times Square (Map 8)

A spare facility just off Times Square, the ***Big Apple Hostel*** (*☎ 212-302-2603, fax 302-2605, 119 W 45th St*), between Sixth and Seventh Aves, offers beds for $30 and private rooms for $80. Rates include access to the kitchen, laundry room and backyard barbecue. The hostel's open 24 hours. Ⓜ N, R, S, 1, 2, 3, 7, 9 to Times Square-42nd St.

Upper West & East Sides (Map 9)

Hostelling International-New York (*☎ 212-932-2300, fax 932-2574, 891 Amsterdam Ave*), near W 103rd St, books its 620 beds quickly during the summer, especially since it offers air-conditioned rooms. As it's open for check-in 24 hours a day, this hostel is the place to head if you land in town at an odd time. A bed costs $22 to $25 for members (rooms with fewer beds cost more), with a small $3 surcharge for nonmembers. Rates drop slightly in winter. Ⓜ 1, 9 to 103rd St.

Also uptown, the ***International Student Center*** (*☎ 212-787-7706, 38 W 88th St*), near Central Park West, accommodates non-US residents under age 30 for $20. Ⓜ B, C to 86th St.

Overlooking Central Park, the new ***Park View Hotel*** (*☎ 212-369-3340, 55 Central Park North*), near Lenox Ave, offers beds in simple but colorful dormitory-style rooms for $26. Private rooms in the recently refurbished building rent for $60 to $80. Ⓜ B, C to 110th St.

Harlem (Map 10)

The reliable ***Sugar Hill International House*** (*☎ 212-926-7030, fax 283-0108, 722 St Nicholas Ave*) and its sister hostel, ***Blue Rabbit*** (*☎ 212-491-3892, 730 St Nicholas Ave*), near 146th St, offer a total of 60 dorm beds ($20) in two renovated limestone homes that date back to the 19th century. Private rooms that sleep two cost $25 per person. Ⓜ B, C to 145th St.

B&BS & APARTMENTS

Several rival companies vie for the B&B reservations business, many offering spots in 'outlaw' B&Bs not registered with the city or any organization. Rooms tend to cost the same as those at the cheapest hotels – about $75 to $120 a night, with two-night minimum stays in the summer. Most services offer reduced rates for monthly rentals of studios and apartments.

Even though you're not calling the B&B directly when you contact one of these services, don't hesitate to ask about the degree of contact you'll have with the host, the nature of the neighborhood or the kinds of attractions you'll find nearby. Whoever answers the phone should know the answers to these questions. You may hear the terms 'hosted' and 'unhosted' thrown around; the hosted variety most closely resembles traditional B&B–style accommodations in a private home with hosts who can offer advice on the city and who may actually serve breakfast (but don't count on it). Unhosted accommodations include vacant apartments that the locals rent out while they're not using them. (The tight hotel market in New York has given birth to a cottage industry, of sorts, with enterprising New Yorkers turning into part-time innkeepers.)

Urban Ventures (☎ 212-594-5650) has 600 rooms in its registry, many priced from $80 to $125. For more information, visit www.nyurbanventures.com.

Bed and Breakfast Network of New York (☎ 800-900-8134) offers singles/doubles starting at $70/100, with a good selection of rooms in Greenwich Village. The phone lines are open 8 am to 6 pm weekdays.

Bed and Breakfast in Manhattan (☎ 212-472-2528) offers a more specialized service, with staff who take the time to match visitors up with hosts according to their individual needs. Prices range from $90 to $110 for hosted accommodations.

For those with deep pockets, City Lights Bed and Breakfast (☎ 212-737-7049) rents private apartments in uptown locations for as much as $300 a night. But the service also offers single rooms for $90 and up.

The Gamut Realty Group (☎ 212-879-4229) handles a number of long-term apartment rentals, with prices starting at $110 for studios and $125 for one-bedroom apartments. Weekly rates range from $700 to $2000. For more details, visit the Web site www.gamutnyc.com.

A group of 10 East Side hotels has formed the network Manhattan East Side Suites Hotels (☎ 800-637-8483), which rents out kitchen-equipped suites for $170 and up on weekdays ($150 on weekends).

As for specific B&Bs, the ***Broadway Inn Bed & Breakfast*** *(Map 8; ☎ 212-997-9200, 264 W 46th St)*, near Eighth Ave, has become a popular choice in the Times Square area. It edges into the hotel category with rates that range from $100 to $190, including breakfast. Ⓜ N, R, S, 1, 2, 3, 7, 9 to Times Square.

The charming ***Inn at Irving Place*** *(Map 7; ☎ 212-533-4600, 56 Irving Place)*, at E 17th St, has a reputation for romance. Rates at the 12-room townhouse, a few blocks south of Gramercy Park, begin at $250. Ⓜ L, N, R, 4, 5, 6 to 14th St-Union Square.

Inn New York City *(Map 9; ☎ 212-580-1900, fax 580-4437, 266 W 71st St)*, near West End Ave, features four beautifully appointed suites inside an elaborate and well-regarded townhouse. Luxury, however, comes at a price: Daily rates start at $415 (with a free night for every weekly stay). Ⓜ 1, 2, 3, 9 to 72nd St.

On City Island in the Bronx, try ***Le Refuge Inn*** *(☎ 718-885-2478, fax 885-1519, 620 City Island Ave)*, a B&B run by transplanted French chef Pierre Saint-Denis. The eight rooms (four with shared bath) cost $95 and up.

Brooklyn's premier B&B is the romantic ***Bed and Breakfast on the Park*** *(Map 12; ☎ 718-499-8961, fax 499-1385, 113 Prospect Park West)*, between 6th and 7th Sts. It's housed in a beautiful brownstone in Park Slope. Rooms range from $125 to $300 and include breakfast in the formal dining room. To see a 360° rotating view of the various rooms, visit www.bbnyc.com. Ⓜ F to 7th Ave-Park Slope.

For more information on Brooklyn B&Bs, contact the Fund for the Borough of Brooklyn (☎ 718-855-7882, www.brooklynx.org), which publishes a list of locations.

You'll find a basic list of New York B&Bs, with their contact information, at the B&B Locator Web site (www.bnb-locator.com/NewYork/newyork.htm), but the site offers no details on the properties.

HOTELS

Lower Manhattan (Map 5)

Most of the available hotels below Houston St cater to a business clientele, so most offer very good deals on weekends. But don't expect to find a lively scene here on Saturday or on Sunday: The neighborhood dies once the office workers go home. The ***Best Western Seaport Inn*** *(☎ 212-766-6600, fax 766-6615, 800-468-3569, 33 Peck Slip)*, between Front and Water Sts, sits in the shadow of the Brooklyn Bridge at the South Street Seaport. Singles rent for $150. Ⓜ A, C, 2, 3, 4, 5 to Fulton St-Broadway Nassau.

The business-oriented ***Millennium Hilton*** *(☎ 212-693-2001, 800-445-8667, 55 Church St)* rises above the street like a black plinth, though it's still dwarfed by the World Trade Center across the street. Free-spending travelers who want great views pay as much as $400 a night to stay here; rates drop to $250 on weekends and include a buffet breakfast. If you like nightlife, though, look elsewhere. Ⓜ 1, 9, N, R to Cortlandt St.

Tribeca & SoHo (Map 6)

The recently renovated ***Cosmopolitan Hotel*** *(☎ 212-566-1900, 888-895-9400, 95 West Broadway)*, near Chambers St, is taking advantage of the boom in downtown tourism. This 103-room hotel, right above the Chambers St stop on the subway, is cheap for the location. Doubles cost $110 to $140. Ⓜ 1, 2, 3, 9 to Chambers St.

Zoning laws kept hotels out of this neighborhood for years, but a savvy real estate magnate built the ***SoHo Grand Hotel*** *(☎ 212-965-3000, fax 965-3200, 800-965-3000, 310 West Broadway)*, just outside the restricted zone; it's in a well-located spot near Canal St. The exterior of this 367-room facility looks like a college dorm, but inside you'll find Eurotrash central: a cast-iron staircase, a staff dressed in black and models lounging in overstuffed couches along the 2nd-floor bar area. Singles range from $250 to $300, with doubles starting at $250. You can book online at www.sohogrand.com. Ⓜ A, C, E to Canal St.

Chinatown, Little Italy & Lower East Side (Map 6)

If you're on a strict budget, you might try the ***World Hotel*** *(☎ 212-226-5522, fax 219-9498, 101 Bowery)*, between Grand and Hester Sts, which most closely resembles a Chinese-run hotel in Southeast Asia. To stay in one of the 130 tiny rooms at this fairly clean transient place will cost $50/60 for a single/double with shared bath. You'll find several other closet-like 'hotels' near here, but they're flophouses to be avoided. Ⓜ B, D, Q to Grand St; J, M to Bowery.

The ***Pioneer Hotel*** *(☎ 212-226-1482, fax 226-3525, 800-737-0702, 341 Broome St)*, near the Bowery, is a pleasant find on the outskirts of Chinatown. Basic rooms, with sinks and TVs, start at about $75 (slightly more in summer). Ⓜ B, D, Q to Grand St; J, M to Bowery.

If you can ignore the garish interior design, the ***Off SoHo Suites*** *(☎ 212-979-9808, 800-633-7646, 11 Rivington St)*, between Chrystie St and the Bowery on the Lower East Side, offers efficiencies starting at $130, though you may have to share a kitchen with another room. A party of four can book adjoining suites for $200. Ⓜ F to Second Ave.

Holiday Inn Downtown *(☎ 212-966-8898, 138 Lafayette St)*, between Canal and Howard Sts near Chinatown, offers standard chain-motel accommodations in a large 225-room facility. Rates start at $180 for a double, $250 for a suite in summer. Ⓜ J, M, N, R, Z, 6 to Canal St.

Greenwich Village & East Village (Map 6)

A number of hotels and inns downtown cater to gay travelers; see the 'Gay-Friendly Hotels & Inns' boxed text, later in this chapter, for more information.

Appropriately enough, the ***Riverview Hotel*** *(☎ 212-929-0060, 113 Jane St)*, near West St, overlooks the Hudson River. The best feature of this transient hotel is its location in the West Village, just west of some of the neighborhood's most beautiful blocks. Its 220 rooms are spare but cheap, at $43.50/70 for singles/doubles. Ⓜ A, C, E to 14th St; L to Eighth Ave.

RICHARD I'ANSON

Greenwich Village

PLACES TO STAY

A charming 12-room inn, the ***Incentra Village*** *(☎ 212-206-0007, fax 604-0625, 32 Eighth Ave)*, near W 12th St, is booked solid every weekend, partly due to its popularity with gay and lesbian travelers. This well-maintained, quiet place features a lovely parlor. Rates start at $100 for smaller rooms, $130 for suites. Ⓜ A, C, E to 14th St; L to Eighth Ave.

Despite its name, the ***Larchmont Hotel*** *(☎ 212-989-9333, fax 989-9496, 27 W 11th St)* is more of an inn, with shared baths and communal kitchens. The hotel's 52 rooms include sinks and cost $80 to $120. You'll find the Larchmont on a great block just off Fifth Ave. Ⓜ F to 14th St.

The 160-room ***Washington Square Hotel*** *(☎ 212-777-9515, 800-222-0418, 103 Waverly Place)*, between MacDougal St and Sixth Ave, has earned a good reputation for its location and price, but its popularity makes last-minute booking difficult. This used to be a mid-range choice, but rates have climbed in recent years; singles/doubles now cost $150/200. Ⓜ A, B, C, D, E, F to W 4th St.

The ***St Marks Hotel*** *(☎ 212-674-2192, 2 St Marks Place)*, at Third Ave, sits at a great location in the East Village, but the block is noisy and you won't want to inquire about the activities of your neighbors. Rooms start at $80.

Chelsea, Flatiron District & Gramercy Park (Map 7)

The ***Chelsea Inn*** *(☎ 212-645-8989, 46 W 17th St)*, between Fifth and Sixth Aves, consists of a set of joined townhouses that contain both private and shared bathrooms. Rates at this clean and popular spot range from $100 to $160. Ⓜ L, N, R, 4, 5, 6 to 14th St-Union Square.

Once a low-cost hangout, the ***Chelsea Hotel*** *(☎ 212-243-3700, 222 W 23rd St)*, near Seventh Ave, is now cashing in on its fame as a literary landmark. Some rooms are better than others, and you never know what

Gay-Friendly Hotels & Inns

Several hotels cater almost exclusively to gays and lesbians, and you'll find the bulk of them in SoHo, Greenwich Village and Chelsea. Be sure to make reservations at least a month in advance for these popular gay-friendly spots.

In Greenwich Village, try ***Incentra Village*** and the ***Washington Square Hotel*** (for more on both of these, see Greenwich Village & East Village in the Hotels section). The ***East Village B&B*** *(Map 6; ☎ 212-260-1865, 252 E 7th St)* tends to attract lesbians.

Fast eclipsing Greenwich Village as the city's prime gay neighborhood, Chelsea contains a number of accommodations where gay and lesbian travelers should feel particularly comfortable. ***Chelsea Pines Inn*** *(Map 7; ☎ 212-929-1023, 317 W 14th St)*, between Eighth and Ninth Aves, and the ***Colonial House Inn*** *(Map 7; ☎ 212-243-9669, 800-689-3779, 318 W 22nd St)*, between Eighth and Ninth Aves, both offer rooms for around $150 a night. The famous ***Chelsea Hotel*** is a pricier option (see Chelsea, Flatiron District & Gramercy Park under Hotels). Closer to Midtown, ***Grand Union*** *(Map 7; ☎ 212-683-5890, 34 E 32nd St)*, between Park and Madison Aves, offers comfortable accommodations starting at $130.

For more information, contact the Lesbian & Gay Community Services Center (Map 6; ☎ 212-620-7310, www.gaycenter.org), temporarily located at 1 Little W 12th St. (At press time, the center's headquarters at 208 W 13th St were undergoing a lengthy renovation, scheduled to be completed in summer or fall of 2001). The *Out & About Newsletter* (☎ 800-929-2268, www.outandabout.com) also provides information about gay-friendly hotels in New York City (as well as restaurants, clubs, gyms and shops).

you'll get. Whatever you do, don't ask for Sid Vicious' room (since remodeled and renumbered) – the front desk clerk will snicker. A limited number of shared bathrooms cost $80 a night, but they're nearly always booked. Prices for rooms with private baths have climbed in recent years and now start at $140. Ⓜ 1, 9 to 23rd St.

Near the Chelsea Hotel is the lower-priced ***Chelsea Savoy Hotel*** *(☎ 212-929-9353, fax 741-6309, 204 W 23rd St)*, near Seventh Ave. Rooms range from $115 to $180. Ⓜ 1, 9 to 23rd St.

The ***Senton Hotel*** *(☎ 212-684-5800, 39-41 W 27th St)*, near Sixth Ave, has attracted travelers with its central location, but overwhelming complaints about its staff and the condition of its rooms mean we can't recommend it, even at just $50 a night. Ⓜ 6 to 28th St.

The ***Gramercy Park Hotel*** *(☎ 212-475-4320, 800-221-4083, 2 Lexington Ave)*, at the corner of E 21st St and Lexington Ave, overlooks Gramercy Park. Be sure to check out the dark bar off the lobby. Singles start at $165. Ⓜ 6 to 23rd St.

Hotel 17 *(☎ 212-475-2845, 225 E 17th St)*, between Second and Third Aves, remains a popular Gramercy Park choice, although its bad reputation for overbooking has triggered a number of complaints. Rooms start at $100. Ⓜ 6 to 23rd St.

If you're not lucky enough to get a spot in the Gershwin Hotel (see Hostels, earlier), you can always resort to the cheap, but far less desirable, ***Madison Hotel*** *(☎ 212-532-7373, fax 686-0092, 800-962-3476, 21 E 27th St)*, near Madison Ave, just a few steps away from the Gerswhin. Very spare rooms with private bath cost $60/80 for a single/double. (No matter what the desk clerk demands, don't pay for your entire stay in advance. Continue trying to book a room at the Gershwin for subsequent nights.) Ⓜ 6 to 28th St.

You'll find a number of reasonably priced hotels on Park Ave south of Grand Central Terminal, an unremarkable but busy stretch of road between Midtown and the Flatiron District. ***Howard Johnson on Park Ave*** *(☎ 212-532-4860, fax 545-9727, 800-446-4656, 429 Park Ave South)*, between E 28th and 29th Sts, offers comfortable rooms starting at $119. Ⓜ 6 to 28th St.

Midtown (Map 7)

Budget & Mid-Range Budget travelers will find several inexpensive places near Herald Square. The non-chain choices are generally okay, so long as you don't expect luxury accommodations for less than $100 a night.

The ***Wolcott Hotel*** *(☎ 212-268-2900, 4 W 31st St)*, near Fifth Ave, is a 280-room beaux arts hotel designed by John Duncan, the architect of Grant's Tomb. Rates start at $100. Ⓜ B, D, F, N, Q, R to 34th St-Herald Square.

The no-frills ***Herald Square Hotel*** *(☎ 212-279-4017, 800-727-1888, 19 W 31st St)*, between Broadway and Fifth Ave, hasn't raised its rates too much in the last several years. A small room with a shared bath runs about $50 ($55 for a private bath). Doubles begin at $75. Ⓜ B, D, F, N, Q, R to 34th St-Herald Square.

A short walk away from the Empire State Building, ***Hotel 31*** *(☎ 212-685-3060, 120 E 31st St)*, between Park Ave South and Lexington Ave, offers rooms in an 80-year-old building. Comfortable rooms with private bath go for about $110. Ⓜ B, D, F, N, Q, R to 34th St-Herald Square.

Hotel Stanford *(☎ 212-563-1500, fax 643-0157, 800-365-1114, 43 W 32nd St)*, between Broadway and Fifth Ave, is a good choice right in the middle of Little Korea near Herald Square. Rooms run $110 to $160, including continental breakfast. You can eat at all hours at the 24-hour restaurant on the premises. Ⓜ B, D, F, N, Q, R to 34th St-Herald Square.

Holiday Inn Broadway *(☎ 212-736-3800, fax 631-0449, 800-465-4329, 49 W 32nd St)*, at Broadway, shows how much this neighborhood has improved in recent years. Once a notoriously filthy welfare hotel, it now offers 525 decent, if uninspiring, chain-motel rooms. Rates begin at $100. Ⓜ B, D, F, N, Q, R to 34th St-Herald Square.

The ***Hotel Metro*** *(☎ 212-947-2500, fax 279-1310, 800-356-3870, 45 W 35th St)*, between Fifth and Sixth Aves, combines '30s art deco (its lobby walls feature movie posters from Hollywood's golden era) with the comfort of a gentlemen's club in its attractive lounge and library area. Upstairs you'll find rather plain rooms, but the price ($145 to $195) and location (near the Morgan Library and the Empire State Building) make this 160-room hotel a worthy choice. Ⓜ B, D, F, N, Q, R to 34th St-Herald Square.

The Italian-owned ***Jolly Madison Towers*** *(☎ 212-802-0600, fax 447-0747,800-225-4340, 22 E 38th St)*, between Park and Madison Aves, attracts a lot of Latin American tourists, who like to hang out in its wonderfully tacky Whaler Bar. Rates start at $150, but these are gradually rising as the hotel undergoes a complete renovation (it remains to be seen whether the hotel will do away with the Whaler's kitschy charm). Ⓜ 4, 5, 6, 7 to Grand Central.

Just around the corner from the New York Public Library, you'll find the ***Clarion Hotel*** *(☎ 212-447-1500, 800-252-7466, 3 E 40th St)*, between Fifth and Madison Aves. The 186-room business hotel discounts its $180 regular rates on weekends, when occupancy drops. Ⓜ 4, 5, 6, 7 to Grand Central.

Furnishings are a bit frayed at the 400-room ***Pickwick Arms Hotel*** *(☎ 212-355-0300, fax 755-5029, 800-742-5945, 230 E 51st St)*, between Second and Third Aves, but European budget travelers like the place anyway. Rates start at $100. Ⓜ 6 to 51st St; E, F to Lexington Ave.

Best Western operates the ***Woodward Hotel*** *(☎ 212-247-2000, fax 581-2248, 800-336-4110, 210 W 55th St)*, near Seventh Ave. Rooms at this quiet spot not far from Carnegie Hall start at $160/180. The hotel also offers access to a good local gym. Ⓜ N, R to 57th St.

A block south of Carnegie Hall, the ***Hotel Wellington*** *(☎ 212-247-3900, 800-652-1212, 871 Seventh Ave)*, at 55th St, has 700 rather unremarkable rooms that cost $155. Ⓜ N, R to 57th St.

Whether you're in the mood for high-brow or low-brow entertainment, you'll find both within a few feet of the ***Salisbury Hotel*** *(☎ 212-246-1300, 888-692-5757, 123 W 57th St)*, between Sixth and Seventh Aves. It stands virtually across from Carnegie Hall and Planet Hollywood. Rooms start at $189. Ⓜ N, R, B, Q to 57th St.

Just south of Columbus Circle is the ***Westpark Hotel*** *(☎ 212-246-6440, fax 246-3131, 800-248-6440, 308 W 58th St)*, between Eighth and Ninth Aves. Its word-of-mouth popularity with European travelers makes it tough to book a room here in the summer. Suites start at $180. Ⓜ A, B, C, D, 1, 9 to 59th St-Columbus Circle.

Top End Rates at most of the expensive Midtown hotels start at $200 but fluctuate greatly according to seasonal demand – ie, they often go up, but they don't usually fall below that mark.

The European *gliterati* like to stay at ***Morgan's*** *(☎ 212-686-0300, fax 779-8352, 800-334-3408, 237 Madison Ave)*, between 37th and 38th Sts, a sleek hotel with no sign. Rates start at $280 for singles, $320 for doubles and $350 for suites. Ⓜ 4, 5, 6, 7 to Grand Central.

Publishing executives still love to lunch at the ***Royalton*** *(☎ 212-869-4400, fax 869-8965, 800-635-9013, 44 W 44th St)*, between Fifth and Sixth Aves, which makes the A-list restaurant difficult to book, but hotel reservations are easier to come by. Rates for doubles start at $315. Ⓜ B, D, F, Q to 42nd St.

Across the street, the ***Algonquin*** *(☎ 212-840-6800, fax 944-1419, 800-555-8000, 59 W 44th St)*, between Fifth and Sixth Aves, still attracts visitors with its romantic reputation as the home of the 1930s literary circle known as the Algonquin Round Table, but some of its small, cramped rooms might disappoint, especially at $300-plus per night. Ⓜ B, D, F, Q to 42nd St.

Formerly a poorer version of the Algonquin, the 1920s-era ***Hotel Iroquois*** *(☎ 212-840-3080, fax 719-0006, 800-332-7220, 49 W 44th St)*, between Fifth and Sixth Aves, has undergone a complete renovation that overlooked no detail, including the attire of the hotel staff (they now wear designer clothes). Rates for the 100-plus rooms and suites range from $275 to $575. Ⓜ B, D, F, Q to 42nd St.

The legendary ***Waldorf Astoria*** *(☎ 212-355-3000, 800-925-3673, 301 Park Ave)*, between 49th and 50th Sts, has hosted fundraising dinners for members of the British royal family, among other notable events. The hotel features a quietly elegant lobby (surprisingly not as grand as you would expect) and restaurants and bars that charge prices befitting the Waldorf's reputation; middle-aged executives frequent the smoky Bull & Bear pub, in search of a bit of company for the evening. Rates range from $199 to $330 for a standard room, though weekend specials bring the price down to about $200. Ⓜ 6 to 51st St; E, F to Lexington Ave.

A storied old Midtown hotel near Rockefeller Center, the ***Warwick*** *(☎ 212-247-2700, fax 489-3926, 800-223-4099, 65 W 54th St)*, near Sixth Ave, has been renovated in recent years and offers 400-plus rooms that count as spacious by Manhattan standards. Rates start at $230. Ⓜ B, D, F, Q to 47th-50th Sts/Rockefeller Center.

Once known as the Gotham Hotel, the ***Peninsula*** *(☎ 212-956-2888, 800-262-9467, 700 Fifth Ave)*, at 55th St, dates back to 1904, making it one of the oldest surviving grand hotels in Midtown. The totally renovated hotel includes a spa and athletic club that sprawls over three floors; the pool is almost big enough for laps. Rates are $340 and up for doubles only. Ⓜ E, F to Fifth Ave.

Across the street, the beaux arts ***St Regis*** *(☎ 212-753-4500, 800-759-7550, 2 E 55th St)*, at Fifth Ave, is well-known for its huge electronic taxi call sign and its King Cole bar, which features a Maxfield Parrish mural that was moved from the old Knickerbocker Hotel in Times Square. Its double rooms start at $425. Ⓜ E, F to Fifth Ave.

IM Pei designed the ***Four Seasons*** *(☎ 800-332-3442, 57 E 57th St)*, at Park Ave, a limestone monolith with 52 floors, all full of spacious rooms that don't come cheap. Rates begin at $495 (on a weekend) and continue up to $2500 or more for a suite. Ⓜ N, R to Fifth Ave.

Home of the famous Oak Room, the ***Plaza Hotel*** *(☎ 212-759-3000, fax 546-5324, 800-527-4727, 768 Fifth Ave)*, between 58th

MICHELLE BENNETT

No shirt, no shoes, no service

PLACES TO STAY

and 59th Sts, has attracted some high-profile customers, including none other than the Beatles, Cary Grant and Grace Kelly. Rates begin at $350. Ⓜ N, R to Fifth Ave.

For information on hotels above 59th St, see the Upper West Side and Upper East Side sections, later.

Times Square (Map 8)

Budget & Mid-Range If you need a room on short notice, try the ***Hotel Carter*** *(☎ 212-944-6000, fax 398-8541, 800-553-3415, 250 W 43rd St)*, between Seventh and Eighth Aves. This huge old hotel has steadfastly lagged behind the rest of the neighborhood in gentrification, which means that rates drop as low as $90. But stay here only at your own risk: In the summer of 1999, a front desk clerk died at the hotel after a fellow employee stabbed him. Ⓜ N, R, S, 1, 2, 3, 7, 9 to Times Square.

The Ramada chain owns the 1300-room ***Milford Plaza*** *(☎ 212-869-3600, fax 944-8357, 800-272-6232, 270 W 45th St)*, near Eighth Ave. The standard hotel often attracts out-of-town bus tours and airline crews. Rooms start at $100, with discounts for special three-day-weekend deals. Ⓜ N, R, S, 1, 2, 3, 7, 9 to Times Square.

Across the street from Restaurant Row, the ***Broadway Bed and Breakfast Inn*** *(☎ 212-997-9200, fax 768-2807, 800-826-6300, 264 W 46th St)*, near Eighth Ave, used to be a rundown Times Square hotel, but it's now a reasonably priced small inn with 42 neat rooms. Room rates range from $135 to $225. Ⓜ N, R, S, 1, 2, 3, 7, 9 to Times Square.

Just steps away from the middle of Times Square, the renovated and clean ***Portland Square Hotel*** *(☎ 212-382-0600, fax 382-0684, 800-388-8988, 132 W 47th St)*, between Sixth and Seventh Aves, offers a limited number of rooms with shared bath for $60; private rooms start at $99. Ⓜ B, D, F, Q to Rockefeller Center.

Once a high-class spot for Broadway stars, the ***Hotel Edison*** *(☎ 212-840-5000, fax 596-6868, 800-637-7070, 228 W 47th St)*, between Broadway and Eighth Ave, caters to tourists now, though theater people still hang out in its colorful coffee shop. Rates start at $130. Ⓜ 1, 9 to 50th St; N, R to 49th St.

Operated by the Days Inn chain, ***Days Hotel Midtown*** *(☎ 212-581-7000, 800-544-8313, 790 Eighth Ave)*, at W 48th St, offers bland rooms for $120 to $180. Ⓜ N, R, S, 1, 2, 3, 7, 9 to Times Square.

The ***Ameritania Hotel*** *(☎ 212-247-5000, fax 751-7868, 800-664-6835, 230 W 54th St)*, at Broadway, stands next door to the Ed Sullivan Theater, where David Letterman's *Late Show* is taped. European bus tours in particular like this moderately priced hotel, which looks like a futuristic disco. The desk clerks usually knock off 10% from the regular room rates, which start at $130, if you tell them that you heard about the hotel in a guidebook. The hotel's Web site (www.nycityhotels.net) also offers Internet discounts, which can drop the price of a basic room as low as $99. Ⓜ B, D, E to Seventh Ave.

Top End Top-end hotels around Times Square charge $200 or more a night but don't really offer much distinction; you're paying for their location. These places do offer certain security features: loud lighting and lobbies set back from the street to discourage loitering. They include the ***Marriott Marquis*** *(☎ 212-398-1900, 800-843-4898, 1535 Broadway)*, between 45th and 46th Sts; the ***Novotel*** *(☎ 212-315-0100, 800-668-6835, 226 W 52nd St)*, near Broadway; and the more luxurious ***Doubletree Guest Suites*** *(☎ 212-719-1600, 800-222-8733)*, at the corner of Seventh Ave and 47th St. Ⓜ N, R, S, 1, 2, 3, 7, 9 to Times Square.

If you're looking for more character, try the ***Paramount Hotel*** *(☎ 212-764-5500, fax 575-4892, 800-225-7474, 235 W 46th St)*, between Broadway and Eighth Ave. It's an artsy place that prides itself on the small details, including flowers in every room. The hotel houses the Whiskey Bar, an ultra-hip hangout spot in the early '90s. Rooms average $200. Ⓜ 1, 9 to 50th St.

Upper West Side (Map 9)

You'll find a good selection of mid-range hotels in this part of town. Most of them charge $90 to $200.

ANGUS OBORN

View of the Upper West Side from Central Park

The slightly stodgy ***Mayflower*** *(☎ 212-265-0060, 15 Central Park West)*, near W 61st St, contains more than 500 rooms and often offers special deals for three-day weekends. Rates go as low as $169 and as high as $400. Ⓜ A, B, C, D, 1, 9 to 59th St-Columbus Circle.

The ***Hotel Olcott*** *(☎ 212-877-4200, 27 W 72nd St)*, between Columbus Ave and Central Park West, enjoys a nice location, just steps away from the W 72nd St entrance to Central Park. Permanent residents occupy most of this old residence hotel, but visitors who secure a room will enjoy a relative bargain. Singles start at $90. Book early. Ⓜ B, C to 72nd St.

The ***Broadway American Hotel*** *(☎ 212-362-1100, 800-509-7598, 2178 Broadway)*, near W 77th St, attracts visitors with its moderate rates starting at $145. Ⓜ 1, 9 to 79th St.

The ***Excelsior Hotel*** *(☎ 212-362-9200, fax 721-2994, 800-368-4575, 45 W 81st St)*, near Columbus Ave, overlooks the American Museum of Natural History. Rates at this old, 169-room hotel start at $160 for a single, $200 for a two-room suite. Ⓜ B, C to 81st St-Museum of Natural History.

The 96-room ***Newtown*** *(☎ 212-678-6500, 800-463-5553, 2528 Broadway)*, between 94th and 95th Sts, offers a more intimate alternative to the big West Side hotels. Rates start at $99. Ⓜ 1, 2, 3, 9 to 96th St.

Upper East Side (Map 9)

Some of New York's most elegant and expensive hotels are near Fifth and Madison Aves on the Upper East Side. The elegant ***Sherry-Netherland Hotel*** *(☎ 212-355-2800, 800-247-4377, 781 Fifth Ave)*, between 59th and 60th Sts, features Central Park views from many of its 70-plus rooms. Regular rooms start at $310, and suites go as high as $875. Ⓜ N, R to Fifth Ave.

If you have $300 or more to spend, you can enjoy the quiet elegance of the ***Pierre Hotel*** *(☎ 212-838-8000, 800-332-3442, 2 E 61st St)*, at Fifth Ave. Ⓜ N, R to Fifth Ave.

The intimate and quiet 61-room ***Lowell Hotel*** *(☎ 212-838-1400, fax 319-4230, 800-221-4444, 28 E 63rd St)*, between Park and Madison Aves, ranks as the of-the-moment place favored by celebrities such as Brad Pitt. Rates start at $350. Ⓜ B, Q to Lexington Ave.

The storied ***Carlyle Hotel*** *(☎ 212-744-1600, 35 E 76th St)*, at Madison Ave, ranks among the crown jewels of Upper East Side hotels. The *très* elegant, European-style hostelry features cabaret singer Bobby Short in its lounge. Rates range from $300 to more than $1000. Ⓜ 6 to 77th St.

For a cheaper alternative, try the 12-room ***Gracie Inn*** *(☎ 212-628-1700, fax 628-6420, 800-404-2252, 502 E 81st St)*, between York and East End Aves. Rooms at this undiscovered country-style inn near the East River start at $175, including a good breakfast.

The ***Franklin*** *(☎ 212-369-1000, 164 E 87th St)*, between Third and Lexington Aves, is a standard hotel with 53 rooms that cost $245 and up. Ⓜ 4, 5, 6 to 86th St.

The century-old ***Hotel Wales*** *(☎ 212-876-6000, fax 860-7000, 877-847-4444, 1295 Madison Ave)*, at 92nd St, returned to its former glory a few years ago, when architects reintroduced some Victorian architectural details that'll make you wonder if you're in San Francisco. Its 100 rooms start at $245 and include a continental breakfast. You can make reservations online at www.waleshotel.com. Ⓜ B, C to 96th St.

Brooklyn (Map 11)

It's a real indication of the hotel boom that Brooklyn has gotten its first full-service hotel in more than 50 years. The impressive ***New York Brooklyn Marriott*** *(☎ 718-246-7000, fax 246-0563, 800-436-3759, 333 Adams St)*, between Tillary and Willoughby Sts, contains 376 rooms, a restaurant and a health club, all spread out on the lower floors of an office building. This Brooklyn Heights spot offers strategic advantages: It's closer to JFK International Airport than any hotels in Manhattan, and it's only a short subway ride away from Midtown. Rooms average $145 to $310, with some discounts available. Ⓜ M, N, R to Lawrence St; A, C, F to Jay St-Borough Hall.

Places to Eat

FOOD

If you decided to eat in a different restaurant every night in New York City, 46 years would pass before you ran out of options. Only Paris offers a greater selection of elegant culinary experiences; and at the opposite end of the spectrum, absolutely no other city can beat New York's selection of reasonably priced restaurants. As French chef Alain Ducasse has observed, 'The two most pampered and spoiled publics in the world – the two cities where the meals to be had are the most sophisticated, the most varied, the most intelligent – are New York and Paris.' But even the master admits that 'in absolute terms, there is more variety in New York. I myself am seduced by what's offered there.'

Although New York offers plenty of culinary bargains, a number of the restaurants here could also put a serious dent in your vacation budget. Don't be shy about asking about the cost of a meal; most waiters, whatever the price level of a restaurant, neglect to tell you the cost of off-menu 'specials' or recommended wines. And if you're looking for a night of drinking, do it at a bar, not a restaurant, where proprietors make a healthy profit on drink markups.

Visitors with extremely limited funds can always cobble together a decent and healthy lunch from one of the fruit stands set up on major avenues all over the city. At the numerous stands along Broadway on the Upper West Side, you can stock up on provisions for a picnic or quick snack.

For a comprehensive list of the city's better bets in dining, pick up a copy of the ever-popular *Zagat Survey*, available at bookstores all over the city. Restaurant reviews also appear weekly in *Time Out* and *New York* magazine and in the Weekend section of Friday's *New York Times)*.

DRINKS

You'll be able to get every kind of libation in the city, but this is a particularly good era for beer, as New York leads the microbrewery movement. The first 'new' beer to be brewed in the city was Brooklyn Lager, now a successful nationally distributed brand. If you head to ***Chumley's*** *(☎ 212-675-4449, 86 Bedford St)*, at the corner of Barrow St in Greenwich Village, or the ***Brooklyn Brewery*** *(☎ 718-486-7422, 79 N 11th St)*, between Wythe Ave and Berry St in Williamsburg, Brooklyn, you'll be able to sample home-grown stuff.

The ***Blind Tiger Ale House*** *(☎ 212-675-3848, 518 Hudson St)*, at W 10th St in the West Village, may be the single best place to sample an array of interesting beer. Look out for the brands Yellow Taxi, Neptune and

Five-Star Dining at Two-Star Prices

Most budget travelers can't even consider eating at the temples of New York cuisine, many of which keep out the riffraff by charging $50 and up per person for a meal. But the rich and famous must have started to bore New York's more elite restaurateurs, and in a stunning democratic move they've begun opening their dining rooms to the little people during the biannual 'Restaurant Week.' Held for one week in February and one week in June each year, Restaurant Week offers some elaborate three-course lunches to those with a mere $20 in their pocket. More than 85 restaurants participate, including such premier spots as Tavern on the Green, Aquavit and Union Pacific. True foodies travel to the city just for this event, then spend each Restaurant Week dashing around town with a well-thumbed Zagat's guide in hand. But you must book your tables in advance, often on the first day that these restaurants start accepting reservations for Restaurant Week. For more information, visit the Web site www.newyork.citysearch.com and search for 'Restaurant Week.'

Knickerbocker. Other new microbreweries are opening all over the place, so you probably won't have to look far and wide to find one.

For detailed listings of places to drink in New York, see the Bars & Lounges section of the Entertainment chapter.

LOWER MANHATTAN (Map 5)

The no-frills Indian restaurant ***Pearl Palace*** *(☎ 212-482-0771, 60 Pearl St)*, near Broad St, fuels brokers from nearby Wall St firms. The bargain all-you-can-eat buffet lunch (offered 11 am to 2:30 pm weekdays) costs only $8 and includes a salad bar. Pearl Palace is open around the clock daily. Ⓜ N, R to Whitehall St.

A few steps away, ***Zigolini's*** *(☎ 212-425-7171, 66 Pearl St)*, near Broad St, specializes in filling focaccia sandwiches, all for under $8. (Some of the specials are named after customers who suggested them.) Ⓜ N, R to Whitehall St.

The touristy South Street Seaport features a number of restaurants, few of them better than an average McDonald's. The ***North Star Pub*** *(☎ 212-509-6757, 93 South St)*, near Fulton St, fashions itself after a British pub and serves traditional pub fare like bangers and mash. Office workers pack the place on weekdays. Ⓜ 2, 3 to Fulton St.

If you can afford to spend a few more bucks, take a little detour to the more worthwhile ***Bridge Cafe*** *(☎ 212-227-3344, 279 Water St)*, at Dover St, a homey haven underneath the Brooklyn Bridge. Certified as the oldest pub in the city, the restaurant offers an extensive wine list and pasta, meat and seafood entrees that average $16. Ⓜ 4, 5, 6 to Brooklyn Bridge-City Hall.

Those on expense accounts should ride the elevator to the 107th floor of the World Trade Center and try the pricey ***Windows on the World*** *(☎ 212-524-7011, One World Trade Center)*, near the intersection of Vesey and West Sts. You won't find a more spectacular view anywhere in the city. The menu favors trendy experiments in New American cuisine. Sunday brunch is also offered. Ⓜ N, R, 1, 9 to Cortlandt St.

TRIBECA (Map 6)

In recent years, Tribeca has overtaken SoHo as the trendiest dining spot in the city, but despite the neighborhood's rise in status, you can still find a healthy selection of moderately priced restaurants.

Bubby's *(☎ 212-219-0666, 120 Hudson St)*, at N Moore St, packs 'em in on weekends with its breakfast fare. At lunch and dinner, the big, breezy restaurant features healthy salads, sandwiches, pastas and what some claim are New York's best burgers. Entrees, which include a number of vegetarian options, range from $9 to $20. If you have kids, the crayons handed out here should keep them occupied for hours. Ⓜ 1, 9 to Franklin St.

The dark watering hole ***Walkers*** *(☎ 212-941-0142, 16 N Moore St)*, at Varick St, serves tasty straightforward fare – turkey sandwiches and burgers with a gourmet twist for under $10. A laid-back, homey feel pervades the three dining rooms, with tables covered in checkered cloths and poems taped up in the bathrooms. Sunday may be the best time to visit: In the morning, come for the reasonable brunch; at night, stop by to hear live jazz combos (no cover charge). Ⓜ 1, 9 to Franklin St.

Odeon *(☎ 212-233-0507, 145 West Broadway)*, between Thomas and Dwayne Sts, buzzes with a smart, happy crowd feasting on lamb sandwiches or risotto with truffle oil, wild mushrooms and the like. Unlike some of its trendy '80s counterparts, this fancy diner has managed to thrive all the way through the 1990s and still attracts crowds with moderately priced bistro fare (dinner entrees range from $16 to $30). Odeon stays open until at least 2 am daily (3 am on Friday and Saturday, so you can enjoy the view of the World Trade Center until well into the night. Ⓜ 1, 2, 3, 9 to Chambers St.

Riverrun *(☎ 212-966-3894, 176 Franklin St)*, between Hudson and Greenwich Sts, considers itself a pioneer in the Tribeca dining scene, but the quality of its trendy American cuisine has seriously declined in recent years. You're better off going here for a drink after dinner, since it's still a great neighborhood bar – the jukebox is the cheapest in the city at 10¢ per play. Ⓜ 1, 9 to Franklin St.

The spare ***Montrachet*** *(☎ 212-219-2777, 239 West Broadway)*, between Walker and White Sts, doesn't offer much in the way of decor, but its Friday-only lunchtime specials ($20) do come at a relative bargain for Tribeca. Here you'll find more of the gourmet French-American cuisine the neighborhood tends to favor (offerings include warm braised rabbit salad and roasted sweetbreads with Parmesan jus). The extravagant tasting menu costs $75 for dinner. Ⓜ 1, 9 to Franklin St.

Make reservations weeks or months in advance at ***Chanterelle*** *(☎ 212-966-6960, 2 Harrison St)*, near Hudson St, a romantic French restaurant that offers a fixed-price dinner menu for around $80 per person. Its changing menu often features a heavenly seafood sausage, among other examples of world-class cuisine. Finish off your dinner with the sublime cheese platter. Ⓜ 1, 9 to Franklin St.

This oh-so-trendy sushi restaurant ***Nobu*** *(☎ 212-219-0500, 105 Hudson St)*, at the corner of Franklin St, has taken chichi dining in Manhattan to a new level of insanity. In order to make a mere reservation, you must give out your credit card number – you'll face a $25-per-person charge if anyone neglects to show up. Nobu's tasting menu *(omakase)*, prepared by hot chef Nobuyuki Matsuhisa, begins at $75, and while some say it's worth the price, the sometimes inattentive service can make the whole evening feel like a complete rip-off – you're better

ANGUS OBORN

PLACES TO EAT

The Classics

In a town with no shortage of museums and theaters, a handful of restaurants have managed to become major cultural attractions in their own right. People now make pilgrimages to famous spots like Tavern on the Green as much for the experience of eating there as for the food itself – which can mean that some chefs at these classic restaurants are starting to sit back and rake in the tourist dollars instead of producing innovative cuisine. Still, a memorable meal at one of these famous places sure makes a good story for the folks back home, even if the food doesn't taste quite as exotic as the great kimchi and mung-bean pancakes you had in Little Korea. Be prepared for big bills at these celebrated standbys.

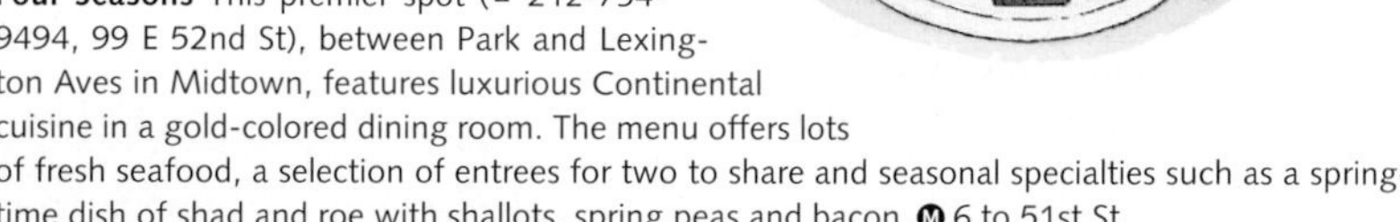

Four Seasons This premier spot (☎ 212-754-9494, 99 E 52nd St), between Park and Lexington Aves in Midtown, features luxurious Continental cuisine in a gold-colored dining room. The menu offers lots of fresh seafood, a selection of entrees for two to share and seasonal specialties such as a springtime dish of shad and roe with shallots, spring peas and bacon. Ⓜ 6 to 51st St.

Le Cirque 2000 Filled with fine crystal and china settings lightened up by amusing touches (especially those of pastry chef Jacques Torres), this elegant spot in the Palace Hotel (☎ 212-303-7788, 455 Madison Ave), between 50th and 51st Sts in Midtown, features a nightly 'classic' as well as a menu full of innovative, serious cuisine. Ⓜ 6 to 51st St.

21 The classic spot for ladies who lunch, this club-like place (☎ 212-582-7200, 21 W 52nd St), between Fifth and Sixth Aves in Midtown, serves traditional fare and flaming desserts to business people and tourists who sit in leather banquettes and pretend they're characters in a Prohibition-era novel. Ⓜ E, F to Fifth Ave.

Russian Tea Room Remodeled in 1999, the Russian Tea Room (☎ 212-974-2111, 150 W 57th St), between Sixth and Seventh Aves in Midtown, conjures an over-the-top opulence in a two-story mirrored room hung with giant chandeliers and upholstered in plush red and purple. It serves 'modern Russian cuisine' that's heavy on meat, caviar and smoked fish. Ⓜ N, R to 57th St.

Tavern on the Green The most profitable restaurant in the USA, Tavern on the Green (☎ 212-873-3200), Central Park West at W 67th St on the Upper West Side, pulls in an astounding $35 million annually from visitors who want to admire the crystal chandeliers and topiary statues in the back garden. Despite a new chef in 1999 and some positive reviews, it's still largely a tourist trap – and an expensive one, at that. Ⓜ B, C to 72nd St.

– Erin Corrigan

off going to the far cheaper sushi restaurants on E 9th St off Third Ave (see the 'Culinary Corners' boxed text). Ⓜ 1, 9 to Franklin St.

CHINATOWN (Map 6)

As you might expect, Chinatown features quite a cluster of Asian restaurants, all within a few blocks of each other. Most Chinatown restaurants (including those listed here) offer bargain meals, with appetizers for around $5 and entrees for $10 or less.

To reach any of the following spots, take the subway to the Canal St stations at Broadway, Lafayette or Centre Sts (Ⓜ J, M, N, R, Z, 6 to Canal St).

Everyone in New York has a favorite restaurant in Chinatown. Former mayor Ed Koch seems to like ***Peking Duck House*** *(☎ 212-227-1810, 28 Mott St)*, between Pell and Mosco Sts. If you decide to follow his example, stick with the standard fare; this restaurant may have seen better days.

Vegetarians who still pine for the taste of meat should head to ***Vegetarian Paradise 3*** *(☎ 212-406-6988, 33 Mott St)*, near Pell St, a good and cheap option that serves faux versions of just about every meat you can imagine, from ham to lamb. In a similar vein, the vegan-oriented ***House of Vegetarian*** *(☎ 212-226-6572, 68 Mott St)*, near Bayard St, prepares barbecue 'pork' and 'duck' dishes ($7 to $12) that taste so much like the real thing you'll wonder if the entire menu is a trick.

Hay Wun Loy *(☎ 212-285-8686, 28-30 Pell St)*, near Doyers St, specializes in fresh fish right out of the tank and also offers dim sum. The basement-level ***Hong Ying Rice Shop*** *(☎ 212-349-6126, 11 Mott St)*, near Chatham Square, serves classic dishes, such as shrimp with black bean sauce, for around $9.

In recent years, a number of Vietnamese restaurants have also found a home in Chinatown. ***Nha Trang*** *(☎ 212-233-5948, 87 Baxter St)*, near Bayard St, attracts a lunchtime crowd of jurors and lawyers from the nearby city courthouses; they eat at crowded tables with other strangers. You can enjoy a filling meal for less than $10 if you stick with basic dishes like barbecued beef on rice vermicelli and shrimp spring rolls. Wash it all down with the super-rich but delicious Vietnamese-style coffee with sweetened condensed milk. Next door, ***New Pasteur*** *(☎ 212-608-3656, 85 Baxter St)*, near Bayard St, serves a virtually identical menu.

The food at ***Pho Viet Huong***, *(☎ 212-233-8988, 73 Mulberry St)*, near Canal St, far surpasses the decor, so don't be scared away by the dinky little bamboo courtyard theme. The menu here will overwhelm you with great choices, none of them too greasy. The Vietnamese clay-pot curries and fondues arrive burbling, and the vegetables come crispy and glistening. Entree prices range from $7 to $12.

The ***Thailand Restaurant*** *(☎ 212-349-3132, 106 Bayard St)*, between Baxter and Mulberry Sts, offers the most authentic Thai dishes outside of Bangkok, including the particularly good spicy vegetarian soup for two – it's the closest thing to a cure for the common cold.

Just a bit farther afield, on the stretch of East Broadway that runs east from Chatham Square to the Manhattan Bridge, you'll find a number of ethnic restaurants and food stands that cater to locals. The ***Nice Restaurant*** *(☎ 212-406-9776, 35 East Broadway)*, between Catherine and Market Sts, offers fancy Hong Kong–style food. While you're there, you might see wedding parties heading toward the popular 2nd-floor banquet room.

LITTLE ITALY (Map 6)

A good rule of thumb while looking for a restaurant in Little Italy is to avoid any place where the manager hangs out in the street trying to drum up business.

During summer months, the two blocks of Mulberry St north of Canal St close to traffic so that the small restaurants here can set up outdoor tables. Most of the places with al fresco dining offer entrees for $15 and under, and if you stick with pasta, you can't go far wrong. When the bill comes, though, examine it carefully: Some Little Italy restaurants add a 25% service charge to the bill if the waiter pegs you for a tourist.

A local institution, ***Benito One*** *(☎ 212-226-9171, 174 Mulberry St)*, between Grand and Broome Sts, bills itself as the neighborhood's last authentic Italian restaurant. Entrees range from your basic spaghetti ($7) to a grilled seafood plate with shrimp, mussels and clams ($24, all served in a colorful dining room). Ⓜ 6 to Spring St; J, M to Bowery.

For pizza, try the truly legendary ***Lombardi's*** *(☎ 212-941-7994, 32 Spring St)*, between Mott and Mulberry Sts, indisputably the oldest pizza restaurant in New York. Established in 1905, this brick-oven pizzeria serves only pizza pies and huge calzones, delicious half-moon dough shells stuffed with ricotta cheese and herbs. The fresh mushroom pie comes with three different types of mushrooms. Ⓜ 6 to Spring St.

By far, the best spot to sit down for a while is ***Caffe Roma*** *(☎ 212-226-8413, 385 Broome St)*, near Mulberry St, where you can have cannoli and espresso in a quiet setting after a Chinatown or SoHo meal. If you're in the mood for a chat, strike up a conversation with the natives at one of the bench-style tables. Ⓜ 6 to Spring St; J, M to Bowery.

Many of the storied old eateries in this neighborhood now cater almost exclusively to the tourists, which means that you'll probably pay more than you would elsewhere. These include ***Vincent's*** *(☎ 212-226-8133, 119 Mott St)*, at the corner of Hester St, and ***Puglia*** *(☎ 212-226-8912, 189 Hester St)*, between Mulberry and Mott Sts, with its raucous singing (audience participation!) and huge crowds.

KIM GRANT

LOWER EAST SIDE (Map 6)

Katz's Deli *(☎ 212-254-2246, 205 E Houston St)*, at Ludlow St, serves heaping pastrami sandwiches that have been known to make women cry out in ecstasy (at least in the movies – the famous fake orgasm scene in *When Harry Met Sally* took place here), but you'll probably be able to contain your excitement. Still, if you're looking for a basic New York deli experience, complete with kosher pickles and egg creams, you can't go wrong. Ⓜ F to Second Ave.

Yonah Shimmel Bakery *(☎ 212-477-2858, 137 E Houston St)*, between Eldridge and Forsyth Sts, offers just what you'd expect from a Jewish bakery: knishes, bagels and bialys. On Sunday morning, this local institution attracts an interesting mix of Yiddish-speaking seniors who've lived in the Lower East Side for years and young urbanites who've begun colonizing the neighborhood. Ⓜ F to Second Ave.

Bereket *(☎ 212-475-7700, 187 E Houston St)*, at Orchard St, serves Turkish kebabs and a good selection of vegetarian dishes. Since it's open 24 hours, late-night clubbers like to start their hangover cures here. Ⓜ F to Second Ave.

SOHO (Map 6)

If you're on a budget, you might want to make up your own lunch at SoHo's branch of ***Gourmet Garage*** *(☎ 212-941-5850, 453 Broome St)*, at Mercer St. It offers a good selection of fruit, breads and cheeses. Ⓜ A, C, E to Canal St.

Lupe's East LA Kitchen *(☎ 212-966-1326, 110 Sixth Ave)*, between Watts and Broome Sts, also attracts those with limited funds. The good burritos and enchiladas here cost $7 to $8. Locals like to lunch here. Ⓜ A, C, E to Canal St.

At ***Abyssinia*** *(☎ 212-226-5959, 35 Grand St)*, at Thompson St, diners perch on stools and feast on excellent, authentic Ethiopian cuisine, including *atakilt* (vegetables sautéed in spicy herbs, *shuro* (chick pea and vegetable puree) and *ye'beg tibs* (juicy lamb fried with rosemary and black pepper), accompanied by *injera* (pancake bread). A filling meal here costs $10 to $20. Ⓜ A, C, E to Canal St.

Culinary Corners

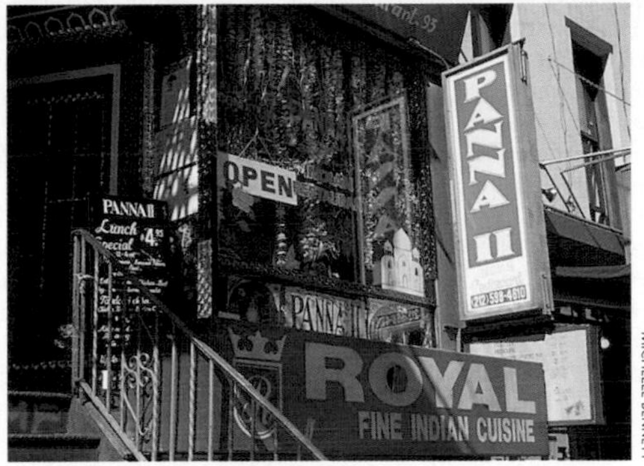

MICHELLE BENNETT

Manhattan features a number of distinct areas where one type of ethnic cuisine predominates. Beyond the famous Little Italy and Chinatown, some of the lesser-known areas offer exotic culinary adventures for bargain rates.

Little India Since the late 1970s, almost two dozen Indian restaurants have popped up on E 6th St between Second and First Aves. (Don't bother asking the proprietors if all the restaurants share the same kitchen – it's a tired joke they've heard a million times before.) At one time, these spots all drew crowds on weekend nights, but as Indian restaurants have spread throughout town (and the Indian population has shifted to the Jackson Heights section of Queens), these eateries have hit slower times. They now engage in a mad war for lunch business, with many offering four- and five-course meals, including a beverage, for as little as $5. In general, the restaurants offering live Indian music and/or a wine list wind up being more expensive than their alcohol-free counterparts. Arrive at the dry places with your own store-bought beer – you can buy some at the Indian markets on First Ave near 6th St. Despite the block's 'Little India' nickname, most of the immigrants who operate shops here actually hail from Bangladesh.

Little Korea Korean-owned fashion and accessories shops fill the streets near Herald Square in Midtown, with food shops and restaurants clustered between Broadway and Fifth Ave from 31st to 36th Sts. Go to one of the 24-hour joints along 32nd St for some Korean barbecue (meat cooked at your table on gas or coal-fired grills), accompanied by kimchi, an array of pickled vegetables.

Little Tokyo In the East Village, the two-block stretch of E 9th St between First and Third Aves has become a gathering spot for young Japanese who've moved to the neighborhood over the past few years. Excellent sushi restaurants line the street. ***Hasaki*** *(Map 6; ☎ 212-473-3327, 210 E 9th St)*, between Second and Third Aves, has the best reputation. Try there first, but if you find you have a long wait ahead of you, then go across the street to ***Sharaku*** *(Map 6; ☎ 212-598-0403, 14 Stuyvesant St)*, near E 9th St, where you'll find plenty of tables and a large menu featuring many Japanese specialties aside from sushi.

In SoHo, vegetarians have their pick of three notable vegetarian restaurants. ***Souen*** *(☎ 212-807-7421, 210 Sixth Ave)*, at Prince St, offers a wide selection of macrobiotic menu items, as well as less stringent vegetarian dishes. Nearby, ***Helianthus Vegetarian*** *(☎ 212-598-0387, 48 MacDougal St)*, between King and W Houston Sts, features Chinese and Japanese food, with a lunch deal that includes main courses like lemon mock chicken and sautéed udon plus a dumpling and rice (around $5.50). Ⓜ 1, 9 to Houston St.

The louder and busier ***Spring St Natural*** *(☎ 212-966-0290, 62 Spring St)*, near the corner of Lafayette St, serves a large menu of vegetarian selections (pastas, stir-fries and salads), plus healthy fish and organic chicken dishes for $15 or less. The large space suffers from a slight cafeteria feel, but you never ate food this fresh in a cafeteria. Ⓜ 6 to Spring St.

One of the grittier places in the neighborhood, ***Fanelli Cafe*** *(☎ 212-226-9412, 94 Prince St)*, at Mercer St, offers a glimpse of the old SoHo, before modern-day gentrification. Fanelli's is New York's second oldest restaurant, established in 1872, and was at one time a speakeasy. The dark, smoky bar features a pressed tin ceiling and a century-old dining room full of tables covered in red checkered cloths. A burger here will set you back about $10. Ⓜ N, R to Prince St.

Lucky Strike *(☎ 212-941-0479, 59 Grand St)*, between West Broadway and Wooster, serves moderately priced French bistro fare to a youthful crowd. The menu, painted on mirrors above the table, features pasta, salads, burgers and vegetarian options. Some of its better-known patrons might have tired of it (Madonna doesn't come here anymore), but plenty of others can't get enough of this hip spot. Crowds come late on Friday and Saturday; a DJ plays the front room nightly. Ⓜ A, C, E to Canal St.

When you call the exclusive ***Balthazar*** *(☎ 212-965-1414, 80 Spring St)*, between Broadway and Crosby St, don't expect a live person to answer the telephone. Some critics allege that only the restaurant's 'friends' (ie, celebrity patrons) know the number for the real reservation line. Still, nobodies like us can try to get a table at this mock Parisian bistro during the day. The top-rate menu features oysters from the raw bar, along with other seafood and meat specialties ($15 to $25). The onsite bakery churns out fresh bread and pastries. Ⓜ 6 to Spring St.

At the intimate ***Kitchen Club*** *(☎ 212-274-0025, 30 Prince St)*, at Mott St in the Nolita-SoHo area, owner-chef Marja Samson works in full view of diners. She's a bit eccentric – if you spot a worm in your salad, she will respond with a lecture on the wonders of organic foods. The mushroom dumplings, Japanese box dinners and pumpkin ice cream taste sublime. Entrees range from $15 to $25.

An austere white space, ***Quilty's*** *(☎ 212-254-1260, 177 Prince St)*, between Sullivan and Thompson Sts, takes its name from Humbert Humbert's adversary in the Vladimir Nabokov novel *Lolita*. Butterflies under

ANGUS OBORN

The Restaurant Reservations Game

Theoretically, New York (also known as, the great melting pot) is a town where everyone's born equal. But democracy seems to end at the door of a hot restaurant. These snobby eateries might not have bouncers, but they hardly shy at turning 'nobodies' away, especially at peak times.

To get yourself a table at seriously popular restaurants like the Union Square Cafe, Tabla and Picoline, you must make reservations a month in advance for Friday or Saturday night. But at least these places pride themselves on providing the same standard of service to all customers. Others, hungry for celebrity clientele and the publicity that goes with them, treat Joe Public with disdain. These offenders include the overpriced sushi den Nobu, the trendy Greenwich Village spot Moomba and the neo-Parisian SoHo cafe Balthazar. Indeed, both Nobu and Balthazar are notorious for never answering their listed telephone lines, and the latter eatery has been accused of having a 'secret' phone line available only to a select group of 3,000 of the beautiful people.

Even if you do get through to a human being, it's helpful if you know the many ways these people can politely say 'no.' If, for example, they tell you the restaurant is 'fully committed,' it's hot-spot speak for 'the only way you're getting into this place is by hiding under Leonardo DiCaprio's coat.'

glass decorate the walls – an allusion to Nabokov's passionate nonliterary pursuit. The menu features a solid selection of fish and game items, including steamed black sea bass, dry-aged New York sirloin and roasted venison. Entrees average $25. Ⓜ C, E to Spring St.

Raoul's *(☎ 212-966-3518, 180 Prince St)*, between Sullivan and Thompson Sts, has both the attitude and pulse of a classic late-night bistro. The menu, written in chalk on a blackboard, is exclusively in French, accompanied by Parisian-level prices – $40 or more per person with wine. Ⓜ C, E to Spring St.

GREENWICH VILLAGE (Map 6)

You'll have your pick of cafes in Greenwich Village, but don't pass up the lip-smacking window display at ***Bleecker St Pastry*** *(☎ 212-242-4959, 245 Bleecker St)*, near Cornelia St, where you can linger over a cappuccino and sweet Italian croissant among locals reading their morning papers. Ⓜ A, B, C, D, E, F, Q to W 4th St.

Don't count calories at ***Jon Vie*** *(☎ 212-242-4440, 492 Sixth Ave)*, between 12th and 13th Sts, a traditional French bakery that offers rich pastries and coffee for breakfast. The 24-hour cafe ***French Roast*** *(☎ 212-533-2233, 458 Sixth Ave)*, at W 11th St, serves breakfasts, sandwiches and desserts as well as more substantial meals such as steak frites and chicken or vegetable couscous for reasonable prices. Ⓜ L to Sixth Ave; F to 14th St.

For the makings of a picnic lunch, stop in at ***Gourmet Garage*** *(☎ 212-941-1664, 117 Seventh Ave)*, near Christopher St. Here you'll find a good selection of fresh fruit, breads and cheeses. Ⓜ A, B, C, D, E, F, Q to W 4th St.

Self-proclaimed 'ice cream artisans' practice their craft at ***Cones*** *(☎ 212-414-1795, 272 Bleecker St)*, between Seventh Ave South and Jones St, where the Italian-style ice creams and sorbets offer a great respite from the summer heat. A double scoop costs $2. Ⓜ A, B, C, D, E, F, Q to W 4th St.

Passersby can watch homemade noodles being prepared at ***Sammy's Noodle Shop*** *(☎ 212-924-6688, 453-461 Sixth Ave)*, near W 11th St, which sprawls over several storefronts. Lunch specials start at $4.50, and none of the noodle dishes cost more than $7. Ⓜ L to Sixth Ave; F to 14th St.

Despite its trendiness, ***Bar Six*** *(☎ 212-691-1363, 502 Sixth Ave)*, between 12th and 13th Sts, offers reasonable lunch deals. Grilled chicken, fish or vegetable sandwiches start at $7, including soup or salad. The lunch

ANGUS OBORN

Whiling away the afternoon at a Greenwich Village cafe

entrees range from vegetable couscous ($11) to New York–strip steak ($18), but you can also order something as simple as an omelette ($8). Bar Six is open late: to 2 am Monday to Thursday, 3 am Friday and Saturday. Ⓜ L to Sixth Ave; F to 14th St.

The Village also contains many mid-range Italian restaurants. Among the best is ***Trattoria Spaghetto*** *(☎ 212-255-6752, 232 Bleecker St)*, at Carmine St, a converted old coffee shop with traditional red-checked vinyl tablecloths. Almost all the pasta dishes cost $10. Ⓜ A, B, C, D, E, F, Q to W 4th St.

Slightly more expensive, and certainly more colorful, is ***Rocco*** *(☎ 212-677-0590, 181 Thompson St)*, between Bleecker and Houston Sts, where the friendly and attentive wait staff will be happy to provide your favorite dish even if it's not on the menu. This gathering place for local Village eccentrics has been around for 60 years. Ⓜ 1, 9 to Houston St.

Marinella *(☎ 212-807-7472, 49 Carmine St)*, near Bedford St, not only has a multipage menu, but it also displays extensive daily specials on a blackboard that's wheeled from table to table. The Northern Italian chicken, fish and veal entrees cost about $14. Ⓜ A, B, C, D, E, F, Q to W 4th St.

Grange Hall *(☎ 212-924-5246, 50 Commerce St)*, a block off Bedford St, is the modern reincarnation of an old neighborhood speakeasy once called the Blue Mill. Decorated with a large harvest mural, the renovated tavern-restaurant features hearty American meals (roasted, baked or grilled meats) with organic vegetables and Amish potatoes. Reasonably priced entrees average $14, but you can always make a meal out of the generous smoked trout salad appetizer (about $8). Or just stop in for a drink at the beautiful wooden bar. Ⓜ 1, 9 to Christopher St-Sheridan Square.

The tiny Village gem ***Little Havana*** *(☎ 212-255-2212, 30 Cornelia St)*, between Bleecker and W 4th Sts, serves earthy and filling but still delicate dishes ($14 to $16) in a cozy setting. Try the first-rate tamales or the spicy roast pork with green tomato sauce. Everything goes well with a Cuban Hatuey beer (made in Florida). Ⓜ A, B, C, D, E, F, Q to W 4th St.

The wildly popular ***Tomoe Sushi*** *(☎ 212-777-9346, 172 Thompson St)*, in between Bleecker and W Houston Sts, always seems to have a line. The sushi here, reputed to be the best in the city, costs $15 to $25 for a full meal. Ⓜ 6 to Bleecker St.

Quentin Tarantino's investment in ***Do Hwa*** *(☎ 212-414-2815, 55 Carmine St)*, near the corner of Bedford St between Sixth and Seventh Aves, has no doubt helped to boost the popularity of this Korean barbecue spot in the heart of the Village. Harvey Keitel, Wesley Snipes and Uma Thurman have stopped by for a taste of the flavorful beef ribs and kimchi in the spare Asian dining room. Entrees range from $15 to $25 but often can feed two. Ⓜ 1, 9 to Houston St.

The French bistro ***Caffe Lure*** *(☎ 212-473-2642, 169 Sullivan St)*, between Bleecker and W Houston Sts, has attracted its share of celebrities, especially models like Naomi Campbell and film heartthrob Leonardo DiCaprio. Yet amazingly enough, they let mere mortals in, too. (Caffe Lure doesn't take reservations, which improves your odds of getting a table.) Although the affordable gourmet cuisine has fallen off a bit in recent years, you still can't go wrong with the delicious pizzas (about $11, made in a wood-burning oven). Ⓜ 1, 9 to Houston St.

El Faro *(☎ 212-929-8210, 823 Greenwich St)*, at the corner of Horatio St, is a classic old Spanish restaurant that's quiet during the week but impossibly crowded on Friday and Saturday nights. The decor hasn't changed in 20 years, nor have the waiters. Main dishes, such as the spicy shrimp diablo, may seem pricey at $16, but they're enough to feed two people. Ⓜ A, C, E to 14th St; L to Eighth Ave.

In the far reaches of the West Village sits ***Florent*** *(☎ 212-989-5779, 69 Gansevoort St)*, between Greenwich and Washington Sts, one of the first bistros to go where no other trendsetters had gone before: to the heart of the meatpacking district. The bustling 24-hour spot draws clubbers at all hours with its hangar steak, hamburgers and breakfast selections. Try the praiseworthy blood sausage, pork chops or mussels. On the weekend closest to July 14th, the restaurant takes over Gansevoort St for an open-air Bastille Day celebration. Ⓜ A, C, E to 14th St; L to Eighth Ave.

EAST VILLAGE (Map 6)

The East Village abounds with many delis and diners that can provide you with a filling meal at low prices. The standouts include ***Veselka*** *(☎ 212-228-9682, 144 Second Ave)*, at the corner of 9th St, a Ukranian diner with a strong local following. Murals by local artists decorate the walls, and the grill chefs treat making pancakes as another kind of art form. Ⓜ 6 to Astor Place; N, R to 8th St-NYU.

The late French-Italian actor Yves Montand's favorite hangout in New York was the ***Second Ave Deli*** *(☎ 212-677-0606, 156 Second Ave)*, at the corner of 10th St, a quintessential deli offering great fare (the matzo ball soup comes with sprigs of fresh dill). Ⓜ 6 to Astor Place; N, R to 8th St-NYU.

Benny's Burritos *(☎ 212-254-2054, 93 Ave A)*, near 6th St, looks like it survived from the '60s; lava lamps, pink walls and Formica tables make up the decor. This local pioneer in low-fat Cal-Mex food serves super-filling burritos and enchiladas ($8 and under, with plenty of options for vegetarians). But watch out for the lethal margaritas. (You'll find a larger and more crowded Benny's at 113 Greenwich Ave in the West Village.) Ⓜ 6 to Astor Place.

Curious out-of-towners have virtually taken over ***Lucky Cheng's*** *(☎ 212-473-0516, 24 First Ave)*, between 1st and 2nd Sts, a

ANGUS OBORN

Hmm...borscht or farina...?

PLACES TO EAT

Thai restaurant featuring drag queen 'waitresses.' Note that reservations are often not respected – you can encounter an hour-long wait even if you call ahead. The Asian fusion entrees range from $6 to $16. Ⓜ F to Second Ave.

The renowned Vietnamese restaurant ***Cyclo*** *(☎ 212-673-3957, 203 First Ave)*, between 12th and 13th Sts, serves some tasty pho (the classic Vietnamese beef soup) and spring rolls, among other authentic Asian dishes. A little more expensive than its Chinatown counterparts, Cyclo charges $7 to $14 for entrees. Ⓜ L to First Ave.

A Swiss restaurant on a predominantly Polish block, ***Roettele AG*** *(☎ 212-674-4140, 126 E 7th St)*, between First Ave and Ave A, clings to its Alpine traditions. The menu at this Manhattan chalet offers creamy cheese fondue and authentic Wiener schnitzel, complemented by European wines. Entrees cost $7 to $17. Ⓜ 6 to Astor Place.

With its pressed-tin ceilings and faded paintings, ***Lanza's*** *(☎ 212-674-7014, 168 First Ave)*, between 10th and 11th Sts, will take you back to an earlier time in the East Village. Its five-course Italian dinner (just $11.95) includes a selection of delicious desserts. If you're not hungry but want a strong espresso and an Italian pastry, try the nearby ***DeRobertis*** *(☎ 212-674-7137, 176 First Ave)*, between 10th and 11th Sts, a *pasticceria* (bakery) that's been in business since 1904. Ⓜ 6 to Astor Place.

Time Cafe *(☎ 212-533-7000, 380 Lafayette St)*, at the corner of E 3rd St (Great Jones St), is a pleasant surprise: a trendy nightspot, popular with models, that actually serves tasty organic food, although the service can sometimes be inattentive. The varied menu includes everything from pasta to tapas, seafood to quesadillas. Entrees range from $10 for a smoked chicken pizza to $18 for Black Angus steak. You can eat outside under umbrellas or join the indoor hubbub. Ⓜ 6 to Bleecker St.

At the stylish ***Raga*** *(☎ 212-388-0957, 433 E 6th St)*, between First Ave and Ave A, Indian and Western cooking meet in inventive combinations like beef curry stew and swordfish over basmati rice. More sophisticated than a lot of inexpensive Indian places you'll find in Manhattan, this spot features a tasteful setting (complete with votive candles and earth-toned walls) and artful dishes at reasonable prices ($11 to $17). Best of all, the pastry chef wisely decided to look to France for inspiration. Ⓜ 6 to Astor Place; N, R to 8th St-NYU.

Plentiful wood trim and enormous mirrors make up the decor at ***Astor Restaurant & Lounge*** *(☎ 212-253-8644, 316 Bowery)*, at Bleecker St, a sleek bistro with a great airy dining room fashioned from an old warehouse. Downstairs, the colorful lounge features a Moroccan theme, with candles and festive tiles. Expect all the typical trendy bistro fare (grilled meats and seafood dressed up with chutneys and the like), all artfully presented, with entrees under $20. Ⓜ 6 to Bleecker St.

CHELSEA, FLATIRON DISTRICT & UNION SQUARE (Map 7)

Chelsea offers some of the best and most varied dining experiences in the city. But the neighborhood's become so popular that you may have to make weekend reservations weeks in advance, especially at some of the pricier restaurants.

For some classic New York people-watching, try the ***Empire Diner*** *(☎ 212-243-2736, 210 Tenth Ave)*, between 22nd and 23rd Sts, one of the neighborhood's prominent all-night hangouts. Club-hoppers work their way through burgers and omelettes all night long. Ⓜ C, E to 23rd St.

Noisy ***America*** *(☎ 212-505-2110, 9 E 18th St)*, between Fifth Ave and Broadway, sounds as if the whole country has decided to eat in one huge restaurant. And the chefs have designed a voluminous menu to suit just about everybody, with dishes inspired by a variety of regions across the USA, from Maine (clam chowder) to Texas (chili). Entrees cost $7 to $20. A skylight covers the elevated bar in back. Ⓜ N, R to 23rd St.

For a quieter experience, go to the nearby ***Caffe Bondi*** *(☎ 212-691-8136, 7 W 20th St)*, near Fifth Ave, an isolated spot with a back garden. In an effort to produce the most authentic Sicilian cooking possible, the chef here has gone so far as to recreate dishes from the 12th century. The recipe for chicken soup with pounded almonds predates Columbus (and the tomatoes he brought back from the New World). Entrees ($14 to $28), which include rabbit in orange sauce and a seafood brioche, favor meat eaters, but at lunch you can order vegetarian pizzas (about $12). Ⓜ N, R to 23rd St.

Tabla *(☎ 212-889-0667, 11 Madison Ave)*, at 25th St, heralds a resurgence in creative cuisine in the Madison Square area. The menu fuses Indian spices and fresh North American ingredients in such mind-blowing combinations as lobster and coconut curry. The prix-fixe dinner costs $52, but you can also order from the à la carte lunch and dinner menus. This extremely popular eatery requires reservations well in advance, but it's worth the wait. Ⓜ 6 to 23rd St; N, R to 23rd St.

You'll find several sublime places near Union Square, including the famous ***Union Square Cafe*** *(☎ 212-243-4020, 21 E 16th St)*, between Fifth Ave and Union Square West, which features fine American cuisine, top-flight service and a reasonably priced menu. The offerings range all the way from gourmet potato chips ($4.50) to filet mignon ($27), all prepared by a chef who's often been voted one of the best in the country. Ⓜ L, N, R, 4, 5, 6 to 14th St-Union Square.

The ***Gramercy Tavern*** *(☎ 212-477-0777, 42 E 20th St)*, between Park Ave South and Broadway, also provides five-star dining at relatively low prices: The nightly fixed-price menu costs $60, while the gourmet Continental entrees on the changing daily menu run $17 to $35. The excellent service and exquisite food make this a top choice among New Yorkers; thus, you'll have to book weeks beforehand to eat on a weekend. Ⓜ L, N, R, 4, 5, 6 to 14th St-Union Square.

The extraordinary ***Union Pacific*** *(☎ 212-995-8500, 111 E 22nd St)*, between Park Ave South and Lexington Ave, speaks the last word in fresh American cuisine, which makes it worth the price (entrees cost $20 to $35). Praised all over town, the menu combines the flavors of France and the Pacific Rim, with an emphasis on fish dishes. Asian-inspired details, including a wall of falling water, contribute to the sublime atmosphere. Ⓜ 6 to 23rd St.

MIDTOWN (Map 7)

Throughout Midtown, you'll find dozens of delis, pubs and moderately priced restaurants that cater to area office workers. You should have no problems finding an affordable lunch in this part of town.

The ***Pan Bagnat*** *(☎ 212-765-7575, 54 W 55th St)*, between Fifth and Sixth Aves, offers coffee, pastries and fresh baguette sandwiches ($7.25). Ⓜ B, Q to 57th St; E, F to Fifth Ave.

La Bonne Soupe *(☎ 212-586-7650, 48 W 55th St)*, between Fifth and Sixth Aves, features lunch specials with a French flavor and dinner choices that include soups, salads, steaks and fondue. The colorful bistro draws praise for its French onion soup, among other Gallic specialties. Ⓜ B, Q to 57th St; E, F to Fifth Ave.

While New York's soup-for-lunch craze seems to be dying down recently, the ***Soup Kitchen International*** *(☎ 212-757-7730, 259A W 55th St)*, near Eighth Ave, may survive, thanks to its chicken chili and other tasty soups, not to mention the publicity it got from the hit TV series *Seinfeld*. That show nicknamed this spot's gruff owner, Al Yeganeh, the 'Soup Nazi,' since he demands that customers know just what they want by the time they reach the head of the line. Beware of the idiosyncratic hours: This place shuts down during summer and opens again in September. Ⓜ B, D, E to Seventh Ave.

The ***Carnegie Deli*** *(☎ 212-757-2245, 854 Seventh Ave)*, at the corner of W 55th St, keeps packing them in, although why tourists love this tired place so much remains a mystery – maybe it's the star endorsements all over the walls or the stream of film crews shooting here. The food does come in enormous portions, but the prices match; expect to pay $15 for a pastrami sandwich bigger than your head. Ⓜ B, D, E to Seventh Ave.

The granddaddy of all theme restaurants, the ***Hard Rock Cafe*** *(☎ 212-489-6565, 221 W 57th St)*, between Seventh Ave and Broadway, started in London and arrived in New

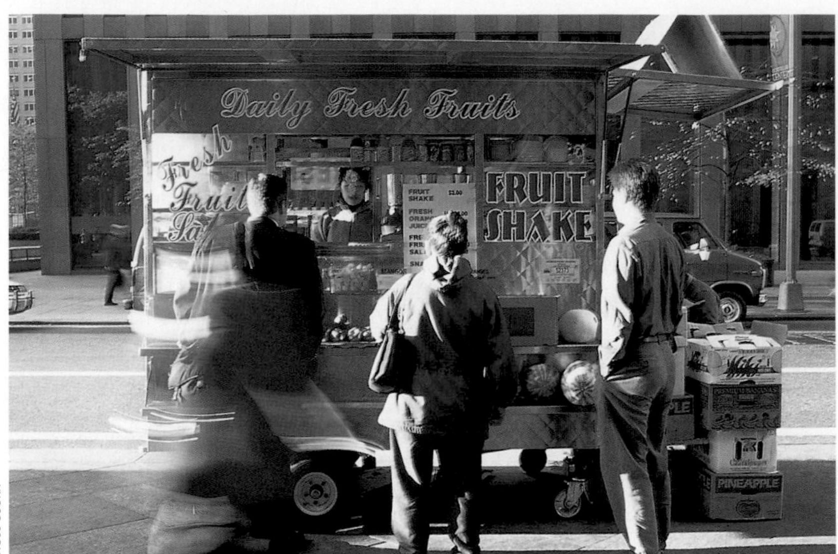

ANGUS OBORN

For snacks on the run

York in 1983. Like all the other Hard Rock Cafes around the world, this one offers glimpses of rock memorabilia of dubious provenance. Just how many times did Elvis really strum that guitar, anyway? The basic fare includes burgers, sandwiches and salads sold at overly inflated prices – you're really paying for the atmosphere here. Ⓜ N, R to 57th St.

At the unpretentious but authentic French bistro ***Le Quercy*** *(☎ 212-265-8141, 52 W 55th St)*, between Fifth and Sixth Aves, you can fortify yourself with hangar steak or grilled swordfish, accompanied by a good glass of steely Vouvray or Sancerre. Entrees range from $12 to $20. Ⓜ B, Q to 57th St; E, F to Fifth Ave.

Vong *(☎ 212-486-9592, 200 E 54th St)*, on the southeast corner of Third Ave, offers pricey East-West fusion fare that combines French and Thai cuisine in such unusual dishes as rabbit curry. The elegant setting here brings to mind the Bangkok hotel where chef Jean-Georges Vongerichten learned some of his craft. A fixed-price lunch menu costs $28. Ⓜ E, F to Lexington Ave.

Modern art hangs on the walls of ***Michael's*** *(☎ 212-767-0555, 24 W 55th St)*, between Fifth and Sixth Aves, an expensive option not far from MoMA. The light and airy dining room (with one glass wall that overlooks a garden) offers just the right setting for the chef's California cuisine. Entrees range from $24 for a vegetable plate or Cobb salad to $35 for 'Big Eats' portion of steak. The fixed-price pre-theater menu costs $32.50. Ⓜ B, Q to 57th St.

Michael Jordan's Steakhouse *(☎ 212-655-2300, 23 Vanderbilt Ave)*, at 43rd St, sits smack in the middle of Grand Central Terminal, on a balcony overlooking the concourse. The mahogany walls and leather chairs here add elegance to the restored train station. Despite its celebrity owner (usually a sign of poor food), this place has earned raves for its broiled steak and lobster, though you pay for the setting and the name – about $50 per person without drinks. Ⓜ S, 4, 5, 6, 7 to Grand Central-42nd St.

Plenty of Midtown restaurants rely on expense account executives, but few produce high-quality meals to match their prices.

One that certainly does is ***Aquavit*** *(☎ 212-307-7311, 13 W 54th St)*, between Fifth and Sixth Aves. A stunning six-story glass atrium, complete with a silent waterfall, encloses the main dining room. The $62 fixed-price menu may seem steep, but you'll think it's worth every penny when you taste such sublime entrees as the venison with pomegranate sauce. Swedish touches make Aquavit's menu unique among the A-list Manhattan restaurants that specialize in Continental cuisine. Ⓜ B, D, F, Q to Rockefeller Center; E, F to Fifth Ave.

Hell's Kitchen (Map 7)

The waitress will call you 'Hon' at the ***Munson Diner*** *(☎ 212-246-0964, 600 W 49th St)*, at Eleventh Ave, which must be one of the most authentic restaurants in the city. Before and after their shifts, cab drivers come here for the greasy burgers. Ⓜ C, E to 50th St.

A little worn around the edges, ***Mike's*** *(☎ 212-246-4115, 650 Tenth Ave)*, between 45th and 46th Sts, is a cheap bistro with ever-changing decorative themes that have turned the place into a pinball machine and a Christmas shrine to Madonna (the singer, not the Virgin). The basic American menu features some Cajun influences in dishes like the pan-friend blackened redfish. Burgers and grilled vegetable sandwiches start at $8; entrees top out at $14. Ⓜ A, C, E to 42nd St.

More a restaurant than a bar, ***Landmark Tavern*** *(☎ 212-757-8595, 626 Eleventh Ave)*, at the corner of 46th St, serves the best fish and chips in the city and the world's best Irish soda bread, warm and fresh from the oven. This 1868 structure once housed the tavern owner's family (see the 2nd-floor living room); this means that you can enjoy your steak and grilled fish in a historic setting. But don't expect to find a cramped, dull replica of bygone days. This spacious eatery buzzes with the energy of modern-day Manhattan. Entrees start at $14. Ⓜ A, C, E to 42nd St.

Bricco *(☎ 212-245-7160, 304 West 56th St)*, near the corner of Eighth Ave, is a standout in this neighborhood. This two-story place offers reasonable prices (the dishes tend to be $18 and under; the wine, $20 a bottle) plus high-quality service and great Italian-inspired fare. Fresh ravioli stuffed with crabmeat is a house specialty, but the pasta primavera and other vegetable choices make Bricco a good choice for vegetarians, too. Ⓜ A, B, C, D, 1, 9 to 59th St-Columbus Circle.

Times Square (Map 8)

Hamburger joints and mid-range ethnic restaurants fill up the side streets off Times Square. The quality of these places varies widely, but you'll do okay as long as you're not too adventurous. Stick to the basics.

Part of the city's best chain of cheap Chinese restaurants, ***Mee Noodle Shop*** *(☎ 212-765-2929, 795 Ninth Ave)*, near W 53rd St, serves a hearty bowl of broth, noodles and meat for just $5. (You can find the same offerings at Mee's two other locations: 922 Second Ave at E 49th St and 219 First Ave at E 13th St.) Ⓜ 1, 9 to 50th St.

Island Burgers and Shakes *(☎ 212-307-7934, 766 Ninth Ave)*, between W 51st and 52nd Sts, specializes in *churascos*, a juicy breast of chicken sandwich that comes in more than 50 different varieties for under $8. Ⓜ C, E to 50th St.

Popular with tourists, the ***Stage Deli*** *(☎ 212-245-7850, 834 Seventh Ave)*, between W 53rd and W 54th Sts, offers huge sandwiches for about $12. Ⓜ B, D, E to Seventh Ave.

You'll discover many moderately priced Italian places along Eighth and Ninth Aves. These include ***Basilica*** *(☎ 212-489-0051, 676 Ninth Ave)*, between W 46th and 47th Sts. Homemade pasta entrees cost about $10, with meat dishes for $10 to $12. Ⓜ A, C, E to 42nd St.

Zen Palate *(☎ 212-582-1669, 663 Ninth Ave)*, on the corner of 46th St, serves an exclusively vegetarian menu of Asian-inspired dishes. In addition to tofu, though, the menu also features plenty of pasta. Dishes run about $10.

Restaurant Row Restaurant Row is officially the block of W 46th St between Eighth and Ninth Aves, but locals use the name to refer to almost all the restaurants west of

Times Square. To reach all of the following places, take the subway (Ⓜ N, R, S, 1, 2, 3, 7, 9) to Times Square-42nd St.

Some mediocre places – usually those serving glorified pub grub – survive thanks to their proximity to the theater district, but you'll find a few gems here, too. ***Joe Allen*** *(☎ 212-581-6464, 326 W 46th St)*, between Eighth and Ninth Aves, serves everything from mashed potatoes and meatloaf to goat-cheese ravioli in a brick-walled room lined with the posters of famous Broadway flops. At dinner, it's impossible to get into the place without a reservation unless you wait until 8 pm; by then, all of the pre-theater diners have left to see a Broadway show.

Also run by Joe Allen, ***Orso*** *(☎ 212-489-7212, 322 W 46th St)* serves more expensive Tuscan food at about $17 to $20 per entree. It's popular with theater people and offers a daily late night seating at 10:30 pm for those coming out of performances.

Barbetta *(☎ 212-246-9171, 321 W 46th St)* sits in an old townhouse that may have once been a brothel. In warm weather, you can enjoy the Italian dishes in Barbetta's quiet garden. Entrees, which include specialties like beef braised in red wine and halibut with sweet peppers and leeks, cost about $30, with a fixed-price menu for $43.

The tiny ***Hourglass Tavern*** *(☎ 212-265-2060, 375 W 46th St)*, between Eighth and Ninth Aves, the same one featured in John Grisham's novel *The Firm*, serves reasonably priced stews and fish dishes. A full meal, including soup and salad, costs less than $15. As the saying goes, though, time is money – this restaurant can afford to deliver cheaper meals because waiters hustle people through dinner. If you head here before a Broadway show, be ready to finish eating in an hour; when the hourglass on your table runs out, you'd better be done.

Take a Taste of the Melting Pot

The stretch of Ninth Ave from W 38th to 40th Sts may be unique in the city, as it offers at least 12 different types of food within three blocks. The many recent immigrants who work as cab drivers or pushcart vendors like to frequent the area after their shifts, which has led to a profusion of international eateries. Along the avenue, or just off it, you'll have your pick of Italian, Indian, Chinese, West African, Haitian, Filipino, Pakistani, Mexican, Cuban or Cajun cuisine.

The area's mainstays include the ***Cupcake Cafe*** *(☎ 212-465-1530, 522 Ninth Ave)*, on the southeast corner of W 39th St, which makes specialty wedding cakes and serves an array of fancy pastries. It's not 'international,' but it is pretty famous locally for its buttercream-frosted cakes. Across the street in the Supreme Macaroni Company building, the pasta restaurant ***Guido's*** *(☎ 212-564-8074, 511 Ninth Ave)* offers a taste of Italy, as does ***Manganaro's*** *(☎ 212-563-5331, 488 Ninth Ave)*, near W 38th St, a wood-floored Italian grocery that serves cheap pasta dishes and heroes for about $5.

For authentic Mexican, try ***Los Dos Rancheros*** *(☎ 212-868-7780, 507 Ninth Ave)*, at the corner of W 39th St. Up the street a bit is ***Jam's Jamaican*** *(☎ 212-967-0730, 518 Ninth Ave)*, between W 38th and 39th Sts. If you're looking for something you won't find in many American cities, try the delicious home-style Senegalese food at ***Chez Gnagna Koty's*** *(☎ 212-279-1755, 530 Ninth Ave)*, between W 39th and 40th Sts. Lamb and chicken are favorites, as is *thiebu djen*, or '*cheb*,' the national dish of vegetables and fish with spicy tomato rice. A little farther afield, ***Bali Nusa Indah*** (☎ 212-974-1875, 651 Ninth Ave), between W 45th and 46th Sts, specializes in Javanese-Malaysian food such as the classic *rendang* (a type of curry), *ayam opor* (coconut chicken curry), *sambals* (chile relish) and *otak otak* (a kind of spiced coconut fish cake steamed in a banana leaf). Ⓜ N, R, S, 1, 2, 3, 7, 9 to Times Square-42nd St.

UPPER WEST SIDE (Map 9)

If you're looking for a grocery store, you've come to the right neighborhood. The city's most popular food emporium, ***Zabar's*** *(☎ 212-787-2000, 2245 Broadway)*, at W 80th St, offers very good prices on smoked salmon, cheeses and other gourmet items. Slicing salmon is something of an art form here – experienced slicers earn up to $80,000 a year! Ⓜ 1, 9 to 79th St.

The ***Fairway Market*** *(☎ 212-595-1888, 2127 Broadway)*, between W 74th and 75th Sts, sells items such as cheese and prepared salads for the lowest prices in the area. Ⓜ 1, 2, 3, 9 to 72nd St.

The Upper West Side contains dozens of cheap Chinese restaurants, pubs and coffee shops. The most reliable Chinese selection is ***Empire Szechuan***, with two Upper West Side locations: *(☎ 212-496-8460, 251 W 72nd St)*, between Broadway and West End Ave, and *(☎ 212-496-8778, 193 Columbus Ave)*, between W 68th and 69th Sts. These bustling places serve generally healthy fare, with lunch specials for around $7. Ⓜ 1, 2, 3, 9 to 72nd St.

Tibet Shambala *(☎ 212-721-1270, 488 Amsterdam Ave)*, between 83rd and 84th Sts, features a menu split evenly between meat and vegetarian dishes. Entrees cost $5 to $9. Ⓜ 1, 9 to 86th St.

At ***Cafe Lalo*** *(☎ 212-496-6031, 201 W 83rd St)*, between Amsterdam and Broadway, you can spend an entire rainy afternoon reading dozens of newspapers and magazines – or just the 14-page menu of expensive pastries. Ⓜ 1, 9 to 86th St.

This neighborhood's moderately priced restaurants tend to have mediocre food and inattentive service. The better choices include ***Cafe con Leche*** *(☎ 212-595-7000, 424 Amsterdam Ave)*, at 80th St, an easy-going neighborhood place with fast service and a spicy Creole menu dominated by eggs at breakfast, chicken and seafood dishes the rest of the day (but it also serves a good variety of vegetarian dishes). The feisty paella can feed two. Entrees average $10 to $15. Ⓜ 1, 9 to 79th St.

Dim sum meets sushi at the larger-than-life ***Ruby Foo's*** *(☎ 212-724-6700, 2182 Broadway)*, between 77th and 78th Sts, an extravagant red-and-black Asian theme park that can seat 400. Despite the volume of diners, the waiters manage not to keep anyone waiting long, but the lavish (some might say campy) decor should keep you entertained in any idle moments. The pan-Asian menu ranges from baby back ribs with black bean sauce to a tangy green papaya salad, with entrees costing $10 to $20. Ⓜ 1, 9 to 79th St.

If you're looking to splurge, try one of the Upper West Side's well-known and expensive restaurants. ***Cafe Luxembourg*** *(☎ 212-873-7411, 200 W 70th St)*, between Amsterdam and West End Aves, attracts the pre-performance crowd from Lincoln Center with its French-inspired food: cassoulet, escargots and interesting salads. Prices range from $15 at lunch to $25 at dinner for main courses. Don't even try getting in here without a reservation. Ⓜ 1, 2, 3, 9 to 72nd St.

Big crowds love ***Carmine's*** *(☎ 212-362-2200, 2450 Broadway)*, near 90th St, a zoo-like Italian restaurant that serves huge, community-style pasta and roasted meat entrees. Try the rigatoni with sausage and broccoli. You'll pay $20 for a portion of pasta that feeds several people. Ⓜ 1, 9 to 86th St.

The romantic ***Cafe des Artistes*** *(☎ 212-877-3500, 1 W 67th St)*, between Central Park West and Columbus Ave, has seen countless marriage proposals over the years, not to mention a few appearances by none other than President Bill Clinton. The restaurant features a famous mural of naked nymphs prancing through Central Park; the mural almost obscures the generally high quality of the food. The meaty entrees, which include osso bucco served with fettucine, average $27. There are also several vegetarian offerings and a three course prix-fixe dinner for $37.50. Men must wear jackets after 6 pm. Ⓜ B, C to 72nd St.

Picholine *(☎ 212-724-8585, 35 W 64th St)*, near Central Park West, offers first-rate Mediterranean-flavored cuisine that celebrities seem to love. It's one of the few restaurants in the city to maintain an after-dinner cheese course, with cheeses kept in a special cellar on the premises. House specialties include the Moroccan lamb with vegetable couscous and lobster bisque. At dinner, the two-course fixed-price meal costs $50, and the three-course option is $59. Ⓜ 1, 9 to 66th St-Lincoln Center.

UPPER EAST SIDE (Map 9)

Although this neighborhood tends to be an expensive one, you'll find dozens of moderately priced restaurants along Second and Third Aves between 60th and 86th Sts; many of these offer lunch specials for under $10.

To make your own sandwiches or snacks, go to the Upper East Side's branch of ***Gourmet Garage*** *(☎ 212-535-5880, 301 E 64th St)*, between First and Second Aves. It offers a good selection of fruit, breads and cheeses. Ⓜ B, Q to Lexington Ave.

The ***Lexington Candy Shop*** *(☎ 212-288-0057, 1226 Lexington Ave)*, at E 83rd St, is a picture-perfect lunch spot complete with an old-fashioned soda fountain. Here, school kids suck up malteds all afternoon while neighborhood folk nurse a coffee or a famed fresh lemonade. Best of all, this place sells burgers and other classic diner fare at reasonable prices in one of the city's most expensive neighborhoods. Ⓜ 4, 5, 6 to 86th St.

Cafe Greco *(☎ 212-737-4300, 1390 Second Ave)*, between E 71st and 72nd Sts, serves decent Greek fare (try the fresh fish entrees, like swordfish and flounder, both about $15) and also offers a reasonable three-course fixed-price menu and weekend brunch choices. Ⓜ 6 to 68th St-Hunter College.

KIM GRANT

Cheapest eats on the Upper East Side

The health-oriented Italian restaurant ***Favia Lite*** *(☎ 212-223-9115, 1140 Second Ave)*, at E 60th St, serves surprisingly tasty pasta entrees, considering the low calorie and fat content for every menu item. The large grilled chicken pizza costs $15, with skim-milk or soy mozzarella available at no extra charge. Ⓜ 4, 5, 6 to 59th St; N, R to Lexington Ave.

Many small, wood-paneled restaurants with a French flavor line Madison Ave north of 60th St and several nearby side streets. Places to find a bit of Paris (including pricey entrees in the $20-to-$30 range and a well-dressed clientele) are ***La Goulue*** *(☎ 212-988-8169, 746 Madison Ave)*, between 64th and 65th Sts, and ***Madame Romaine de Lyon*** *(☎ 212-759-5200, 132 E 61st St)*, between Lexington and Park Aves. At either place, you can enjoy a moderately priced meal by sticking to the appetizer side of the menu or by ordering lighter fare like omelettes (Madame Romaine features hundreds of varieties). Ⓜ B, Q to Lexington Ave.

Within Central Park, ***Park View Restaurant at the Boathouse*** *(☎ 212-517-2233)*, E 72nd St at Park Drive North, offers a pastoral view of boaters on the lake in summertime. In winter, the dining room crackles with a wood fire, making this spot a prime choice in all seasons. The lunch menu couples unusual offerings like Thai pork and rice cake ($10) with such standards as roasted chicken ($19). Dinner entrees top out at $35. Ⓜ 6 to 77th St.

HARLEM (Map 10)

Justifiably famous for its soul food, Harlem is now developing a reputation as the place to go for tasty West African fare. Whatever your appetites, be prepared to eat huge portions of fried chicken and other meaty selections, often available for incredibly cheap prices. Vegetarians or those seeking low-fat choices, beware.

At ***Pan Pan*** *(☎ 212-926-4900, 500 Malcolm X Blvd)*, at the corner of 135th St, less than $2 will buy you spicy Jamaican meat patties or a coffee-and-roll breakfast. But with a little more cash, you can feast on the diner's eggs, grits, pancakes and such or on a dinner with southern accents. On Sunday, after-church crowds fill the stools here. Ⓜ 2, 3 to 135th St.

For a soul-food bargain, head to ***Singleton's Barbecue*** *(☎ 212-694-9442, 525 Malcolm X Blvd)*, between W 136th and 137th Sts, where the $7 lunch specials offer chopped barbecue, pigs feet, 'smother' chicken livers and other delicacies with a choice of two vegetables. Ⓜ 2, 3 to 135th St.

Just a short stroll from the Apollo Theater, the ***M&G Soul Food Diner*** *(☎ 212-864-7326, 383 W 125th St)*, near Morningside Ave, offers one of the cheapest options in a low-cost neighborhood. (Try the delicious fried chicken.) A huge amount of food costs about $8. Ⓜ A, B, C, D to 125th St.

To taste the best fried chicken in Harlem, head way up north to ***Charles' Southern Style Kitchen*** *(☎ 212-926-4313, 2839 Frederick Douglass Blvd)*, between W 151st and 152nd Sts. The batter is perfection. You also can't go wrong with the salmon cakes and the macaroni and cheese. Hungry budget travelers shouldn't miss the all-you-can-eat buffet, an astounding bargain at $9.95. Ⓜ A, B, C, D to 145th St.

By far the most famous restaurant in Harlem is ***Sylvia's*** *(☎ 212-996-0660, 328 Malcolm X Blvd)*, between W 126th and 127th Sts, where the finger-licking meals include fried chicken and ribs, plus candied yams and collard greens. Generous entrees cost $9 to $18. On Sunday, you can feast on an array of food at the rousing Sunday gospel brunch ($16, but you must have a reservation). Ⓜ A, B, C, D, 2, 3 to 125th St.

Like Sylvia's, ***Copeland's*** *(☎ 212-234-2357, 547 W 145th St)*, between Broadway and Amsterdam Ave, offers a popular Sunday gospel brunch (make reservations a month ahead). Copeland's also features an all-you-can-eat jazz buffet ($18.65) during the week. An à la carte soul-food dinner will cost you about $25. Ⓜ 1, 9 to 145th St.

In the old Italian enclave of East Harlem, the tiny ***Rao's Restaurant*** (pronounced **ray**-o's) *(☎ 212-722-6709, 455 E 114th St)*, near First Ave, contains only 12 tables, which makes it next to impossible to score a reservation here unless you're Martin Scorsese or another one of Rao's favorite patrons. Closed on weekends, Rao's only offers one seating weekdays. A full-course authentic Italian meal could cost you over $50. Ⓜ 6 to 116th St.

But you don't have to spend a fortune to enjoy a taste of genuine Italian cooking, New York style. With a few dollars in your pocket, head to the nearby ***Patsy's Pizzeria*** *(☎ 212-534-9783, 2291 First Ave)*, between E 117th and 118th Sts, for a big slice of some historic pizza. Still one of the city's contenders for 'best pie,' Patsy's creation pioneered the use of coal-fired pizza ovens in New York, back in the 1930s, though the restaurant was sold off and franchised fairly recently. A nephew of the original owner, Patsy Grimaldi, now runs Patsy Grimaldi's Pizzeria in Brooklyn (see that section later in this chapter for details). A block away, ***Morrone's Bakery*** *(☎ 212-722-2972, 324 E 116th St)*, between First and Second Aves, sells delicious peasant bread. Ⓜ 6 to 116th St.

Conran Comes to Town

British design guru Terence Conran, progenitor of the 'big' London dining experience, has recently opened ***Guastavino*** *(☎ 212-980-2455, 409 E 59th St)*, between York and First Aves, in a refurbished arcade under the Queensboro Bridge. This massive, 300-seat restaurant with a wide-ranging menu takes over a landmark space designed by Rafael Guastavino in 1908. Guastavino's company also designed the tile work seen in several historic city sites, including the Oyster Bar in Grand Central Terminal and the Immigration Station on Ellis Island. The 98,000-square-foot bridge arcade, which had been abandoned for several decades, underwent a $25 million renovation and now holds the restaurant, a club, Conran's new furnishing store and a big supermarket. The jury's out, however, as to whether New Yorkers will accept the offhand service and barn-like atmosphere that some Londoners consider chic.

THE BRONX

The Bronx's most famous culinary neighborhood is Belmont, an Italian enclave just south of Fordham University. Some of the restaurants in this eight-block neighborhood have been in business since WWI, including ***Mario's*** *(☎ 718-584-1188, 2342 Arthur Ave)*, serving robust Neapolitan food, and ***Ann & Tony's*** *(☎ 718-933-1469, 2407 Arthur Ave)*, a family-style Neapolitan restaurant with pasta specials for $12 or less.

You'll often find a line outside the more famous ***Dominick's*** *(☎ 718-733-2807, 2335 Arthur Ave)*, a cash-only place where the crusty waiters serve large portions at long tables for around $12 a dish. (You won't find prices on the menu; the waiters simply present you with a final figure at the end of the meal. Expect to pay about $15 per person, depending on your wine consumption.)

In City Island, locals hang out at the ***Rhodes Restaurant*** *(☎ 718-885-1538, 288 City Island Ave)*, which serves standard pub specials and burgers for under $10. If you're looking for something to do late at night on City Island, you won't have many other options besides a meal at this spot, which stays open until 3 am daily.

For detailed information on getting to these neighborhoods on public transportation, see the Bronx section of the Things to See & Do chapter.

BROOKLYN

Brooklyn Heights (Map 11)

Many of Brooklyn's restaurants are located on Court St. The bar ***Cousin's Cafe*** *(☎ 718-596-3514, 160 Court St)*, between Pacific and Amity Sts, serves steaks, chops, hamburgers and pasta in the $17 range. A more casual, less-expensive pub menu features favorites such as chicken wings. On weekend nights, Cousin's hosts live jazz combos. Ⓜ F, G to Bergen St.

You can also find a bargain at the no-frills ***Sam's Restaurant*** *(☎ 718-596-3458, 238 Court St)*, between Baltic and Kane Sts. Here, you'll find a '40s-style atmosphere, including the menu recommendation that 'if your wife can't cook, don't divorce her – eat at Sam's.' Pizzas average $10 to $12, with standard pasta dishes around $8 and meat entrees like veal shank for $12. Ⓜ F, G to Bergen St.

For dessert, try ***Court Pastry*** *(☎ 718-875-4820, 298 Court St)*, near DeGraw St, where the famously filling pastries include the cream-filled lobster tail. Ⓜ A, C to High St.

At Fulton Landing, ***Patsy Grimaldi's Pizzeria*** *(☎ 718-858-4300, 19 Old Fulton St)*, between Front and Water Sts, offers cheap but tasty fare prepared by one of the descendants of a pioneering Manhattan pizza maker (see Patsy's Pizzeria in the Harlem section). Like his uncle before him, Patsy Grimaldi uses a coal-fired oven to produce a crispy crust on his popular pies. This friendly family place makes a great stop for kids. Ⓜ A, C to High St.

Budget travelers can also head to the local microbrewery for a moderately priced meal. The ***Park Slope Brewing Co*** *(☎ 718-522-4801, 62 Henry St)*, between Orange and Cranberry Sts, serves a dozen local microbrews and sandwiches for $7 or less. Ⓜ A, C to High St.

For even cheaper pints and basic pub grub (chicken wings and the like), go to ***Waterfront Ale House*** *(☎ 718-522-3794, 155 Atlantic Ave)*, which proclaims itself the 'home of warm beer, lousy food and an ugly owner.' The bar features live music at night, and happy hour runs from 4 to 7 pm. Ⓜ 2, 3, 4, 5 to Borough Hall.

If you don't mind bringing your own alcohol to dinner, try the excellent ***Acadia Parish*** *(☎ 718-624-5154, 148 Atlantic Ave)*, between Clinton and Henry Sts, which serves dinners of filling Cajun fare like jambalaya and fried oysters. Entrees average $14. Ⓜ 2, 3, 4, 5 to Borough Hall.

At nearby ***La Bouillabaisse*** *(☎ 718-522-8275, 145 Atlantic Ave)*, the signature dish and other French fare often attract lines out the door. This comfy bistro now features a small wine list to complement the seafood dishes. Expect to pay about $12 for an entree, although the popular bouillabaisse will cost you more. Ⓜ 2, 3, 4, 5 to Borough Hall.

In downtown Brooklyn, not far from the Brooklyn Academy of Music, ***Junior's*** *(☎ 718-852-5257, 386 Flatbush Ave Exten-*

sion), at DeKalb Ave, serves some of New York's best cheesecake, along with other high-calorie pleasures such as an enormous burger that weighs in at more than half a pound. The large diner-style menu includes an eclectic assortment of items, from soul food platters to kosher corned beef sandwiches. Entrees range from $10 to $30. Ⓜ D, M, N, Q, R to DeKalb Ave.

Established in 1879, ***Gage & Tollner*** *(☎ 718-875-5181, 372 Fulton St)*, at Smith St, is one of New York's oldest restaurants. A meal here doesn't come cheap (about $35), but you're paying for both the romantic, gaslight atmosphere and the solid seafood fare, which includes huge clams and crab cakes. Ⓜ M, N, R to Lawrence St.

At Fulton Landing stands the famous ***River Cafe*** *(☎ 718-522-5200, 1 Water St)*, near Old Fulton St, a romantic restaurant with delicately prepared American cuisine and a $65 fixed-price dinner menu – you'll need to make early reservations for a window seat, but the view of Manhattan makes the wait worth it. Ⓜ A, C to High St.

Park Slope (Map 12)

Local writers do their scribbling at the coffee shop cum literary hangout ***Ozzie's*** *(☎ 718-398-6695, 57 7th Ave)*, near Lincoln Place, one of several cafes along the street. Ⓜ D, Q to 7th Ave; F to 7th Ave-Park Slope.

The ***Lemongrass Grill*** *(☎ 718-399-7100, 61A 7th Ave)*, between Lincoln and Berkeley Places, serves spicy and generous Thai dishes, including a wide selection of meatless choices, for $12 or less. Ⓜ 2, 3, 4 to Grand Army Plaza.

The original ***Park Slope Brewing Co*** *(☎ 718-788-1756, 356 6th Ave)*, at 5th St, serves hearty pub grub and local brews. Burgers and sandwiches cost $6 to $12. Ⓜ F to 7th Ave-Park Slope.

Eastern Parkway (Map 12)

The legendary ***Tom's Restaurant*** *(☎ 718-636-9738, 782 Washington Ave)*, on the corner of Sterling Place, has survived for 65 years on the strength of its egg cream sodas and hearty breakfasts. This luncheonette serves kid-friendly hamburgers and fries or a tasty egg salad, too. Ⓜ 2, 3, 4 to Eastern Parkway-Brooklyn Museum.

Coney Island

Totonno's *(☎ 718-372-8606, 1524 Neptune Ave)*, two blocks away from the boardwalk, is one of the city's best and oldest brick-oven pizza restaurants. Totonno's is open only Wednesday to Sunday from noon to whenever he runs out of fresh mozzarella cheese.

A noisy family-style place, ***Gargiulos*** *(☎ 718-266-4891, 2911 W 15th St)* first attracted crowds with a huge styrofoam octopus, reputedly stolen from the aquarium. Unfortunately, it's gone now. But people still come for the filling southern Italian dishes, which cost about $15.

Brighton Beach

Some of Brighton Beach's restaurants cater to regional sectors of the Soviet emigré population. At night, several raucous nightclub-restaurants offer elaborate floor shows. The ***Winter Garden*** *(☎ 718-934-6666, 3152 Brighton 6th St)*, right on the boardwalk, attracts Muscovites with its $40 prix-fixe dinner, which includes two shots of vodka and a live nightclub act of music and dancing.

The ***National*** *(☎ 718-646-1225, 273 Brighton Beach Ave)* charges $55 per person on Friday, Saturday and Sunday nights for its completely over-the-top variety show and dinner, well oiled by carafes of vodka. ***Primorski*** *(☎ 718-891-3111, 282 Brighton Beach Ave)* offers a cheaper set menu – $22 ($25 on weekends) – but if you lose track of the vodka consumption, the bill is sure to be much larger. As with Winter Garden and National, the price of your dinner includes the nightclub act, and if you don't fancy the Russian dinner, expect to pay extra for a 'French' version.

The bakeries on Brighton Beach Ave sell fantastic dark Russian sourdough bread for about $1.50 a loaf.

Williamsburg

Plan-eat Thailand *(☎ 718-599-5758, 141 N 7th St)*, near Bedford Ave and the Bowery in northern Williamsburg, has grown into a massive industrial Thai-Japanese theme park.

Sushi now complements the Thai menu. While you eat, you can listen to live jazz. Most entrees range from $8 to $10. Ⓜ L to Bedford Ave.

The most famous steak house in the city, ***Peter Luger Steakhouse*** *(☎ 718-387-7400, 178 Broadway)*, between Bedford and Driggs Aves, sits in a century-old warehouse. Side dishes like creamed spinach and German potatoes complement huge entrees; the juicy Porterhouse can feed more than two people. This place takes cash only, and dinner with a drink can cost up to $60 per person with wine. Ⓜ J, M, Z to Marcy Ave.

QUEENS

Astoria (Map 13)

For a cheap dinner, head to ***Uncle George's*** *(☎ 718-626-0593, 33-19 Broadway)*, between 33rd and 34th Sts, a 24-hour spot that serves daily specials of barbecue pork and potatoes for $8 and red snapper for $12. Try the restaurant's *tzatziki*, a Greek dip made of yogurt, garlic and cucumber. Ⓜ N to Broadway; G, R to Steinway St.

At the smoky and sleek patisserie ***Omonia Cafe*** *(☎ 718-274-6650, 32-20 Broadway)*, between 32nd and 33rd Sts, it's possible to linger over an espresso, close your eyes and hear nothing but Greek spoken around you. The pastries, both French and Greek, and ice-cream treats each cost about $4. Ⓜ N to Broadway; G, R to Steinway St.

You'll have a similar cafe experience at the ***Galaxy Cafe*** *(☎ 718-545-3951, 34-02 Broadway)*, between 35th and 36th Sts, which has great baklava, and the ***Kolonaki Cafe*** *(☎ 718-932-8222, 33-02 Broadway)*, between 33rd and 34th Sts, which takes its name from Kolonaki Square in Athens, the meeting place for Greece's idle rich. Ⓜ N to Broadway; G, R to Steinway St.

The more expensive and out-of-the-way ***Elias Corner*** *(☎ 718-932-1510, 24-02 31st St)*, at 24th Ave near Hoyt Ave North, merits a special trip. It's famous for its floppingly fresh grilled fish and bracing *retsina*, a potent Greek wine. There is no menu at this moderately priced, cash-only, seafood-only spot; you get what was caught fresh early that morning. Ⓜ N to Astoria Blvd.

Jackson Heights

At the low end of the spectrum, the fast-food restaurant ***Taco Mexico*** *(☎ 718-899-5800, 88-12 Roosevelt Ave)*, near Elbertson St, offers homemade salsa and tortilla chips. Ⓜ 7 to 90th St.

Many consider the legendary ***Jackson Diner*** *(☎ 718-672-1232, 37-47 74th St)*, between 37th and Roosevelt Aves, to be the city's best southern Indian restaurant. This dingy converted coffee shop is famous for its *masala dosa* (a massive crepe with potato, onion and peas) and *seekh kabob* (a long sausage made of tender lamb). Entrees average $7 to $10. Ⓜ 7 to 74th St.

Around the corner from the Jackson Diner, ***La Porteña*** *(☎ 718-458-8111, 74-25 37th Ave)*, between 74th and 75th Sts, offers a spicy taste of Argentina, serving Buenos Aires–style barbecue entrees ($8 to $12) prepared in the storefront window. Meals come to the table with *chimichurri*, a garlic-laden oil and vinegar sauce. Ⓜ 7 to 74th St.

The large Colombian population in this neighborhood frequents such restaurant-nightclubs as ***Chibcha*** *(☎ 718-429-9033, 79-05 Roosevelt Ave)*, between 78th and 79th Sts, which features salsa and jazz shows on Friday and Saturday nights beginning at 11 pm. It also offers what one critic has dubbed the 'cardiac special,' a sampler of grilled sausages, beef, cracked pork skin topped with an egg, plus plantains, rice and beans ($10.50). Ⓜ 7 to 82nd St.

Inti Raymi *(☎ 718-424-1938, 86-14 37th Ave)*, between 86th and 87th Sts, serves Peruvian specialties like grilled cow's heart ($8) and does seafood particularly well. They don't serve alcohol here, but they also don't mind if you bring your own. It's open only Thursday to Sunday. Ⓜ 7 to 90th St.

Corona

Several Latino subcultures exist side by side here at the dividing line between Jackson Heights and Corona, so you'll find a strong Latin influence in the cuisine.

The ***Broadway Sandwich Shop*** *(☎ 718-898-4088, 96-01 Roosevelt Ave)*, near Junction Blvd, serves garlicky Cuban pork sandwiches (under $5) and steaming hot cups of *cafe con leche*, which make it worth the trip out to Queens. Ⓜ 7 to Junction Blvd.

One block away, ***Quisqueya Restaurant*** *(☎ 718-478-0704, 97-03 Roosevelt Ave)*, near 97th St, offers sweet plantain plates and Dominican specialties like young goat stew for $8.

Tomas Gonzalez offers a taste of Mexico at ***La Espiga*** *(☎ 718-779-7898, 42-13 102nd St)*, near 42nd Ave; it's a combination bakery, taco bar, restaurant and grocery store. People line up for the fresh tortillas (2lb for $1), made several times a day. The shop also sells Mexican embroidery and foodstuffs for home cooking. Ⓜ 7 to 103rd St.

For dessert, head to the ***Lemon Ice King of Corona*** *(☎ 718-699-5133, 52-02 108th St)*, near Corona Ave, which serves homemade ices. The signature ice has chunks of lemon and is the perfect refresher for a summer day. The shop's open all year (in winter, it closes at 6 pm). Ⓜ 7 to 103rd St. The Lemon Ice King is about a mile from the subway. Walk south on 104th St to Corona Ave, turn left and walk two blocks to 52nd Ave. You can also take the Q23 bus to Forest Hills and get off at 108th St and 52nd Ave, on the opposite corner from the shop.

Flushing (Map 14)

You'll find plenty of decent Chinese food in Flushing, all at reasonable prices; most entrees at the following spots cost less than $10, although whole-fish dishes at seafood restaurants usually fall in the $10-to-$15 range. ***Joe's Shanghai*** *(☎ 718-539-3838, 136-21 37th Ave)*, near Main St, has earned a reputation throughout the city for its steaming bowls of handmade dumplings and noodle dishes.

The sleekest place in Flushing is the inexpensive ***Shanghai Tang*** *(☎ 718-661-0900, 135-20 40th Rd)*, between Roosevelt and 41st Aves. The waiters enthusiastically guide newcomers through the Shanghai-style menu choices (all under $6).

Golden Pond *(☎ 718-886-1628, 37-17A Prince St)*, on the corner of 38th Ave, specializes in whole-fish meals ($12 to $17). For a dim sum feast on Sunday afternoon, head to ***KB Garden*** *(☎ 718-961-9088, 136-28 39th Ave)*. Dishes cost $3 to $8.

To reach any of these places listed here, take the No 7 subway all the way to the last stop at Main St.

STATEN ISLAND

It's bleak and unattractive near the ferry terminal, but if you venture a little farther, you'll find some worthwhile dining spots. The ***Sidestreet Saloon*** *(☎ 718-448-6868, 11 Schuyler St)*, just a few minutes' walk from the ferry, is a popular lunch spot for workers from the borough courthouse across the street. Three blocks east of the ferry terminal, the ***Cargo Cafe*** *(☎ 718-876-0539, 120 Bay St)*, at Slossen Terrace, has inexpensive lunch specials.

La Caleta *(☎ 718-447-0397, 75 Bay St)*, offers Spanish seafood specials and chicken dishes for $8 and under. ***The Rare Olive*** *(☎ 718-273-5100, 981 Bay St)* serves an interesting combination of Italian and southern Creole food. Lunch entrees cost about $7 and dinner runs from $13 to a max of $23 for lobster. There's a full bar here.

Gilly's Luncheonette *(☎ 718-448-0579, 9 Hyatt St)*, immediately behind the Staten Island Borough Hall, is a classic working-class breakfast and lunch spot. ***RH Tug's*** *(☎ 718-447-6369, 1115 Richmond Terrace)*, offers waterfront al fresco lunching just a few minutes' walk west from the Snug Harbor Cultural Center.

Entertainment

No single source could possibly list everything that happens in the city, but *Time Out* offers the best guide to nightlife. For high-culture events, check out the Sunday and Friday editions of the *New York Times*, as well as *New York* magazine and the *New Yorker*. Dance clubs and smaller music venues take out numerous ads in the weekly *Village Voice*. The free papers, including *Metro* and *New York Press*, feature blurbs about a range of cultural events.

The Department of Cultural Affairs' 24-hour hotline (☎ 212-777-2787) lists events and concerts at major museums and other cultural institutions. You can also call NYC On Stage (☎ 212-768-1818), a 24-hour information line that publicizes music and dance events.

THEATER

The heart of Broadway runs right through Times Square, which has long served as the center of New York's theater world. For years, though, overblown spectaculars created by Andrew Lloyd Webber *(Cats, Phantom of the Opera, Miss Saigon)* have dominated the scene. And the arrival of film spin-offs produced by Disney *(The Lion King, Beauty and the Beast)* hasn't helped New York regain its reputation as a serious theater town. Some premier new American plays, including Arthur Miller's latest work, began opening in London.

Then the Brits came back across the Atlantic to change all that. In the late '90s, new dramas from Britain and Ireland *(The Weir, The Blue Room* and *Closer)* met with great acclaim. At the same time, some classic American revivals *(The Iceman Cometh, Death of a Salesman)* starring big-name film actors attracted ever-larger crowds to the Broadway stage. New and revived musicals saw success, too, including *Titanic*, *Chicago* and *Fosse*.

All this has added up to a great era of success for Broadway. More than 11 million people buy tickets to shows each year, and the average age of patrons has finally begun to drop after years of worries about the graying of the audience. Now there's even a shortage of theaters to meet the demand. In fact, the high cost of producing a play on Broadway forced even Broadway giant Neil Simon – who has a theater named after him on 52nd St – to debut his *London Suite* in Union Square.

The costs have risen so high that some Broadway venues may soon follow the example of sports teams and rename themselves after corporate investors in order to attract more money. The Selwyn Theater has signed an $8.5-million deal to become the American Airlines Theater, and the famous Winter Garden Theater (former home to *Cats)* flirted with the idea of becoming the Cadillac Theater until public outcry discouraged that idea.

RICHARD I'ANSON

Broadway Theaters

In general, 'Broadway' productions are staged in the large theaters around Times Square. Some of the major venues include the following. (If you're looking for the location of a particular Broadway theater not listed here, consult Map 8 in the map section at the back of this book.) You can reach all of these theaters via subway (Ⓜ N,

R, S, 1, 2, 3, 7, 9 to Times Square-42nd St). To purchase tickets for the spots listed below, see Tickets, later.

The ***Eugene O'Neill Theater*** *(Map 8; 230 W 49th St)*, between Broadway and Eighth Ave, has staged top theatrical productions like Neil Simon's *A Thousand Clowns* and *Prisoner of Second Avenue* and Arthur Miller's *All My Sons*. Its recent production of *Death of a Salesman* earned rave reviews. The pleasant theater seats 1100.

Arguably Broadway's best theater, the ***Majestic Theater*** *(Map 8; 247 W 44th St)*, near Eighth Ave, has staged the blockbuster musicals *Carousel*, *South Pacific* and *Camelot* with Julie Andrews. Its wildly popular current production, *Phantom of the Opera*, may play until the sky falls down. Most of the 1600 seats here offer good views.

A 1771-seat jewel, the ***New Amsterdam Theatre*** *(Map 8; ☎ 212-282-2900, 214 W 42nd St)*, near Seventh Ave, was rescued from decrepitude by the Disney corporation, which stages upbeat, kid-friendly productions like *The Lion King* here. The lobby, rest rooms and auditorium are lavish, but the seating is a bit cramped.

Off-Broadway Theaters

'Off Broadway' usually refers to shows performed in smaller spaces (200 seats or fewer) elsewhere in town, although you'll find some in the Times Square area. 'Off-off Broadway' events include readings, experimental performances and improvisations held in spaces with fewer than 100 seats.

A big business in itself, off-Broadway theater now attracts four million people a year. Some prominent spots include the following.

The ***Circle in the Square Theater*** *(Map 8; ☎ 212-307-2705, 1633 Broadway)*, at 50th St, staged groundbreaking productions like Eugene O'Neill's *The Iceman Cometh* at its original 159 Bleecker St premises. The company takes an active role in New York's thespian scene, training new actors at its theater school. Ⓜ 1, 9 to 50th St.

The ***Joseph Papp Public Theater*** *(Map 6; ☎ 212-260-2400, 425 Lafayette St)*, between E 4th St and Astor Place in the East Village, presents its famous Shakespeare in Central Park productions at the park's Delacorte Theater every summer. Meryl Streep, Robert DeNiro, Kevin Kline and many other stars have performed at the Public, one of the city's most important cultural centers. For information on upcoming shows, visit www.publictheater.org. Ⓜ N, R to 8th St-NYU; 6 to Astor Place.

Founded in the '60s, the ***Performing Garage*** *(Map 6; ☎ 212-966-3651, 33 Wooster St)*, between Broome and Grand Sts in SoHo, remains one of the most consistent of the avant-garde performance spaces. It's home to the Wooster Group, whose members have included Willem Dafoe, Spalding Gray and Steve Buscemi. Ⓜ A, C, E to Canal St.

PS 122 *(Map 6; ☎ 212-477-5288, 150 First Ave)*, near E 9th St in the East Village, has been committed to fostering new artists and their way-out ideas since its inception in 1979. Its two stages have hosted such avant-garde performers as Meredith Monk, Eric Bogosian and the Blue Man Group. For a schedule, visit www.ps122.org. Ⓜ 6 to Astor Place.

The ***Samuel Beckett Theater*** *(Map 8; ☎ 212-594-2826, 410 W 42nd St)*, near Ninth Ave, tends to hold small-scale productions of mainstream new plays and high-quality revivals in a nice theater with good views and comfy seats. Ⓜ N, R, S, 1, 2, 3, 7, 9 to Times Square-42nd St.

Tickets

The Broadway Show Line (☎ 212-302-4111, www.broadway.org) provides descriptions of plays and musicals both on and off the Great White Way; you can use it to obtain information on ticket prices and to make credit card purchases.

For most Broadway and off-Broadway shows, you can also purchase tickets through Telecharge (☎ 212-239-6200, 800-432-7250). To buy same-day standing room tickets for sold-out shows, contact theaters directly. For \$10 to \$15, you'll get great views and sore feet (but you can always look for vacant seats at intermission).

KIM GRANT

Discount tickets The TKTS booth in Times Square (Map 8; ☎ 212-768-1818), Broadway and W 47th St, sells same-day tickets to Broadway and off-Broadway musicals and drama. Tickets sell at either 50% or 75% off regular box-office rates, plus a $2.50 service charge per ticket. The booth's electric marquee lists available shows; availability depends on the popularity of the show you're looking to see. (Before you go, check out the Friday *New York Times* and *Time Out* to make selections, but you'll have to be willing to be flexible.)

On Wednesday and Saturday, matinee tickets go on sale at 10 am, and on Sunday the windows open at noon for afternoon performances. Evening tickets go on sale every day at 3 pm, and a line begins to form up to an hour before the booth opens. Note that TKTS accepts cash or traveler's checks only. (You'll find a smaller, less crowded TKTS outlet at 2 World Trade Center; it maintains the same hours.)

BARS & LOUNGES

Bars have always been a fixture of New York nightlife, but in the '90s, lounges popped up all over the city. What makes a lounge different from a plain old bar? Couches, cigars and classy clientele. Downtown lounges tend to attract high-paid office workers who while away their evenings with bourbon and cigars; uptown, you'll find yourself in the company of old money. In SoHo, artsy types fill the lounges, while Chelsea's spots draw a predominantly gay crowd.

But if you can't be bothered with the latest trends, you'll still find plenty of old-fashioned, unpretentious bars throughout the city that never sleeps. A proper listing of New York City's best bars could fill an entire book, but here's a highly selective list of bars that stay open until 2 am most nights. (New York's bars can stay open until 4 am, and on weekends, most of them do.)

Lower Manhattan (Map 5)

The Greatest Bar on Earth *(☎ 212-524-7011)*, at Windows on the World on the 107th floor of One World Trade Center, enjoys an unparalleled view of the city skyline. A gin and tonic runs a high $9, while a bottle of wine can soar up to $15,000. The "casual but neat" dress code means no dirty jeans and t-shirts. Ⓜ 1, 9 to Cortlandt St.

Expect to work up a sweat at ***Cafe Remy*** *(☎ 212-267-4646, 104 Greenwich St)*, between Carlisle and Rector Sts, which features a wild dance floor with salsa and other Latin music nightly. DJs also play plenty of reggae and R&B at this two-level lounge. Ⓜ 1, 9 to Rector St.

Tribeca (Map 6)

The well-heeled Wall Street crowd patronizes the ***Bubble Lounge*** *(☎ 212-431-3433, 228 West Broadway)*, between White and Franklin Sts, which features 280 varieties of champagne and sparkling wine. It's the place to drop $2000 on a bottle of champagne, but you can also order champagne by the glass for $8 and up. Ⓜ A, C, E to Canal St.

Lower East Side (Map 6)

You'll find many bars in the Ludlow St area of the Lower East Side. ***Barramundi*** *(☎ 212-529-6900, 147 Ludlow St)*, between Stanton and Rivington Sts, makes a good place to start a Lower East Side bar crawl. This Australian-owned arty place features convivial booths, reasonably priced drinks and a lovely shady garden. Ⓜ F, J, M, Z to Delancey St.

SoHo (Map 6)

A block from the Hudson River, ***The Ear Inn*** *(☎ 212-226-9060, 326 Spring St)*, between Greenwich and Washington Sts, sits in the old James Brown House (the James Brown who was an aide to George Washington, not the Godfather of Soul), which dates back to 1817. A number of sanitation workers and office dwellers come here on their lunch hours or after their shifts end. Tuesday is biker's night; Saturday is poetry night; every night is Guinness night. The bar menu features a great shepherd's pie. Ⓜ C, E to Spring St.

At ***Cafe Noir*** *(☎ 212-431-7910, 32 Grand St)*, you can munch on North African appetizers while watching the passing SoHo parade from the open-air bar railing. Ⓜ A, C, E to Canal St.

The owners of ***Pravda*** *(☎ 212-226-4696, 281 Lafayette St)*, between Prince and Houston Sts, have tried to make their spot hard to find, but the lines outside mean the secret's out. If you dress trendy enough and look sufficiently intense, you'll make it past the gatekeepers and enter clouds of cigar smoke in this mock Eastern European speakeasy. The martinis make all the hassle worth it, though; the two-page vodka list includes Canada's Inferno Pepper and a homegrown Rain Organic. Ⓜ B, D, F, Q to Broadway-Lafayette St.

Greenwich Village (Map 6)

Chumley's *(☎ 212-675-4449, 86 Bedford St)*, between Grove and Barrow Sts, is a hard-to-find, storied speakeasy that serves decent pub grub to a sometimes rowdy crowd of

ANGUS OBORN

That city that never sleeps

jocks and their friends. You can sample some homegrown beers here, since Chumley's serves American microbrews exclusively. Look for the unmarked brown door in a white wall. Ⓜ 1, 9 to Christopher St-Sheridan Square.

The ***Corner Bistro*** *(☎ 212-242-9502, 331 W 4th St)*, between Jane St and W 12th St, a famous bar from the bohemian days, contains carved wooden tables where you can eat charred hamburgers until 2 am. The enormous, half-pound bistro burger with bacon and onions has won some awards in the local press. Ⓜ 1, 9 to Christopher St-Sheridan Square.

The friendly and unpretentious ***Blind Tiger Ale House*** *(☎ 212-675-3848, 518 Hudson St)*, between W 10th and Christopher Sts, may be the single best place to sample an array of interesting beer. Ⓜ 1, 9 to Christopher St-Sheridan Square.

The ***Liquor Store Bar*** *(☎ 212-226-7121, 235 West Broadway)*, between White and Walker Sts, is a popular nighttime hangout in a small Federal-style building that its owners proudly claim has been in continuous commercial use since 1804. Big windows offer plenty of opportunity to watch the street traffic, and you can also people-watch from outdoor tables when the weather's nice. The bar takes its name from a previous business at the same site; locals, inspired by the furry animals often seen scampering down the street, call it the Rat Bar. Ⓜ A, C, E to Canal St.

Be prepared for some pretentiousness at ***Hudson Bar & Books*** *(☎ 212-229-2642, 636 Hudson St)*, between Jane and Horatio Sts, a narrow faux library with free jazz on weekend evenings. Ⓜ A, C, E to 14th St.

The smoky retro lounge ***Bar d'O*** *(☎ 212-627-1580, 29 Bedford St)*, near Downing St, features drag acts several nights a week. It attracts a chic mixed crowd of gays and straights. Ⓜ 1, 9 to Houston St.

Okay, ***Bowlmor Lanes*** *(☎ 212-255-8188, 110 University Place)*, between E 12th and 13th Sts, doesn't technically qualify as a lounge, but it's still a hip nightspot. The disco soundtrack and the glow-in-the-dark bowling (on Monday nights) produce a retro atmosphere worthy of a club. You're more likely to spot cocktail-drinking urbanites here than championship bowlers, and visits by Julia Roberts and other celebrities have lent Bowlmor plenty of cachet. Ⓜ L, N, R, 4, 5, 6 to 14th St-Union Square.

East Village (Map 6)

The Scratcher *(☎ 212-477-0030, 209 E 5th St)*, near Third Ave, attracts a large Irish clientele because it looks like a true Dublin pub: a quiet place to sip coffee and read the newspaper during the day but a crowded and raucous spot at night. Ⓜ 6 to Astor Place.

Church pews and candles complete the Irish atmosphere at ***Swift's Hibernian Lounge*** *(☎ 212-260-3600, 34 E 4th St)*, near the Bowery, a wildly popular bar with live folk music and probably the best pint of Guinness in New York City. The musicians cozy up to their audiences here, since they can't perform on the nonexistent stage. Ⓜ 6 to Bleecker St.

A relic from days of yore, ***McSorley's Old Ale House*** *(☎ 212-473-9148, 15 E 7th St)*, between Second and Third Aves, predates the Civil War and bears the dubious distinction of resisting the modern age; it barred women from its doors until the 1970s. This cramped and stodgy old bar often served as a setting for Joseph Mitchell's well-known *New Yorker* short stories. These days, you'll often find a long line of tourists waiting outside. Ⓜ 6 to Astor Place.

For a nice slice of East Village life, have a late-night drink in ***Vazac's*** *(☎ 212-473-8840, 108 Ave B)*, at E 7th St, a horseshoe-shaped bar at the southeast end of Tompkins Square Park. Also called 7B's, it's been featured in a number of films, including *The Verdict* and *Crocodile Dundee*. Ⓜ L to First Ave.

Tribe *(☎ 212-979-8965)*, St Marks Place at First Ave, tells you everything you need to know about the hip East Village today. Formerly the storied old St Marks Bar & Grill, this place now features a DJ, dance-floor lighting and pricey pints. Ⓜ 6 to Astor Place.

The ***Beauty Bar*** *(☎ 212-539-1389, 231 E 14th St)*, between Second and Third Aves, isn't full of supermodels, just old hairdryers that'll make you look like a conehead while you sip your martini. This not-quite-converted beauty salon still offers manicures a couple of nights a week, in addition to DJ dance tunes. Ⓜ L to Third Ave.

Tired of the trendy East Village scene? Try ***WCOU Radio*** *(no phone, 115 First Ave)*, at E 7th St, a low-key hangout that bears a slight resemblance to a bathroom, thanks to the old tiles on the floor. Sit in the window and watch life pass by with a Bud or a bud and listen to the tunes on the cool jukebox. Ⓜ 6 to Astor Place.

Union Square (Map 7)

The famous short story writer O Henry used to do some of his scribbling at ***Pete's Tavern*** *(☎ 212-473-7676, 129 E 18th St)*, near Irving Place. It's said that he wrote his classic Christmas story 'The Gift of the Magi' in a front booth. You can get a decent burger and beer here or find the same fare by walking a block away to the equally popular ***Old Town Bar and Grill*** *(☎ 212-529-6732, 45 E 18th St)*, between Broadway and Park Ave, a wood-paneled 1890s pub with grumpy barmen but decent eats in its booths and upstairs dining area. Ⓜ L, N, R, 4, 5, 6 to 14th St-Union Square.

The hip ***Belmont Lounge*** *(☎ 212-533-0009, 117 E 15th St)*, near Irving Place, features plenty of nooks for those with an eye for romance or gossip. You can stargaze in the garden or nosh your way through the night, picking from a selection of sandwiches, salads and appetizers. Ⓜ L, N, R, 4, 5, 6 to 14th St-Union Square.

Midtown & Times Square (Maps 7 & 8)

At the Rainbow Grill's ***Rainbow Room*** *(☎ 212-632-5000, 30 Rockefeller Plaza)*, on the 65th floor of the GE Building, you must wear a jacket, but for the price of admission to the Empire State Building, you get a stunning view that includes that landmark and a drink to go along with it. The Rainbow Room is open Friday nights and some Saturdays for dinner and dancing. You must make reservations. Ⓜ B, D, F, Q to 47th-50th Sts/Rockefeller Center.

44 *(☎ 212-944-8844, 44 W 44th St)*, between Fifth and Sixth Aves, sits in the lobby of the Royalton Hotel. Look beyond the snooty atmosphere here and head to the tiny circular bar located immediately to the right after the entrance; it makes a great hideaway spot for a martini. Ⓜ B, D, F, Q to 42nd St.

Rudy's Bar & Grill *(☎ 212-974-9169, 627 Ninth Ave)*, between 44th and 45th Sts, practically glories in its reputation as a spot for booze hounds. But that doesn't stop this old dive from turning away any of the trendy twentysomethings who stop in for the free hot dogs during a night of club-hopping in Hell's Kitchen. The drinks come pretty cheap here ($2 for a draft beer). Ⓜ A, C, E to 42nd St.

The slightly more upscale ***Film Center Cafe*** *(☎ 212-262-2525, 635 Ninth Ave)*, between 44th and 45th Sts, offers happy-hour discounts on pints from 4 to 6 pm weekdays. Ⓜ A, C, E to 42nd St.

Old guys have been hanging out around the wooden bar at ***McHale's Bar & Cafe*** *(☎ 212-997-8885, 750 Eighth Ave)*, at 46th St, for years now. The actors and theater people who frequent this unpretentious spot also lend it character. Look for McHale's great neon sign, which should take you back at least a half-dozen decades. Ⓜ A, C, E to 42nd St.

Mercury Bar *(☎ 212-262-7755, 659 Ninth Ave)*, between 45th and 46th Sts, attracts the after-work crowd with a decent menu of bar snacks, plus a few more filling options. A sleek new spot in an up-and-coming West Side neighborhood near Port Authority, the Mercury packs in patrons on Thursday and Friday nights, or whenever a major sporting event plays on the two big-screen TVs here. Ⓜ A, C, E to 42nd St.

Perched on the 26th floor of the Beekman Tower Hotel, the ***Top of the Tower*** *(☎ 212-355-7300, 3 Mitchell Place)*, at First Ave, offers a clear view of the East Side, including the Chrysler Building and the fabulous '30s-era Pepsi ad across the East River. Ⓜ E, F to Lexington Ave; 6 to 51st St.

In a city packed with Irish pubs, the ***British Open*** *(☎ 212-355-8467, 320 E 59th St)*, between First and Second Aves in the shadow of the Queensboro Bridge, draws fans of golf and the Royal Family. Ⓜ 4, 5, 6 to 59th St.

Upper West Side (Map 9)

The Evelyn *(☎ 212-724-2363, 380 Columbus Ave)*, at 78th St, a roomy cellar-level space with plenty of couches, includes a classy cigar lounge and a martini list with more options than the dinner menu. A laid-back crowd frequents this spot during the week but makes room for hobnobbing students on the weekend. Ⓜ 1, 9 to 79th St.

The old-school Irish bar ***Dublin House*** *(☎ 212-874-9528, 225 W 79th St)*, between Broadway and Amsterdam Ave, shouldn't be remarkable, but it is, thanks to the odd combination of old men and Columbia University undergrads who patronize the place. Ⓜ 1, 9 to 79th St.

Columbia's grad students tend to hang out at the colorful dive called the ***Night Cafe*** *(☎ 212-864-8889, 938 Amsterdam Ave)*, at W 106th St. Answer the obscure trivia questions, and you'll get a free drink. Ⓜ 1, 9 to 103rd St.

The quiet spot ***Saints*** *(☎ 212-222-2431, 992 Amsterdam Ave)*, between W 109th and 110th Sts, welcomes a mixed crowd, though it's a predominantly gay bar. Ⓜ 1, 9 to Cathedral Parkway (110th St).

Upper East Side (Map 9)

The old ***Subway Inn*** *(☎ 212-223-8929, 143 E 60th St)*, between Lexington and Third Aves, looks like it hasn't changed in 40 years, right down to the barmen's white shirts and thin black ties. Ⓜ 4, 5, 6 to 59th St.

Inside the Carlyle Hotel, ***Bemelmans Bar*** *(☎ 212-744-1600, 35 E 76th St)*, between Madison and Park Aves, is an elegant space where you'll feel uncomfortable without a jacket. Tuesday through Saturday, you'll have to pay a cover charge for evening jazz performances. Ⓜ 6 to 77th St.

The quiet lounge at the ***Mark Hotel*** *(☎ 212-774-4300, 22 E 77th St)*, between Madison and Fifth Aves, epitomizes Upper East Side elegance. Ⓜ 6 to 77th St.

The ***Kinsale Tavern*** *(☎ 212-348-4370, 1672 Third Ave)*, between 93rd and 94th Sts, attracts European rugby and soccer fanatics with early-morning live satellite broadcasts of European matches during the winter months. This place features more than 20 beers on tap. Ⓜ 1, 2, 3, 9 to 96th St.

CLUBS

Constantly changing, the New York club scene defies efforts to pin down what's hot and what's not. For the up-to-the-minute news on clubs, check out the monthly magazine *Paper* ($3.50 at newsstands); the publication also offers the very latest entertainment listings at www.papermag.com. You should also keep an eye out for club and band flyers on walls and billboards while walking through the East Village – sometimes that's the best way to find out about clubs that don't have phones or advertise. You can also check out the latest club information on the Web site www.scenetrack.com.

Don't even think about going to any of these places before 11 pm, even on a weeknight; things don't truly pick up until 1 am or later.

Tribeca & SoHo (Map 6)

Vinyl *(☎ 212-206-1590, 6 Hubert St)*, between Hudson and Greenwich Sts in Tribeca, hosts a unique, alcohol-free dance party called 'Body and Soul,' from 4 pm to midnight on Sunday. So put on your comfortable clothes and get into the house-music groove with the most diverse group of clubbers you'll find in the city. This warehouse space also features dance parties on Wednesday, Friday and Saturday. The cover varies. Ⓜ 1, 9 to Franklin St.

Double Happiness *(☎ 212-941-1282, 173 Mott St)*, between Broome and Grand Sts in the Nolita area, is a cavernous basement retreat that has become très popular among a young and trendy urban crowd. Mingle and lounge with the hip crowd early on and get down to house music later on in the evening. Ⓜ N, R, J, M, Z to Canal St.

Despite its name, ***Culture Club*** *(☎ 212-243-1999, 179 Varick St)*, between King and Charlton Sts in SoHo, isn't Boy George's paradise. While this downtown warehouse spins '80s dance music every night, it attracts a humdrum crowd of recent-college-grads-turned-Wall-St-types. The decor is nothing to admire either, but if '80s music gets you into the groove, then this is the place to go. The cover is $15. Ⓜ 1, 9 to Houston St.

Although it's primarily a bar, ***Naked Lunch*** *(☎ 212-343-0828, 17 Thompson St)*, at Grand St in SoHo, can turn into a rockin' dance party on a good night, but it still offers a more relaxing atmosphere than a hardcore nightclub. The DJ spins a good mix of house music and Top 40. While the scene inside is pretty laid-back, leave your sneakers at home because you might not get in the door. The cover is usually $5. Ⓜ A, C, E to Canal St.

Greenwich Village (Map 6)

Baktun *(☎ 212-206-1590, 418 W 14th St)*, between Ninth Ave and Washington St, borders on the psychedelic, with an array of

Crash of a Club King

The late '90s were tough times for New York City's dance clubs. Fresh from their crackdowns on the street drug trade, the city cops turned their attention to the clubs. Unfortunately for the club owners and those who love partying all night, Mayor Giuliani turned out to be right when he called the dance clubs all-night drug supermarkets. The clubs also didn't benefit from recent press coverage of the city's 'club kids,' an odd mixture of the idle rich, drug addicts, and hangers-on who live for the nightlife.

No one has suffered more from the crackdown that Peter Gatien, the self-proclaimed 'Club King' and owner of Limelight and the Tunnel. A Canadian entrepreneur with an eye patch that lends him an air of malevolent mystery, Gatien has long been a target of the crackdowns. Life got particularly hairy for Gatien in 1996, when a club kid named Angel Melendez disappeared following a dispute over drug debts. (His mutilated body was later found floating in the river.) After being convicted of the murder, a Limelight party planner named Michael Alig turned on his boss Gatien in exchange for a lesser sentence. Gatien survived the accusation of drug dealing but did serve a 90-day sentence for not paying $1.4 million in taxes.

Both Limelight and the Tunnel reopened but again shut their doors in 1999, when a teenager died after a taking both ecstasy and Special K. (At the trial, the judge hearing evidence uttered the immortal line: 'You mean Special K is not a cereal?')

Today, the ***Tunnel*** *(☎ 212-695-7292, 220 Twelfth Ave)*, at W 27th St in Midtown, and ***Limelight*** *(☎ 212-807-7850, 660 Sixth Ave)*, at E 20th St in the Flatiron District, remain open (but for who knows how long?). No matter what club you go to in the city, don't forget that the cops are keeping a close eye on who sells what to whom.

cutting-edge sound that ranges from underground to house to electronic. The big-screen TV in the middle of the bar shows multimedia art performances. Friday night usually features a house party, while drum and bass performances happen on Saturday. The cover is $5 to $10. Ⓜ A, C, E to 14th St; L to Eighth Ave.

The Cooler (*☎ 212-229-0785, 416 W 14th St*), between Ninth Ave and Washington St, began as a meat locker in New York's meat-packing district but now hosts punk, rock, electronic, surf, indie rock, reggae, and hip-hop performances. The Monday night 'free series' is a great place to catch local bands for free. Other nights, be prepared to pay a cover (usually $8 to $15) for more well-known bands and for house parties on Friday and Saturday. Ⓜ A, C, E to 14th St; L to Eighth Ave.

Chelsea (Map 7)

Centro-Fly (*☎ 212-627-7770, 45 W 21st St*), between Fifth and Sixth Aves, plays house music from Thursday to Saturday and attracts a mix of urban clubgoers and Euro trash. The funky op art, the waitresses in galactic gowns and the guards in orange space suits give this hip spot a style all its own. Dance to 'subliminal sessions' on Thursday, be in the mood to lounge on Friday and get down to house music on Saturday. The cover is $10 to $20. Ⓜ 1, 9, F to 23rd St.

Roxy (*☎ 212-645-5156, 515 W 18th St*), between Tenth and Eleventh Aves, plays disco and house music for those in tight black t-shirts and leather pants. A former roller-skating paradise, the place still hosts roller discos on Tuesday and Wednesday. On the weekend, the dance floor offers plenty of space to try out all your moves, and Saturday night is sheer party madness. Scantily clad drag queens entertain in the lounge. The cover varies. Ⓜ A, C, E to 14th St; L to Eighth Ave.

Twirl (*☎ 212-691-7685, 208 W 23rd St*), between Seventh and Eighth Aves, offers plenty of space for hard-core clubbers to strut their stuff and for loungers to mingle and observe. This chic and trendy Chelsea hot spot plays house music and hosts special events. The cover varies. Ⓜ C, E to 23rd St.

True (*☎ 212-254-6117, 28 E 23rd St*), between Madison Ave and Park Ave South near Midtown, is an intimate one-room dance club that attracts an older crowd. This spot stays mellow during weeknights, with lounge music and a Tuesday night Latin Club, but on the weekend house music is the order of the day. Ⓜ N, R, 6 to 23rd St.

Midtown & Times Square (Maps 7 & 8)

Twilo (*☎ 212-268-1600, 503 W 27th St*), between Tenth and Eleventh Aves in Midtown, spins house music every Saturday, as DJ Junior Vasquez invites clubbers of all ages (including those with glow sticks) to dance all night into the early afternoon. On Friday, be prepared for everything from trance to progressive to Euro. Though the bleachers on one side of the warehouse and the oversized spiral balloons falling from the ceiling are tacky, the music is hip and the space is large. The cover is $20 if you call in advance, $25 at the door. Ⓜ C, E to 23rd St.

Wear your designer best if you dare to go to ***Float*** (*☎ 212-581-0055, 240 W 52nd St*), between Eighth Ave and Broadway in the Times Square area. Arguably Manhattan's most popular scene among the beautiful and famous these days, this tri-level megaclub features a lighted runway on the dance floor and leather-strutting, caged dancing girls. If you're worthy enough to enter, be on the lookout for Leonardo, Ben Affleck and the like on the 3rd floor, reserved for those with the right stuff. Cover is $15 to $25. Ⓜ B, D, E to Seventh Ave.

The four-floor multiplex king of all clubs, ***Exit*** (*☎ 212-582-8282, 610 56th St*), between Eleventh and Twelfth Aves in Midtown, hides its exits well. You'll get lost in the maze of theme rooms on every floor, each equipped with leopard-patterned sofas and its own DJ playing specialty music. Also check out the roof garden. Whatever music you're craving, it's in there somewhere. The cover is $25. Ⓜ A, B, C, D, 1,9 to Columbus Circle.

The East Village: New York's Hottest Neighborhood

The East Village – particularly the area on and around St Marks Place – has long been known as New York's prototypical grunge neighborhood, which has always attracted a number of down-at-the-heels characters, including junkies, Eastern European immigrants and *outré* artists such as Beat poet Allen Ginsberg and eccentric English dandy Quentin Crisp. In the '70s and '80s, it served as ground zero of the US punk movement: The infamous nightclub CBGB, on the Bowery, helped to launch the careers of such famous bands as Talking Heads and the Ramones. By the late '80s, Tompkins Square became a stomping ground (literally) for local punks and anarchists. They congregated at the late, much-lamented Coney Island High, a barn-like bar and performance space on St Marks Place, or at the still-thriving 7B's (see the Bars & Lounges section). During the day, 7B's was a quiet place for old men to hang out; at night, it became nothing less than a grunge pickup joint fueled by malt liquor beer specials.

But by the early '90s, the mean streets of the East Village began a rapid, stunning transformation, which extended even into the notorious 'Alphabet City' (Aves A, B, C and D). The change started with a resurgence in cutting-edge nightlife. A number of groundbreaking cafes opened near Tompkins Square, including Cafe Siné on St Marks Place, a literary-musical hangout that became a magnet for Irish-born immigrants, including doomed folk singer Jeff Buckley. (It's closed now.)

The East Village continued its rise with the refurbishment of once-wrecked apartment buildings in an area that stretched from E 2nd to E 13th Sts east of Third Ave. Funky bars sprang up in the area, often in the place of drunk hangouts – among them the Guinness-dispensing Irish bars Swift and The Scratcher (see the Bars & Lounges section).

The natural progression of the East Village led to the establishment of Internet cafes and more upscale venues that attracted celebrities but served up an attitude and pretty lousy food. Still, there's some grunge life left in the East Village: The Continental (see the Rock section) attracts a heavily pierced crowd with its live rock bands.

These days, even the side streets off Avenues B and C are hopping with lounges that stay open to 2 am nightly. It's yours to explore – check out the listings in *Paper*, the downtown magazine, for more information.

GAY & LESBIAN VENUES

For a list of gay clubs and bars catering to every taste, pick up the free sheets *HX/ Homo Xtra* and *Next*, available at most restaurants and bars. *HX For Her* is a lesbian-oriented free sheet.

On the whole, gay drinking places tend to cater only to men, but the more popular gay dance clubs welcome women, gay or straight. Most mainstream clubs (see Clubs, earlier) feature gay nights either weekly or monthly, and you're likely to find mixed crowds there. Predominantly gay venues populate Chelsea and Greenwich Village, the traditional heart of the gay community.

SoHo & Greenwich Village (Map 6)

At ***Don Hill's*** (*☎ 212-219-2850, 511 Greenwich St*), near Spring St, live soul and pop music might give way to a late-night ostentatious transvestite party with drag shows, go-go boys and anything goes. Ⓜ C, E to Spring St.

The leather bar ***Lure*** (*☎ 212-741-3919, 409 W 13th St*), near Ninth Ave, enforces a strict dress code: leather, denim or uniform. The particularly naughty entertainment on Wednesday night might include body painting, piercing, tattooing or pornographic performances. Ⓜ A, C, E to 14th St; L to Eighth Ave.

Despite its name, ***Hell*** *(☎ 212-727-1666, 59 Gansevoort St)*, between Greenwich and Washington Sts, attracts a largely friendly mixed crowd. The decor here includes luscious red drapery and photos of celebrities sporting devilish horns. Sunday is disco night. Ⓜ A, C, E to 14th St; L to Eighth Ave.

You probably won't find your mom at ***Mother*** *(☎ 212-366-5680, 432 W 14th St)*, near Washington St, where the lively theme nights run the gamut from Friday's 'Clit Club' for lesbians to Thursday's Long Black Veil. At press time, the club planned to relocate in the near future, so visit Mother's Web site (www.mothernyc.com) for more information. Ⓜ A, C, E to 14th St; L to Eighth Ave.

Monster *(☎ 212-924-3558, 80 Grove St)*, at the corner of W 4th St, a comfortable place for all ages, features a piano bar upstairs and a dance floor below. Drag shows take place Monday to Wednesday, with disco on Tuesday. Ⓜ 1, 9 to Christopher St.

The lesbian dive bar ***Henrietta Hudson*** *(☎ 212-924-3347, 438 Hudson St)*, near Morton St, stays open until 4 am every night, so you can play pool or dance to DJ music into the wee hours. Or just nurse a beer all night long at this comfy spot. Ⓜ 1, 9 to Christopher St.

KIM GRANT

Older lesbians frequent ***Rubyfruit*** *(☎ 212-929-3343, 531 Hudson St)*, near W 10th St, a civilized spot with a welcoming regular crowd. Weekend entertainment runs from piano-bar schmaltz to '50s bebop. Dinner is served every night. Ⓜ 1, 9 to Christopher St.

Crazy Nanny's *(☎ 212-366-6312, 21 Seventh Ave)*, near Leroy St, hosts a pool tournament on Monday, karaoke on Wednesday and Sunday, a drag show on Thursday and exotic dance on Saturday. This brash bar for gay women and their friends gets crowded and rather raucous on weekends. Ⓜ 1, 9 to Houston St.

Marie's Crisis *(☎ 212-243-9323, 59 Grove St)*, near Seventh Ave, caters mostly to older gays. This wonderful tavern features piano playing and loud renditions of show tunes that often involve the vocal stylings of everyone in the place. Ⓜ 1, 9 to Houston St.

East Village (Map 6)

The Cock *(☎ 212-777-6254, 188 Avenue A)*, near E 12th St, attracts an old-school, artsy East Village crowd, with the occasional leather-dressed go-go boy thrown in for flair. This boozy, cruisey club hosts wild Saturday night through-the-roof parties with DJs and drag queens. Ⓜ L to First Ave.

A prime lesbian hangout in the East Village, ***Meow Mix*** *(☎ 212-254-0688, 269 E Houston St)*, between Aves A and B, attracts a youthful crowd with live indie girl rock. Happy hours, open jams and DJs all help to get the joint moving and grooving. Ⓜ F to Second Ave.

Chelsea (Map 7)

The video dance bar ***Splash*** *(☎ 212-691-0073, 50 W 17th St)*, at Sixth Ave, attracts an upscale male crowd with its nightly dancers and happy hours. Monday features only videos from Broadway musicals, promising a campy experience. At other times, well-toned boys put on a water show. Ⓜ L to Sixth Ave; F to 14th St.

King *(☎ 212-366-5464, 579 Sixth Ave)*, between 16th and 17th Sts, draws the biggest crowds on Saturday night. This men's cruise joint features a dance floor and theme rooms (sample theme: get naked). Ⓜ L to Sixth Ave; F to 14th St.

Less scene-y than its Chelsea brethren, ***Barracuda*** *(☎ 212-645-8613, 275 W 22nd St)*, between Seventh and Eighth Aves, features a dimly lit front room, where you can grope under cover of darkness, and a smoky back lounge where you can sink into the chairs and chat for a while. Ⓜ 1, 9 to 23rd St.

ROCK

When major singers and 'super groups' that regularly fill arenas play a smaller venue in New York, their record company usually buys up all the tickets and hands them out as freebies, so don't set your heart on catching Whitney Houston's or Prince's surprise club appearance. Instead, New York clubs offer you the chance to see up-and-coming artists and lesser-known bands, many of whom know how to put on a better show in intimate venues than big-name stars who play one huge concert after another.

Big names have turned up at the small ***Mercury Lounge*** *(Map 6; ☎ 212-260-4700, 217 E Houston St)*, near Essex St on the Lower East Side. Jeff Buckley, Lou Reed and Bikini Kill have all played at this comfy venue, which blasts music by local bands and touring indie groups on its quality sound system every night. Ⓜ F to Second Ave.

The convenience-store-turned-club ***Arlene Grocery*** *(Map 6; ☎ 212-358-1633, 95 Stanton St)*, near Orchard St, has heralded a gentrification of the Lower East Side in the late '90s. The one-room hothouse incubates local talent, with great live shows for free every night. Students like to come here for the cheap bottled beer. Look out for hilarious punk rock karaoke. Ⓜ F to Second Ave.

Luna Lounge *(Map 6; ☎ 212-260-2323, 171 Ludlow St)*, near Stanton St on the Lower East Side, hosts garage bands, local musicians and up-and-coming indie darlings in a small room. Since there's never a cover charge at this mellow bar, it's worth poking your head in to check out the night's act. Ⓜ F to Second Ave.

KIM GRANT

Street musicians, Union Square

At the ***Bottom Line*** *(Map 6; ☎ 212-228-6300, 15 W 4th St)*, near Mercer St in the Village, all sorts of live acts perform in a huge cabaret-style music hall. Each night, a single artist or a group usually performs two sets (7:30 and 10:30 pm). Waiters bring pizza and burgers to the table. Ⓜ 6 to Astor Place.

The prototypical punk club ***CBGB*** *(Map 6; ☎ 212-982-4052, 315 Bowery)*, between E 1st and 2nd Sts in the East Village, is still going strong after nearly three decades. The name stands for 'Country, Bluegrass and Blues,' but since the mid '70s, the place has heard more rock than anything else. Some of the luminaries who've sweated through sets here include Debbie Harry, the Talking Heads and the B52s. Today, the bands experiment with rock, Motown, thrash and everything in between. Ⓜ 6 to Bleecker St.

The ***Continental*** *(Map 6; ☎ 212-529-6924, 25 Third Ave)*, off St Marks Place, famous for its cheap drink specials, still hosts unannounced gigs by the likes of Iggy Pop and Jakob Dylan. It keeps the grunge scene alive in the East Village. Ⓜ 6 to Astor Place.

Irving Plaza *(Map 7; ☎ 212-777-6800, 17 Irving Place)*, near E 15th St in the Union Square area, attracts lots of NYU students with well-known indie acts like Luscious Jackson, Everything But the Girl and Pavement. This popular concert venue has reawakened a formerly sleepy neighborhood. Ⓜ L, N, R, 4, 5, 6 to Union Square.

If you're determined to see a rock superstar's concert, you'll find those big shows at ***Madison Square Garden*** *(Map 7; ☎ 212-465-6741)*, Seventh Ave at W 33rd St in

Midtown; ***Radio City Music Hall*** *(Map 7; ☎ 212-247-4777)*, Sixth Ave at W 51st St in Midtown; or the ***Beacon Theater*** *(Map 9; ☎ 212-496-7070, 2124 Broadway)*, between W 74th and 75th Sts on the Upper West Side.

JAZZ & BLUES

For the latest in fringe jazz, head to the ***Knitting Factory*** *(Map 6; ☎ 212-219-3055, 74 Leonard St)*, between Church St and Broadway in Tribeca. Its four performance spaces host all kinds of music, from cosmic space jazz to the occasional traditional gig (the Preservation Hall Jazz Band has taken the stage here), plus rock and hip-hop. Listen to bands on the main floor or the balcony or lounge in the bar downstairs. Ⓜ 1, 9 to Franklin St.

Visiting blues masters play at ***Chicago Blues*** *(Map 6; ☎ 212-924-9755, 73 Eighth Ave)*, at W 14th St in the West Village, which features nightly shows. The up-and-coming also perform at this none-too-flashy club, and if you've got a harmonica in your pocket, you can jump in for Monday night's blues jam. Ⓜ A, C, E to 14th St; L to Eighth Ave.

ANGUS OBORN

The basement-level ***Village Vanguard*** *(Map 6; ☎ 212-255-4037, 178 Seventh Ave)*, at W 11th St in Greenwich Village, may be the world's most prestigious jazz club; it has hosted literally every major star of the past 50 years. The cover charge runs from $15 to $20, with a two-drink minimum. Ⓜ 1, 9 to Christopher St.

Sweet Basil *(Map 6; ☎ 212-242-1785, 88 Seventh Ave)*, between Barrow and Grove Sts in the Village, hosts a well-known Sunday jazz brunch (the music's better than the food), plus weeklong visits by jazz stars like McCoy Tyner. Shows take place every night and usually feature touring artists. Ⓜ 1, 9 to Christopher St.

Despite its lack of a liquor license, ***Smalls*** *(Map 6; ☎ 212-929-7565, 183 W 10th St)*, near Seventh Ave in the Village, still packs them in with its incredible 10-hour jazz marathon every night from 10 pm to 8 am. After top performers wrap up their gigs in mainstream joints, they jam here into the wee hours. Future stars also come to this laid-back spot to prove themselves. The cover is $10 on weekdays, $20 on Saturday. Ⓜ 1, 9 to Christopher St.

By far the most famous (and expensive) jazz club is the ***Blue Note*** *(Map 6; ☎ 212-475-8592, 131 W 3rd St)*, near Sixth Ave in the Village. You might pay as much as $60 to hear big stars play short sets for a throng of tourists. Ⓜ A, B, C, D, E, F, Q to W 4th St.

An authentic smoky joint, the ***55 Bar*** *(Map 6; ☎ 212-929-9883, 55 Christopher St)*, near W 4th St in the Village, hosts jazz, blues and fusion nightly, with performances by first-rate artists-in-residence and stars passing through town. Cover charges range from next-to-nothing to about $15 (but that cover price includes two drinks). Ⓜ 1, 9 to Christopher St.

Inside the Time Cafe, ***Fez*** *(Map 6; ☎ 212-533-2680, 380 Lafayette St)*, near E 3rd St in the East Village, hosts the popular Mingus Big Band every Thursday. On other nights, you can catch drag shows, readings of novels in progress and rock concerts. Ⓜ 6 to Bleecker St.

The splashy ***Iridium*** *(Map 9; ☎ 212-582-2121, 48 W 63rd St)*, between Broadway and Columbus on the Upper West Side, comes with way-out decor and good acoustics. High-quality traditional jazz acts play two sets a night from Sunday to Thursday, three sets on weekends. This spot also hosts a Sunday jazz brunch. Ⓜ A, B, C, D, 1, 9 to 59th St-Columbus Circle.

Although Harlem's Cotton Club era ended long ago, you can still hear some good jazz here, whether your tastes run to the modern or traditional. The old ***Lenox Lounge*** *(Map 10; ☎ 212-427-0253, 288 Malcolm X Blvd)*, between W 124th and 125th Sts, merits a visit for its remarkable art deco interior alone. But those coming for a glimpse of the past have driven a lot of locals away from this vintage spot. Ⓜ 2, 3 to 125th St.

Showman's *(Map 10; ☎ 212-864-8941, 375 W 125th St)*, between Morningside and St Nicholas Aves, features jazz combos and R&B vocalists. Ⓜ A, B, C, D to 125th St.

Nat King Cole got married at ***Wells*** *(Map 10; ☎ 212-234-0700, 2247 Adam Clayton Powell Jr Blvd)*, near W 132nd St, which features progressive jazz combos on Friday, Saturday and Monday evenings, plus a relaxed Sunday jazz brunch. Most folks take in dinner and the show, but you can just prop yourself at the bar and listen to the band. Ⓜ B, C to 135th St.

Lickety Split *(Map 10; ☎ 212-283-9093, 2361 Adam Clayton Powell Jr Blvd)*, near W 137th St, specializes in Caribbean bands. Ⓜ B, C to 135th St.

FOLK & WORLD MUSIC

The ***Fast Folk Cafe*** *(Map 6; ☎ 212-274-1636, 41 N Moore St)*, between Varick and Hudson Sts in Tribeca, features only acoustic music every weekend. Ⓜ 1, 9 to Franklin St.

SOBs *(Map 6; ☎ 212-243-4940, 204 Varick St)*, between King and Houston Sts in the West Village, stands for Sounds of Brazil, but this spot features eclectic sounds from around the world, including Afro-Cuban music, salsa and reggae, both live and on the turntable. SOBs hosts dinner shows nightly but it doesn't really start jumping until 2 am. Be awake and ready to get down with a funky downtown crowd. Ⓜ 1, 9 to Houston St.

Buying Tickets

Ticketmaster (☎ 212-307-7171 for concerts, 307-4100 for the performing arts, www.ticketmaster.com) – and only Ticketmaster – sells tickets to most major concerts and sporting events. This monopoly on sales makes it easier for Ticketmaster to gouge customers. When you call, beware: You may have to pay 'handling,' 'venue' and 'postage' fees, which can add a whopping $20 to the cost of a top-price ticket. To make sure that you only pay face value for a ticket, go to the venue's box office directly.

Telecharge (☎ 212-239-6200, www.telecharge.com) sells tickets to Broadway and off-Broadway shows. See Tickets under Theater for more information.

The World Music Institute (☎ 212-545-7536) brings Algerian folk singers, Zairean congo players and other international artists to the ***Washington Square Church*** *(Map 6; 135 W 4th St)*, between Sixth Ave and MacDougal St, a century-old institution in the Village. Ⓜ A, B, C, D, E, F, Q to W 4th St.

The laid-back ***Back Fence*** *(Map 6; ☎ 212-475-9221, 155 Bleecker St)*, between MacDougal and Sullivan Sts in the center of Greenwich Village, offers folk and blues during the week, classic rock on weekends. Plenty of college students congregate here. Ⓜ A, B, C, D, E, F, Q to W 4th St.

Uptown, head to the ***Latin Quarter*** *(Map 9; ☎ 212-864-7600, 2551 Broadway)*, near W 95th St on the Upper West Side, which attracts a mature Latin crowd with mostly merengue and salsa. Local and international live bands perform Thursday to Saturday, and at least one room features hip-shaking favorites every night. Sunday attracts a younger party crowd with hip-hop and R&B. Leave your jeans and sneakers at home. Ⓜ 1, 2, 3, 9 to 96th St.

CLASSICAL MUSIC

The ***New York Philharmonic*** *(☎ 212-875-5656)* has been getting rave reviews under the direction of German-born conductor Kurt Masur, though the aging Philharmonic audience still resists deviations from the standard repertoire. Tickets range from $15 to $70 and can be purchased through Center Charge (☎ 212-721-6500). All concerts take place at Lincoln Center's Avery Fisher Hall, Broadway at W 64th St (Map 9). For a schedule, visit www.newyorkphilharmonic.org. Ⓜ 1, 9 to 66th St-Lincoln Center.

The ***Chamber Music Society of Lincoln Center*** *(☎ 212-875-5050)* ranks as the foremost chamber music ensemble in the country. Its main concert season takes place in early autumn at Lincoln Center's Alice Tully Hall (Map 9; ☎ 212-721-6500), which is also home to the American Symphony Orchestra and the Little Orchestra Society. Ⓜ 1, 9 to 66th St-Lincoln Center.

Visiting philharmonics and the New York Pops orchestra play at storied ***Carnegie Hall*** *(Map 7; ☎ 212-247-7800, 154 W 57th St)*, at Seventh Ave. Since 1891, the historic performance hall has hosted none other than Tchaikovsky, Mahler and Prokofiev. See the schedule of monthly events in the lobby next to the box office. For nonsubscription events, tickets often come as cheap as $12. Ⓜ A, B, C, D, 1, 9 to 59th St-Columbus Circle.

The city's more intimate venues for classical music include the ***Merkin Concert Hall*** *(Map 9; ☎ 212-501-3330, 129 W 67th St)*, between Broadway and Amsterdam Aves on the Upper West Side; ***Symphony Space*** *(Map 9; ☎ 212-864-5400, 2537 Broadway)*, at W 95th St on the Upper West Side; and ***Town Hall*** *(Map 8; ☎ 212-840-2824, 123 W 43rd St)*, near Sixth Ave in Times Square.

OPERA

New York's premier opera company, the ***Metropolitan Opera*** *(☎ 212-362-6000)* offers a spectacular mixture of classics and premieres. It's nearly impossible to get into the first few performances of operas that feature such big stars as Jessye Norman and Plácido Domingo, but once the B-team moves in, tickets become available. The season runs from September to April in the company's namesake Lincoln Center theater (Map 9). Tickets for center orchestra seats start at $150, but you can buy a seat in the upper balcony for $25. Standing-room tickets cost $12 to $16 and go on sale at 10 am on Saturday for the following week's performances. For a season schedule, visit www.metopera.org. Ⓜ 1, 9 to 66th St-Lincoln Center.

The more daring and lower-cost ***New York City Opera*** *(☎ 212-870-5630)* performs new works, neglected operas and revitalized old standards in the Philip Johnson–designed New York State Theater (☎ 212-870-5570) at Lincoln Center (Map 9). The split season runs for a few weeks in early autumn and again in late spring. You can view the season schedule at www.nycopera.com. Ⓜ 1, 9 to 66th St-Lincoln Center.

DANCE

New York is home to more than half a dozen world-famous dance companies. The ***New York City Ballet*** *(☎ 212-870-5570)*, established by Lincoln Kirstein and George Balanchine in 1948, features a varied season of premieres and revivals, always including a production of *The Nutcracker* during the Christmas holidays. The company performs at the New York State Theater in Lincoln Center, Broadway at W 64th St on the Upper West Side (Map 9). Tickets cost $25 to $62. For a season schedule, visit the Web site www.nycballet.com. Ⓜ 1, 9 to 66th St-Lincoln Center.

During the late spring and summer, the ***American Ballet Theatre*** *(☎ 212-477-3030)* presents its largely classical season at the Metropolitan Opera House at Lincoln Center (Map 9). Tickets range from $20 to $125. For a schedule, go to www.abt.org. Ⓜ 1, 9 to 66th St-Lincoln Center.

City Center *(Map 7; ☎ 212-581-1212, 130 W 56th St)*, between Sixth and Seventh Aves in Midtown, hosts the Alvin Ailey American Dance Theater every December, plus a steady stream of engagements by renowned companies like the Harlem Dance Theatre and American Ballet Theatre. The center's Web site (www.citycenter.org) lists a full schedule of events. The box office is on 55th

Getting Your Culture Fix in the Outer Boroughs

If you should find yourself a bridge away from Carnegie Hall and Lincoln Center, don't despair. Brooklyn boasts its own array of classical music offerings. The prime spot for high culture in the outer boroughs is the ***Brooklyn Academy of Music*** *(☎ 718-636-4100, 30 Lafayette Ave)*, which hosts concerts, operas and plays year-round in the Majestic Theater and the Brooklyn Opera House. The shows here range from formal Shakespeare productions to avant-garde music concerts. For a schedule of events, visit the Web site www.bam.org. Ⓜ D, Q, 2, 3, 4, 5 to Atlantic Ave.

You can also try ***St Ann's Church*** *(Map 11; ☎ 718-858-2424, 157 Montague St)*, near Clinton St in Brooklyn Heights, which features cutting-edge performances for about $25. The church doesn't hold arts programs in the summer, due to a lack of air-conditioning. Ⓜ M, N, R to Court St.

The chamber music program ***Bargemusic*** *(☎ 718-624-4061)*, at Fulton Landing, takes place on a floating barge in the East River during the summer. Ⓜ A, C to High St.

The ***Brooklyn Center for the Performing Arts*** *(☎ 718-951-4500)*, Campus Rd and Hillel Place on the Brooklyn College campus, hosts concerts and performances by small dance companies. For a schedule, visit www.brooklyncenter.com. Ⓜ 2, 5 to Flatbush Ave-Brooklyn College.

St between Sixth and Seventh Aves. Ⓜ N, R, B, Q to 57th St.

An offbeat dance venue, the ***Joyce Theater*** *(Map 7; ☎ 212-242-0800, 175 Eighth Ave)*, at W 19th St in Chelsea, offers non-commercial companies the chance to reach an audience. The Merce Cunningham and Pilabolus dance companies make annual appearances at this renovated cinema, which seats 470. Ticket prices average $35. For a schedule, visit www.joyce.org. Ⓜ A, C, E to 14th St; L to Eighth Ave.

CINEMAS

New York offers the movie lover plenty of choices, many of which range beyond the run-of-the-mill major Hollywood pictures you might find at your hometown cineplex. While it might seem strange to come to New York City to go to the movies, a lot of New Yorkers consider film to be just as much an art form as opera or Broadway drama. What's more, an air-conditioned movie theater offers the perfect respite from New York's sultry summer heat.

Because New Yorkers take film so seriously, you may find long lines at theaters in the evenings and on weekends, despite the fact that tickets now cost $9.50 and might jump to $10 soon. Most first-run films sell out a half hour early on Friday and Saturday nights. You're likely to have to stand in one line to buy a ticket and another to get into the theater, but you can avoid one of these lines by calling ☎ 212-777-FILM(3456) and prepaying for the movie of your choice for an additional $1-per-ticket charge; you get the ticket by swiping a credit card through a machine upon arrival at the theater.

The three-screen ***Film Forum*** *(Map 6; ☎ 212-727-8110, 209 W Houston St)*, between Varick St and Sixth Ave in SoHo, features independent films, revivals and career retrospectives. NYU students love it here, so you might want to bring something to read while you stand in a block-long line. Ⓜ 1, 9 to Houston St.

The ***Angelika Film Center*** *(Map 6; ☎ 212-995-2000, 18 W Houston St)*, near Mercer St in the Village, specializes in foreign and independent films. It always draws big crowds on weekends. The roomy cafe here serves some gourmet sweet treats. Ⓜ B, D, F, Q to Broadway-Lafayette St.

Anthology Film Archives *(Map 6; ☎ 212-505-5181, 32 Second Ave)*, near E 2nd St in the East Village, shows low-budget European and fringe works. Ⓜ F to Second Ave.

The massive, 13-screen ***Loews 42nd St E-Walk Theater*** *(Map 8; ☎ 212-505-6397)*, on 42nd St between Broadway and Eighth Ave in Times Square, sits on a block that became the quintessential porn district in the '70s; this facility, which shows mainstream movies, celebrates the area's restoration to cleaner entertainment. Ⓜ N, R, S, 1, 2, 3, 7, 9 to Times Square.

Lincoln Center's ***Walter Reade Theater*** *(Map 9; ☎ 212-875-5600, 165 W 65th St)*, near Broadway on the Upper West Side, boasts wide, screening room-style seats. Screenings for the New York Film Festival take place here every September. At other times of the year, you can see independent films, career retrospectives and themed series. Ⓜ 1, 9 to 66th St-Lincoln Center.

Sony Theaters Lincoln Square *(Map 9; ☎ 212-336-5000)*, Broadway and W 68th St on the Upper West Side, includes a 3D Imax theater and 12 large screens that play first-run features. Sony also operates other multiplexes throughout Manhattan, as does Cineplex Odeon (☎ 212-505-2463). Ⓜ 1, 2, 3, 9 to 72nd St.

The six-screen ***Lincoln Plaza Cinemas*** *(Map 9; ☎ 212-757-2280)*, Broadway near W 62nd St, is the place to go for artsy independent films on the Upper West Side. Ⓜ A, B, C, D, 1, 9 to 59th St-Columbus Circle.

In Brooklyn, the Brooklyn Academy of Music includes the ***Rose Cinema*** *(☎ 718-623-2770, 30 Lafayette Ave)*, which shows independent and foreign films. Ⓜ D, Q, 2, 3, 4, 5 to Atlantic Ave.

COMEDY CLUBS

Those looking for cutting-edge comedy should head to the Lower East Side and try the nightly shows at ***Surf Reality*** *(Map 6; ☎ 212-673-4182, 172 Allen St)*, between Stanton and Rivington Sts, where the Sunday night open mic attracts young comedians with attitude. Tickets start as low as $3. Ⓜ F to Second Ave.

Edgier comedians like Janeane Garofalo try out their stuff at the ***Luna Lounge*** *(Map 6; ☎ 212-260-2323, 171 Ludlow St)*, near Stanton St on the Lower East Side. But you never know who you'll see, since the comedians aren't announced ahead of time. The Monday night comedy shows cost $5, including a free drink. (On other nights of the week, the Luna Lounge features live music. See Rock, earlier in the chapter.) Ⓜ F to Second Ave.

If you're looking for mainstream material, try the long-established club ***Comedy Cellar*** *(Map 6; ☎ 212-254-3480, 117 MacDougal St)*, between 3rd and Bleecker Sts in Greenwich Village. This spot showcases high-profile comics, a number of whom like to make surprise visits. Robin Williams, Jerry Seinfeld and Chris Rock have all dropped in from time to time. Tickets cost $7 to $12, plus a two-drink minimum. Ⓜ A, B, C, D, E, F, Q to W 4th St.

A number of cable comedy specials have taken place at the well-known ***Caroline's on Broadway*** *(Map 8; ☎ 212-757-4100, 1626 Broadway)*, near W 50th St in Times Square. Tickets start at $15 on weekdays and $17 on weekends, plus a two-drink minimum. Ⓜ N, R to 49th St; 1, 9 to 50th St.

Chicago City Limits *(Map 9; ☎ 212-888-5233, 1105 First Ave)*, at E 61st St on the Upper East Side, features a long-running comedy revue that includes plenty of comic songs and sketches. Tickets cost $20 ($10 on Monday night). Ⓜ N, R to Lexington Ave; 4, 5, 6 to 59th St.

SPECTATOR SPORTS

Baseball

New York's baseball teams have had good years lately, which makes tickets hard to obtain for certain games. However, the Yankees and the Mets play a combined 162 home games during the regular season (April to October), so if you're in town for more than a few days, you shouldn't have problems walking up to the stadium and buying same-day tickets ($5 to $42.50).

The National League ***New York Mets*** *(☎ 718-507-8499)* play in windswept old Shea Stadium in Flushing Meadows, Queens; it's a 40-minute journey by subway from Midtown. Ⓜ 7 to Willets Point-Shea Stadium.

The American League ***New York Yankees*** *(☎ 718-293-6000)* play at their legendary namesake stadium in the South Bronx, just 15 minutes from Midtown by subway. Ⓜ B, D, 4 to 161st St-Yankee Stadium.

The two crosstown rivals play a limited number of regular season inter-league games.

Most games begin at 7:30 pm. (For more on the stadiums, see the Queens and Bronx sections of the Things to See & Do chapter.)

Basketball & Hockey

New York's high-profile basketball and hockey teams play in the famous 19,000-seat Madison Square Garden, Seventh Ave at 33rd St (Map 7), from early fall until early summer. The NBA ***New York Knicks*** *(☎ 212-465-6741)* and the NHL ***New York Rangers*** *(☎ 212-465-6741)* sell a huge number of season tickets, so visitors must buy individual game tickets through Ticketmaster or Madison Square Garden or deal with the many scalpers who hover around the area on game nights.

Scalpers charge a premium on seats that already cost up to $200 for big games. When dealing with scalpers, the best strategy is to wait until after the 7:30 pm game time, when prices drop – or merely head to a nearby bar. All the Knicks and Rangers games air on cable television.

In nearby New Jersey, the NBA ***New Jersey Nets*** *(☎ 800-765-6387)* and the NHL ***New Jersey Devils*** *(☎ 800-653-3845)* play at Continental Airlines Arena in the Meadowlands Sports Complex, Route 120 in East Rutherford, New Jersey. To reach the complex, take the NJ Turnpike to the Meadowlands exit (exit 16W). Public buses also run from the Port Authority Bus Terminal in Midtown to the Meadowlands.

Football

Ironically, New York's two football teams both play home games at a stadium in New Jersey. The ***New York Giants*** *(☎ 201-935-8111)* and the ***New York Jets*** *(☎ 516-560-8200)* share New Jersey's Meadowlands Sports Complex from August to December; they play on alternate weekends.

Tennis

The US Open, the year's final Grand Slam event, takes place over two weeks at the end of August (often including Labor Day weekend) at the ***USTA National Tennis Center*** *(Map 14; ☎ 718-760-6200)* in Flushing Meadows-Corona Park in Queens. Corporations buy up blocks of seats for the Open, so you might have to resort to scalpers for tickets to the big matches. As you approach the main court (Arthur Ashe Stadium), you'll find a gauntlet of hawkers offering tickets at outrageous prices. For early-round matches, try the box office.

The USTA rents out courts to amateurs year-round for $25 an hour and up. With the exception of Open weeks, you play on the same courts the pros use for practice. Ⓜ 7 to Shea Stadium-Willets Point.

Horse Racing

When Off Track Betting (OTB) offices were established in the 1970s, turnstile figures at racetracks in the New York area plummeted. Now the Sport of Kings is the Sport of Cigar-Smoking Retirees. The winter racing season (November to May) takes place at ***Aqueduct Racetrack*** *(☎ 718-641-4700)* in Brooklyn. Ⓜ A to Aqueduct.

The Belmont Stakes, the third leg of thoroughbred racing's Triple Crown, happens in early June at ***Belmont Park*** *(☎ 718-641-4700)*, just beyond the Queens border in Nassau County. A special Long Island Rail Road train (☎ 718-217-5477) leaves Penn Station for Belmont several times each racing day and costs $9 roundtrip.

The ***Meadowlands Racetrack*** *(☎ 201-935-8500)*, Route 120 in East Rutherford, New Jersey, features harness racing from late December to August and thoroughbred racing from Labor Day to early December.

Shopping

WHAT TO BUY

Antiques

Top-level auctions take place at Christie's (Map 7; ☎ 212-636-2000), 20 Rockefeller Plaza (W 49th St between Fifth and Sixth Aves) in Midtown. The premier auction house has sold items that once belonged to John F Kennedy, Marilyn Monroe and Frank Sinatra. Sotheby's (Map 9; ☎ 212-606-7000), 1334 York Ave near E 72nd St on the Upper East Side, specializes in paintings and fine furniture. Both auction houses have also opened up lucrative online auction operations (www.christies.com and www.sothebys.com). Friday's edition of the *New York Times* contains announcements about exhibitions of sale items.

Frequent antiques shows take place at the Park Ave Armory, Park Ave at E 61st St (Map 9). Browsers should head to the antique furniture stores on 59th St between Second and Third Aves. You'll find more stores on Broadway just below Union Square and along E 12th St in the East Village.

The Annex Antique Fair & Flea Market (Map 7; ☎ 212-243-5343) takes place every weekend (10 am to 5 pm) on Sixth Ave between 24th and 27th Sts. It attracts thousands of visitors and hundreds of dealers, who offer a generally high-quality selection of pocket watches, used cameras and one-of-a-kind items like gumball machines at outdoor stalls. Admission is $1, but you can hover on the fence to see if there's anything you like before paying to get in. The popularity of the market has spurred the creation of other markets in empty parking lots nearby; these are free.

The Chelsea Antiques Building (Map 7; ☎ 212-929-0909), 110 W 25th St between Sixth and Seventh Aves in Chelsea, features first edition books, furniture, lighting fixtures and other items at indoor stalls.

KIM GRANT

Bask in shopping heaven.

A Tax Cut!

Low prices, competition and the low values of the dollar against many major currencies make New York City pretty much a shopper's paradise. Now things have gotten even better: The city and state have exempted taxes on shoes and items of clothing under $110, which amounts to an 8.25% cut in price!

Beauty Products

Many Manhattan stores sell perfumes and colognes at steep discounts. But the chain store Cosmetics Plus (Map 7; ☎ 212-247-0444), 1320 Sixth Ave at W 53rd St in Midtown, seems to carry the most reliable supply of the popular scents.

The quirky pharmacy Kiehl's (Map 6; ☎ 212-475-3400), 109 Third Ave between E 13th and 14th Sts in the East Village, has been selling organic skin-care products since 1851, long before the Body Shop. Cosmetics giant L'Oreal bought this shop in mid-2000 for a reported $100 million, but the company promises it will not alter the nature of this shop – including its reputation for personal service and generous sample sizes and its policy of never advertising itself. Celebrities sometimes stop in to buy products or to admire the late owner's eccentric collection of antique Harley-Davidson motorcycles.

PENELOPE RICHARDSON

Take home an Empire State Building.

Books

General In business since 1920, the cluttered Gotham Book Mart (Map 7; ☎ 212-719-4448), 41 W 47th St between Fifth and Sixth Aves in Midtown, has become one of the city's premier shops. Its trademark shingle declares that 'wise men fish here,' and poets W H Auden and Marianne Moore have both dangled a line.

In its several pleasant Manhattan shops, Shakespeare & Co offers an assortment of general interest and academic selections. Its Greenwich Village store (Map 6; ☎ 212-529-1330), 716 Broadway between E 4th St and Astor Place, features a large selection of theater and film books and scripts. You'll find other branches in Lower Manhattan (Map 5; ☎ 212-742-7025), 1 Whitehall St between Stone and Bridge Sts; on the East Side (Map 7; ☎ 212-220-5199), 137 E 23rd St near Third Ave; and on the Upper East Side (Map 9; ☎ 212-570-0201), 939 Lexington Ave between 68th and 69th Sts.

A Greenwich Village institution, Three Lives (Map 6; ☎ 212-741-2069), 154 W 10th St between Waverly Place and Seventh Ave, stocks a good number of biographies. The wall-to-wall wooden shelves lend the place a comfy library feel.

St Marks Bookshop (Map 6; ☎ 212-260-7853), 31 Third Ave between E 8th and 9th Sts in the East Village, specializes in political literature, poetry and academic journals. This lovely big bookshop has become a popular neighborhood stop.

Coliseum Books (Map 7; ☎ 212-757-8381), 1771 Broadway at W 57th St in Midtown, includes a huge selection of paperback fiction and out-of-print titles.

The handsome Rizzoli chain sells great art, architecture and design books (as well as general interest books) in two beautiful shops: 454 West Broadway (Map 6; ☎ 212-674-1616), between Houston and Prince Sts in SoHo; and 31 W 57th St (Map 7; ☎ 212-759-2424), between Fifth and Sixth Aves in Midtown.

You'll also find several Barnes & Noble 'superstores' throughout Manhattan, including the chain's main store (Map 7;

☎ 212-691-3770), 128 Fifth Ave at 18th St. Other locations include Union Square (Map 7; ☎ 212-253-0810), 33 E 17th St between Broadway and Park Ave South; Astor Place (Map 6; ☎ 212-420-1322), 4 Astor Place between Broadway and Lafayette St; Chelsea (Map 7; ☎ 212-727-1227), 675 Sixth Ave between W 21st and 22nd Sts; and the Upper West Side (Map 9; ☎ 212-362-8835), 2289 Broadway at W 82nd St. Each features more than 200,000 titles, a music department, comfortable seating and a cafe where patrons can read magazines for free.

Barnes & Noble's rival chain, Borders, has three locations: in Lower Manhattan (Map 5; 212-839-8049), 5 World Trade Center at the corner of Church and Vesey Sts; in Midtown (Map 7; ☎ 212-685-3938), 550 Second Ave at E 32nd St; and in Midtown near the Upper East Side (Map 7; ☎ 212-980-6785), 461 Park Ave between E 57th and 58th Sts.

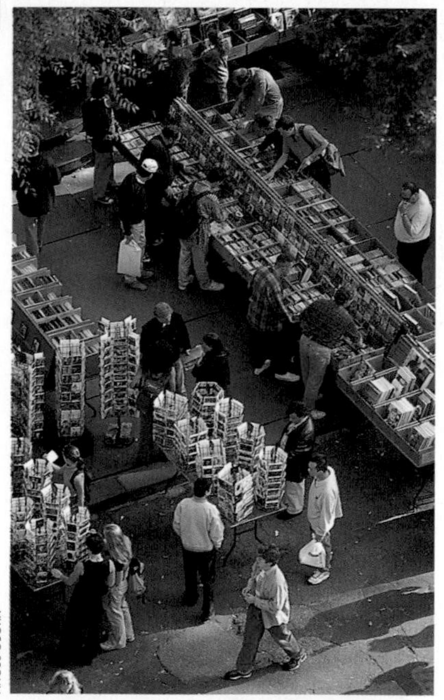

ANGUS OBORN

Book and music stalls, Union Square

Travel Traveler's Choice (Map 6; ☎ 212-941-1535), 2 Wooster St near Canal St in SoHo, sells guides, phrasebooks, dictionaries, maps and travel accessories – everything to inspire you to stay on the road.

The Complete Traveller (Map 7; ☎ 212-685-9007), 199 Madison Ave at W 35th St in Midtown, offers an interesting selection of first editions and old Baedecker guides.

Hagstrom Map & Travel Center (Map 7; ☎ 212-398-1222), 57 W 43rd St between Fifth and Sixth Aves in Midtown, carries a wide assortment of maps and travel guides.

If you're on the Upper West Side, try Civilized Traveler (Map 9; ☎ 212-875-0306), 2003 Broadway.

Gay Every decent bookstore now includes a gay and lesbian department. A Different Light Bookstore (Map 6; ☎ 212-989-4850), 151 W 19th St between Sixth and Seventh Aves in Chelsea, contains 15,000 titles on gay themes. It also features a small cafe, several author readings a week and a free Sunday night movie series.

Creative Visions/Gay Pleasures (Map 6; ☎ 212-255-5756), 548 Hudson St between Perry and Charles Sts in the Village, sells gay titles and stocks magazines and all the entertainment weeklies.

Although it's small, the Oscar Wilde Memorial Bookshop (Map 6; ☎ 212-255-8097), 15 Christopher St between Sixth and Seventh Aves in the Village, is packed with gay and lesbian literature, along with rainbow flags and other souvenirs.

Specialty Titles Applause Books (Map 9; ☎ 212-496-7511), 211 W 71st St near Broadway on the Upper West Side, carries screenplays and film essays. The Drama Bookshop (Map 8; ☎ 212-944-0595), 723 Seventh Ave between W 48th and 49th Sts in Times Square, features the city's largest selection of plays.

Books of Wonder (Map 7; ☎ 212-989-3270), 16 W 18th St between Fifth and Sixth Aves in Chelsea, carries children's titles and young adult fiction.

East-West Books (Map 6; ☎ 212-243-5994), 78 Fifth Ave between E 13th and 14th

Sts, contains a large stock of titles on Buddhism and Asian philosophies.

Whodunit lovers should head to the Mysterious Bookshop (Map 7; ☎ 212-765-0900), 129 W 56th St between Sixth and Seventh Aves in Midtown, and Murder Ink (Map 9; ☎ 212-362-8905), 2486 Broadway between W 92nd and 93rd Sts on the Upper West Side.

If you're interested in architecture, check out Urban Center Books (Map 7; ☎ 212-935-3592), 457 Madison Ave at E 51st St, an impressive shop inside the historic Villard Houses.

Used A well-loved New York institution, the Strand Bookstore (Map 6; ☎ 212-473-1452), 828 Broadway near E 12th in the Village, claims to have 8 miles of used books and review copies. This spot either inspires or crushes the aspiring writer.

The Argosy (Map 7; ☎ 212-753-4455), 116 E 59th St between Park and Lexington Aves in Midtown, features estate sales, rare prints, autographs, old maps, art books, classics and other eclectic books on all topics.

Cameras

New York's camera prices are hard to beat, but some of the camera stores in Midtown have earned reputations for 'bait and switch' tactics, so if you go in to buy a Canon lens and the salesman begins offering a cheaper, no-name alternative that's supposedly 'better,' beware. You should know what kind of camera you want, because most of the following places offer cheap prices but not patient service.

New York's most popular camera store, B&H Photo-Video (Map 7; ☎ 212-444-6615, 800-606-6969), 420 Ninth Ave between W 33rd and 34th Sts in Midtown, suffers from zoo-like crowding and a pay-first, pick-up-second bureaucracy. It does a brisk business with international clients, and even accepts personal checks (drawn on US banks) of up to $15,000. It's closed on Saturday.

Ken Hansen Photo (Map 7; ☎ 212-317-0923), 509 Madison Ave (18th floor) at W 53rd St in Midtown, specializes in Leicas and other top-end equipment. Don't fear coming here even if you need a lot of guidance; the salespeople are most helpful.

Clothing

The Garment District abounds with shops selling off-brand clothing at wholesale prices, mainly on W 37th St between Eighth and Ninth Aves. For funky clothing, head to the East Village, especially E 9th St between Ave A and First Ave. A number of young clothing designers are trying to make a name for themselves in eponymous shops in this neighborhood that attracts plenty of fashion-conscious women. These shops include Amy Downs (Map 6; ☎ 212-598-4189), 103 Stanton St at Ludlow St, which specializes in funky women's hats.

Dollar Bill's (Map 7; ☎ 212-867-0212), 32 E 42nd St between Madison and Fifth Aves near Grand Central Terminal, offers designer closeouts at markdown prices, much like Century 21 (see separate heading under Where to Shop, later).

For jeans, many people head to Canal Jean Company (Map 6; ☎ 212-226-1130), 504 Broadway between Spring and Broome Sts in SoHo, and the nearby Urban Outfitters (Map 6; ☎ 212-475-0009), 628 Broadway between Bleecker and Houston Sts in the Village. But these stores now sell an array of trendy accessories and no longer offer the cheapest prices in town.

For true bargains on casual wear, go to Old Navy (Map 7; ☎ 212-645-0885), 610 Sixth Ave near W 18th St, a chain store owned by the Gap; you'll find a few other Old Navy branches around town. Dave's Army & Navy (Map 7; ☎ 212-989-6444), 581 Sixth Ave between W 16th and 17th Sts in Chelsea, does an extremely brisk business selling jeans and construction boots to tourists; before the store closes on Saturday evening, you'll probably find a long line of airplane-bound foreign visitors stocking up on $35 Levis.

If you're looking for vintage attire, you'll find the best bargains in the East Village and around Ludlow St on the Lower East Side. Resurrection sells some gems from the past at two locations: 123 E 7th St (Map 6; ☎ 212-228-0063), between First Ave and Ave A on the Lower East Side, and 217 Mott St (Map 6; ☎ 212-625-1374), between Prince and Spring Sts in SoHo. Both outlets feature summer-long sales.

Computers & Electronics

Gateway Computers (Map 7; ☎ 212-246-5575), the mail-order firm, has opened a New York retail outlet at 4 Columbus Circle, Eighth Ave between W 57th and 58th Sts, with computers available for far less than European prices.

The massive J&R Music & Computer World (Map 5; ☎ 212-238-9100), 15 Park Row between Ann and Beekman Sts in Lower Manhattan, offers a good selection and reasonable prices, but the level of service depends on the salesperson you encounter. Avoid shopping on busy weekends.

CompUSA (Map 7; ☎ 212-764-6224), 420 Fifth Ave between 37th and 38th Sts in Midtown, features aisles of computer software and a good range of printers. Staples (Map 8; ☎ 212-944-6744), 1075 Sixth Ave between W 40th and 41st Sts in the Times Square area, sells computer peripherals, fax machines, printers and office supplies at decent prices.

If you're looking for light electronics, like extension cords and plugs, head to the stores that line Canal St between Sixth Ave and the Bowery. Avoid purchasing anything that requires a warranty here (such as cameras and stereo equipment), since the shopkeepers do not have good reputations, and *never* buy a phone or video camera from a roving street vendor – the equipment won't work or the box will be empty.

KIM GRANT

Jewelry

Groups of cooperative stalls sell discount diamonds, pearls and other jewelry in the 'Diamond District' on W 47th St between Fifth and Sixth Aves. The vendors here know how to look pained while offering you the 'best deal' possible – even though they're still making a healthy profit. Since Orthodox Jews own many of the stores, the street shuts down early on Friday and stays closed all weekend.

You'll find a similar cluster of Chinese-owned jewelry shops in Chinatown, with the greatest concentration near the intersection of the Bowery and Canal St. These are open weekends.

For first-rate jewelry, head straight to the biggest names in the business. Cartier (Map 7; ☎ 212-446-3460), 653 Fifth Ave near 52nd St in Midtown, sells some eye-popping rocks set in rings, watches, glasses, bags and brooches.

If you look hard enough in Tiffany & Co (Map 7; ☎ 212-755-8000), 727 Fifth Ave at 57th St in Midtown, you can take home a reasonably priced small item and get the impressive Tiffany box.

Kitchenware

It might seem odd to buy cookware and other prosaic domestic items in New York, but you can really beat department-store and catalog prices on items like espresso machines, Kitchenaids, Cuisinarts, chef's knives, pepper mills and even pizza peels (the wooden paddles that slide pizzas into the oven) by shopping the restaurant supply stores on Bowery just below Houston St. Be forewarned, though, that some of these places are closed Saturday. The retail store Bari (Map 6; ☎ 212-925-3845), 240 Bowery between Houston and Prince Sts, stays open all week.

The famous gourmet emporium Zabar's (Map 9; ☎ 212-787-2000), 2245 Broadway at W 80th St, is not only famous for its food but also for its large 2nd-floor kitchenware department, where you'll find some very good prices on gourmet items like espresso machines.

Music & Video

Tower Records (☎ 212-505-1500), 692 Broadway at 4th St, offers a wide selection of music at its huge main store (you'll find other branches around town) but specializes in rock and soul. You can purchase concert tickets at the Ticketmaster outlet here.

HMV, one of Tower's main competitors, generally sells CDs cheaper than Tower. HMV's Manhattan shops include a Midtown store (Map 7; ☎ 212-681-6700), 565 Fifth Ave at 46th St; an Upper East Side store (Map 9; ☎ 212-348-0800), 1280 Lexington Ave at E 86th St; and an Upper West Side store (Map 9; ☎ 212-721-5900), 2081 Broadway at W 72nd St.

Both Tower and HMV face major competition from the massive Virgin Megastore (Map 8; ☎ 212-921-1020), 1540 Broadway between 45th and 46th Sts in Times Square, a huge store with plenty of mainstream CDs, plus a decent selection of dance, jazz, classical and progressive music. Virgin has also opened a Union Square megastore (Map 7; ☎ 212-598-4666), 52 E 14th St at Broadway.

J&R Music & Computer World (Map 5; ☎ 212-238-9100), 15 Park Row between Ann and Beekman Sts in Lower Manhattan, offers a very large selection of jazz, hiphop and other mainstream music.

For discount CDs (less than $10), as well as bootlegs and imports, head to Triton (Map 6; ☎ 212-243-3610), 247 Bleecker St between Carmine and Cornelia Sts, and Route 66 Records (Map 6; ☎ 212-533-2345), 99 MacDougal St between Bleecker St and W 3rd St.

Other Music (Map 6; ☎ 212-477-8150), 15 E 4th St between Broadway and Lafayette St, brazenly opened right across the street from a Tower Records outlet, but it thrives thanks to its selection of offbeat CDs.

Uptown, NYCD (Map 9; ☎ 212-724-4466), 426 Amsterdam Ave between W 80th and 81st Sts, runs a permanent special: Buy four CDs, get the fifth free.

Traditionalists should head to Carmine St in the Village, where stores still sell old LPs. Footlight Records (Map 6; ☎ 212-533-1572), 113 E 12th St between Third and Fourth Aves, features a magnificent collection of out-of-print vinyl and foreign movie soundtracks.

Musical Instruments

Several legendary music shops reside on W 48th St between Sixth and Seventh Aves, including Manny's Music (Map 7; ☎ 800-448-8478), 156 W 48th St, and Sam Ash Music (Map 7; ☎ 212-719-2299), 163 W 48th St. Both of these sell just about anything you can play, new and used. These shops are closed on Sunday.

Guitar lovers will also want to head downtown to Matt Umanov (Map 6; ☎ 212-675-2157), 273 Bleecker St between Jones and Cornelia Sts.

Shoes & Handbags

You'll find low-cost knockoffs of Coach bags and leather backpacks in numerous spots in the Village: along Broadway just above Houston St, on Bleecker St and on W 4th St immediately off Sixth Ave.

ANGUS OBORN

Designer handbag shop, SoHo

TOM SMALLMAN

Manhattan's latest look

Fans of Doc Martens and the rest of the construction-boot crowd head to the stretch of W 8th St between Sixth Ave and Broadway, where some 30 shoe stores offer reasonable prices on workhorse shoes and sneakers. For Timberland and other great hiking shoes, check out the shops on Broadway in the five or six blocks immediately above and below the intersection with Houston St. Check ads in the *Village Voice* for specials.

For more elegant shoes, head to SoHo, where you'll find higher-priced shoe shops among the clothing boutiques.

Sporting Goods

Paragon Athletic Goods (Map 7; ☎ 212-255-8036), 867 Broadway between E 17th and 18th Sts in Union Square, not only offers the best selection of sports merchandise, but it also regularly beats prices at chain stores like Sports Authority. Particularly notable for its end-of-season sales on tennis racquets and running shoes, Paragon also boasts the best selection of in-line skates in the city and helpful staff who will help you choose the best kind.

The NBA Store (Map 7; ☎ 212-407-8000), 645 Fifth Ave between E 51st and 52nd Sts, carries some sports clothing (no sneakers, though) and a handful of sporting goods, including – you guessed it – basketballs. Mostly, though, this spot features memorabilia marketed by the National Basketball Association.

Toys

It may not be the only toy store in the city, but you wouldn't know it from the weekend crowds at FAO Schwarz (Map 7; ☎ 212-644-9400), 767 Fifth Ave between 58th and 59th Sts in Midtown. You'll wait about a half hour just to get into the hot spot during the holiday season. The Barbie salon at the back of the store (enter on Madison Ave) is wildly popular.

The smaller Enchanted Forest (Map 6; ☎ 212-925-6677), 85 Mercer St between Broome and Spring Sts in SoHo, is a delightful spot where you can avoid 'brand-name' toys and commercial tie-ins (eg, action figures from movies). It specializes in teddy bears and hand puppets. Virtually nothing here requires batteries.

The Warner Bros Studio Store (Map 7; ☎ 212-754-0300), 1 E 57th St at Fifth Ave, features stuffed versions of Sylvester, Bugs Bunny and other Warner Bros creations. Not for kids only, it also sells animation cels for $2500 and up. This has become one of the most profitable retail outlets in New York City, so expect a crowd.

A visit to the Disney Store (Map 7; ☎ 212-702-0702), 711 Fifth Ave near 55th St, will probably include some glad-handing with Mickey Mouse and other life-size Disney characters as you browse three floors full of merchandise.

WHERE TO SHOP

If you can't get it in New York, you probably can't get it anywhere. Virtually all neighborhoods in the city contain retail stores of some kind or other, from big-name emporiums to quirky little shops. If you've come to New York just to shop (as many do), you'll be able to browse the stores here for days on end, particularly in the concentrated shopping districts on Fifth and Madison Aves. But if you'd rather limit the time you spend shopping for presents to take home, take yourself to one of New York's famous department stores and get everything you need at once.

Department Stores

Bergdorf Goodman This elegant store (Map 7; ☎ 212-753-7300), 754 Fifth Ave between 57th and 58th Sts, has become a favorite with out-of-town visitors who are looking for classy gifts in prestige wrapping to take home. Bergdorf's features first-rate jewelry and couture collections, plus attentive staff and great sales. Ⓜ E, F, N, R to Fifth Ave.

Bloomingdale's 'Bloomie's' (Map 9; ☎ 212-705-2000), E 59th St and Lexington Ave, may think of itself as a New York version of Harrods, but this cramped, crowded department store matches the London emporium in attitude and almost nothing else. It doesn't duplicate Harrods' architectural splendor, magnificent food hall or grand selection of merchandise.

Still, a good clothing sale makes a visit here worth it. In recent years, snappy young designers have reinvigorated the apparel department. If you stop by, definitely walk through the bizarre 1st-floor perfume section, where dozens of clerks try to spray you with the latest scent while repeating the sales pitch in an automaton-like fashion. Ⓜ 4, 5, 6 to 59th St.

Century 21 This discount store (Map 5; ☎ 212-227-9092), 22 Cortlandt St between Church St and Broadway in Lower Manhattan, is a legend among savvy New York shoppers. It offers big bargains on designer clothing (including Armani shirts and Donna Karan dresses), perfume, sportswear and kitchen products and boasts a selection of men's wear as extensive as the women's department. Located across the street from the World Trade Center, Century 21 opens early for the Wall St crowd, and shopping here has become a ritual for business types and for those serving their two weeks of jury duty at the nearby courthouses. Ⓜ 1, 9 to Cortlandt St.

Henri Bendel This pricey department store (Map 7; ☎ 212-247-1100), 712 Fifth Ave at 56th St in Midtown, specializes in curious, stylish clothing, cosmetics and accessories from newly established and flavor-of-the-moment designers. Ⓜ E, F, N, R to Fifth Ave.

Lord & Taylor The ten floors of fashion at Lord & Taylor (Map 7; ☎ 212-391-3344), 424 Fifth Ave between 38th and 39th Sts in Midtown, feature conservative casual wear prominently. This place also offers a good selection of swimwear. The pleasant sales staff refrains from applying much pressure, even in the cosmetics department. Ⓜ 7 to Fifth Ave; B, D, F, Q to 42nd St.

Macy's Though its claim to be the world's largest store is dubious, Macy's (Map 7; ☎ 212-695-4400), 151 W 34th St at Broadway in Midtown, is certainly massive. Most New Yorkers have an affectionate regard for the storied emporium, in large part because of its sponsorship of a fireworks festival on July 4th and its annual Thanksgiving Day Parade. Though Macy's has experienced financial problems in recent years, the store's stock hasn't diminished, and it continues to hold its famous Wednesday 'One Day Sales.' Ⓜ B, D, F, N, Q, R to 34th St-Herald Square.

Saks Fifth Ave Famous for its January sale, Saks Fifth Ave (Map 7; ☎ 212-753-4000), 611 Fifth Ave at 50th St in Midtown, boasts a vast ground-floor selling space with pleasantly arranged stock and a helpful staff. Although it's a department store, Saks only sells men's and women's fashion items. Ⓜ B, D, F, Q to 47th-50th Sts/Rockefeller Center.

Takashimaya The Japanese owners have brought elegant Eastern style to the stunning Takashimaya (Map 7; ☎ 212-350-0100), 693 Fifth Ave near 55th St, which sells furniture, travel gear, clothing, housewares and other goods from all over the world. This store particularly concentrates on high-quality craftsmanship and gorgeous packaging. Even if you don't tour the whole place, take time to browse through the ground-floor floral department. The Teabox in the basement features a relaxing afternoon tea. Ⓜ E, F to 53rd St.

Madison Ave

For the funkiest boutiques, you'll have to head to SoHo, but Madison Ave shops display some of the latest fashion styles in the world. Strolling up Madison Ave from Midtown to the Upper East Side will bring you close to a Parisian experience, as designers try to outdo each other in their showplace stores. You'll encounter fewer crowds on Sunday, but you won't be able to drop in on any of the avenue's first-rate art galleries, which are closed that day.

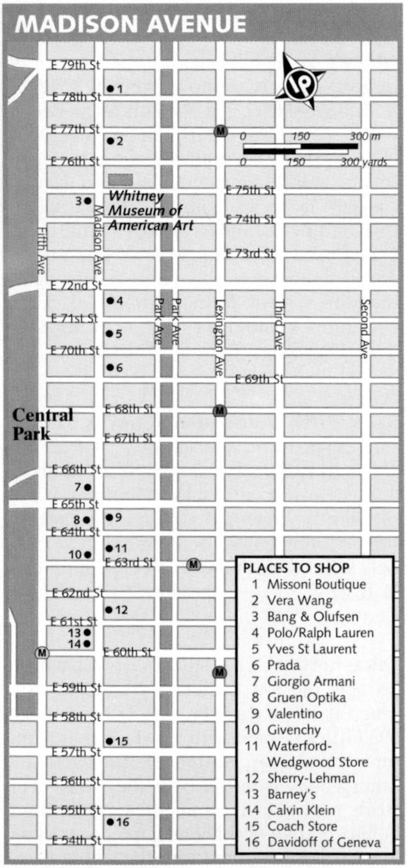

MADISON AVENUE

PLACES TO SHOP
1 Missoni Boutique
2 Vera Wang
3 Bang & Olufsen
4 Polo/Ralph Lauren
5 Yves St Laurent
6 Prada
7 Giorgio Armani
8 Gruen Optika
9 Valentino
10 Givenchy
11 Waterford-Wedgwood Store
12 Sherry-Lehman
13 Barney's
14 Calvin Klein
15 Coach Store
16 Davidoff of Geneva

Walking north on Madison Ave from 42nd St, you'll pass the following shops.

The legendary Brooks Brothers (☎ 212-682-8800), 346 Madison Ave near E 44th St, sells conservative clothing and formal wear for men; it also includes a smaller women's department.

Lederer de Paris (☎ 212-355-5515), 457 Madison Ave near E 51st St, sells fine leather goods and diaries from France.

Davidoff of Geneva (☎ 212-751-9060), 535 Madison Ave near E 54th St, features cigars, pipes, tobacco, cologne, ashtrays and ties – everything for the smoker except Cuban cigars.

The Coach Store (☎ 212-754-0041), 595 Madison Ave at E 57th St, is the place for expensive leather bags, wallets and belts that never go on sale.

Calvin Klein (☎ 212-292-9000), 654 Madison Ave between E 60th and 61st Sts, is a study in elegance by the media savvy designer.

Barney's (☎ 212-826-8900), 660 Madison Ave between E 60th and 61st Sts, has become famous for treating potential customers as too fat, too poor and, in the men's department, too straight. This is the hip and haughty clothing chain's flagship store.

Sherry-Lehman (☎ 212-838-7500), 679 Madison Ave between E 61st and 62nd Sts, is a world-class wine and spirits store with reasonable prices.

Givenchy (☎ 212-772-1040), 710 Madison Ave near E 63rd St, features traditional French suits and accessories.

The Waterford-Wedgwood Store (☎ 212-759-0500), 713 Madison Ave between E 63rd and 64th Sts, is one of Madison Ave's premier shops for fine China and blown glass.

Gruen Optika (☎ 212-988-5832), 740 Madison Ave between E 64th and 65th Sts, specializes in one-of-a-kind eyewear, with a full range of frames, from quirky to serious.

Valentino (☎ 212-772-6969), 747 Madison Ave between E 64th and 65th Sts, displays the creations of one of the world's best-known *couture* designers.

The massive Giorgio Armani (☎ 212-988-9191), 760 Madison Ave between E 65th and 66th Sts, shows that the world-famous designer can't stand to be outdone by anyone. Armani's gorgeous clothes fill four floors.

Prada (☎ 212-327-4200), 841 Madison Ave between E 69th and 70th Sts, showcases the Milan company's expensive and trendy offerings. The shoes start at $300.

Yves St Laurent (☎ 212-472-5299), 855 Madison Ave between E 70th and 71st Sts, features selections by the legendary master of French *couture*.

Polo/Ralph Lauren (☎ 212-606-2100), 867 Madison Ave near E 72nd St, is housed in an old mansion, which makes an appropriate setting for Lauren's clothing aimed at aristocratic wannabes.

Bang & Olufsen (☎ 212-879-6161), 952 Madison Ave near E 75th St, sells the most expensive and the best-designed electronic equipment in the world. The desk consoles are sublime, sexy and somewhat affordable.

Vera Wang (☎ 212-628-3400), 991 Madison Ave near E 77th St, offers bridal wear for New York's high society. You can only try on some of this stylish attire if you have an appointment, though.

Missoni Boutique (☎ 212-517-9339), 1009 Madison Ave near E 78th St, features the popular Italian designer's expensive knitwear.

Excursions

New York State

Just a short drive away from the crowded metropolis of New York City lies the bucolic serenity of New York State. If you're looking for a respite from the city's frenetic pace, you need only go as far as the beaches at the eastern end of Long Island (only a bridge away from Manhattan), where some of the activities include winery tours and bicycling adventures on the back roads. You can also head west from the city and take a scenic drive in the wooded countryside of the Hudson Valley. An upstate day trip in the middle of your New York City visit might just fortify you enough to return to the hustle and bustle of the Big Apple.

LONG ISLAND

The largest island in the US (120 miles from end to end) begins with Brooklyn (Kings County) and Queens (Queens County) on the western shore. New York City then gives way to the suburban housing and strip malls in neighboring Nassau County. The terrain becomes flatter and less crowded in rural Suffolk County, which comprises the eastern end of the island. Suffolk County itself contains two peninsulas – commonly called the North and South Forks – divided by Peconic Bay.

Long Island (population 2,609,212) began as a series of whaling and fishing ports, as well as an exclusive outpost for the ultra-rich, who built estates along the secluded coves on the north shore. In the years following WWII, Nassau County became increasingly more populated, as thousands of middle-class families moved to the suburbs. Many of them migrated to Levittown, built in 1947 in the center of Nassau County. It featured thousands of low-cost homes in huge tracts near major highways and railway lines leading into Manhattan. Named after its developer (Levit & Sons), the town attracted 55,000 residents and became the model for hundreds of similar, boring suburban communities across the USA.

In Suffolk County, economic development patterns were geographically reversed. The North Fork is home to salaried workers and owners of small farms, while the South Fork is dominated by several upscale villages (Hampton Bays, Southampton, Bridgehampton, East Hampton and Amagansett), known collectively as the Hamptons. Actors, writers and entertainment executives gather in the Hamptons to schmooze away the summer season on private estates and in expensive restaurants.

For most visitors, a trip to Long Island means a trip to the beach, whether the destination is crowded Jones Beach, quiet Shelter Island or the more showy Hamptons enclaves. All are within easy reach via public transportation, which is the best option for summer weekends, when traffic jams are particularly hellish. However, if you're interested in exploring Long Island's historic mansions or sampling wine in the vineyards of the North Fork, it's best to have a car.

Information

The Long Island Convention and Visitors Bureau (☎ 516-951-3440 ext 660, 877-368-6654 ext 660) publishes a free travel guide. You can obtain maps, restaurant listings and lodging guides from the local chambers of commerce.

Southampton	☎ 631-283-0402
Shelter Island	☎ 631-749-0399
Parks Information	☎ 516-669-1000
East Hampton	☎ 631-324-0362
Montauk	☎ 631-668-2428
Greenport	☎ 631-477-1383

Getting There & Away

Bus The Hampton Jitney (☎ 516-283-4600, 800-936-0440) leaves several times daily for

EXCURSIONS

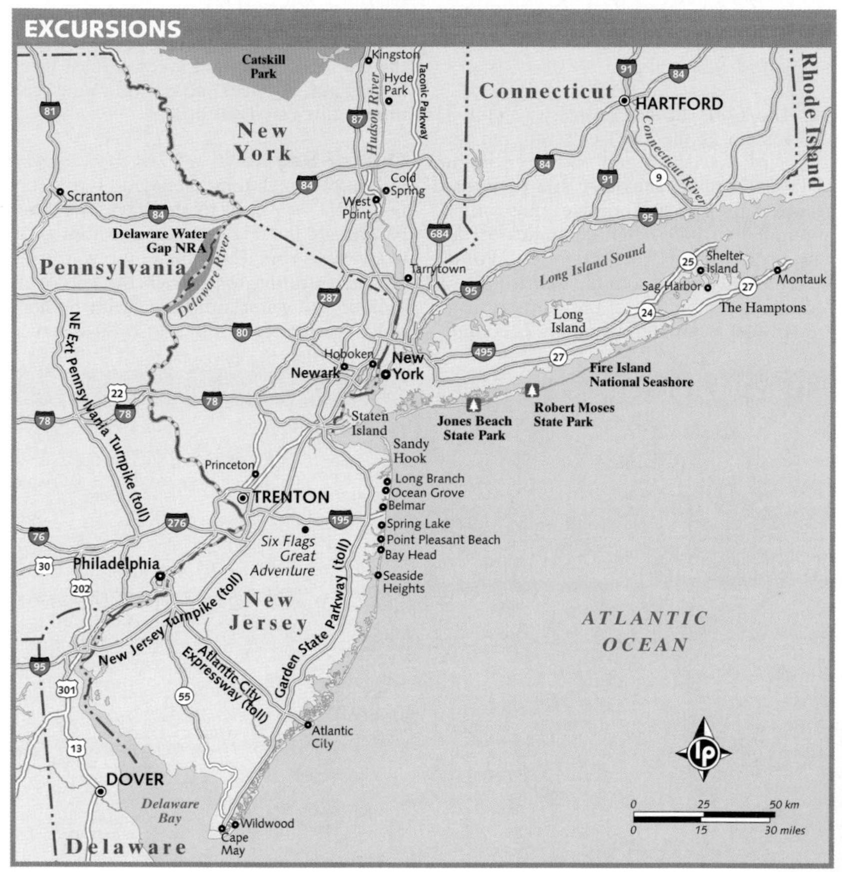

Long Island's South Fork from three locations on the East Side of Manhattan, including 41st St between Lexington and Third Aves. Sunrise Coach Lines (☎ 800-527-7709), which goes to the North Fork, picks up passengers at 44th St and Third Ave in Midtown Manhattan. The fare is $22 one-way, $40 roundtrip. The drivers usually know ways of circumventing summer weekend traffic, which makes riding these buses a good alternative to driving a car.

A number of private bus companies serve points within Long Island – call ☎ 516-766-6722 for information on transportation in Nassau County; for Suffolk County, call ☎ 631-360-5700.

Train The Long Island Rail Road (LIRR; ☎ 516-822-5477, 718-217-5477) carries 275,000 passengers daily to 134 stations throughout Long Island from New York City's Penn Station. Trips to the farthest points on the railroad – Greenport in the North Fork and Montauk in the South Fork – cost about $20 each way. In the summer, the LIRR offers roundtrip deals to the south shore beaches, but be aware that the lines at the station ticket office are very long on Friday night and Saturday morning.

Car The Long Island Expressway (I-495, also known as the LIE) cuts through the center of the island and ends by joining two smaller roads. The older Route 25 (also known as the Jericho Turnpike) runs roughly parallel to I-495, then continues to the end of the North Fork at Orient Point. Route 27 (also known as the Sunrise Hwy) runs along the bottom of Long Island from the Brooklyn border, eventually becoming the Montauk Hwy, and ends up at the tip of the South Fork at Montauk Point. A trip to the end of Long Island takes at least three hours, but on weekends, traffic jams can turn it into a six-hour ordeal.

Oyster Bay

Driving through tony, secluded Oyster Bay may take you back to the days of robber barons and the Jazz Age. Just one hour away from New York City, this quiet, waterside village is a refuge for the rich; the hills overlooking the water are dotted with million-dollar residences built a tasteful distance

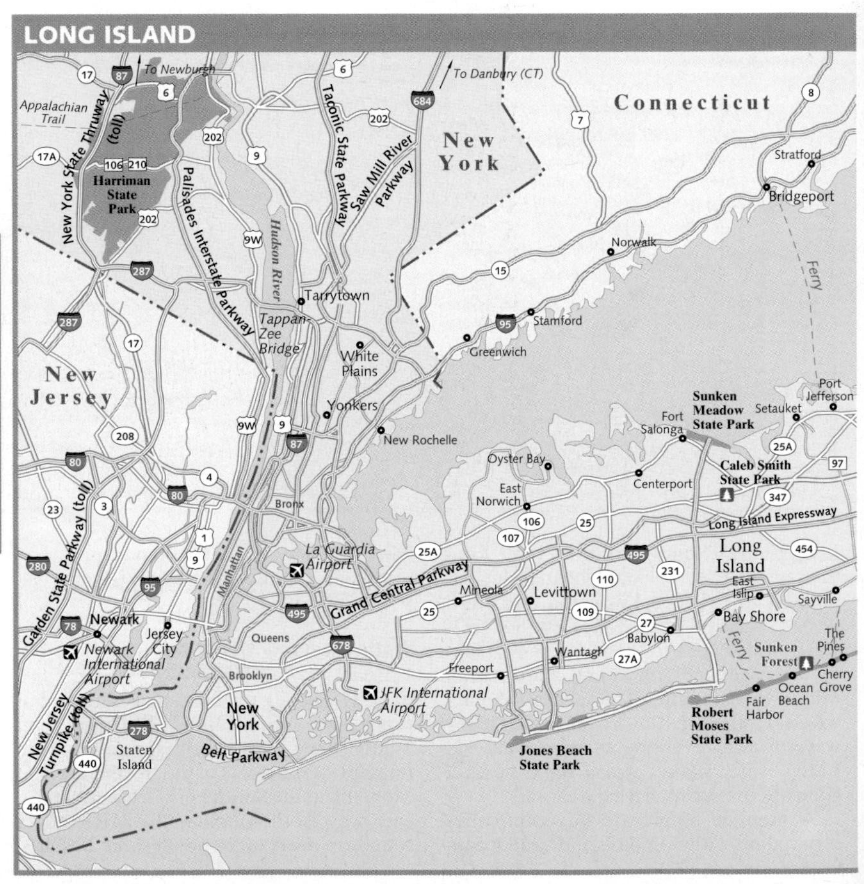

from one another. In 1885, Theodore Roosevelt built a 23-room mansion on **Sagamore Hill** (☎ 631-922-4447), which eventually served as the summer White House during his tenure in office from 1901–09. In this dark Victorian mansion, Roosevelt brokered an end to the Russo-Japanese War, for which he won the Nobel Peace Prize.

Roosevelt was in many ways the first president of the modern era – he used a telephone (still on view in his study) to remain in contact with Washington. Though he was also the first chief executive to concern himself with land conservation, animal rights activists will no doubt turn pale at the many mounted heads, antlers and leopard skins on display, along with the inkwell made from a rhinoceros foot.

Roosevelt died at Sagamore Hill in 1919 and was buried in a cemetery a mile away. A red-brick Georgian house on the grounds houses his gold Nobel medal. Later occupied by Theodore Roosevelt Jr, the home now holds a museum that charts the 26th president's political career.

Sagamore Hill is open 9 am to 5 pm daily from April to October and 9 am to 5 pm Wednesday to Sunday during the winter.

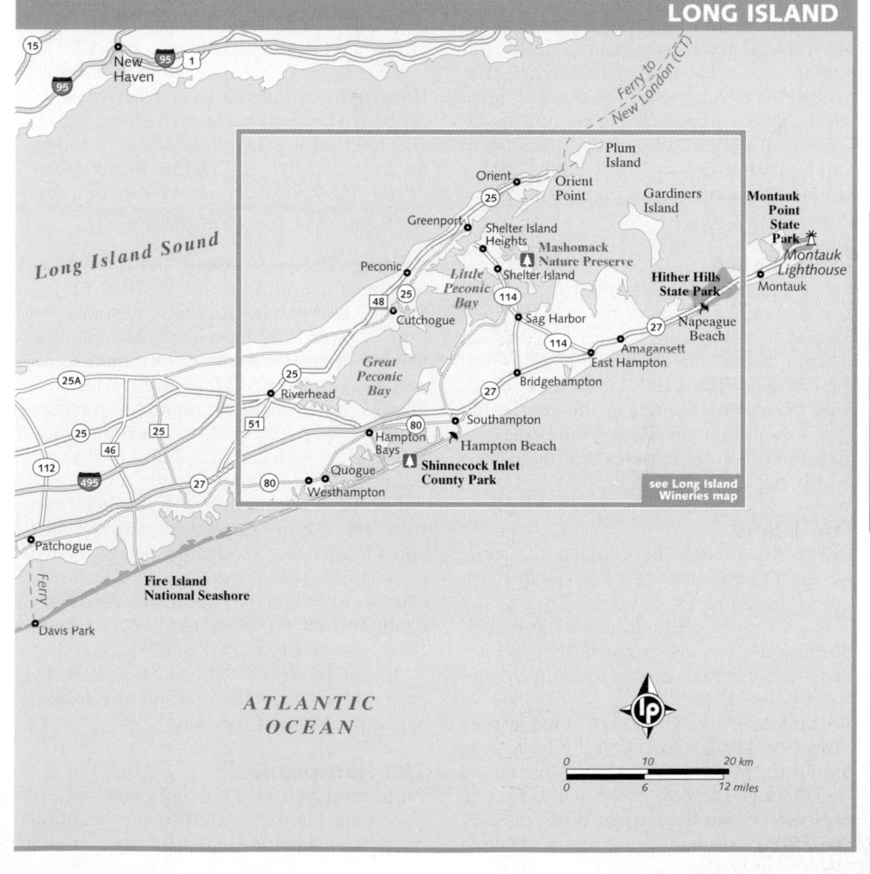

Tours of the Roosevelt home leave on the hour. Admission is $2 for adults, free for seniors and children.

To get to Sagamore Hill, take the 41N exit from the LIE to Route 106, turn right on E Main St and follow the signs on Cove Neck Rd.

In nearby Centerport, the **Vanderbilt Mansion and Planetarium** (☎ 631-854-5555), on Route 25A, once belonged to Willie Vanderbilt, one of the last major heirs to the Staten Island family railroad fortune. Willie spent most of his life – and money – collecting sea creatures and curiosities from the South Pacific and Egypt, many of which are on display at his former estate, also known as Eagle's Nest. A planetarium (☎ 631-854-5533), added to the grounds in 1971, features a 60-foot 'Sky Theater' and telescope. The mansion is now owned by Nassau County, which holds community events on the 43-acre site. It's open 10 am to 4 pm Tuesday to Sunday. Admission is $5 for adults, $3 for seniors, $1 for children; a planetarium laser show costs $7.50.

Jones Beach

Jones Beach (☎ 631-785-1600) is the most crowded public beach in the area. Though it's always mobbed, the sand at Jones Beach is clean, and it's an enjoyable respite from the city heat. The LIRR offers $15 roundtrips from Penn Station in the city to the Freeport station on Long Island; the trip takes less than 40 minutes and includes a shuttle bus to Jones Beach.

Fire Island

Robert Moses State Park, which lies at the westernmost end of the Fire Island National Seashore (☎ 631-289-4810), is the only spot on Fire Island accessible by car. Because it's so easy to reach, the park attracts the same kinds of crowds as neighboring Jones Beach.

The rest of Fire Island is a summer-only cluster of villages accessible by ferry only from three points on mainland Long Island (see Getting There & Away, later). Though the tourist board tries to play down the fact, Fire Island is probably the country's leading gay resort area. The scene tends to get a little wild on summer weekends.

Places to Stay Because Fire Island is a protected national park, you won't find many places to stay here, so it's best to make this spot a day trip. But if you're determined to stay overnight, try the following.

Camping spots include ***Heckscher Park*** *(☎ 631-581-4433)* in East Islip, at the end of the Southern State Parkway. Sites cost $14 at the campground, which is open from May to September. ***Watch Hill*** *(☎ 631-597-6633)* on Fire Island is across the inlet from Patchogue (pronounced **patch**-oog) on the mainland. To get there, take the Davis Park Ferry (☎ 631-475-1665). Dune campgrounds, which attract a lot of bugs in summer, cost $20.

The Ocean Beach area, halfway between Robert Moses State Park and Cherry Grove, contains a few hotels. ***Houser's Hotel*** *(☎ 631-583-7799)*, along Bay Walk, offers 12 rooms for $135 to $200. The ***Ocean Beach Hotel*** *(☎ 631-583-9292)* features 21 rooms that cost up to $225. It's only open in summer.

Getting There & Away The three ferry terminals are all close to the Bay Shore, Sayville and Patchogue LIRR stations. The ferry season runs from early May to November. Trips take about 20 minutes and cost an average of $12 for adults, $6 for children roundtrip, with discount season passes available. Most ferry departures are timed to coincide with the scheduled arrivals of trains from New York City.

Fire Island Ferries (☎ 631-665-3600) run from Bay Shore to Saltaire, Fair Harbor and Ocean Beach. Sayville Ferry Service (☎ 631-589-8980) runs from Sayville to Cherry Grove and the Pines. Davis Park Ferry Company (☎ 631-475-1665) travels from Patchogue to Davis Park and Watch Hill.

To get to Robert Moses State Park by car, take exit 53 off the LIE and travel south across the Moses Causeway.

The Hamptons

Prominent artists, musicians and writers have long been attracted to the beautiful beaches and rustic Cape Cod–style homes in the Hamptons, but the easy-money '80s brought an influx of showier summertime visitors who made their fortunes in the fashion industry and on Wall St. In recent years, the Hamptons have become an even hotter destination, as West Coast entertainment moguls purchase large homes here, following in the footsteps of Steven Spielberg. Year-round residents seem annoyed and amused in equal measures by the show. If you're celebrity-obsessed, you're better off heading to the Hamptons than standing in line at Planet Hollywood in New York City.

Many of the attractions, restaurants and hotels in the Hamptons close during the last week in October and remain shut until late April. B&B prices drop – and traffic jams along the Montauk Hwy disappear – about two weeks after Labor Day.

Southampton Southampton village doesn't have half the flash of its neighbors to the east, but it's a pleasant place to spend an afternoon in search of history and art. Pick up maps and brochures about the town at the Southampton Chamber of Commerce office (631-283-0402), 76 Main St, located among a group of high-priced craft shops and decent restaurants.

Just a few steps away from the chamber office is the **Halsey Homestead** (☎ 631-283-3527), a saltbox house built in 1648, eight years after the first of the European settlers arrived in the area. It's open to the public 11 am to 4:30 pm Tuesday to Saturday and 2 to 4:30 pm Sunday from June to September.

The **Parrish Art Museum** (☎ 631-283-2111), 25 Jobs Lane, is just a short walk away from Main St. It has been open to the public since 1898, and its gallery features the work of major artists like the late Roy Lichtenstein, who owned a nearby house.

The museum is open 11 am to 5 pm Monday to Saturday and 1 to 5 pm Sunday. In the winter, it's closed on Tuesday and Wednesday. Suggested admission is $4.

Sag Harbor Sag Harbor, 7 miles north of Bridgehampton on Peconic Bay, is an old whaling town that's far less beach-oriented than the other Hampton towns. The **Whaling Museum** (☎ 631-725-0770), just west of the shops on Main St, celebrates Sag Harbor's history. It's open 10 am to 5 pm Monday to Saturday and 1 pm to 5 pm Sunday from May to October. Admission is $3 for adults, $1 for children.

East Hampton & Amagansett The heart of trendy Long Island is East Hampton, where you can shop at the Coach leather store and attend readings and art exhibitions at the **Guild Hall** (☎ 631-324-0806).

Drive or bike down Main Beach along Ocean Ave to catch glimpses of the larger saltbox estates with water views. You can see some other grand (private) houses by turning right at Lily Pond Lane and peeking through the breaks in the high shrubbery.

Amagansett is basically an extension of East Hampton, distinguished by the huge flagpole in the center of the Montauk Hwy.

Montauk Montauk is a long, flat 13-mile drive from Amagansett along Route 27. If you're a biker looking for a challenge, peel off to the right and take the Old Montauk Hwy, an undulating road that overlooks the ocean and passes by several resorts.

Montauk itself is more honky-tonk than the rest of the Hamptons, with reasonably priced restaurants and a rougher bar scene. **Montauk Downs State Park** (☎ 631-668-3781) features a fine public golf course charging $25 per person for a round; there are long waits for tee times in the summer.

If you drive out to **Montauk Point State Park**, stop at the scenic overlook and avoid the parking lot at the very end (you'll have to pay for a view that's not really worth the money), unless you intend to visit the unimpressive **Montauk Lighthouse Museum**. Museum admission is $2.

You can take the LIRR to Montauk, but it's a 10-minute walk from the train station to the center of town.

Places to Stay You can camp near Montauk at ***Hither Hills State Park*** *(☎ 631-668-2461)*, a windswept, 40-acre campground along the Old Montauk Hwy, right on the Atlantic Ocean. Sites cost $16.

In the Hamptons, there's virtually no price difference between places calling themselves B&Bs and smaller inns – most have rates well over $150 a night in high season.

The renovated ***Mill House Inn*** *(☎ 631-324-9766, 33 N Main St)* in East Hampton, run by Dan and Katherine Hartnett, offers eight rooms that start at $100 off-season and $200 in summer.

Since 1957, the Fariel family has run the ***Sea Breeze Inn*** *(☎ 631-267-3692, 30 Atlantic Ave)* in Amagansett. It's just a block away from the LIRR station, and its 12 rooms (some with shared bath) are all clean. Rates are $60 to $140, with weekly discounts available.

The cheaper motels in Montauk run about $125 a night, but many are booked solid on a monthly basis by groups of students employed at the resorts and restaurants. For a list, call the tourist office at ☎ 631-668-2428.

The top hotel choices are the ***Montauk Yacht Club Resort*** *(☎ 888-692-8668, 32 Star Island Rd)*, with suites in summer running up to $400. ***Gurney's Inn*** *(☎ 631-668-3203)*, on Old Montauk Hwy, features 175 rooms and a spa. Rates start at $300.

In Sag Harbor, the ***American Hotel*** *(☎ 631-725-3535)*, on Main St, has eight rooms starting at $200. The ground-floor restaurant and bar attract weekending media types from Manhattan.

EXCURSIONS

Places to Eat It's easier to find reasonably priced places to eat than reasonably priced lodging in the Hamptons. Relatively inexpensive seafood stands line Route 27 near Napeague Beach (between Amagansett and Montauk); these serve fish sandwiches, fresh steamers and fried clams for $10 or less during the summer.

The most popular spots are the ***Lobster Roll*** *(☎ 631-267-3740)*, with its distinctive 'Lunch' sign, and the ***Clam Bar***, which also does a brisk business selling T-shirts to its BMW- and Mercedes-driving clientele. ***Cyril's***, a restaurant started by an ex-Marine with a handlebar mustache, serves an excellent sesame shrimp meal.

In Montauk, the ***Shagwong Restaurant*** *(☎ 631-668-3050)*, on Main St, serves good tavern-style meals year-round.

The ***Laundry*** *(☎ 631-324-3199, 31 Race Lane)*, one block from the LIRR station in East Hampton, was among the first celebrity-spotting restaurants to open in the Hamptons. There's less attitude here than in other places, and the food – generally fresh fish entrees in the $20-to-$25 range – is quite good. The ***Maidstone Arms*** *(☎ 631-324-5006, 207 Main St)* is the most elegant and expensive restaurant in East Hampton.

Entertainment Both Billy Joel and James Taylor have appeared at East Hampton's ***Stephen Talkhouse*** *(☎ 631-267-3117, 161 Main St)*, a 25-year-old concert venue with an active bar scene on nonperformance nights. Also in East Hampton, ***Rowdy House*** *(☎ 631-324-8555, 10 Main St)* is a microbrewery that gets crowded during the summer.

Shelter Island

Nearly a third of Shelter Island is dedicated to the **Mashomack Nature Preserve**, which makes the island a largely quiet retreat that offers a true respite from the crowds in the Hamptons. You'll find a small, attractive town center in Shelter Island Heights, a cluster of Victorian buildings on the north side of the island.

Piccozzi's Bike Shop (☎ 631-749-0045), on Bridge St, rents bikes for $18 a day; these are sturdy enough for a strenuous trek across Shelter Island. You can also take the bikes on the ferry to Greenport and then explore the North Fork and Orient Point. Call ahead in the summer to reserve a bike.

Places to Stay & Eat For such a small place, Shelter Island includes more than its share of B&Bs, including the ***Azalea House*** *(☎ 631-749-4252, 1 Thomas Ave)*, where the five rooms range from $50 to $125. ***Shelter Island B&B*** *(☎ 631-749-0842, 7 St Mary's Rd)* offers four rooms for $60 on weekends.

You can get great off-season rates at the ***Ram's Head Inn*** *(☎ 631-749-0811)*, on Ram Island Drive, a large, columned place overlooking the water. A room with a private

ANGUS OBORN

Mashomack Nature Preserve, Shelter Island

bath costs a mere $70 at off-peak times; during the summer, rates jump to $200 or more.

Almost all the restaurants on Shelter Island are only open during the tourist season. The ***Dory*** *(☎ 631-749-8871)*, near the Shelter Island Heights Bridge, is a smoky bar that serves simple fare on a waterfront patio. ***Shelter Island Pizza*** *(☎ 631-749-0400)*, on Route 114, is just about the only place open every day year-round.

Getting There & Away The North Ferry Company (☎ 631-749-0139) runs boats from the North Fork terminal (near the LIRR station in Greenport) to Shelter Island every 15 minutes from 6 am to 11:45 pm. The fare is $6.50 for a car and driver, and additional passengers cost $1. The trip takes seven minutes.

South Ferry Inc (☎ 631-749-1200) leaves from a dock 3 miles north of Sag Harbor, with boats operating from 6 am to 1:45 am. The cost for a car and driver is $7; additional passengers are $1.

Greenport

The main town in the North Fork, Greenport used to be packed with farmers and workers from the Grumman company, but economic change in the '80s forced a downturn that Greenport is still shaking off today. In recent years, though, weekending city dwellers have started snapping up properties in the area, changing the character of this working-class town.

Efforts to revive the slumping farming and manufacturing economy in the North Fork led to the establishment of several vineyards during the '80s. Today, Greenport makes a perfect base for exploring the Long Island wineries.

While you're in the area, make it a point to visit the tiny hamlet of **Orient**, about 3 miles from the Orient Point ferry terminal; follow the signs for the 'Orient Business District' at the Civil War monument on the side of Route 25. There's not much of a business district in this tiny 17th-century hamlet, just an old wooden post office and a general store, but Orient features a well-preserved collection of white clapboard houses and former inns. Farther out of town, you can bike past the Oyster Ponds just east of Main St and check out the beach at Orient Beach State Park.

Places to Stay & Eat The best place to stay in Greenport is the ***White Lions Inn***

Long Island Wineries

Today there are 14 full-scale wineries on the North Fork and three on the South Fork of Long Island, plus 50 vineyards that take up a collective 1400 acres of land. Long Island seems to have perfected the art of making white wine, but its reds lag behind because the soil and climate aren't conducive to those heartier grapes. Judge for yourself by visiting a few wineries – the vintners are more than happy to pour out a few free glasses of their product.

You'll find most of the major wineries in the North Fork on Route 25. Just look for the distinctive green 'wine trail' road signs that crop up past Riverhead; nine of the vineyards lie within 2 miles of the town of Cutchogue (pronounced **kutch**-oog).

The following wineries offer tastings, usually from 11 am to 5 pm during the summer months. Pindar Vineyards, the largest facility, also offers tours of its 250 acres of vines.

Bedell Cellars	(☎ 631-734-7537)	Palmer Vineyards	(☎ 631-722-9463)
Duck Walk Vineyards	(☎ 631-726-7555)	Paumanok Vineyards	(☎ 631-722-8800)
Hargrave Vineyard	(☎ 631-734-5158)	Peconic Bay Vineyards	(☎ 631-734-7361)
Lenz Winery	(☎ 631-734-6010)	Pelligrini Vineyards	(☎ 631-734-4111)
Osprey's Dominion	(☎ 631-765-6188)	Pindar Vineyards	(☎ 631-734-6200)

For more information on touring the wine trail, contact the Long Island Wine Council (☎ 631-369-5887), PO Box 74, Peconic, NY, 11958. For a *Winery Guide*, call ☎ 800-441-4601.

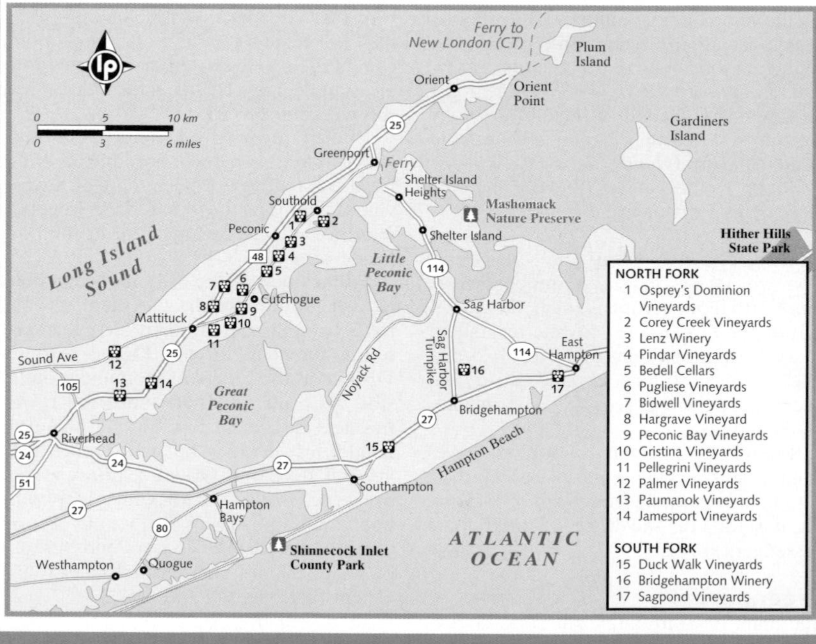

EXCURSIONS

(☎ *631-477-8819, 433 Main St*). This large old home, adorned by two huge stone lions, has five rooms (two with shared baths) and is only a four-block walk from the Shelter Island ferry dock and LIRR train station. Rates are $70 to $110, with free parking.

The ***Seafood Barge*** (☎ *631-765-3010*), just 3 miles from Greenport on Route 25, is one of the best places in the area to taste the sweet Peconic Bay scallops, a local specialty that has made a comeback after being devastated by 'brown tide' in 1994. The restaurant, which overlooks the Port of Egypt Marina, charges $18 for dinner entrees and offers a selection of lunch specials for $8.95.

Within Greenport, most restaurants are clustered around the marina. ***Claudio's*** (☎ *631-477-0715*), on the ferry dock, is a landmark that gets quite noisy at the long wooden bar and that charges a bit much for its food. A better option is ***Aldo's*** (☎ *631-477-1699, 103-105 Front St*), which is also pricey but serves sublime food and is known for its desserts, made in the small bakery next to the restaurant. Reservations are essential.

Getting There & Away The Cross Sound Ferry Company (☎ 631-323-2525, 860-443-5281) takes passengers and cars from Orient Point, at the tip of the North Fork, to New London, Connecticut, several times a day; reservations are recommended. Cars cost $32, including driver; passengers are $9 one-way. The company also offers a car-free hydrofoil shuttle from the terminal to the Foxwoods Casino and Resort in Connecticut ($14 one-way, $22 same-day return).

THE HUDSON VALLEY

You'll find many charming spots just north of New York City in this region, which refers to the villages and towns that dot the Hudson River south of Albany. Autumn is a particularly beautiful time here, and many city dwellers rent cars to see the changing colors.

Remember that even though the towns can easily be reached by the Metro-North commuter train from Grand Central Terminal, you'll find little reliable public transportation between towns or to sites set back from the river. You'll need to have a car for the fullest exploration of the area.

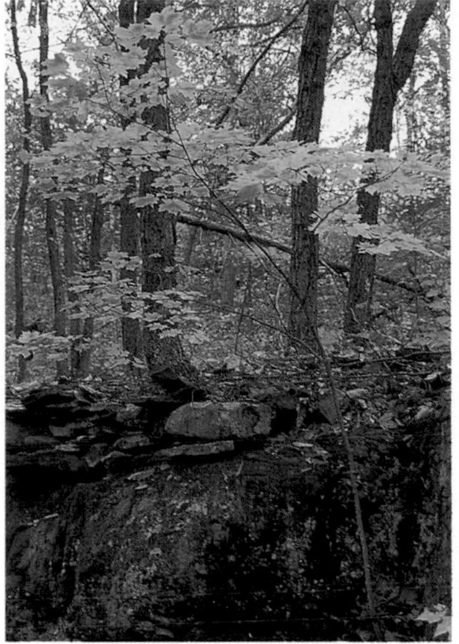
GEORGI SHABLOVSKY

Fall in the Hudson Valley

The regional Hudson Valley Tourist Board (☎ 800-232-4782) issues a guide to attractions and annual events. Orange County, the location of the United States Military Academy, also publishes a guide (☎ 800-762-8687). Most tourist brochures can be obtained at the New York State Information Center at Harriman, exit 16 off I-87 (the New York State Thruway).

Getting There & Around

Train While Amtrak trains (☎ 800-872-7245, www.amtrak.com) run the length of the river and connect with several communities on the eastern shore, your best bet from New York City is the Metro-North commuter train (☎ 212-532-4900, 800-638-7646, www.mnr.org), which departs from Grand Central Terminal (take the 'Hudson Line').

The regular one-way fare from Grand Central to various towns in the Hudson Valley ranges from $5.50 to $9.50 On weekends,

Metro-North runs special summer and autumn tourist packages that include train fare and transportation to and from specific sites such as Hyde Park and the Vanderbilt Mansion.

Car The principal scenic river route is Route 9, which hugs the east side of the river. On the west side of the river, the road is called Route 9W. Most towns can also be reached by taking the faster Taconic State Parkway, which runs north from Ossining and is considered one of the state's prettiest roads when the leaves turn in the autumn. The New York State Thruway runs west of the Hudson River.

Bicycle The country roads east of the Hudson River are perfect for biking. For further information, read *Mountain Biking Destinations in the NY Metropolitan Area* by Joel Sendek (Urban Country Publications) or *25 Bicycle Tours in the Hudson Valley* by Peter Kick (Back Country Books).

West Point

Generations of American soldiers have been groomed at the United States Military Academy since its establishment in 1802, including US Grant, Douglas MacArthur and Dwight Eisenhower. Today the cadet corps are made up of men and women who live on an impressive campus of red-brick and gray-stone Gothic and Federal-style buildings, churches and temples.

For maps and tour information, stop in at the West Point Visitors Center (☎ 914-938-2638), which is actually in Highland Falls, about 100 yards south of the military academy's Thayer Gate. It's open 9 am to 4:45 pm daily.

New York Waterway (☎ 800-533-3779) runs ferries to West Point in the summer months. By car, take the New York State Thruway to Route 9W North and look for the West Point exit, then follow the signs. It's about an hour's drive from Midtown Manhattan.

Hyde Park

The peaceful hillsides of Hyde Park overlook the eastern edge of the Hudson and are home to three significant attractions: the Franklin D Roosevelt Home and Library, the Eleanor Roosevelt National Historic Site and the Vanderbilt Mansion National Historic Site.

The **Franklin D Roosevelt Home and Library** (☎ 914-229-8114, 800-337-8474), 511 Albany Post Rd, was the first US presidential library. FDR (1882–1945) made Hyde Park his summer White House during his four terms. The museum features old photos, FDR's voice on tape (from the fireside chats and several speeches), a special wing in memory of Eleanor Roosevelt (1884–1962) and FDR's famous 1936 Ford Phaeton car, with its special hand controls that enabled the wheelchair-bound president to drive. President and Mrs Roosevelt are interred in the Rose Garden on the grounds.

The museum is open 9 am to 5 pm daily from November through April and 9 am to 6 pm daily from May through October. Admission is $5 for adults, $4 for seniors, free for children.

Because FDR's mother lived at Hyde Park until her death in 1941, Eleanor Roosevelt, who did not get along with her mother-in-law, stayed at her own home, which she called Val-Kill after the Dutch for 'valley stream.' It's now the site of the **Eleanor Roosevelt National Historic Site** (☎ 914-229-9115), 2 miles east of Hyde Park. After the president's death in April 1945, Eleanor made this her permanent home. The peaceful grounds are dotted with sugar maple and pine trees, and a dirt road leads to the cottage from the entrance off Route 9G. It's open daily from May through October and weekends only in April, November and December. Admission is free.

The **Vanderbilt Mansion National Historic Site** (☎ 914-229-9115) is 2 miles north of Hyde Park on Route 9. The spectacular

54-room beaux arts home, with many original furnishings still intact, used to be a mere weekend and summer cottage for members of the railroad dynasty. It's open 9 am to 5 pm daily from April to November (closed Tuesday and Wednesday during the winter). Admission is $2 for adults, free for seniors and children.

New Jersey

It's easy to see why the Garden State is largely ignored and often mocked. It stands in the shadow of confident, popular and powerful New York City. Most Americans think of northern New Jersey as merely a suburb of the Big Apple and southern New Jersey as a suburb of Philadelphia. To many foreign visitors, it looks like a crowded corridor of smelly oil refineries, shipping docks and dirty marshland along the New Jersey Turnpike leading into New York City from Newark International Airport.

This is the New Jersey of punch lines and snickering asides. But in recent years, the state government has made great and largely successful efforts to emphasize the area's varied pleasures – 127 miles of beaches, millions of acres of preserved parkland and historic sites inexorably tied to the nation's colonial history. Indeed, the tourism trade brings in $30 billion a year, largely from weekenders who seek the pleasures of the beaches or want to try their luck at the casinos in Atlantic City. Those who explore New Jersey off the beaten track may find their attitude toward this much-maligned state changing fast.

LIBERTY STATE PARK

This 1200-acre park (☎ 201-915-3403) faces the Statue of Liberty and also offers spectacular views of Manhattan. Ferries depart from here for Ellis and Liberty Islands and are always far less crowded than their counterparts operating from Battery Park (see the Things to See & Do chapter for information on the islands). Well worth a visit, Liberty State Park features a picnic area, a children's playground, paths for walking, jogging, cycling and horseback riding and opportunities for boating, swimming and fishing.

Entering the park, you drive along State Flag Row (with the flags arranged in order of the states' induction into the Union), and some 1750 feet ahead of you stands the Statue of Liberty. Beyond, you can also see the Brooklyn Bridge and, to the right, the bridge linking Staten Island to Brooklyn. Check out the **Liberation Monument**. 'Dedicated to America's role of preserving freedom and rescuing the oppressed,' this statue features a US soldier carrying a WWII concentration camp survivor.

The visitor center is open 6 am to 6 pm daily from May to November and 8 am to 4 pm during the winter.

Statue of Liberty Tours

Ferries (☎ 201-435-0499) travel from Liberty State Park to the Statue of Liberty and Ellis Island every day except Christmas Day. The boats tend to be less crowded than those leaving from Lower Manhattan, but the mobs on both islands mean you won't be able to take in both sites unless you depart well before noon. The trip takes just 15 minutes and costs $7 for adults, $6 for seniors, $3 for children.

Liberty Science Center

This spectacular modern museum (☎ 201-200-1000, www.lsc.org), also located in the state park, bills itself as a family learning center for science, technology and nature, with three of the four floors dedicated to the theme of invention. At the interactive exhibits, you can transmit sound through a laser beam, learn how to see in 3-D or watch a million watts of electricity flow through a coil to create lightning bolts.

The museum's shop, Tools & Toys, sells science-related products, books and toys. The Laser Lights Cafe offers terrific views across the Hudson to the Statue of Liberty and the Manhattan skyline, but you'll probably go mad from the noise of the school kids.

The Science Center is open 9:30 am to 5:30 pm daily from April to September and noon to 5 pm Tuesday to Sunday during the winter. Admission is $9.50 for adults, $7.50 for seniors and children.

HOBOKEN

Hoboken (population 33,397) is a New Jersey version of Brooklyn Heights – a gentrified community of well-preserved brownstones and apartment blocks within easy commuting distance of Manhattan. Young professionals who've moved here looking for cheap rent now live side by side with longtime residents. On Friday night, the younger folks get a bit rowdy as they wind down from the work week at local taverns' happy hours. Because Hoboken has developed a reputation as a weekend party town, the police have become rather aggressive about cracking down on drinking in public, so beware if you're out for a night of fun in Hoboken.

While many come only to indulge themselves, some visitors make something of a cultural pilgrimage to Hoboken. The city holds a small but important place in the history of baseball and popular music. It's generally agreed that the first organized baseball game was played here, on a plain overlooking Manhattan in 1846; a memorial plaque at the corner of Washington and 11th Sts commemorates the event. Hoboken's other claim to fame is its most famous resident: Frank Sinatra. 'The Chairman of the Board' was born here in 1915 and got his start in local clubs.

Orientation & Information

Since it occupies little more than a square mile, Hoboken is easy to explore on foot, and a grid system makes getting around a breeze. Most of Hoboken's shops and restaurants lie within a few blocks of the ornate old Erie Lackawanna Train Terminal, where the PATH trains stop, or along Washington St.

Parking in Hoboken can be a headache, especially at night and on weekends. With the parking police aggressively checking for offenders, you should consider paying to park in a lot rather than leaving your car on the street and risking a ticket.

The city has no tourist office, but you can pick up a copy of the free weekly *Hudson Current*, which covers local arts and special events, at bars and shops all around town. City Hall (see below) offers flyers on local events.

You'll find ATMs all along Washington St. The main post office is on River St between Newark and 1st Sts. Hoboken Books (☎ 201-963-7781), 626 Washington St between 6th and 7th Sts, features a good selection of reading material.

Hoboken City Hall & Museum

Built in 1881, City Hall (☎ 201-420-2026), 1st and Washington Sts, qualifies as an official State and National Historic Landmark. Inside, the Hoboken Historical Museum features display cases about local history, with mementos of Frank Sinatra. (Sinatra's birthplace was torn down some years ago, so this spot is the main Frank shrine.) The museum is open 9 am to 4 pm weekdays.

Places to Eat

A growing array of cafes and fancier restaurants populates Hoboken, especially on Washington St. ***Vito's Italian Deli*** *(☎ 201-792-4944, 806 Washington St)*, between 8th and 9th Sts, makes great submarine sandwiches. ***City Hall Bakery*** *(☎ 201-659-3671, 95 Washington St)*, between Newark and 1st Sts, offers the standard fare of cookies, cakes and coffee.

Schnackenberg's Luncheonette *(☎ 201-659-9834, 1110 Washington St)*, between 11th and 12th Sts, is a wonderfully retro place from the 1940s with prices from the '70s: Most items are under $5, including burgers, sandwiches and thick milkshakes. ***Piccolo's*** *(☎ 201-653-0564, 92 Clinton St)*, between Newark and 1st Sts, has been serving delicious cheese steak sandwiches at this location since 1955.

Established in 1899, ***Clam Broth House*** *(☎ 201-659-6767, 38 Newark St)*, near the train station, specializes in seafood dishes. It's decorated with photos of celebrities who've visited, including Frank Sinatra. ***Helmer's*** *(☎ 201-963-3333, 1036 Washington St)*, at 11th St, is a traditional German bar

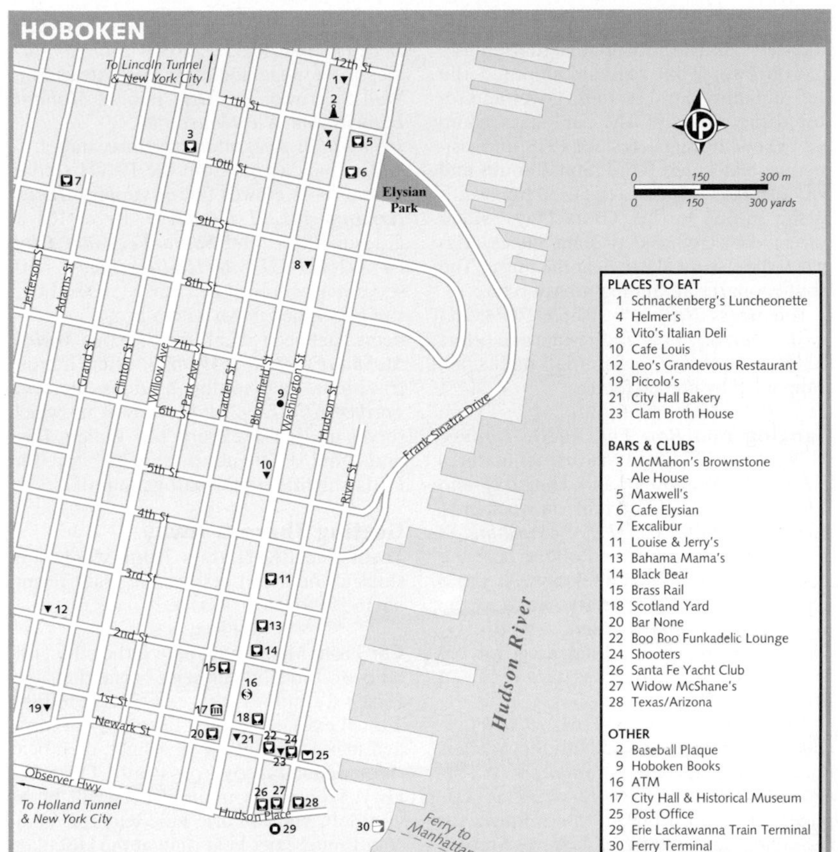

and restaurant from the 1930s. The $7 lunch specials include German specialties like knockwurst sandwiches with sauerkraut.

Leo's Grandevous Restaurant (☎ *201-659-9467, 200 Grand St*), at 2nd St, is another classic. Located in the neighborhood where Frank Sinatra grew up, it features pictures of the singer and still attracts Frank's old neighbors with its standard Italian dishes ($20 to $30). ***Cafe Louis*** (☎ *201-659-9542, 505 Washington St*), between 5th and 6th Sts, features varying cuisines, including Cajun and Spanish, and serves consistently good food in a pleasant room for less than $20.

Entertainment

Hoboken's lively music scene has even spawned a few independent record labels. The indie group Yo La Tengo launched itself here, and many big-name groups appear at Maxwell's, the city's most legendary club. At last count, Hoboken had 40 clubs and bars!

Most dance clubs stay open until 3 am on Friday and Saturday, and at least one club on Washington St seems to be rocking during the weekdays.

Rock ***Maxwell's*** (☎ *201-798-4064, 1039 Washington St*), at 11th St, is the reason many people visit this town. In the mid-'90s, Maxwell's disastrously re-created itself as a microbrewery, but regulars shunned the club and music loyalists took it over and restored the old ways. The bar's back room has been featuring acts since 1978, and visitors have included REM, Sonic Youth and Nirvana. Bruce Springsteen used Maxwell's as the setting for his 'Glory Days' video (directed by city resident John Sayles). Expect to pay about $12 to hear the music. The front-room restaurant features pub fare.

The ***Brass Rail*** *(☎ 201-659-7074, 135 Washington St)*, a bar and restaurant, offers live jazz Thursday to Saturday nights, accompanied by French food.

Dancing ***Boo Boo Funkadelic Lounge*** *(☎ 201-659-5527, 40-42 Newark St)* features live bands Wednesday and Thursday and DJs spinning house and funk on weekends. ***Bar None*** *(☎ 201-420-1112, 84 Washington St)* plays Top 40 music and offers 'beat the clock' drink specials on weekdays. As you'd expect, the crowd gets pretty rowdy as the night goes on. ***Bahama Mama's*** *(☎ 201-217-1642, 215 Washington St)* has no cover before 10 pm and $1 margaritas until 11 pm on Friday.

Excalibur *(☎ 201-795-1161, 1000 Jefferson St)*, between 9th and 10th Sts, attracts a largely gay clientele. At ***Shooters*** *(☎ 201-656-3889, 92 River St)*, at Newark St, DJs play house and drum and bass music for the college crowd from Hoboken's Stevens Institute of Technology.

Bars Built in 1896, the ***Cafe Elysian*** *(☎ 201-659-9110, 1001 Washington St)*, at 10th St, features a beautiful old bar that became a beauty salon and an ice-cream parlor to survive the Prohibition years. Some of the regulars – many of whom park their motorcycles out front – look like extras in the movie *On the Waterfront* (some scenes from that classic film were shot in Hoboken).

An old Hoboken standby from the beginning of the 20th century, ***Louise & Jerry's*** *(☎ 201-656-9698, 329 Washington St)*, between 3rd and 4th Sts, is a classic basement-level hangout with a coin-operated pool table and happy-hour specials. The ***Black Bear*** *(☎ 201-656-5511, 205 Washington St)*, a sports lounge and cigar bar, attracts the Wall St crowd. The Irish pub ***McMahon's Brownstone Ale House*** *(☎ 201-798-5650, 1034 Willow Ave)* offers a Sunday buffet.

The bars across from the PATH station attract large crowds full of yuppies. ***Texas/Arizona*** *(☎ 201-420-0304)*, River Rd at Hudson Place, and ***Santa Fe Yacht Club*** *(☎ 201-420-8317, 44 Hudson Place)* both serve reasonably priced Tex-Mex food that can be washed down with a broad range of beers. Between them, the raucous ***Widow McShane's*** *(☎ 201-659-9690)* offers a more traditional pub setting, as does ***Scotland Yard*** *(☎ 201-222-9273, 72 Hudson St)*, which serves up British exports like Fullers, Bass and Double Diamond from the tap. On Friday night, people quaff gallons of ale.

Getting There & Away

Train The PATH train from Manhattan stops at the Erie Lackawanna Train Terminal in Hoboken.

Car From Manhattan, take either the Holland or Lincoln Tunnels. From the New Jersey Turnpike, take exit 14C (Holland Tunnel exit), go to the bottom of the ramp and make a left at the first light, then bear right under the overpass onto Observer Hwy; Hoboken's main streets will be to your left. You can also take exit 16E (Lincoln Tunnel exit), bear right at the Hoboken exit and continue through the first light to the bottom of the ramp; turn right onto Park Ave, then left onto 14th St. You'll find Washington St three blocks later on the right.

Boat New York Waterway (☎ 800-533-3779) operates between Hoboken (near the Erie Lackawanna Train Terminal) and the World Financial Center in Lower Manhattan. Ferries leave every 10 minutes during rush hours and every 20 minutes at off-peak times (every hour, on the half hour, on weekends from 10 am to 10 pm). The trip takes eight minutes and costs $2 each way; a monthly pass is $75.

PRINCETON

Princeton (population 13,016) is known throughout the world for its Ivy League college, which educates 6000 students on an attractive, wall-enclosed campus. In addition to the beautiful campus, the town has some lovely architecture, interesting historic sites and a nice selection of shops and restaurants along Nassau St.

Princeton is particularly sleepy on Monday, when many of the places of interest are closed, and you should avoid the town in late May and June, since hotels are booked solid months in advance for graduation. During the summer, when most of the students leave town, you'll find peace and quiet, but it's often accompanied by hot and humid weather. The fall is the best time to visit – for what is a university town without students?

Information

The Princeton Convention and Visitors Bureau (☎ 609-683-1760), 20 Nassau St, offers maps and brochures for those planning a trip to Princeton, but it doesn't provide much helpful information for those already in town – the phone line is almost never

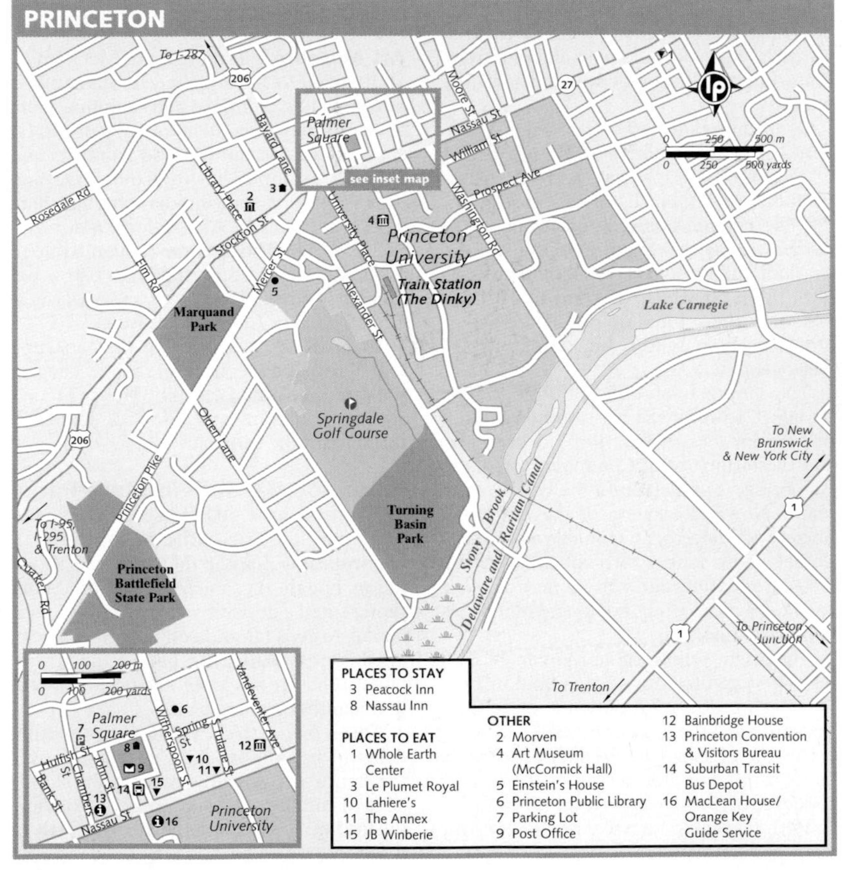

answered by a live person. But two other groups can assist you in town: the Historical Society of Princeton (☎ 609-921-6748) and, for university information, the Orange Key Guide Service & Campus Information Office in MacLean House (☎ 609-452-6303).

A map of literary Princeton that immortalizes the homes and hangouts of local writers is available for $10 at the town's bookstores.

Historic Houses

Albert Einstein's home sits at 112 Mercer St, but the house now belongs to a member of the Institute for Advanced Studies (where Einstein himself studied). Einstein's 2nd-floor study at the back of the house enjoyed a woodsy view of some pine and oak trees. Unfortunately, this spot isn't open to the public.

Drumthwacket (☎ 609-683-0057), on Route 206, was built in 1835 by Charles Olden, a Civil War governor, and refurbished by the New Jersey Historical Society. Today the historic home is the residence of the New Jersey governor. Free tours of the 1st-floor public rooms take place from noon until 2 pm on Wednesday. Be sure to call ahead, as these tours do not always operate. Admission is free, but donations are welcome.

The Georgian-style **Bainbridge House** (☎ 609-921-6748), 158 Nassau St, was built in 1766 for local tanner Job Stockton and was the birthplace of Commodore William Bainbridge, commander of the USS *Constitution*. Now the location of the Historical Society of Princeton, it contains a museum, library and a shop where you can pick up free information and self-guided walking tour maps, plus various books and other souvenirs of Princeton.

The bright yellow estate **Morven** (☎ 609-683-4495), 55 Stockton St, was built in 1750 for Declaration of Independence signer Richard Stockton. It later belonged to Robert Wood Johnson (the founder of Johnson & Johnson) and then served as the official residence of New Jersey governors from 1953 to 1981. It's open 11 am to 2 pm Wednesday or by appointment.

Princeton University

Orange Key Tours (☎ 609-258-3603) offers free tours of the campus. Student volunteers lead these walks, which include a history of the university along with some information for any prospective students about academic and social life on campus.

Look for the tour office in MacLean House, which is not well marked – it's the light-mustard colored building adjacent to the gate across from Palmer Square. The office is open 9 am to 5 pm Monday to Saturday and 1 to 5 pm on Sunday; tours operate at 10 and 11 am, 1:30 and 3:30 pm Monday to Saturday, at 1:30 and 3:30 pm on Sunday. You don't need reservations.

Art Museum This museum in McCormick Hall (☎ 609-452-3787) merits a visit. Exhibits include paintings and sculpture from ancient times to contemporary periods. Of special note are the Chinese paintings and bronzes, examples of pre-Columbian and African art and some modern art, including works by Picasso, Alexander Calder and Andy Warhol. The museum is open 10 am to 5 pm Tuesday to Saturday and 1 to 5 pm Sunday. A free guided tour takes place at 2 pm Saturday. Admission is free.

In addition to the art in the museum, you'll also find a collection of 20th-century sculpture, including works by Henry Moore, Jacques Lipchitz and Picasso, scattered throughout the campus.

Princeton Battlefield State Park

This historic park, 500 Mercer St, commemorates the historic battle of Princeton, a major turning point in the American Revolution. Fought on January 3, 1777, the fight represented a decisive victory for the Continental Army's famous commander, George Washington. After the battle, the triumphant rebel troops looted Princeton, a predominantly Loyalist town.

This is one of the few colonial-era battlefields to remain virtually unchanged over the centuries. An illustrated plan stands next to the flagpole, and graves of soldiers killed during the battle lie to the north of the memorial columns.

The park, about a mile southwest of downtown Princeton, is open daily from dawn to dusk. Admission is free. Stop at Bainbridge House (see Historic Homes, earlier) for a copy of the free leaflet describing the battle.

Places to Stay & Eat

There are few budget places to stay in Princeton. The motels along Route 1 are the closest, but they're far enough away that you'll need a car to reach them from downtown.

The Route 1 choices include the moderately priced ***Red Roof Inn*** *(☎ 908-821-8800, 208 New Rd)*, at Monmouth Junction off Route 1, where singles start at $55. The ***McIntosh Inn of Princeton*** *(☎ 609-896-2544)*, near the Quaker Bridge Mall about 5 miles south of Princeton, offers rooms for $60 and up. About a mile south of town, the ***Best Western Palmer Inn****(☎ 609-452-2500)* , on Route 1, has rooms for about $100. Also try the ***Days Inn*** *(☎ 908 329-4555)* and the ***Ramada Inn*** *(☎ 609-452-2400)*.

A little pricier, the ***Hyatt Regency Princeton*** *(☎ 609-987-2584, 102 Carnegie Center)*, off Route 1, charges $180 on weekdays and less than $100 on weekends. At the ***Marriott Residence Inn*** *(☎ 908-389-8100)*, on Route 1, rooms begin at $150 on weekdays.

Bed & Breakfast of Princeton (☎ 609-924-3189, fax 921-6271) provides information on the town's inns and B&Bs. The ***Nassau Inn*** *(☎ 609-921-7500)*, on Palmer Square, is a 1756 structure with modern additions. Famous visitors to the inn have included Fidel Castro, Indira Ghandi and just about anyone who's ever received an honorary degree at the university.

The 1775 ***Peacock Inn*** *(☎ 609-924-1707, 20 Bayard Lane)* offers a good location and reasonable rates, with 17 rooms for $100, including continental breakfast. It has the comfortable feel of an informal wealthy home.

The restaurant and bar ***JB Winberie*** *(☎ 609-921-0700, 1 Palmer Square)* features entrees under $15, a daily happy hour and an all-you-can-eat Sunday brunch buffet. ***The Annex*** *(☎ 609-921-7555, 128 Nassau St)* offers pub grub for less than $10. No college town would be complete without a veggie place, and the best in Princeton is the ***Whole Earth Center*** *(☎ 609-924-7429, 360 Nassau St)*, which offers organic choices.

ANGUS OBORN

The Gothic halls of Princeton University

Lahiere's *(☎ 609-921-2798, 11 Witherspoon St)* is probably the toniest place in town. French-Continental meals cost $30 per person. ***Le Plumet Royal*** *(☎ 609-924-1707, 20 Bayard Lane)*, at the Peacock Inn, offers a special $30 fixed-price menu, with à la carte meals for $40 per person and up. Both Le Plumet Royal and Lahiere's require that men wear jackets at dinner.

Getting There & Away

Bus Suburban Transit buses (☎ 609-249-1100) travel from New York City's Port Authority Bus Terminal to Palmer Square, Princeton. The trip takes about 90 minutes and costs $15.80.

Train NJ Transit (☎ 973-762-5100) and Amtrak (☎ 800-872-7245, www.amtrak.com) offer several daily trains to Princeton Junction from New York City. The fare on NJ Transit is $9 one-way, $13 roundtrip. The faster Amtrak train costs $28 one-way. Passengers must then cross over to a smaller train (known to locals as 'the dinky') to make the five-minute trip to Princeton itself. That train stops right next to the university campus.

Car From New York and northern New Jersey, take the New Jersey Turnpike to exit 9; follow Route 1 south to Princeton and take the Washington Rd exit (Route 571) to Nassau St. You can also take Route 1 (instead of the New Jersey Turnpike) all the way from northern New Jersey to Princeton, but be prepared to encounter a lot of stop lights.

ATLANTIC CITY

Since casino gambling came to Atlantic City on the Jersey Shore in 1977, the town has become one of the most popular tourist destinations in the USA, with 37 million annual visitors spending some $4 billion at its 13 casinos and numerous restaurants. But even though the casino industry has created 45,000 jobs and experienced record profits, little of this money has benefited Atlantic City itself. Homelessness and crime are still big problems, and the four-block stretch of town from the end of the Atlantic City Expressway to the beachfront casinos is still a depressing collection of empty lots, rough-looking bars and abandoned warehouses. The boardwalk itself includes a string of fortress-like casinos punctuated by the odd T-shirt shop and gyro stand. Since the self-contained casinos have their own restaurants, bars and nightclubs (the better to keep players entertained and spending in one place), few people mill about the streets.

The bottom line is that for non-gamblers, there is no reason to visit Atlantic City unless you're on your way to the Cape May resort area or Philadelphia. But if you want to gamble, you can't beat Atlantic City's selection of 700 blackjack tables and nearly 30,000 slot machines. If you visit, plan on trying your luck at something – even if you wish to spend only $10 or $15 – and remember that it's no sin to walk away if you're ahead of the game.

Information

The Visitors Information Center (☎ 609-344-8338) is at 1716 Pacific Ave between Indiana Ave and Martin Luther King Jr Blvd. Five information booths stand along the Boardwalk between the Taj Mahal to the north and the Grand Casino to the south. Also, a desk inside the old Convention Center provides many brochures for local hotels from 10 am to 7 pm daily.

The best of the free guides to the area are the monthly *AC Shoreline* and the weeklies *Whoot* and *At the Shore*.

Not surprisingly, you can find banks and ATMs near the gaming areas of all the casinos. Casinos will also do foreign-currency exchange and give advances against credit cards.

Casinos

Atlantic City's casinos are obviously the major attractions here, and though high rollers all seem to have a favorite, the gaming areas tend to look alike (garish) and sound alike (loud).

Most of the casinos in 'AC' are dedicated to gaming and, beyond the Taj Mahal, do not emphasize glitz and showmanship like their Las Vegas counterparts. But all that could change when Las Vegas showman Steve Wynn opens a brand-new casino at the marina.

Note: You must be at least 21 years old to gamble or be on the gambling floor.

The city's many casinos include the following. The southernmost casino, **Atlantic City Hilton** (☎ 609-340-7100), Boardwalk at Boston Ave, has more than 500 hotel rooms.

Bally's Park Place Casino Hotel & Tower (☎ 609-340-2000), Park Place at the Boardwalk, occupies the site of the 1860 Dennis Hotel, which is incorporated into the newer, 1200-room facility. It's the site of many heavyweight boxing matches.

Caesar's Atlantic City (☎ 609-348-4411), Arkansas Ave at the Boardwalk, contains

1000 rooms and Atlantic City's Planet Hollywood theme restaurant, which is just off the gaming area.

Popular with low-rolling senior citizens, the **Claridge Casino Hotel** (☎ 609-340-3400), on Indiana Ave one block west of the Boardwalk, is accessible by a moving walkway that operates in one direction only – into the casino, not out. The casino has 500 rooms and a three-floor, claustrophobic gaming area.

Harrah's Marina Hotel Casino (☎ 609-441-5000), Brigantine Blvd, contains 760 rooms in its two towers.

Resorts Casino Hotel (☎ 609-340-6000), North Carolina Ave at the Boardwalk, is a 670-room Victorian hotel that served as a hospital during WWII.

Sands Hotel, Casino & Country Club (☎ 609-441-4000, 800-257-8580), Indiana Ave near the Boardwalk, looks like a big black glass box.

Showboat Casino (☎ 609-343-4000), Delaware Ave and the Boardwalk, features a riverboat theme interior in its 700 rooms.

Tropicana Casino & Entertainment Resort (☎ 609-340-4000), Iowa Ave at the Boardwalk, is one of the biggest places in town, with its own indoor theme park (Tivoli Pier), a 90,000-sq-foot casino and 1020 rooms.

Trump's Marina Resort (☎ 609-441-2000), Huron Ave near Brigantine Blvd, overlooks the Farley State Marina and features an art deco theme. Away from the Boardwalk, the two casino hotels here offer a more relaxed setting.

Trump Plaza Casino Hotel (☎ 609-441-6700), Mississippi Ave at the Boardwalk, features a Warner Bros Studio Store overlooking the Boardwalk and 560 rooms.

Once the most extravagant property in Atlantic City, the garish **Trump Taj Mahal** (☎ 609-449-1000), 1000 Boardwalk, is now being eclipsed by the newer Mirage resorts at the marina. Nine 2-ton limestone elephants welcome visitors, and 70 bright minarets crown the rooftops. The German crystal chandeliers in the casino and lobby alone cost $15 million, but despite the garish nature of the interior, the room rates are similar to those found in more modest facilities.

The Boardwalk

Atlantic City Historical Museum On the site of the restored Garden Pier, this museum (☎ 609-347-5839), New Jersey Ave at the Boardwalk, provides a look at the city's colorful past, taking visitors back to the heyday of Atlantic City, when such stars as Benny Goodman, Frank Sinatra and Duke Ellington headlined at the casinos. The Florence Valore Miller Arts Center, part of the same complex as the museum, features changing exhibits of regional and local art. It occupies the building on the north of the pier. The center is open 10 am to 4 pm daily.

Steel Pier This amusement pier, directly in front of the Taj Mahal casino, belongs to Donald Trump's empire. It used to be the place where the famous diving horse plunged

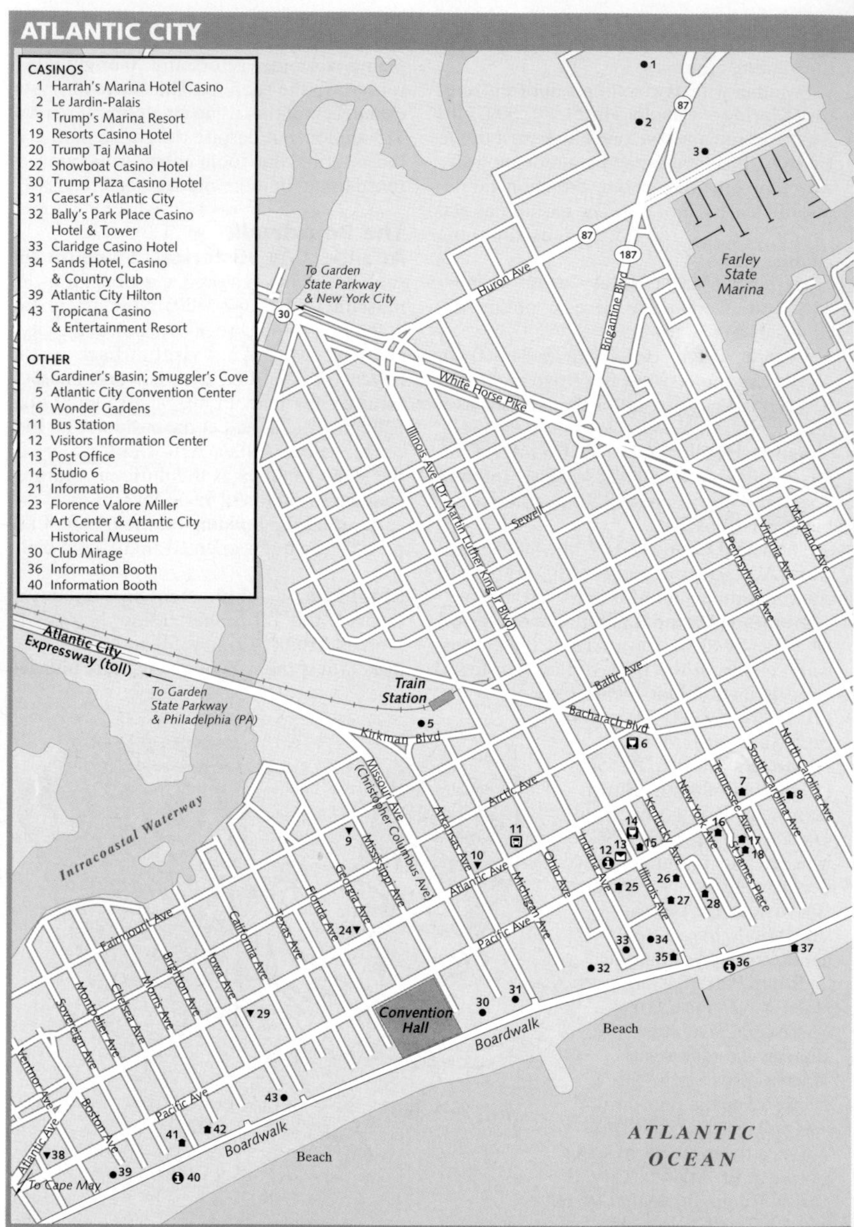
ATLANTIC CITY
CASINOS
1 Harrah's Marina Hotel Casino
2 Le Jardin-Palais
3 Trump's Marina Resort
19 Resorts Casino Hotel
20 Trump Taj Mahal
22 Showboat Casino Hotel
30 Trump Plaza Casino Hotel
31 Caesar's Atlantic City
32 Bally's Park Place Casino Hotel & Tower
33 Claridge Casino Hotel
34 Sands Hotel, Casino & Country Club
39 Atlantic City Hilton
43 Tropicana Casino & Entertainment Resort
OTHER
4 Gardiner's Basin; Smuggler's Cove
5 Atlantic City Convention Center
6 Wonder Gardens
11 Bus Station
12 Visitors Information Center
13 Post Office
14 Studio 6
21 Information Booth
23 Florence Valore Miller Art Center & Atlantic City Historical Museum
30 Club Mirage
36 Information Booth
40 Information Booth
To Garden State Parkway & New York City
Farley State Marina
Huron Ave
Brigantine Blvd
White Horse Pike
Illinois Ave (Dr Martin Luther King Jr Blvd)
Sewell
Pennsylvania Ave
Virginia Ave
Maryland Ave
Atlantic City Expressway (toll)
To Garden State Parkway & Philadelphia (PA)
Train Station
Baltic Ave
Bacharach Blvd
Kirkman Blvd
Missouri Ave (Christopher Columbus Ave)
Arctic Ave
Arkansas Ave
Atlantic Ave
Intracoastal Waterway
Mississippi Ave
Georgia Ave
Florida Ave
Texas Ave
California Ave
Iowa Ave
Brighton Ave
Morris Ave
Chelsea Ave
Montpelier Ave
Sovereign Ave
Ventnor Ave
Boston Ave
Fairmount Ave
Michigan Ave
Ohio Ave
Indiana Ave
Illinois Ave
Kentucky Ave
New York Ave
Tennessee Ave
South Carolina Ave
North Carolina Ave
St James Place
Pacific Ave
Convention Hall
Boardwalk
Beach
ATLANTIC OCEAN
To Cape May

EXCURSIONS

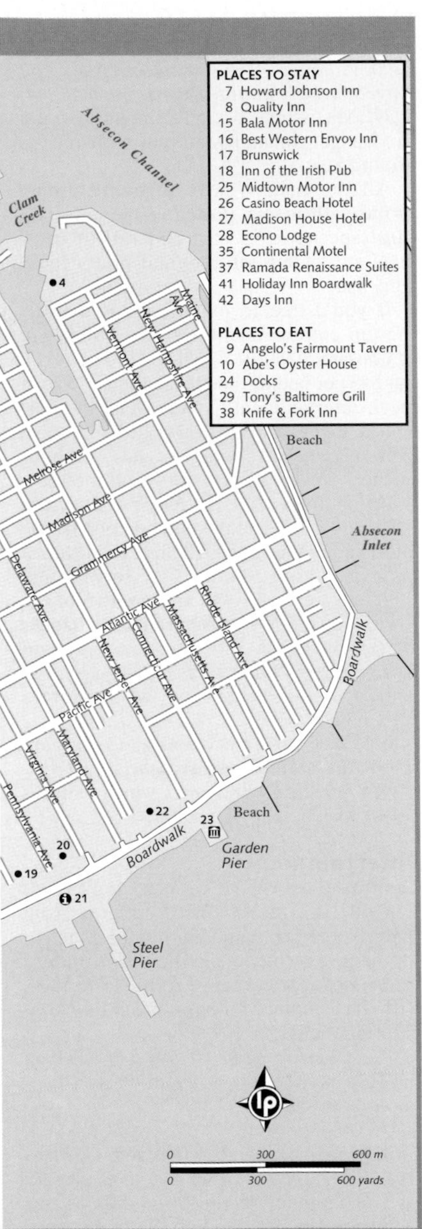

into the Atlantic before crowds of spectators, but today it's just a collection of small amusement rides and candy stands.

Convention Hall The former site of the annual Miss America pageant was the largest auditorium in the world without interior roof posts or pillars when it opened in 1929. If there's no event in progress, see if you can take a look at the superb interior of the main hall, home to the world's largest pipe organ. Every year, Miss America contestants line up for publicity shots amid the columns by the Convention Hall's entrance.

Atlantic City Convention Center

A $300-million convention center (☎ 888-222-3838) opened above the train station in 1998 and houses a non-casino hotel with 12,000 rooms, plus shops, theaters and restaurants. The center, built by the company responsible for New York's successful South Street Seaport complex and Baltimore's Inner Harbor, now hosts the Miss America pageant every September.

Places to Stay

Atlantic City itself offers a good reservations service (☎ 800-447-6667), with rooms at all price levels and package deals. The town's room rates vary considerably depending on the season. In winter, it's possible to stay in a hotel such as Resorts Casino for as little as $50 a night. In summer, the rates run much higher, especially during the week of Miss America festivities in the fall. If you plan to gamble and want a good mid-range hotel, book a package deal through a casino hotel or travel agent. The AmeriRoom Reservations hotline (☎ 800-888-5825) specializes in these packages, which usually include meals, show tickets and complimentary chips.

Budget Shoestring travelers will have a hard time in Atlantic City, since the cheaper motels a few blocks off the boardwalk tend to be pickup spots for prostitutes.

The ***Inn of the Irish Pub*** *(☎ 609-344-9063, 164 St James Place)* is right off the Boardwalk but on one of the city's gamiest blocks.

Rooms with shared baths cost $25 to $60; rooms with private baths cost $75 and up. Just next door is the ***Brunswick*** *(☎ 609-344-8098)*, which has similar rates.

Mid-Range The motels listed here charge about the following rates: $25 to $30 midweek in the winter, $50 to $80 on winter weekends, $35 to $45 midweek in the summer, $60 to $100 on summer weekends. Holiday weekend rates range from $60 to $200.

Bala Motor Inn (☎ 609-348-3031), Martin Luther King Jr Blvd at Pacific Ave

Best Western Envoy Inn (☎ 609-344-7117), Pacific Ave at New York Ave

Casino Beach Hotel (☎ 609-348-4000, 154 Kentucky Ave), between the Boardwalk and Pacific Ave

Continental Motel (☎ 609-345-5141), the Boardwalk at Martin Luther King Jr Blvd

Days Inn (☎ 609-344-6101), the Boardwalk at Morris Ave

Econo Lodge (☎ 609-344-9093, 800-323-6410, 117 S Kentucky Ave), between the Boardwalk and Pacific Ave

Holiday Inn Boardwalk (☎ 609-348-2200), the Boardwalk at Chelsea Ave

Howard Johnson Inn (☎ 609-344-4193), Tennessee Ave at Pacific Ave

Midtown Motor Inn (☎ 609-348-3031), Indiana Ave at Pacific Ave

Madison House Hotel (☎ 609-345-1400, 123 Martin Luther King Jr Blvd)

Ramada Renaissance Suites (☎ 609-344-1200), the Boardwalk at New York Ave

Quality Inn (☎ 609-345-7070), South Carolina Ave at Pacific Ave

Top End Atlantic City's casino hotels (see Casinos) dominate the expensive choices. Rates run from $120 to $370 depending on the season and day of the week, usually with meals, shows, free use of the health spa and casino chips. In the winter, rates can be as low as $50 – the trick is to walk up to the reception desk and act uncertain if you plan to stay the night. You will most likely be offered a room at a deep discount, provided you look well dressed enough to spend money in the casino.

Places to Eat

Tony's Baltimore Grill *(☎ 609-345-5766, 2800 Atlantic Ave)*, at Iowa Ave, and ***Angelo's Fairmount Tavern*** *(☎ 609-344-2439)*, Mississippi Ave at Fairmount Ave, are two budget Italian restaurants with entrees around $10.

All the casinos have high-end dining rooms with menus posted at the entrance. Most specialize in 'surf and turf' items – huge steaks, big lobsters and pretty lousy wine lists.

If you'd like to experience real over-the-top entertainment, try ***The Bacchanal*** at Caesar's Atlantic City (☎ 609-348-4411). For $45 per person, you'll get a seven-course meal, entertainment by 'Augustus' and possibly a higher level of service than you've ever experienced: 'Wine wenches' will pour pitchers of wine directly into your mouth.

Dating from 1927, the ***Knife & Fork Inn*** *(☎ 609-344-1133)*, at the junction of Atlantic and Pacific Aves near Albany Ave, offers a taste of the old Atlantic City, serving seafood and steaks for $45 and up. Two of the town's top seafood restaurants are ***Docks*** *(☎ 609-345-0092, 2405 Atlantic Ave)* and ***Abe's Oyster House*** *(☎ 609-344-7701)*, Atlantic Ave at Arkansas Ave, where entrees start at $30.

In Venice Park, away from all the casinos, stands the ***Old Waterway Inn*** *(☎ 609-347-1793, 1700 Riverside Drive)*, which features a deck overlooking the water.

Entertainment

Casinos Each of the casinos offers a full schedule of entertainment, ranging from ragtime and jazz bands in hotel lobbies to top-name entertainers in the casino auditoriums. Ticket prices range from $15 to $400, with the smaller lounges providing free entertainment.

The ***Comedy Stop*** *(☎ 609-340-4000)* in the Tropicana Casino is Atlantic City's leading comedy club.

Clubs For jazz, head to ***Wonder Gardens*** *(☎ 609-347-1466)*, Arctic Ave at Kentucky Ave, a reminder of the busy strip of jazz nightspots that used to line Kentucky Ave.

One Way to Win in Atlantic City

If you're hungry, some of the best bargains can be found at the various buffets offered by the casinos to keep patrons inside the premises. Wander around and you'll find all sorts of all-you-can-eat bargains, most between $6 and $15. With names such as the Epic Buffet and Sultan's Feast and special events like the '50s Experience, these buffets offer plentiful choices, and all vie for the title of best boardwalk bargain. (Repeat visitors will readily share tips on the best place to go.)

You'll also find some reasonable restaurants that offer waiter service at the resorts. Caesar's includes the ***Boardwalk Cafe***. Tropicana's ***Pasta Pavilion***, ***Pickles*** in Bally's Park Place Casino and the ***New Delhi Deli*** in the Taj Mahal all offer moderately priced fare.

The club ***Studio 6*** *(☎ 609-348-3310)*, on Mount Vernon between Pacific and Atlantic Aves, attracts a gay and straight crowd. ***Club Mirage***, in front of Trump Plaza on the Boardwalk near Mississippi Ave, is a standard disco.

Spectator Sports The ***Atlantic City Surf*** minor league baseball team plays in the spanking new $15-million Sandcastle Stadium throughout the summer. Call ☎ 609-344-8873 for schedules and tickets.

The ***Atlantic City Seagulls*** basketball team plays in less exalted confines – the Atlantic City High School gym (☎ 609-466-7797). College basketball tournaments and various car shows take place at Convention Hall (☎ 609-355-7155) during the winter months.

Getting There & Away

Air Atlantic City International Airport (☎ 609-645-7895), off Tilton Rd in Pomona, is used by airlines servicing the city's casino industry. Spirit Airlines (☎ 800-772-7117) and USAir Express (☎ 800-428-4322) connect the town with Cleveland, Detroit, Philadelphia and several Florida cities.

The Royal Airport Shuttle (☎ 609-748-9777) and Sky Shuttle (☎ 800-825-3759) offer service to the JFK, LaGuardia, and Newark airports several times a day.

Bus NJ Transit runs buses from New York City to the depot on Atlantic Ave between Michigan and Ohio Aves. For a better deal, check out the casino buses from New York; these cost about $20 roundtrip but include food vouchers and quarters for the slots.

Academy (☎ 212-971-9054) and Greyhound (☎ 800-231-2222) buses depart for Atlantic City from the Port Authority Bus Terminal in Midtown. Fares are cheaper Monday to Thursday. Gray Line (☎ 212-397-2620) operates from 900 Eighth Ave between W 53rd and 54th Sts in Midtown.

Car Atlantic City is exit 38 of the Garden State Parkway. The Atlantic City Expressway runs directly to Atlantic City from Philadelphia.

CAPE MAY

Cape May (population 4700), which stands at the southern tip of the New Jersey shore, is one of the oldest seashore resorts in the USA. A quiet collection of more than 600 gingerbread Victorian homes, the entire town was designated a National Historic Landmark in 1976. In addition to its attractive architecture, accommodations and eating places, Cape May boasts a lovely beach, a famous lighthouse, craft shops and bird watching. It's the only place in New Jersey where you can watch the sun both rise and set over the water.

Cape May is divided into Cape May City, where you find the hotels, main beach and boardwalk, and Cape May Point State Park, which includes the lighthouse, Sunset Beach and a bird refuge.

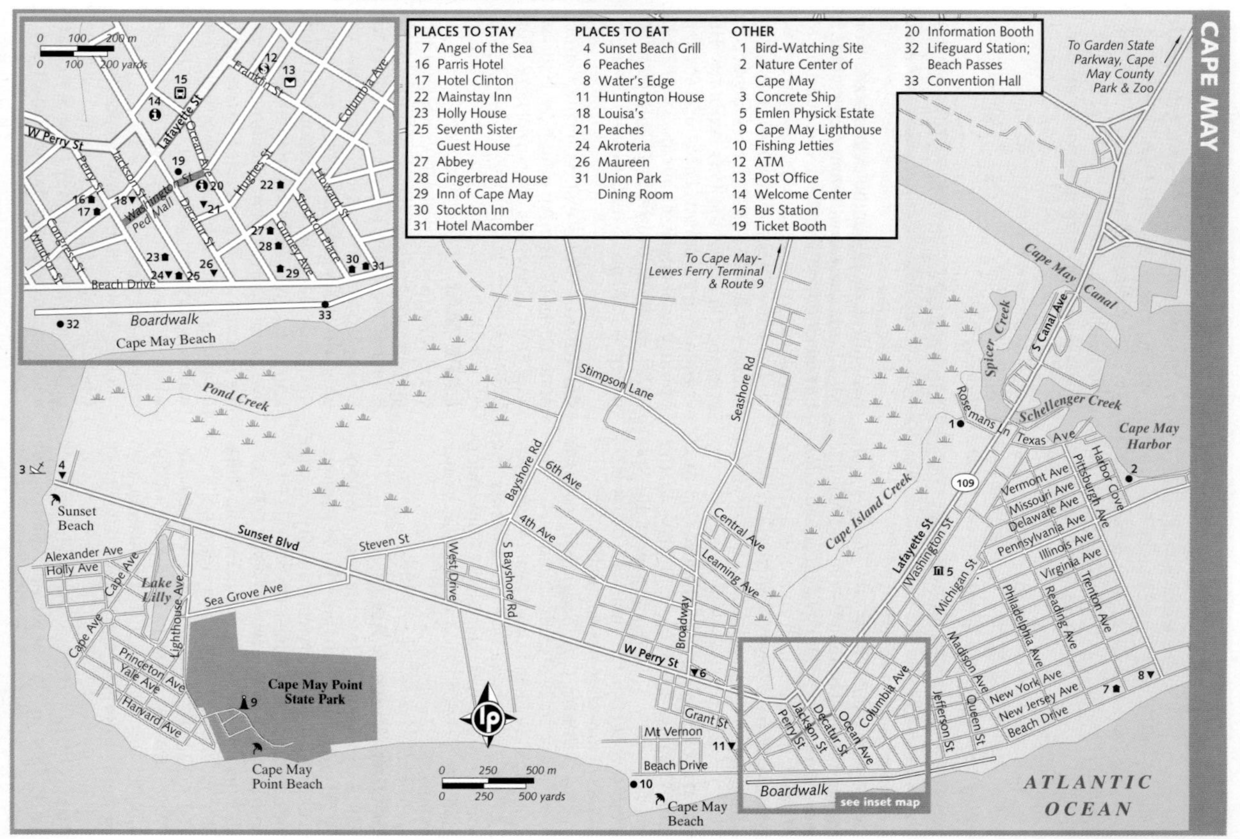
CAPE MAY
PLACES TO STAY
7 Angel of the Sea
16 Parris Hotel
17 Hotel Clinton
22 Mainstay Inn
23 Holly House
25 Seventh Sister Guest House
27 Abbey
28 Gingerbread House
29 Inn of Cape May
30 Stockton Inn
31 Hotel Macomber
PLACES TO EAT
4 Sunset Beach Grill
6 Peaches
8 Water's Edge
11 Huntington House
18 Louisa's
21 Peaches
24 Akroteria
26 Maureen
31 Union Park Dining Room
OTHER
1 Bird-Watching Site
2 Nature Center of Cape May
3 Concrete Ship
5 Emlen Physick Estate
9 Cape May Lighthouse
10 Fishing Jetties
12 ATM
13 Post Office
14 Welcome Center
15 Bus Station
19 Ticket Booth
20 Information Booth
32 Lifeguard Station; Beach Passes
33 Convention Hall
To Garden State Parkway, Cape May County Park & Zoo
To Cape May-Lewes Ferry Terminal & Route 9
Cape May Canal
Cape May Harbor
Schellenger Creek
Spicer Creek
Cape Island Creek
Pond Creek
Lake Lilly
Cape May Point State Park
ATLANTIC OCEAN
Sunset Beach
Cape May Point Beach
Cape May Beach
Boardwalk
see inset map
S Canal Ave
Lafayette St
Washington St
Michigan St
Texas Ave
Rosemans Ln
Harbor Cove
Pittsburgh Ave
Vermont Ave
Missouri Ave
Delaware Ave
Pennsylvania Ave
Illinois Ave
Virginia Ave
Trenton Ave
Reading Ave
Philadelphia Ave
Madison Ave
New York Ave
New Jersey Ave
Beach Drive
Queen St
Jefferson St
Columbia Ave
Ocean Ave
Decatur St
Jackson St
Perry St
Seashore Rd
Central Ave
Leaming Ave
Broadway
W Perry St
Grant St
Mt Vernon
Stimpson Lane
6th Ave
4th Ave
Bayshore Rd
S Bayshore Rd
West Drive
Steven St
Sunset Blvd
Sea Grove Ave
Lighthouse Ave
Cape Ave
Alexander Ave
Holly Ave
Princeton Ave
Yale Ave
Harvard Ave
109
0 250 500 m
0 250 500 yards
0 100 200 m
0 100 200 yards
Howard St
Stockton Place
Gurney Ave
Franklin St
Hughes St
Washington St Ped Mall
Congress St
Windsor St
Cape May Beach

Information

For comprehensive information on Cape May county attractions, stop at the Welcome Center at milepost 11 on the Garden State Parkway.

The local Welcome Center (☎ 609-884-9562) is at 405 Lafayette St. *This Week*, a publication of the Mid-Atlantic Center for the Arts, lists all activities in town.

The post office is at 700 Washington St.

Things to See & Do

The **Emlen Physick Estate** (☎ 609-884-5404), 1048 Washington St, an 18-room mansion built in 1879, now houses the Mid-Atlantic Center for the Arts. You can book a tour for nearby historic Cold Spring Village and buy Victoriana and history books at the museum shop. It's open year-round.

The **Concrete Ship** dates from WWI, when twelve experimental concrete ships were built to compensate for a shortage of steel. The *Atlantis*, with a 5-inch concrete aggregate hull, began its seagoing life in 1918, but eight years later it broke free in a storm and ran aground on the western side of the Cape May Point coast. A small chunk of the hull still sits a few feet from shore on Sunset Beach at the end of Sunset Blvd.

The 18-acre **Nature Center of Cape May** (☎ 609-898-8848), 1600 Delaware Ave, is the best place to get information on the different types of fowl that pass through southern New Jersey. It features a bird-watching site with open-air observation platforms over the marshes and beaches.

Cape May Point State Park

This state park (☎ 609-884-2736), 707 E Lake Drive (just off Lighthouse Ave), includes the famous **Cape May Lighthouse** (☎ 609-884-2159). Built in 1859, the 157-foot lighthouse still operates, its light visible 25 miles out to sea. You can climb to the top in the summer months. It's open 10 am to 5 pm daily; admission is $3.50.

The Cape May peninsula is a resting place for millions of migratory birds each year, and the bird-watching hotline (☎ 609-884-2626) offers information on the latest sightings. The bird observatory also offers tours of Reed's Beach, 12 miles north of Cape May on the Delaware Bay, where migrating shorebirds swoop down to feed on the eggs laid by thousands of horseshoe crabs each May.

To get to the park, drive west from Cape May on Sunset Blvd about 2 miles to Lighthouse Ave. Make a left and drive half a mile to the lighthouse. The park is open 9 am to 5 pm daily.

Cape May County Park & Zoo

One of this area's nicest discoveries is the Cape May County Park and Zoo (☎ 609-465-5271), a few miles north of town. The beautifully maintained 200-acre facility features 250 different species of animals, many of which wander freely across a re-created African savanna and other natural habitats while humans observe the action from the elevated boardwalk.

The park, which is busy but not crowded even in summer, also offers nature and bike trails, a playground and a fishing pond. It's open 10 am to 4:30 pm daily. Admission is free. To get there, take the Garden State Parkway to exit 11.

Beaches

The narrow **Cape May Beach** (☎ 609-884-9525) requires passes, which cost $4 per day or $10 per week and are sold at the lifeguard station on the boardwalk at the end of Grant St. The **Cape May Point Beach** is free and accessible from the parking lot at Cape May Point State Park near the lighthouse. **Sunset Beach**, at the end of Sunset Blvd, is also free.

Organized Tours

The Mid-Atlantic Center for the Arts (☎ 609-884-5404), 1048 Washington St, offers a range of walking, trolley and boat tours. You can buy tickets at the ticket booth on the western end of the Washington St Mall, just before Decatur St. Prices are around $5 for walking tours and $15 or less for special events.

Places to Stay

Cape May is packed with expensive B&Bs and inns, and you can't walk 50 feet in the center of town without passing one.

ANGUS OBORN

Victorian buildings line the streets of Cape May.

If you're looking for modest hotels, try the ***Hotel Clinton*** (*☎ 609-884-3993, 202 Perry St*), near Lafayette St. Next door at the ***Parris Hotel*** (*☎ 609-884-8015, 204 Perry St*), most rooms have private baths and some have TVs.

Many places in town offer rooms for less than $120 in high season. ***Holly House*** (*☎ 609-884-7365, 20 Jackson St*) is an 1890 cottage run by a former mayor of Cape May. It's one of the so-called Seven Sisters, a group of seven identical homes; five of them are along Jackson St. The Holly House has six rooms, each with three windows and a shared bath.

The ***Seventh Sister Guest House*** (*☎ 609-884-2280, 10 Jackson St*) is a few doors down from Holly House. The ***Hotel Macomber*** (*☎ 609-884-3020, 727 Beach Drive*), on the corner of Howard St, contains one of the best restaurants in Cape May (see Places to Eat).

The ***Gingerbread House*** (*☎ 609-884-0211, 28 Gurney St*) is a six-room B&B with rates from $100 to $150. The ***Stockton Inn*** (*☎ 609-884-4036, 800-524-4283, 809 Beach Drive*) includes both a motel and a 'manor house.' The motel has standard motel furnishings and a pool; rooms cost up to $100. The manor is a converted Victorian house with 10 rooms and three suites, all with private bath, and is slightly more expensive.

The ***Inn of Cape May*** (*☎ 800-257-0432*), at the corner of Beach Drive and Ocean Ave, is a sprawling white wooden structure with lavender trim. Rooms come in a wide variety of sizes and generally have high ceilings and white wicker furniture.

Built in 1872 as a men's gambling club, the ***Mainstay Inn*** (*☎ 609-884-8690, 635 Columbia Ave*) features rooms furnished in opulent dark woods and large beds; all have private baths. The ***Abbey*** (*☎ 609-884-4506, 34 Gurney St*), at the corner of Columbia Ave, is one of the more elegant places in town. Like the Mainstay, it features plenty of antique furniture, has high ceilings and offers a tour with tea ($5). Rates, including breakfast, are $90 to $175.

Angel of the Sea (*☎ 609-884-3369, 800-848-3369, 5-7 Trenton Ave*) is renowned for its service. All rooms have private baths, ceiling fans and access to wraparound porches. Rooms range from $150 to $250, including breakfast.

Places to Eat

Akroteria, on Beach Drive between Jackson and Perry Sts, is a collection of small fast-food shacks with fare for under $10.

The ***Sunset Beach Grill*** is at the end of Sunset Blvd on Sunset Beach overlooking the sunken *Atlantis* and the ocean. It's the perfect place to order a sandwich and watch the waves.

Louisa's *(☎ 609-884-5882, 104 Jackson St)*, an excellent small restaurant, serves dinner only Tuesday to Saturday. ***Huntington House*** *(☎ 609-884-5868)*, Grant and North Sts, offers an all-you-can-eat buffet for $15.

Cape May is known for fine and ambitious restaurants, including the ***Union Park Dining Room*** *(☎ 609-884-8811, 727 Beach Ave)* at the Hotel Macomber. The menu features French fare with some Asian accents, and the desserts are a house specialty. Reservations are essential in summer.

Water's Edge *(☎ 609-884-1717)*, Beach Drive at Pittsburgh Ave, looks out on the Atlantic and serves seafood with something of a Mediterranean flavor. You can also get a good steak here. A full dinner, including wine, costs about $35. ***Maureen*** *(☎ 609-884-3774)*, Beach Drive at Decatur St, is a good place to splurge on seafood or steak (under $20).

Peaches *(☎ 609-884-0202, 322 Carpenter's Lane)* offers contemporary American dining at relatively high prices for this area; main courses cost $15 to $25. Peaches also has another location at 1 Sunset Blvd (☎ 609-898-0100).

Getting There & Away

Bus NJ Transit (☎ 201-762-5100, 800-772-2222) runs buses to and from New York City. The bus station is next to the Chamber of Commerce building, near the corner of Lafayette and Elmira Sts.

Car Cape May is at the southern extreme of the Garden State Parkway, which leads right into town.

Boat A ferry runs daily between North Cape May and the Delaware coastal town of Lewes (pronounced 'Lewis'); call ☎ 800-643-3779 for recorded information, ☎ 800-717-7245 for reservations, which should be made a day in advance in the high season. The 17-mile trip across the Delaware Bay takes about 70 minutes and saves New York–based travelers heading south some time if they're leaving Cape May for a visit to Washington, DC, and points south (see Lonely Planet's *Virginia & the Capital Region)*.

The North Cape May ferry terminal is on Route 9, west of the Garden State Parkway.

Acknowledgments

THANKS

Many thanks to the travelers who used the last edition and wrote to us with helpful hints, useful advice and interesting anecdotes:

Jorg Ausfelt, Sandra Badelt, Rosemary Behan, Matt Bellingham, Tim Bewer, Margaret Boulos, Lesley Brett, Isabelle Broz, Gretel Butcher, David Butler, Eileen M Cannaday, Emma Chadd, Anita J Cunningham, Peter & Gabrielle De Saeger, Dave Del Rocco, Bianca Eckert, Madelaine Eisenlauer, Mike Evans, Zorana Fabrici, David Fahey, Jeff Fair, Chris Falkous, Bert Flower, Kille & Miguel Fontes, Joe & Rachel Friedman, NL Fulston, Yves & Isabelle Gensane, Esther Hardiman, Hans Heerens, Kristi Hofman, Sarah Holland, Mary Windsor House, Ahsan & Jafri Jamal, Polly Jantzen, Céline Jobert, Judith Jones, Sade Jones, Rebecca Kane, Patricia Kempf, Barbara Kingsman, Kristina Lindermann, Andrea MacLeod, Diego Marin, Agnes Martens, Nina Maynard, Claire Muller, Jono Nienaber, AJ Norman, Kaja Nyhuus, Louise O'Sullivan, Nobu Oda, Richard Owen, Anthony Park, Mag Phang, Mark W Pickens, Sue Pittam, Amanda Roll-Pickering, Mariette Rommers, Nicolas Rossier, Orla Savage, Simran Sehmi, Brant Sextro, Tom Stojanovic, Nan Storms, Harvey Taylor, Greg Tuck, Susanne Unger, Nicole Vina, Jeroen Vreenegoor, Neville Walker, AJ Wells, Claire Wells & Mike Kenyon, Scott Weston, David Williams, C Wootton, Gea Wortelboer, Justin Zaman.

LONELY PLANET

You already know that Lonely Planet produces more than this one guidebook, but you might not be aware of the other products we have on this region. Here is a selection of titles which you may want to check out as well:

USA
ISBN 0 86442 513 9
US$24.95 • UK£14.99

New England
ISBN 0 86442 570 8
US$ 19.95 • UK£ 12.99

Virginia & the Capital Region
ISBN 0 86442 769 7
US$21.99 • UK£13.99

New York, New Jersey & Pennsylvania
ISBN 1 86450 138 3
US$21.99 • UK£13.99

New York Condensed
ISBN 1 86450 046 8
US$9.95 • UK£5.99

New York City map
ISBN 1 86450 010 7
US$5.95 • UK£3.99

Available wherever books are sold.

Guides by Region

Lonely Planet is known worldwide for publishing practical, reliable and no-nonsense travel information in our guides and on our web site. The Lonely Planet list covers just about every accessible part of the world. Currently there are fifteen series: travel guides, Shoestrings, Condensed, Phrasebooks, Read This First, Healthy Travel, Walking guides, Cycling guides, Pisces Diving & Snorkeling guides, City Maps, Travel Atlases, Out to Eat, World Food, Journeys travel literature and Pictorials.

AFRICA Africa on a shoestring • Africa – the South • Arabic (Egyptian) phrasebook • Arabic (Moroccan) phrasebook • Cairo • Cape Town • Cape Town city map • Central Africa • East Africa • Egypt • Egypt travel atlas • Ethiopian (Amharic) phrasebook • The Gambia & Senegal • Healthy Travel Africa • Kenya • Kenya travel atlas • Malawi, Mozambique & Zambia • Morocco • North Africa • Read This First Africa • South Africa, Lesotho & Swaziland • South Africa, Lesotho & Swaziland travel atlas • Swahili phrasebook • Tanzania, Zanzibar & Pemba • Trekking in East Africa • Tunisia • West Africa • Zimbabwe, Botswana & Namibia • Zimbabwe, Botswana & Namibia travel atlas • World Food Morocco

Travel Literature: The Rainbird: A Central African Journey • Songs to an African Sunset: A Zimbabwean Story • Mali Blues: Traveling to an African Beat

AUSTRALIA & THE PACIFIC Auckland • Australia • Australian phrasebook • Bushwalking in Australia • Bushwalking in Papua New Guinea • Fiji • Fijian phrasebook • Healthy Travel Australia, NZ and the Pacific • Islands of Australia's Great Barrier Reef • Melbourne • Melbourne city map • Micronesia • New Caledonia • New South Wales & the ACT • New Zealand • Northern Territory • Outback Australia • Out to Eat – Melbourne • Out to Eat – Sydney • Papua New Guinea • Pidgin phrasebook • Queensland • Rarotonga & the Cook Islands • Samoa • Solomon Islands • South Australia • South Pacific • South Pacific Languages phrasebook • Sydney • Sydney city map • Sydney condensed • Tahiti & French Polynesia • Tasmania • Tonga • Tramping in New Zealand • Vanuatu • Victoria • Western Australia

Travel Literature: Islands in the Clouds • Kiwi Tracks: A New Zealand Journey • Sean & David's Long Drive

CENTRAL AMERICA & THE CARIBBEAN Bahamas, Turks & Caicos • Bermuda • Central America on a shoestring • Costa Rica • Cuba • Dominican Republic & Haiti • Eastern Caribbean • Guatemala, Belize & Yucatán: La Ruta Maya • Jamaica • Mexico • Mexico City • Panama • Puerto Rico • Read This First Central & South America • World Food Mexico • Yucatán

Travel Literature: Green Dreams: Travels in Central America

EUROPE Amsterdam • Amsterdam city map • Andalucía • Austria • Baltic States phrasebook • Barcelona • Berlin • Berlin city map• Britain • British phrasebook • Brussels, Bruges & Antwerp • Budapest city map • Canary Islands • Central Europe • Central Europe phrasebook • Corfu & Ionians • Corsica • Crete • Crete condensed • Croatia • Cyprus • Czech & Slovak Republics • Denmark • Dublin • Eastern Europe • Eastern Europe phrasebook • Edinburgh • Estonia, Latvia & Lithuania • Europe on a shoestring • Finland • Florence • France • French phrasebook • Germany • German phrasebook • Greece • Greek Islands • Greek phrasebook • Hungary • Iceland, Greenland & the Faroe Islands • Istanbul city map • Ireland • Italian phrasebook • Italy • Krakow • Lisbon • London • London city map • London condensed • Mediterranean Europe • Mediterranean Europe phrasebook • Munich • Norway • Paris • Paris city map • Paris condensed • Poland • Portugal • Portugese phrasebook • Portugal travel atlas • Prague • Prague city map • Provence & the Côte d'Azur • Read This First Europe • Romania & Moldova • Rome • Russia, Ukraine & Belarus • Russian phrasebook • Scandinavian & Baltic Europe • Scandinavian Europe phrasebook • Scotland • Slovenia • Spain • Spanish phrasebook • St Petersburg • Switzerland • Trekking in Spain • Ukrainian phrasebook • Venice • Vienna • Walking in Britain • Walking in Ireland • Walking in Italy • Walking in Spain • Walking in Switzerland • Western Europe • Western Europe phrasebook • World Food Italy • World Food Spain

Travel Literature: The Olive Grove: Travels in Greece

LONELY PLANET

Mail Order

Lonely Planet products are distributed worldwide. They are also available by mail order from Lonely Planet, so if you have difficulty finding a title please write to us. North and South American residents should write to 150 Linden St, Oakland, CA 94607, USA; European and African residents should write to 10a Spring Place, London, NW5 3BH; and residents of other countries to Locked Bag 1, Footscray, Victoria 3011, Australia.

INDIAN SUBCONTINENT Bangladesh • Bengali phrasebook • Bhutan • Delhi • Goa • Hindi/Urdu phrasebook • India • India & Bangladesh travel atlas • Indian Himalaya • Karakoram Highway • Kerala • Mumbai • Nepal • Nepali phrasebook • Pakistan • Rajasthan • Read This First: Asia & India • South India • Sri Lanka • Sri Lanka phrasebook • Trekking in the Indian Himalaya • Trekking in the Karakoram & Hindukush • Trekking in the Nepal Himalaya
Travel Literature: In Rajasthan • Shopping for Buddhas • The Age of Kali

ISLANDS OF THE INDIAN OCEAN Madagascar & Comoros • Maldives • Mauritius, Réunion & Seychelles

MIDDLE EAST & CENTRAL ASIA Bahrain, Kuwait & Qatar • Central Asia • Central Asia phrasebook • Dubai • Hebrew phrasebook • Iran • Israel & the Palestinian Territories • Israel & the Palestinian Territories travel atlas • Istanbul • Istanbul city map • Istanbul to Cairo on a shoestring • Jerusalem • Jerusalem city map • Jordan • Jordan, Syria & Lebanon travel atlas • Lebanon • Middle East • Oman & the United Arab Emirates • Syria • Turkey • Turkey travel atlas • Turkish phrasebook •Yemen
Travel Literature: The Gates of Damascus • Kingdom of the Film Stars: Journey into Jordan • Black on Black: Iran Revisited

NORTH AMERICA Alaska • Backpacking in Alaska • Baja California • Boston • California & Nevada • California condensed • Canada • Chicago • Chicago city map • Deep South • Florida • Hawaii • Las Vegas • Los Angeles • Miami • New England • New Orleans • New York City • New York city map • New York condensed • New York, New Jersey & Pennsylvania • Oahu • Pacific Northwest USA • Puerto Rico • Rocky Mountain States • San Francisco • San Francisco city map • Seattle • Southwest USA • Texas • USA • USA phrasebook • Vancouver • Washington, DC & the Capital Region • Washington, DC city map
Travel Literature: Drive Thru America

NORTH-EAST ASIA Beijing • Cantonese phrasebook • China • Hong Kong • Hong Kong city map • Hong Kong, Macau & Guangzhou • Japan • Japanese phrasebook • Japanese audio pack • Korea • Korean phrasebook • Kyoto • Mandarin phrasebook • Mongolia • Mongolian phrasebook • North-East Asia on a shoestring • Seoul • South-West China • Taiwan • Tibet • Tibetan phrasebook • Tokyo
Travel Literature: Lost Japan • In Xanadu

SOUTH AMERICA Argentina, Uruguay & Paraguay • Bolivia • Brazil • Brazilian phrasebook • Buenos Aires • Chile & Easter Island • Chile & Easter Island travel atlas • Colombia • Ecuador & the Galapagos Islands • Healthy Travel Central & South America • Latin American Spanish phrasebook • Peru • Quechua phrasebook • Rio de Janeiro • Rio de Janeiro city map • South America on a shoestring • Trekking in the Patagonian Andes • Venezuela
Travel Literature: Full Circle: A South American Journey

SOUTH-EAST ASIA Bali & Lombok • Bangkok • Bangkok city map • Burmese phrasebook • Cambodia • Hanoi • Healthy Travel Asia & India • Hill Tribes phrasebook • Ho Chi Minh City • Indonesia • Indonesia's Eastern Islands • Indonesian phrasebook • Indonesian audio pack • Jakarta • Java • Laos • Lao phrasebook • Laos travel atlas • Malay phrasebook • Malaysia, Singapore & Brunei • Myanmar (Burma) • Philippines • Pilipino (Tagalog) phrasebook • Read This First Asia & India • Singapore • South-East Asia on a shoestring • South-East Asia phrasebook • Thailand • Thailand's Islands & Beaches • Thailand travel atlas • Thai phrasebook • Thai audio pack • Vietnam • Vietnamese phrasebook • Vietnam travel atlas • World Food Thailand • World Food Vietnam

ALSO AVAILABLE: Antarctica • The Arctic • Brief Encounters: Stories of Love, Sex & Travel • Chasing Rickshaws • Lonely Planet Unpacked • Not the Only Planet: Travel Stories from Science Fiction • Sacred India • Travel with Children • Traveller's Tales

ON THE ROAD

Travel Guides explore cities, regions and countries and supplies information on transport, restaurant and accommodation, regardless of your budget. They come with reliable, easy-to-use maps, practical advice, cultural and historical facts and a run down on attractions both on and off the beaten track. There are over 200 titles in this classic series covering nearly every country in the world.

Lonely Planet Upgrades extend the shelf lives of existing travel guides by detailing any changes that may affect travel in a region since the book has been published. Upgrades can be downloaded for free on **www.lonelyplanet.com/upgrades**

For travelers with more time than money, **Shoestring** guides offer dependable, first-hand information with hundreds of detailed maps, plus insider tips for stretching money as far as possible. Covering entire continents in most cases, the six-volume shoestring guides have been known as 'backpackers' bibles' for over 25 years.

For the discerning short-term visitor, **Condensed** guides highlight the best a destination has to offer in a full-color pocket-sized format designed for quick access. From top sights and walking tours to opinionated reviews of where to eat, stay, shop and have fun.

CitySync lets travelers use their Palm™ or Visor™ handheld computers to guide them through a city's highlights with quick tips on transport, history, cultural life, major sights and shopping and entertainment options. It can also quickly search and sort hundreds of reviews of hotels, restaurants and attractions and pinpoint the place on scrollable street maps. CitySync can be downloaded from www.citysync.com

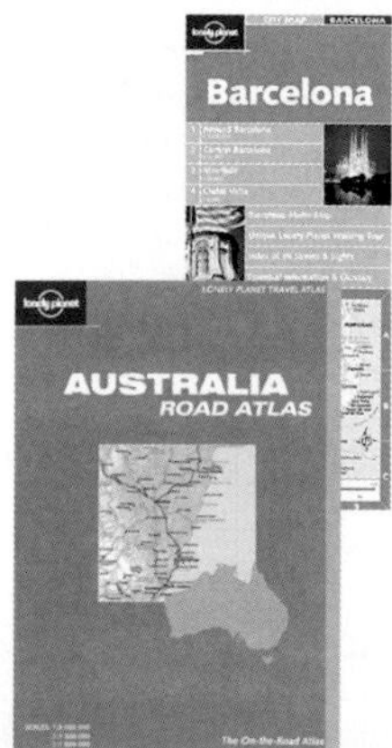

MAPS & ATLASES

Lonely Planet's **City Maps** feature downtown and metropolitan maps as well as transit routes, and walking tours. The maps come complete with an index of streets, a listing of sights and a plastic coat for extra durability.

Road Atlases are an essential navigation tool for serious travelers. Cross-referenced with the guidebooks, they also feature distance and climate charts and a complete site index.

LONELY PLANET

ESSENTIALS

Read This First books help new travelers to hit the road with confidence. These invaluable pre-departure guides give step-by-step advice on preparing for a trip, budgeting, arranging a visa, planning an itinerary and staying safe while still getting off the beaten track.

Healthy Travel pocket guides offer a regional run down on disease hot spots and practical advice on pre-departure health measures, staying well on the road and what to do in emergency situations. The guides come with a user-friendly design and helpful diagrams and tables.

Lonely Planet's **Phrasebooks** cover the essential words and phrases travelers may need when they're strangers in a strange land. It comes in a pocket-sized format with color tabs for quick reference, extensive vocabulary lists, easy-to-follow pronunciation keys and two-way dictionaries.

Lonely Planet's **Travel Journal** is a lightweight but sturdy travel diary for jotting down all those on the road observations and significant travel moments. It comes with a handy time zone wheel, world maps and useful travel information.

Lonely Planet's eKno is an all-in-one communication service developed especially for travelers, with low-cost international calls, free email and voicemail so that you can keep in touch while on the road. Check it out on **www.ekno.lonelyplanet.com**

FOOD & RESTAURANT GUIDES

Lonely Planet's **Out to Eat** guides recommend the brightest and best places to eat and drink in the top international cities. These gourmet companions are arranged by neighborhood, packed with dependable maps, garnished with scene-setting photos and served with quirky features.

For people who live to eat, drink and travel, **World Food** guides are full of lavish photos good enough to eat. They come packed with details on regional cuisine, guides to local markets and produce, sumptuous recipes, useful phrases for shopping and dining, and a comprehensive culinary dictionary.

OUTDOOR GUIDES

For those who believe the best way to see the world is on foot, Lonely Planet's **Walking Guides** detail everything from family strolls to difficult treks, with 'when to go and how to do it' advice supplemented by reliable maps and essential travel information.

Cycling Guides map a destination's best bike tours, long and short, in day-by-day detail. They contain all the information a cyclist needs, including advice on bike maintenance, places to eat and stay, innovative maps with detailed cues to the rides and elevation charts.

The **Watching Wildlife** series is perfect for travelers who want authoritative information but don't want to tote a field guide. Packed with advice on where, when and how to view a region's wildlife, each title features photos of over 300 species and contains engaging comments and insights into local flora and fauna.

With underwater color photos throughout, **Pisces Books** explore the world's best diving and snorkeling areas. Each book contains listings of diving services and dive resorts and detailed information on depth, visibility, difficulty of dives and a round up of the marine life you're likely to see through your mask.

LONELY PLANET

OFF THE ROAD

Journeys, the travel literature series written by renowned travel authors, capture the spirit of a place or illuminate a culture with a journalist's attention to detail and a novelistic flair for words. These are tales to soak up while you're actually on the road or dip into as an at-home armchair indulgence.

The new range of lavishly illustrated **Pictorial** books is just the ticket for both travelers and dreamers. Off-beat tales and vivid photographs bring the adventure of travel to your doorstep long before the journey begins and long after it is over.

The Lonely Planet **Videos** encourage the same independent tough-minded approach as the guideboks. Currently airing throughout the world, this award-winning series features innovative footage and an all-original soundtrack.

Yes, we know, work is tough, so do a little bit of desk side-dreaming with the spiral bound Lonely Planet **Diary,** the tear away page-a-day **Day to Day Calendar** or any Lonely Planet **Wall Calendar,** filled with great photos from around the world.

TRAVELERS NETWORK

Lonely Planet online, Lonely Planet's award-winning web site has insider information on hundreds of destinations from Amsterdam to Zimbabwe complete with interactive maps and relevant links. The site also offers the latest travel news, recent reports from travelers on the road, guidebook upgrades, a travel links site, an online book buying option and a lively traveler's bulletin board. It can be viewed at www.lonelyplanet.com or AOL keyword: lp

Planet Talk is the quarterly print newsletter full of gossip, advice, anecdotes and author articles. It provides an antidote to the being-at-home blues and lets you plan and dream for the next trip. Contact the nearest Lonely Planet office for you free copy.

Comet, the free Lonely Planet newsletter, comes via email once a month. It's loaded with travel news, advice, dispatches from authors, travel competitions and letters from readers. To subscribe, click on the Comet subscription link on the front page of the web site.

Index

Text

A

Bold indicates maps.

Bold indicates maps.

N

O

Bold indicates maps.

Bold indicates maps.

Bold indicates maps.

Boxed Text

New York City Map Section

PENELOPE RICHARDSON

MAP 1 NEW YORK CITY

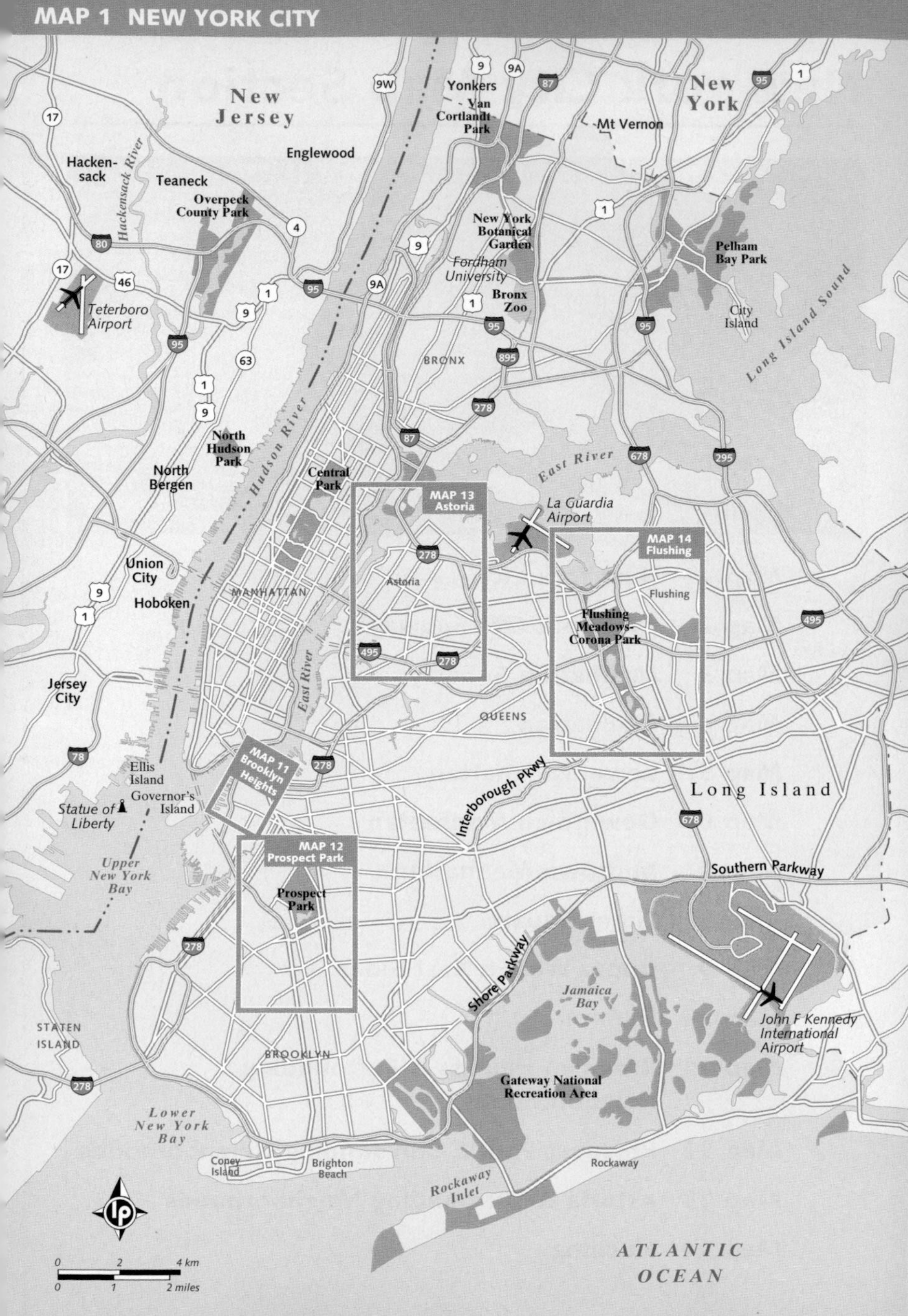

BROOKLYN
STATEN ISLAND
Atlantic Ocean
Jamaica Bay
Staten Island Ferry
Highlands Ferry
Atlantic Highlands Ferry
Weehawken Ferry
Port Liberté Ferry
Coast Guard Only
Brooklyn Army Terminal Ferry
Accessible Stations
The following subway stations are accessible to wheelchair passengers. For further information, call our dedicated phone line for accessible service at 718-596-8585. Customer service representatives are available from 6am to 9pm daily to advise customers and inform them about accessible stations that are unavailable due to construction projects.
For update information regarding the accessibility status of elevators and escalators, call 800-734-6772, 24 hours a day.
Routes Station
MANHATTAN
Inwood - 207 St
175 St
50 St/8 Av southbound only
42 St/8 Av (Port Authority Bus Terminal)
World Trade Center
Roosevelt Island
Lexington Av/63 St
34 St/Herald Sq
Cortlandt St southbound only
66 St-Lincoln Center
34 St/Penn Station express platform only
125 St/Lexington Av
51 St/Lexington Av
42 St/Grand Central
Brooklyn Bridge/City Hall
BRONX
Pelham Bay Park
Simpson St
3 Av/149 St
QUEENS
Jamaica Center (Parsons/Archer)
Sutphin Blvd/Archer Av
Jamaica/Van Wyck
Metropolitan Av
Howard Beach/ JFK Airport northbound only
Rockaway Park/Beach 116 St
21 St/Queensbridge
Flushing-Main Street
Woodside-61 St
BROOKLYN
Coney Island/Stillwell Av
Atlantic Av northbound only
Borough Hall (northbound only)
Flatbush Av/Brooklyn College
Franklin Av
Park Pl
Church Av

MAP 3 MANHATTAN SUBWAY

Hudson River
MANHATTAN
HARLEM
EAST HARLEM
UPPER WEST SIDE
UPPER EAST SIDE
WEST SIDE
CENTRAL PARK
METROPOLITAN MUSEUM OF ART
RANDALL'S ISLAND
ROOSEVELT ISLAND
UNITED NATIONS
LONG ISLAND CITY
ASTORIA
JAVITS CENTER
LaGuardia Airport Ferry
Weehawken Ferry (Port Imperial)
Weehawken Ferry (Lincoln Harbor)
LINCOLN TUNNEL
QUEENS MIDTOWN TUNNEL
QUEENSBORO BRIDGE
TRAMWAY
New Jersey Transit • Amtrak
Amtrak
LIRR
Hunterspoint
Hunterspoint Av
Long Island City
M60
125 St
33 St
116 St Columbia University 1·9
Cathedral Pkwy (110 St) 1·9
103 St 1·9
96 St 1·2·3·9
86 St 1·9
79 St 1·9
72 St 1·2·3·9
66 St Lincoln Center 1·9
125 St A·B·C·D M60 LaGuardia Airport
116 St B·C
Cathedral Pkwy (110 St) B·C
103 St B·C
96 St B·C
86 St B·C
81 St–Museum of Natural History B·C
72 St B·C
59 St Columbus Circle A·B·C·D·1·9
50 St C·E
42 St Port Authority Bus Terminal A·C·E
34 St Penn Station A·C·E
125 St 2·3 · M60 LaGuardia Airport
116 St 2·3
Central Park North (110 St) 2·3
125 St 4·5·6
116 St 6
110 St 6
103 St 6
96 St 6
86 St 4·5·6
77 St 6
68 St Hunter College 6
Lexington Av N·R
59 St 4·5·6
Lexington Av E·F
51 St 6
Grand Central 42 St S·4·5·6·7
33 St 6
Lexington Avenue B·Q
Roosevelt Island B·Q
21 St Queensbridge B·Q
57 St B·Q
5 Av N·R
57 St N·R
7 Av B·D·E
49 St N·R
50 St 1·9
5 Av E·F
47–50 Sts/ Rockefeller Ctr B·D·F·Q
42 St B·D·F·Q
5 Av 7
Times Sq 42 St N·R·S·1·2·3·7·9
34 St Penn Station 1·2·3·9
34 St Herald Sq
Astoria Ditmars Blvd N
Astoria Blvd N
M60 LGA Airport
30 Av N
Broadway N
36 Av N
39 Av N
Queensboro Plaza N·7
Steinway St G·R
46 St G·R
36 St G·R
Queens Plaza E·F·G·R
33 St 7
40 St 7
23 St–Ely Av E·F
Court Sq G
45 Rd Court House Sq 7
21 St G
Hunters Point Av 7
Vernon Blvd–Jackson Av 7
RIVERSIDE DR
AMSTERDAM AV
WEST END AV
BROADWAY
COLUMBUS AV
CENTRAL PARK WEST
EIGHTH AV
SEVENTH AV
SIXTH AV
FIFTH AV
MADISON AV
PARK AV
LEXINGTON AV
THIRD AV
SECOND AV
FIRST AV
YORK AV
1 AV
2 AV
3 AV
9 AV
10 AV
11 AV
12 AV
ST NICHOLAS AV
CENTRAL PARK SOUTH
125 ST
79 ST
72 ST
66 ST
63 ST
60 ST
59 ST
53 ST
50 ST
41 AV
20 AV
21 ST
31 ST
36 ST
VERNON BLVD
STEINWAY ST
ASTORIA BLVD
QUEENS BLVD
GREENPOINT AV
LONG ISLAND EXPWY

Metropolitan Transportation Authority
MTA New York City Subway
June 2000
© 2000 Metropolitan Transportation Authority
Design: Michael Hertz Associates, New York City
Map is subject to change
Used with permission
Local service only
All trains stop (local and express service)
Station served by one of two lines
Free subway transfer
Normal service
Rush hour service
Commuter rail service
Station Name
Full time service
Part time service
Terminal
QUEENS
THE BRONX
MANHATTAN
East River
Harlem River
Hudson River

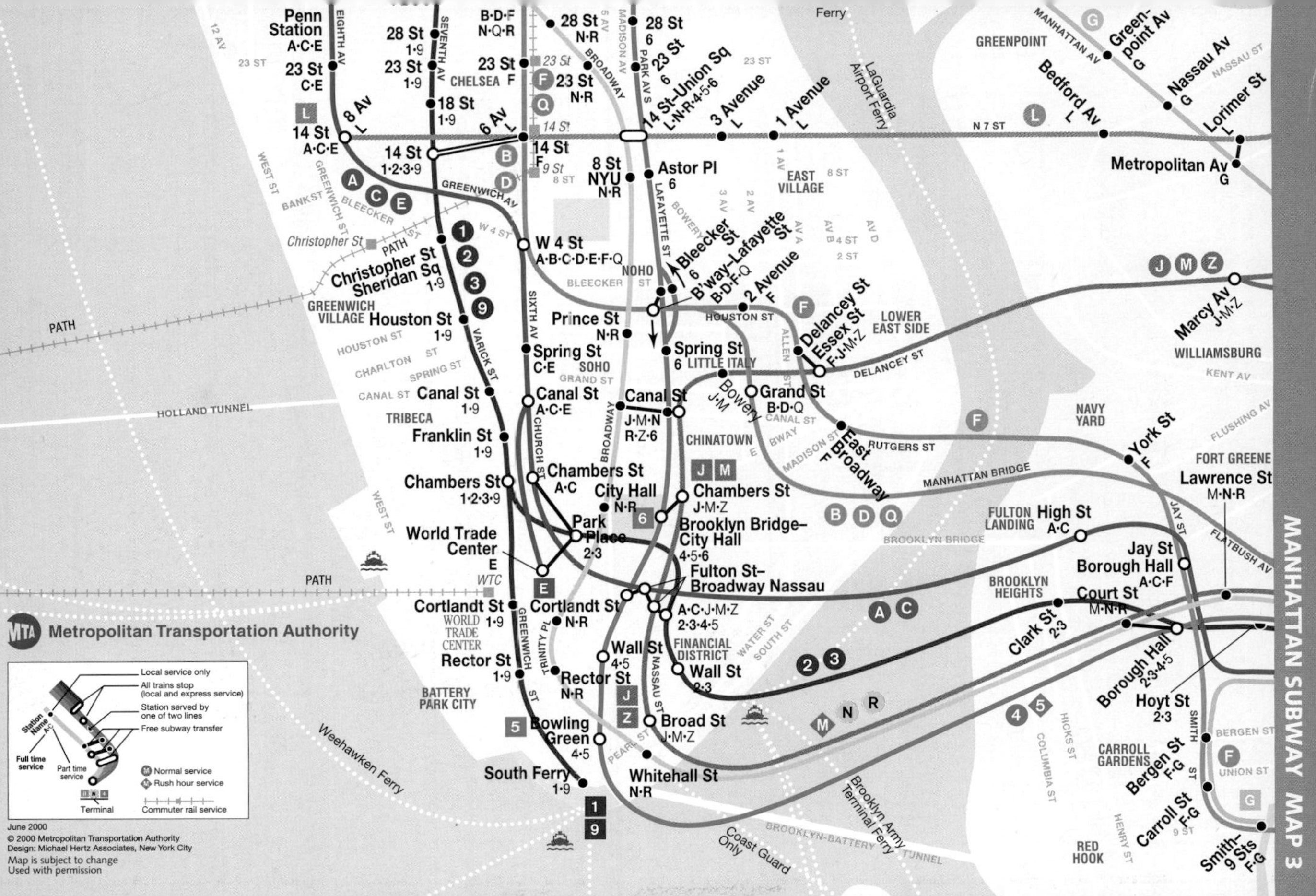

Penn Station A·C·E
23 St C·E
14 St A·C·E
8 Av L
28 St 1·9
23 St 1·9
18 St 1·9
14 St 1·2·3·9
6 Av L
14 St F
B·D·F N·Q·R
23 St F
CHELSEA
28 St N·R
23 St N·R
28 St 6
23 St 6
14 St–Union Sq L·N·R·4·5·6
3 Avenue L
1 Avenue L
Bedford Av L
Green-point Av G
Nassau Av G
Lorimer St L
Metropolitan Av G
GREENPOINT
LaGuardia Airport Ferry
Ferry
8 St NYU N·R
Astor Pl 6
EAST VILLAGE
W 4 St A·B·C·D·E·F·Q
Christopher St Sheridan Sq 1·9
Houston St 1·9
GREENWICH VILLAGE
Bleecker St 6
B'way–Lafayette St B·D·F·Q
2 Avenue F
Prince St N·R
Spring St C·E
Spring St 6
SOHO
LITTLE ITALY
NOHO
Delancey St Essex St F·J·M·Z
LOWER EAST SIDE
Marcy Av J·M·Z
WILLIAMSBURG
Canal St 1·9
Canal St A·C·E
Canal St J·M·N R·Z·6
Bowery J·M
Grand St B·D·Q
TRIBECA
CHINATOWN
Franklin St 1·9
East Broadway F
York St F
NAVY YARD
FORT GREENE
Lawrence St M·N·R
Chambers St 1·2·3·9
Chambers St A·C
City Hall N·R
Chambers St J·M·Z
Brooklyn Bridge–City Hall 4·5·6
Park Place 2·3
World Trade Center E
Fulton St–Broadway Nassau A·C·J·M·Z 2·3·4·5
FULTON LANDING
High St A·C
Jay St Borough Hall A·C·F
Court St M·N·R
BROOKLYN HEIGHTS
Clark St 2·3
Borough Hall 2·3·4·5
Hoyt St 2·3
Cortlandt St 1·9
WORLD TRADE CENTER
Cortlandt St N·R
Rector St 1·9
Rector St N·R
Wall St 4·5
Wall St 2·3
FINANCIAL DISTRICT
BATTERY PARK CITY
Bowling Green 4·5
Broad St J·M·Z
South Ferry 1·9
Whitehall St N·R
CARROLL GARDENS
Bergen St F·G
Carroll St F·G
Smith–9 Sts F·G
RED HOOK
Weehawken Ferry
Brooklyn Army Terminal Ferry
Coast Guard Only
HOLLAND TUNNEL
BROOKLYN-BATTERY TUNNEL
MANHATTAN BRIDGE
BROOKLYN BRIDGE
PATH
Metropolitan Transportation Authority
Local service only
All trains stop (local and express service)
Station served by one of two lines
Free subway transfer
Station Name
Full time service
Part time service
Normal service
Rush hour service
Terminal
Commuter rail service
June 2000
© 2000 Metropolitan Transportation Authority
Design: Michael Hertz Associates, New York City
Map is subject to change
Used with permission

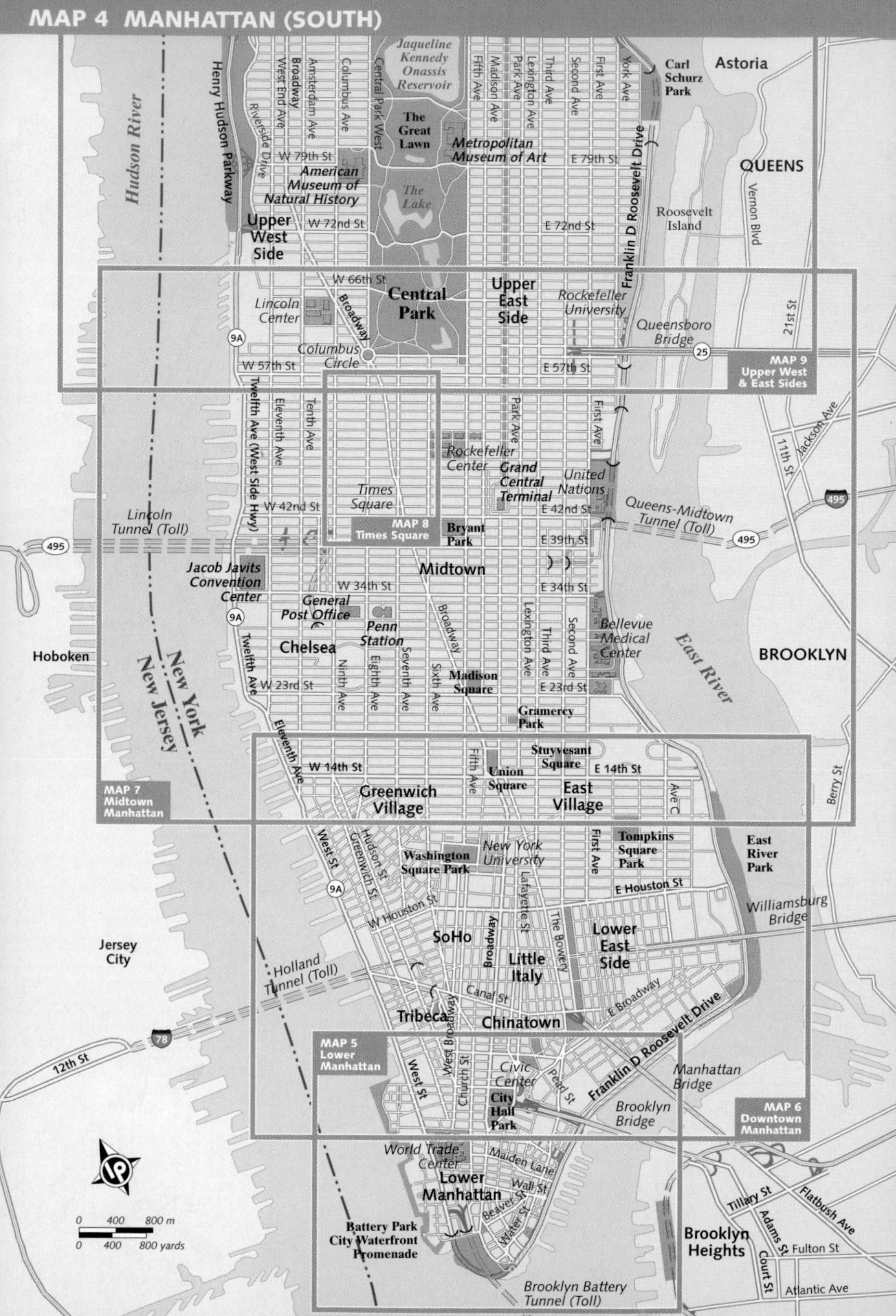

Jaqueline Kennedy Onassis Reservoir
Carl Schurz Park
Astoria
Hudson River
Henry Hudson Parkway
Riverside Drive
West End Ave
Broadway
Amsterdam Ave
Columbus Ave
Central Park West
Fifth Ave
Madison Ave
Park Ave
Lexington Ave
Third Ave
Second Ave
First Ave
York Ave
The Great Lawn
Metropolitan Museum of Art
W 79th St
E 79th St
Franklin D Roosevelt Drive
QUEENS
American Museum of Natural History
The Lake
Vernon Blvd
Roosevelt Island
Upper West Side
W 72nd St
E 72nd St
W 66th St
Central Park
Upper East Side
Rockefeller University
Lincoln Center
Queensboro Bridge
21st St
9A
Columbus Circle
25
W 57th St
E 57th St
MAP 9 Upper West & East Sides
Twelfth Ave (West Side Hwy)
Eleventh Ave
Tenth Ave
Park Ave
First Ave
Jackson Ave
11th St
Rockefeller Center
Grand Central Terminal
United Nations
Times Square
Queens-Midtown Tunnel (Toll)
495
Lincoln Tunnel (Toll)
W 42nd St
E 42nd St
MAP 8 Times Square
Bryant Park
E 39th St
Jacob Javits Convention Center
Midtown
W 34th St
E 34th St
General Post Office
Penn Station
Broadway
Lexington Ave
Third Ave
Second Ave
Bellevue Medical Center
East River
Hoboken
Chelsea
BROOKLYN
New York
New Jersey
Twelfth Ave
W 23rd St
Ninth Ave
Eighth Ave
Seventh Ave
Sixth Ave
Madison Square
E 23rd St
Gramercy Park
Eleventh Ave
Stuyvesant Square
W 14th St
Fifth Ave
Union Square
E 14th St
MAP 7 Midtown Manhattan
Greenwich Village
East Village
Ave C
Berry St
West St
Hudson St
Greenwich St
New York University
First Ave
Tompkins Square Park
East River Park
Washington Square Park
E Houston St
W Houston St
Williamsburg Bridge
Jersey City
SoHo
Broadway
Lafayette St
The Bowery
Lower East Side
Little Italy
Holland Tunnel (Toll)
Canal St
E Broadway
Tribeca
Chinatown
78
12th St
MAP 5 Lower Manhattan
West St
West Broadway
Church St
Civic Center
Pearl St
Manhattan Bridge
City Hall Park
Brooklyn Bridge
MAP 6 Downtown Manhattan
World Trade Center
Maiden Lane
Lower Manhattan
Wall St
Beaver St
Water St
Tillary St
Flatbush Ave
Adams St
Battery Park City Waterfront Promenade
Brooklyn Heights
Fulton St
Court St
Atlantic Ave
Brooklyn Battery Tunnel (Toll)
0 400 800 m
0 400 800 yards

New York Botanical Garden
Fordham University
Bronx Zoo
Kingsbridge Rd
Fordham Rd
187th St
Henry Hudson Bridge (Toll)
Inwood Hill Park
Inwood
The Cloisters
Fort Tryon Park
Hudson River
Harlem River
Henry Hudson Parkway
Broadway
Tenth Ave
St Nicholas Ave
Amsterdam Ave
Martin Luther King Blvd
Jerome Ave
Webster Ave
Grand Concourse
3rd Ave
Arthur Ave
W Tremont Ave
E Tremont Ave
Crotona Park
Claremont Park
George Washington Bridge (Toll)
Washington Heights
Harlem River Driveway
BRONX
E 167th St
Boston Rd
Prospect Ave
Westchester Ave
Fort Washington Park
E 161st St
Macombs Dam Bridge
W 155th St
Yankee Stadium
Morris Ave
New York
New Jersey
MAP 10 Harlem
Riverside Park
145th St Bridge
E 149th St
W 145th St
Frederick Douglass Blvd
Adam Clayton Powell Jr Blvd
Lenox Ave
Madison Ave Bridge
Third Ave
Willis Ave
E 138th St
Fifth Ave
Madison Ave
Third Ave Bridge
Bruckner Blvd
St Nicholas Park
W 131st St
Willis Ave Bridge
W 125th St
Harlem
E 125th St
Triborough Bridge (Toll)
Randalls Island Park
Morningside Heights
Marcus Garvey Park
Park Ave
Second Ave
First Ave
Downing Memorial Stadium
Columbia University
E 116th St
MAP 9 Upper West & East Sides
Morningside Park
Jefferson Park
Cathedral Pkwy
Central Park North
E 110th St
Spanish Harlem
Randalls Island
Harlem Meer
Franklin D Roosevelt Drive
Riverside Drive
West End Ave
Manhattan Ave
Central Park West
Central Park
Lexington Ave
Wards Island Park
Upper West Side
W 96th St
Upper East Side
E 96th St
East River
Mill Rock
Astoria

ANGUS OBORN

ANGUS OBORN

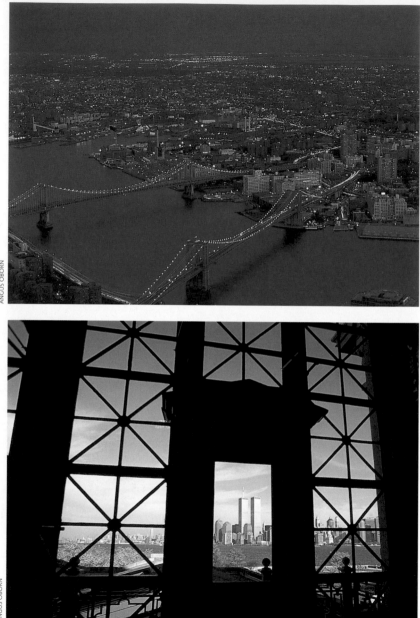

Top: Aerial view of the Brooklyn and Manhattan Bridges
Bottom: The Twin Towers, as seen from Ellis Island

ANGUS OBORN

City sidewalks, busy sidewalks

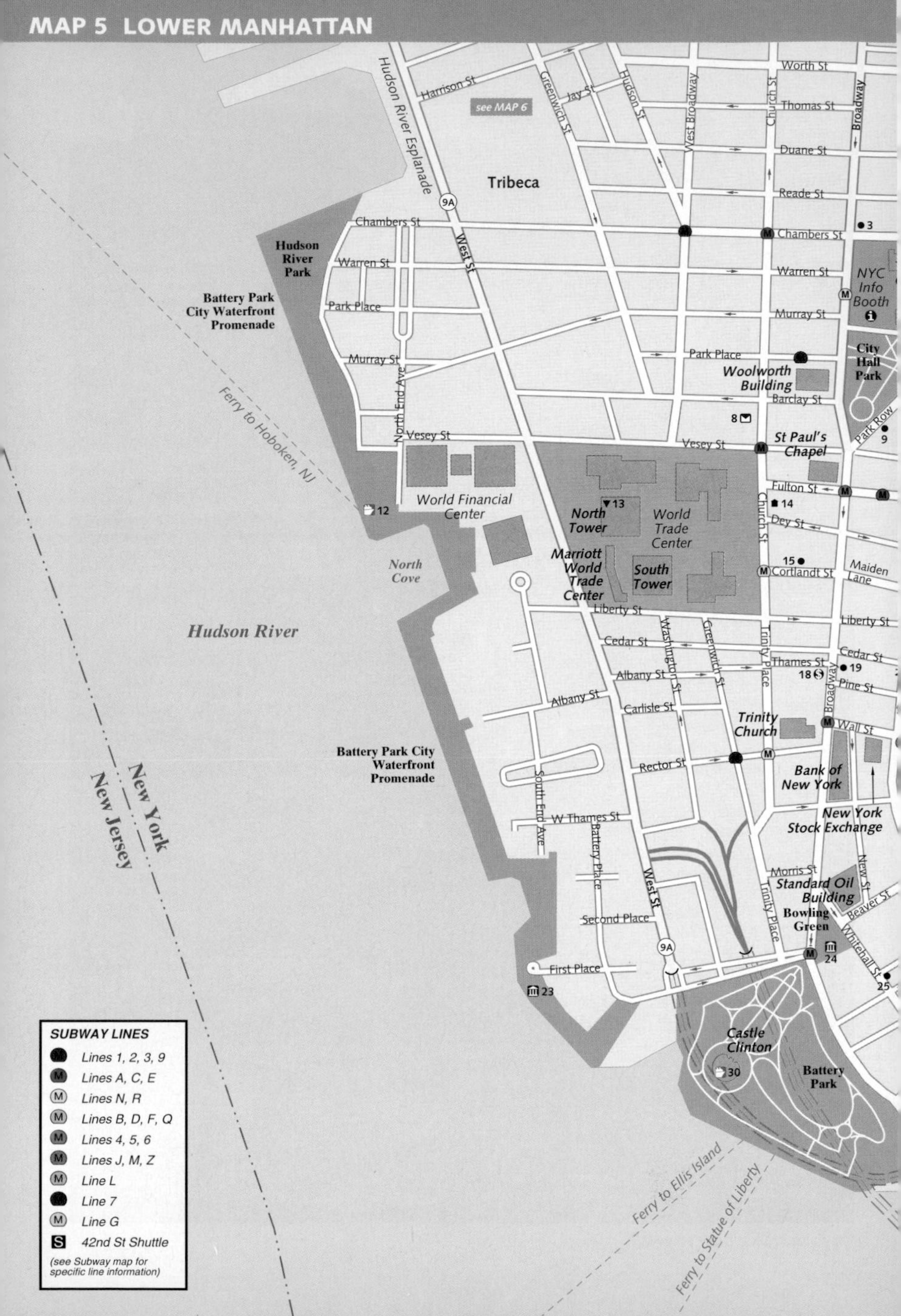

Worth St
Harrison St
Jay St
Thomas St
see MAP 6
Hudson River Esplanade
Greenwich St
Hudson St
West Broadway
Church St
Broadway
Duane St
Tribeca
Reade St
9A
Chambers St
Chambers St
Hudson River Park
West St
Warren St
Warren St
NYC Info Booth
Battery Park City Waterfront Promenade
Park Place
Murray St
Murray St
Park Place
City Hall Park
Woolworth Building
North End Ave
Barclay St
Ferry to Hoboken, NJ
8
Park Row
Vesey St
Vesey St
St Paul's Chapel
9
3
Fulton St
World Financial Center
12
13
14
North Tower
World Trade Center
Dey St
North Cove
Marriott World Trade Center
South Tower
15
Cortlandt St
Maiden Lane
Hudson River
Liberty St
Liberty St
Cedar St
Washington St
Greenwich St
Trinity Place
Cedar St
Thames St
19
18
Albany St
Albany St
Pine St
Carlisle St
Trinity Church
Wall St
Battery Park City Waterfront Promenade
Rector St
Bank of New York
New York
New Jersey
South End Ave
W Thames St
New York Stock Exchange
Battery Place
West St
Morris St
New St
Standard Oil Building
Trinity Place
Beaver St
Second Place
Bowling Green
Whitehall St
24
First Place
25
23
Castle Clinton
30
Battery Park
Ferry to Ellis Island
Ferry to Statue of Liberty
SUBWAY LINES
Lines 1, 2, 3, 9
Lines A, C, E
Lines N, R
Lines B, D, F, Q
Lines 4, 5, 6
Lines J, M, Z
Line L
Line 7
Line G
42nd St Shuttle
(see Subway map for specific line information)

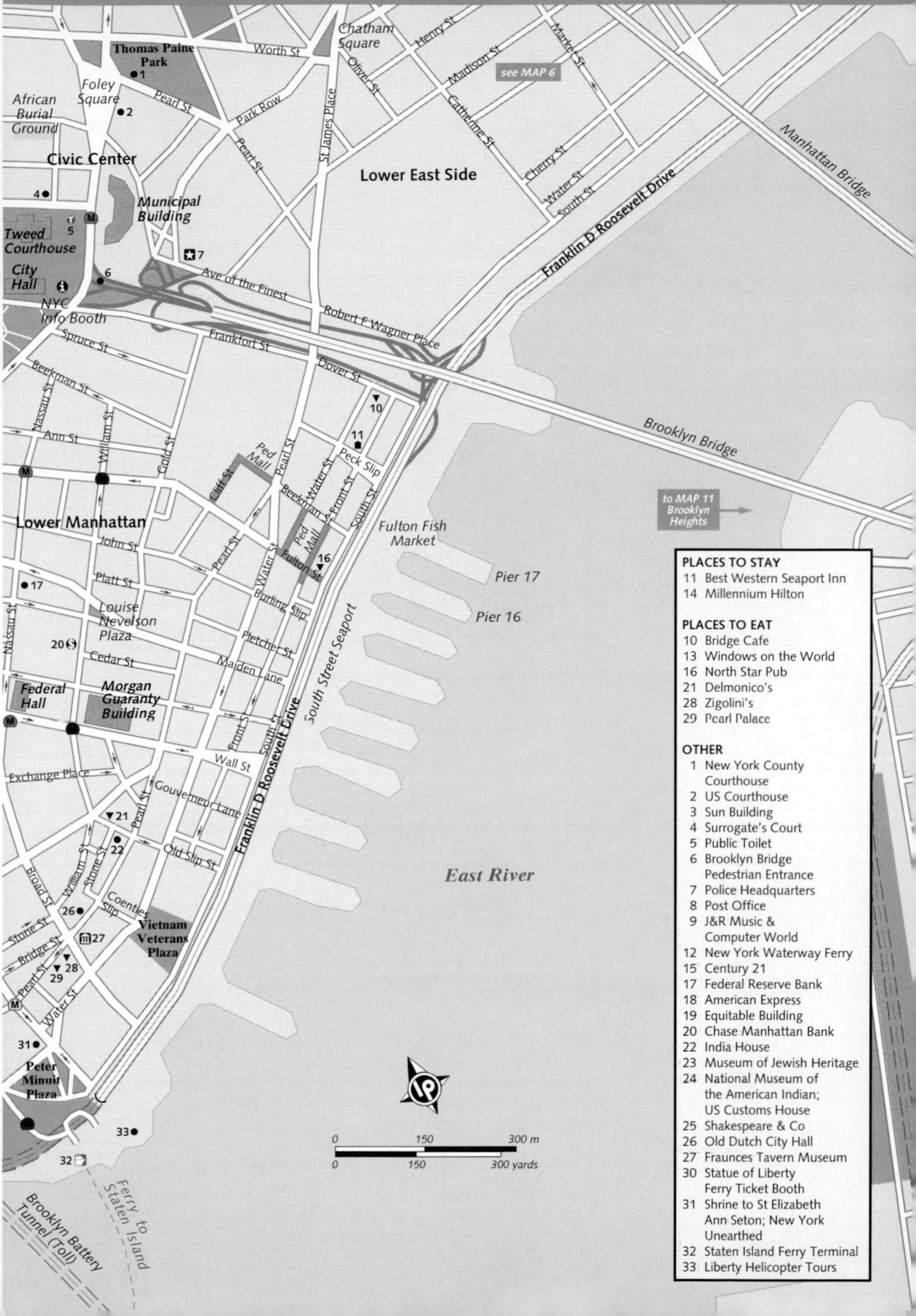

PLACES TO STAY

11 Best Western Seaport Inn
14 Millennium Hilton

PLACES TO EAT

10 Bridge Cafe
13 Windows on the World
16 North Star Pub
21 Delmonico's
28 Zigolini's
29 Pearl Palace

OTHER

1 New York County Courthouse
2 US Courthouse
3 Sun Building
4 Surrogate's Court
5 Public Toilet
6 Brooklyn Bridge Pedestrian Entrance
7 Police Headquarters
8 Post Office
9 J&R Music & Computer World
12 New York Waterway Ferry
15 Century 21
17 Federal Reserve Bank
18 American Express
19 Equitable Building
20 Chase Manhattan Bank
22 India House
23 Museum of Jewish Heritage
24 National Museum of the American Indian; US Customs House
25 Shakespeare & Co
26 Old Dutch City Hall
27 Fraunces Tavern Museum
30 Statue of Liberty Ferry Ticket Booth
31 Shrine to St Elizabeth Ann Seton; New York Unearthed
32 Staten Island Ferry Terminal
33 Liberty Helicopter Tours

Chelsea
West Village
Greenwich Village
Abington Square
Union Square
Washington Square Park
New York University
SoHo
Tribeca
Hudson Square
Lower Manhattan
Battery Park City
Civic Center
Hudson River
Hudson River Park
Hudson River Esplanade
Holland Tunnel (Toll)
Battery Park City Waterfront Promenade
African Burial Ground
Thomas Paine Park
Foley Square
Municipal Building
Tweed Courthouse
City Hall
City Hall Park
Woolworth Building
see MAP 7
see MAP 5
W 17th St
W 16th St
W 15th St
W 14th St
W 13th St
Little W 12th St
Eleventh Ave
Seventh Ave
Sixth Ave (Avenue of the Americas)
Fifth Ave
Broadway
Fourth Ave
Irving Place
E 12th St
E 11th St
E 10th St
E 9th St
E 8th St
University Place
Mercer St
Astor Place
Waverly Place
Washington Place
W 4th St
W 3rd St
Bleecker St
W Houston St
Prince St
Spring St
Broome St
Grand St
Canal St
Howard St
Lispenard St
Walker St
White St
Franklin St
Leonard St
Worth St
Thomas St
Duane St
Reade St
Chambers St
Warren St
Murray St
Park Place
Barclay St
Spruce St
West St
Hudson St
Greenwich St
Washington St
Varick St
Church St
W Broadway
Lafayette St
Centre St
Crosby St
Mulberry St
Mott St
Baxter St
Cortlandt Alley
Thompson St
La Guardia Place
Sullivan St
MacDougal St
Minetta Lane
Wooster St
Greene St
Eighth Ave
Jane St
W 12th St
Bank St
W 11th St
Perry St
Charles St
W 10th St
Christopher St
Greenwich Ave
Gansevoort St
Horatio St
Bethune St
Barrow St
Morton St
Leroy St
Clarkson St
Grove St
Bedford St
Commerce St
Jones St
Cornelia St
Carmine St
Downing St
King St
Charlton St
Vandam St
Dominick St
Watts St
Desbrosses St
Vestry St
Laight St
Hubert St
Beach St
N Moore St
Harrison St
Jay St
9A
78
0
200
400 m
0
200
400 yards

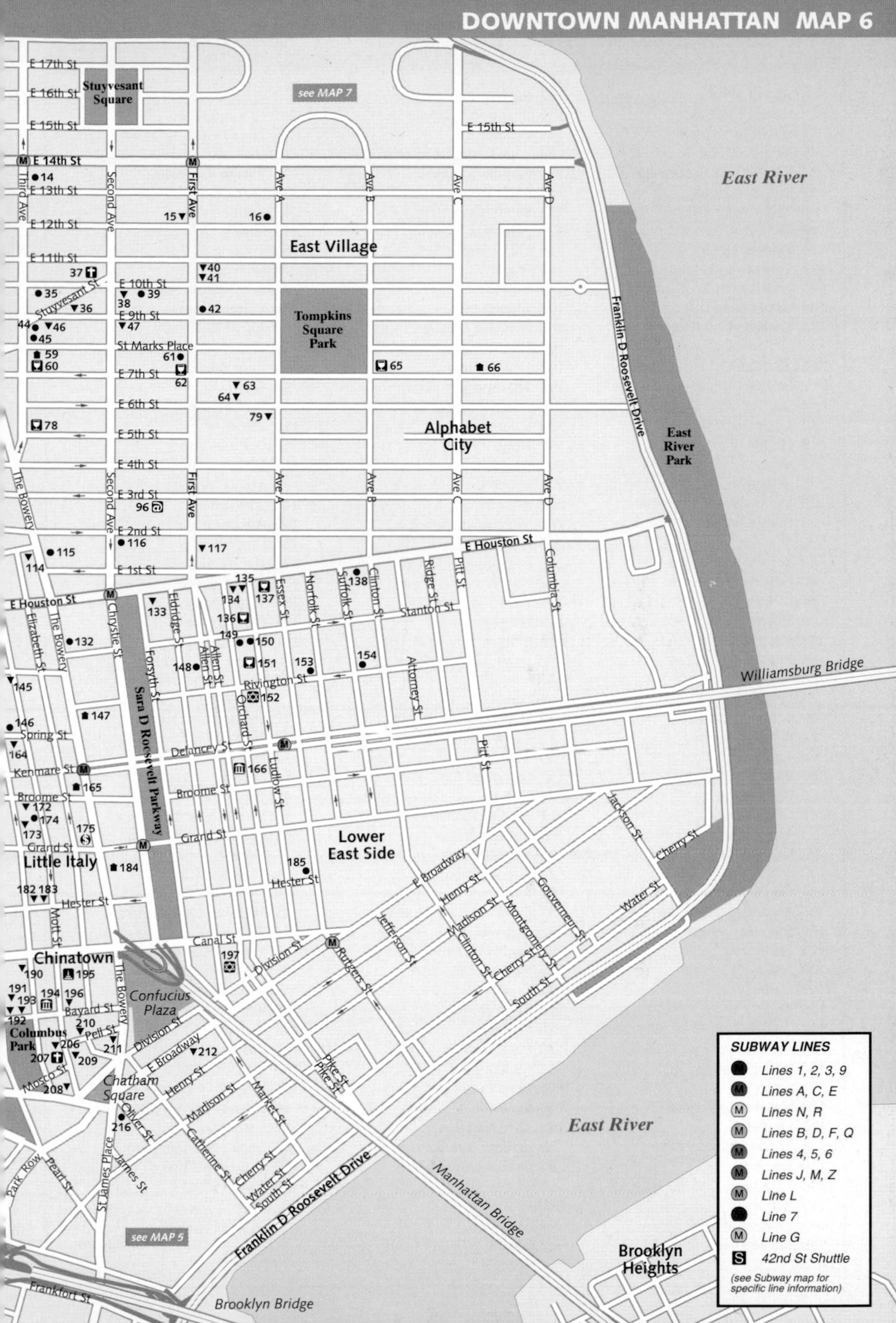
see MAP 7
Stuyvesant Square
E 17th St
E 16th St
E 15th St
E 14th St
E 13th St
E 12th St
E 11th St
E 10th St
E 9th St
St Marks Place
E 7th St
E 6th St
E 5th St
E 4th St
E 3rd St
E 2nd St
E 1st St
E Houston St
Third Ave
Second Ave
First Ave
Ave A
Ave B
Ave C
Ave D
Stuyvesant St
East Village
Tompkins Square Park
Alphabet City
East River
East River Park
Franklin D Roosevelt Drive
The Bowery
Elizabeth St
Chrystie St
Eldridge St
Forsyth St
Allen St
Orchard St
Ludlow St
Essex St
Norfolk St
Suffolk St
Clinton St
Ridge St
Attorney St
Pitt St
Columbia St
Stanton St
Rivington St
Williamsburg Bridge
Sara D Roosevelt Parkway
Spring St
Kenmare St
Delancey St
Broome St
Grand St
Little Italy
Hester St
Mott St
Lower East Side
Jackson St
Cherry St
E Broadway
Henry St
Madison St
Montgomery St
Gouverneur St
Water St
Jefferson St
Rutgers St
Division St
South St
Canal St
Chinatown
Confucius Plaza
Bayard St
Pell St
Columbus Park
Mosco St
Chatham Square
Oliver St
Market St
Catherine St
Pike St
Park Row
Pearl St
St James Place
James St
Manhattan Bridge
see MAP 5
Frankfort St
Brooklyn Bridge
Brooklyn Heights
SUBWAY LINES
Lines 1, 2, 3, 9
Lines A, C, E
Lines N, R
Lines B, D, F, Q
Lines 4, 5, 6
Lines J, M, Z
Line L
Line 7
Line G
42nd St Shuttle
(see Subway map for specific line information)

DOWNTOWN MANHATTAN

PLACES TO STAY

21 Incentra Village
31 Larchmont Hotel
43 Riverview Hotel
54 Washington Square Hotel
59 St Marks Hotel
66 East Village B&B
147 Off SoHo Suites
165 Pioneer Hotel
178 SoHo Grand Hotel
181 Holiday Inn Downtown
184 World Hotel
215 Cosmopolitan Hotel

PLACES TO EAT

7 Bar Six
8 Jon Vie
15 Cyclo
18 Florent
19 El Faro
23 Benny's Burritos
25 Sammy's Noodle Shop
28 French Roast
36 Sharaku
38 Second Ave Deli
40 DeRobertis
41 Lanza's
46 Hasaki
47 Veselka
63 Roettele AG
64 Raga
67 White Horse Tavern
69 Gourmet Garage
79 Benny's Burritos
84 Cones
86 Bleecker St Pastry
88 Little Havana
90 Caffe Reggio
94 Time Cafe
97 Grange Hall
100 Marinella
101 Do Hwa
103 Trattoria Spaghetto
104 Minetta Tavern
106 Caffe Borgia
108 Le Figaro
109 Caffe Lure
110 Rocco
111 Tomoe Sushi
114 Astor Restaurant & Lounge
117 Lucky Cheng's
121 Souen
122 Helianthus Vegetarian
123 Quilty's
133 Yonah Shimmel Bakery
134 Bereket
135 Katz's Deli
139 Raoul's
143 Fanelli Cafe
145 Kitchen Club
162 Balthazar
163 Spring St Natural
164 Lombardi's
167 Lupe's East LA Kitchen
170 Gourmet Garage
172 Caffe Roma
173 Benito One
177 Abyssinia
179 Lucky Strike
182 Puglia
183 Vincent's
188 Montrachet
190 Pho Viet Huong
191 Nha Trang
192 New Pasteur
193 Thailand Restaurant
196 House of Vegetarian
198 Riverrun
199 Nobu
200 Chanterelle
201 Bubby's
202 Walkers
206 Vegetarian Paradise 3
208 Hong Ying Rice Shop
209 Peking Duck House
210 Hay Wun Loy
211 Joe's Shanghai
212 Nice Restaurant
214 Odeon

BARS

4 Lure
20 Hudson Bar & Books
22 Corner Bistro
50 55 Bar
51 Stonewall Bar
60 McSorley's Old Ale House
62 WCOU Radio
65 Vazac's (7B's)
70 Marie's Crisis
78 The Scratcher
80 Rubyfruit
81 Blind Tiger Ale House
82 Chumley's
95 Swift's Hibernian Lounge
98 Henrietta Hudson
99 Crazy Nanny's
102 Bar d'O
128 Pravda
136 Luna Lounge
137 Mercury Bar
151 Barramundi
155 Ear Inn
168 Cafe Noir
189 Liquor Store Bar
203 Bubble Lounge

CLUBS

1 Mother
2 Baktun
3 The Cooler
5 Chicago Blues
16 The Cock
17 Hell
24 Village Vanguard
34 Webster Hall
45 Continental
48 Smalls
61 Tribe
71 Monster
72 Washington Square Church
74 Bottom Line
83 Sweet Basil
89 Blue Note
91 Cafe Wha?
94 Fez
107 Back Fence
115 CBGB
118 Culture Club
119 SOBs
138 Meow Mix
148 Surf Reality
149 Arlene Grocery
156 Don Hill's
174 Double Happiness
176 Naked Lunch
186 Vinyl
187 Fast Folk Cafe
204 Knitting Factory

SHOPS

9 East-West Books
12 Strand Bookstore
13 Footlight Records
14 Kiehl's
44 St Mark's Bookshop
49 Three Lives
55 Barnes & Noble
68 Creative Visions/Gay Pleasures
75 Shakespeare & Co
76 Other Music
85 Matt Umanov Guitars
87 Triton
93 Tower Records
105 Route 66 Records
113 Urban Outfitters
124 Rizzoli
132 Bari
146 Resurrection
150 Amy Downs
153 Schapiro's Wines
154 Streit's Matzoh Company
158 Enchanted Forest
160 Canal Jean Company
180 Traveler's Choice
185 Essex Pickles

continued...

DOWNTOWN MANHATTAN

MUSEUMS

32 Forbes Galleries
77 Old Merchant's House Museum
125 Museum for African Art
126 New Museum of Contemporary Art
127 Guggenheim SoHo
157 New York City Fire Museum
166 Lower East Side Tenement Museum
194 Museum of Chinese in the Americas

OTHER

6 Lesbian & Gay Community Services Center
10 Cyberfeld's
11 Bowlmor Lanes
26 Patchin Place
27 Jefferson Market Library
29 Second Cemetery of Spanish & Portuguese Synagogue
30 Andrew Lockwood House
33 Grace Church
35 Renwick Triangle
37 St Mark's in-the-Bowery
39 10th St Baths
42 PS 122
52 Northern Dispensary
53 Electric Lady Studios
56 Colonnade Row
57 Joseph Papp Public Theater
58 Cooper Union
73 Arch in Washington Square Park
92 Judson Memorial Church
96 Internet Cafe
112 Angelika Film Center
116 Anthology Film Archives
120 Film Forum
129 Cyber Cafe
130 Puck Building
131 Old St Patrick's Cathedral
140 Ward-Nasse Gallery
141 Howard Greenberg Gallery
142 Haas' Mural
144 Singer Building
152 First Roumanian-American Congregation
159 St Nicholas Hotel
161 Haughwout Building
169 Performing Garage
171 Old Police Headquarters
175 Bowery Savings Bank
195 Eastern States Buddhist Temple
197 Eldridge St Synagogue
205 Clocktower Gallery
207 Church of the Transfiguration
213 Harrison St Houses
216 First Shearith Israel Graveyard

ANGUS OBORN

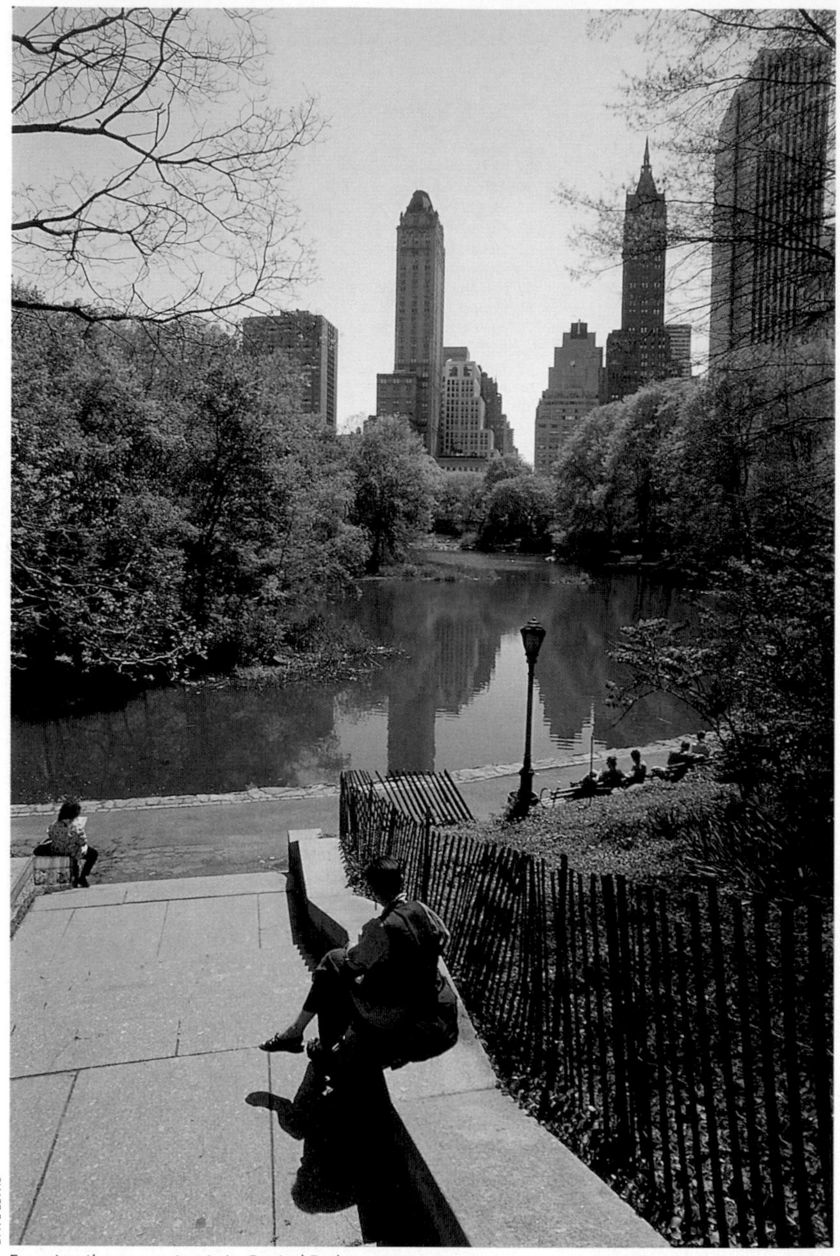

DAVE LEWIS

Escaping the mean streets in Central Park

ANGUS OBORN

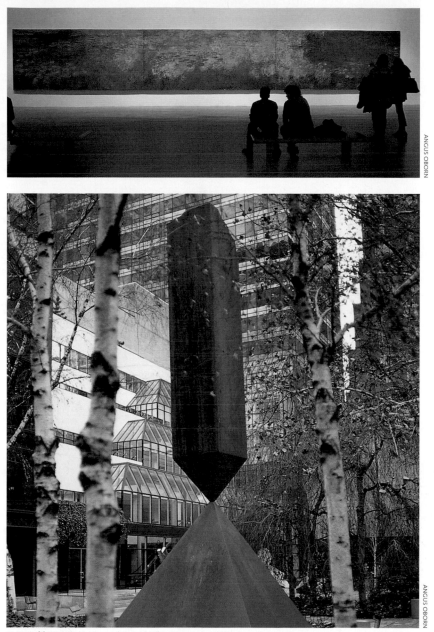

Top and bottom: Inside and outside the Museum of Modern Art, Midtown

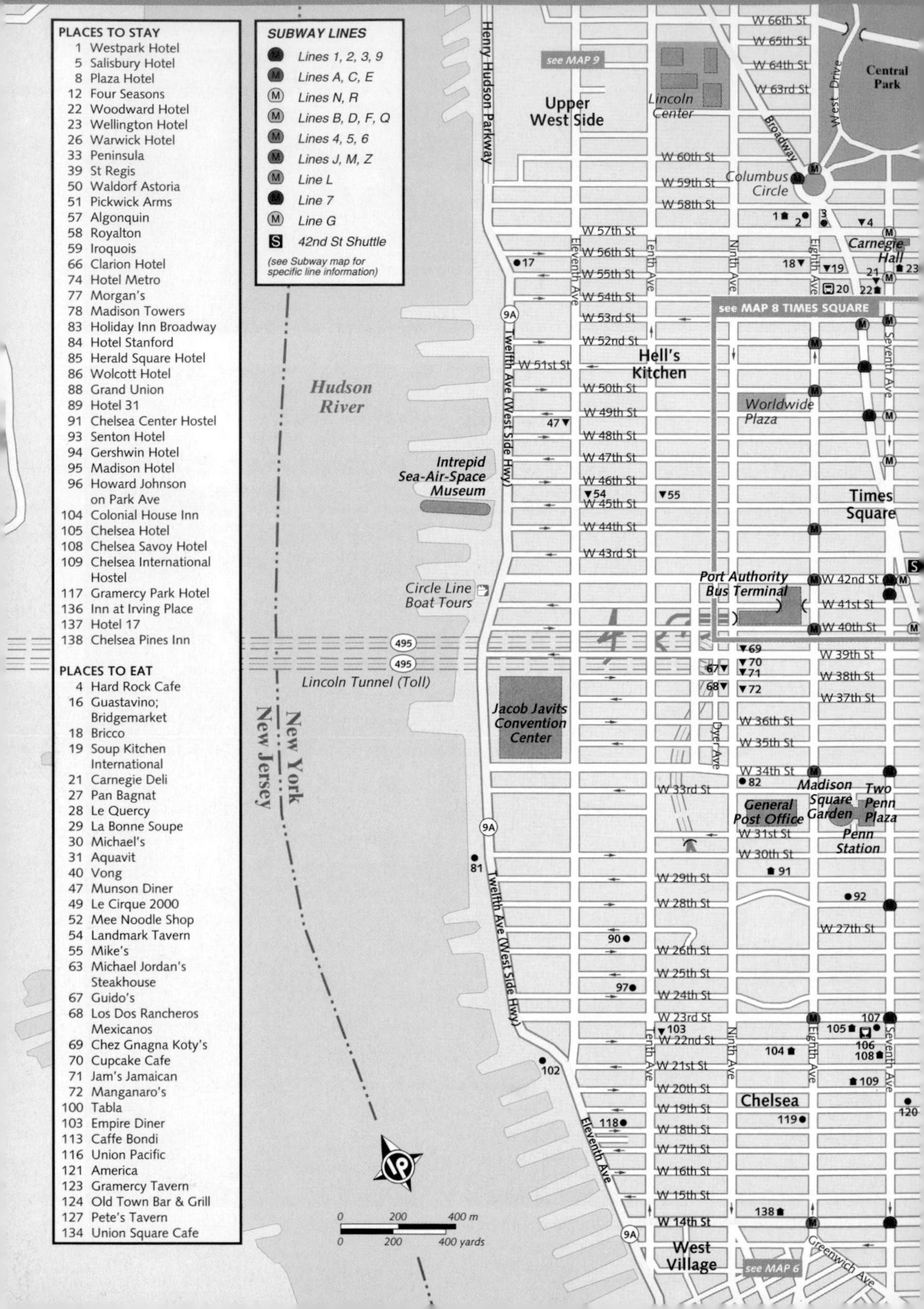

PLACES TO STAY

1 Westpark Hotel
5 Salisbury Hotel
8 Plaza Hotel
12 Four Seasons
22 Woodward Hotel
23 Wellington Hotel
26 Warwick Hotel
33 Peninsula
39 St Regis
50 Waldorf Astoria
51 Pickwick Arms
57 Algonquin
58 Royalton
59 Iroquois
66 Clarion Hotel
74 Hotel Metro
77 Morgan's
78 Madison Towers
83 Holiday Inn Broadway
84 Hotel Stanford
85 Herald Square Hotel
86 Wolcott Hotel
88 Grand Union
89 Hotel 31
91 Chelsea Center Hostel
93 Senton Hotel
94 Gershwin Hotel
95 Madison Hotel
96 Howard Johnson on Park Ave
104 Colonial House Inn
105 Chelsea Hotel
108 Chelsea Savoy Hotel
109 Chelsea International Hostel
117 Gramercy Park Hotel
136 Inn at Irving Place
137 Hotel 17
138 Chelsea Pines Inn

PLACES TO EAT

4 Hard Rock Cafe
16 Guastavino; Bridgemarket
18 Bricco
19 Soup Kitchen International
21 Carnegie Deli
27 Pan Bagnat
28 Le Quercy
29 La Bonne Soupe
30 Michael's
31 Aquavit
40 Vong
47 Munson Diner
49 Le Cirque 2000
52 Mee Noodle Shop
54 Landmark Tavern
55 Mike's
63 Michael Jordan's Steakhouse
67 Guido's
68 Los Dos Rancheros Mexicanos
69 Chez Gnagna Koty's
70 Cupcake Cafe
71 Jam's Jamaican
72 Manganaro's
100 Tabla
103 Empire Diner
113 Caffe Bondi
116 Union Pacific
121 America
123 Gramercy Tavern
124 Old Town Bar & Grill
127 Pete's Tavern
134 Union Square Cafe

SUBWAY LINES

Lines 1, 2, 3, 9
Lines A, C, E
Lines N, R
Lines B, D, F, Q
Lines 4, 5, 6
Lines J, M, Z
Line L
Line 7
Line G
S *42nd St Shuttle*

(see Subway map for specific line information)

Upper West Side
Lincoln Center
Central Park
West Drive
Broadway
Columbus Circle
Carnegie Hall
Hell's Kitchen
Worldwide Plaza
Times Square
Hudson River
Intrepid Sea-Air-Space Museum
Circle Line Boat Tours
Port Authority Bus Terminal
Lincoln Tunnel (Toll)
Jacob Javits Convention Center
New York
New Jersey
Madison Square Garden
Two Penn Plaza
Penn Station
General Post Office
Chelsea
West Village
Henry Hudson Parkway
Twelfth Ave (West Side Hwy)
Eleventh Ave
Tenth Ave
Ninth Ave
Eighth Ave
Seventh Ave
Dyer Ave
Greenwich Ave
W 66th St, W 65th St, W 64th St, W 63rd St, W 60th St, W 59th St, W 58th St, W 57th St, W 56th St, W 55th St, W 54th St, W 53rd St, W 52nd St, W 51st St, W 50th St, W 49th St, W 48th St, W 47th St, W 46th St, W 45th St, W 44th St, W 43rd St, W 42nd St, W 41st St, W 40th St, W 39th St, W 38th St, W 37th St, W 36th St, W 35th St, W 34th St, W 33rd St, W 31st St, W 30th St, W 29th St, W 28th St, W 27th St, W 26th St, W 25th St, W 24th St, W 23rd St, W 22nd St, W 21st St, W 20th St, W 19th St, W 18th St, W 17th St, W 16th St, W 15th St, W 14th St

see MAP 9
see MAP 8 TIMES SQUARE
see MAP 6

0 200 400 m
0 200 400 yards

SHOPS

2 Gateway Computers
3 Coliseum Books
7 Rizzoli
9 Bergdorf Goodman
10 FAO Schwartz
11 Warner Bros Studio Store
13 Argosy
14 Borders
24 Mysterious Bookshop
32 Henri Bendel
34 Tiffany & Co
35 Trump Tower
37 Disney Store
38 Takashimaya
41 Cosmetics Plus
45 NBA Store
46 Cartier
48 Saks Fifth Avenue
56 Gotham Book Mart
60 HMV
61 Brooks Brothers
62 Worth & Worth
65 Dollar Bill's
73 Macy's
75 Lord & Taylor
76 CompUSA
80 Complete Traveller
82 B&H Photo-Video
98 Chelsea Antiques Building
99 Annex Antique Fair & Flea Market
110 Barnes & Noble
120 A Different Light Bookstore
129 Dave's Army & Navy
130 Old Navy
132 Books of Wonder
133 Paragon Athletic Goods
135 Barnes & Noble

OTHER

6 Chequepoint
15 British Open
17 Exit
20 Gray Line Tours
25 City Center
36 Newseum New York
42 Museum of Television & Radio
43 Museum of Modern Art
44 American Craft Museum
49 Villard Houses; Urban Center Books
53 Top of the Tower
64 American Express
79 Pierpont Morgan Library
81 Liberty Helicopter Tours
87 Chase Manhattan Bank
90 Twilo
92 Catch a Rising Star
97 Metro Pictures
101 Metropolitan Life Tower
102 Chelsea Piers
106 Barracuda
107 Twirl
111 Limelight
112 Centro-Fly
114 Flatiron Building
115 True
118 Roxy
119 Joyce Theater
122 Theodore Roosevelt's Birthplace
125 National Arts Club
126 Players Club
128 King
131 Splash
139 Belmont Lounge
140 Irving Plaza
141 Beauty Bar

TIMES SQUARE

PLACES TO STAY

1 Ameritania Hotel
12 Novotel
18 Days Hotel Midtown
33 Paramount Hotel
34 Hotel Edison
37 Doubletree Guest Suites
39 Portland Square Hotel
45 Broadway Inn Bed & Breakfast
49 Marriott Marquis
52 Big Apple Hostel
56 Milford Plaza
73 Hotel Carter

PLACES TO EAT & DRINK

3 Stage Deli
4 Mee Noodle Shop
9 Island Burgers & Shakes
28 Basilica
29 Hourglass Tavern
30 Barbetta
32 McHale's Bar & Cafe
40 Zen Palate
41 Mercury Bar
42 Bali Nusa Indah
43 Joe Allen
44 Orso
53 Film Center Cafe
54 Rudy's Bar & Grill

OTHER

7 NYC & Company Information Center
8 Post Office
11 Float
17 Caroline's on Broadway
21 Drama Bookshop
22 Sam Ash Music
25 Thomas Cook
26 Manny's Music
36 TKTS Booth
38 Times Square Visitors Center
50 Virgin Megastore
64 MTV Studios
70 ABC Studios
71 Town Hall
72 ICP Gallery Midtown
74 Loews 42nd St – E Walk Theater
76 Ford Center Theater
77 One Times Square
79 Post Office
82 Staples

THEATERS

2 Ed Sullivan
5 Victoria
6 Broadway
10 Neil Simon
13 Gershwin
14 Circle in the Square
15 Winter Garden
16 Ambassador
19 Eugene O'Neill
20 Walter Kerr
23 Longacre
24 Ethel Barrymore
27 Cort
31 Brooks Atkinson
35 Lunt-Fontanne
37 Palace
46 Imperial
47 Music Box
48 Richard Rodgers
49 Marquis
51 Lyceum
55 Martin Beck
57 John Golden
58 Royale
59 Plymouth
60 Booth
61 Majestic
62 Broadhurst
63 Schubert
65 Minskoff
66 Criterion Center Stage Right
67 Belasco
68 St James
69 Helen Hayes
75 New Victory
78 Samuel Beckett
80 New Amsterdam
81 Nederlander

TOM SMALLMAN

NYPD, Times Square

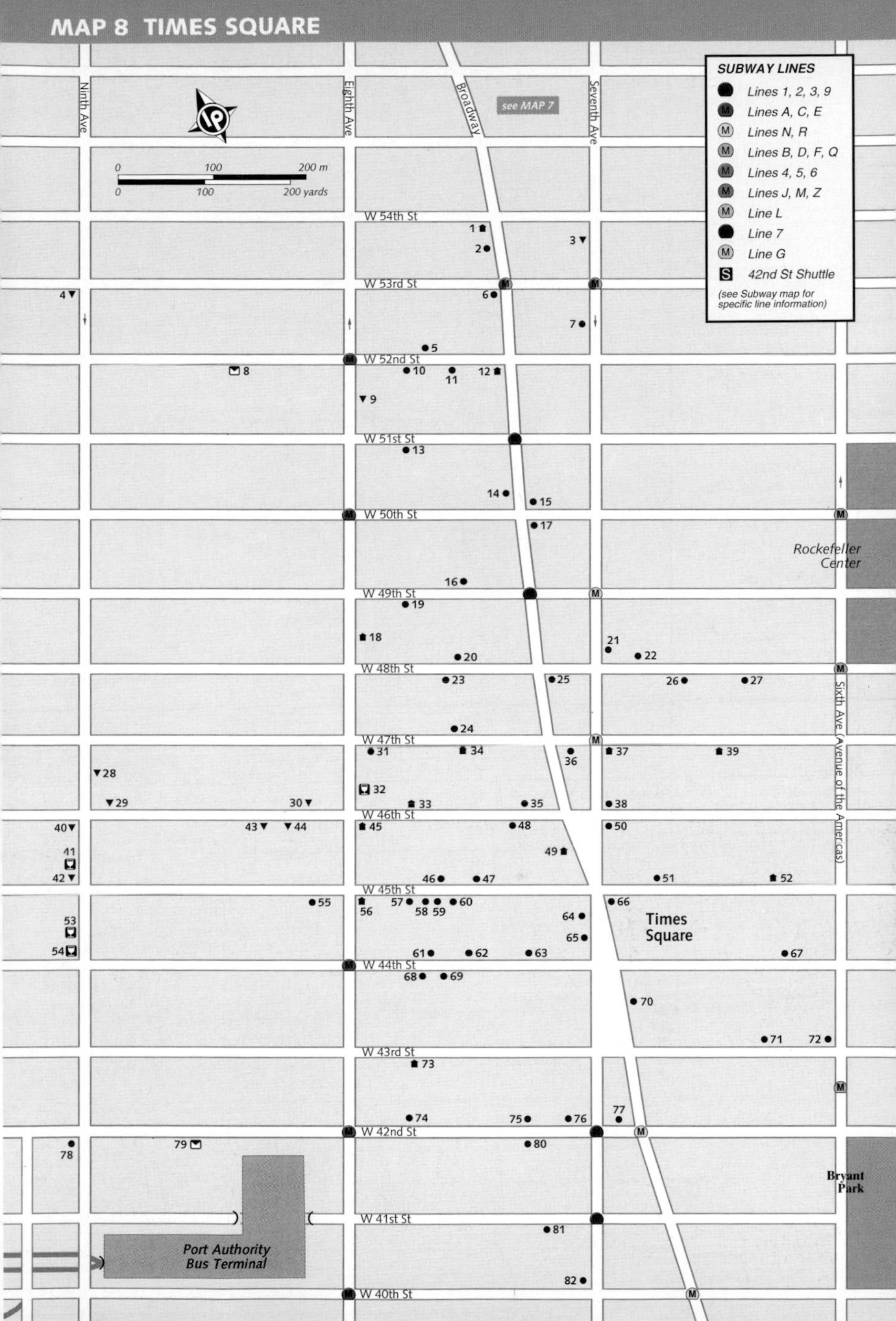
SUBWAY LINES
Lines 1, 2, 3, 9
Lines A, C, E
Lines N, R
Lines B, D, F, Q
Lines 4, 5, 6
Lines J, M, Z
Line L
Line 7
Line G
42nd St Shuttle
(see Subway map for specific line information)
see MAP 7
Ninth Ave
Eighth Ave
Broadway
Seventh Ave
Sixth Ave (Avenue of the Americas)
W 54th St
W 53rd St
W 52nd St
W 51st St
W 50th St
W 49th St
W 48th St
W 47th St
W 46th St
W 45th St
W 44th St
W 43rd St
W 42nd St
W 41st St
W 40th St
Rockefeller Center
Times Square
Bryant Park
Port Authority Bus Terminal
0 100 200 m
0 100 200 yards

PLACES TO STAY

2 Park View Hotel
4 Hostelling International - New York
7 Newtown
10 Hotel Wales
13 International Student Center
16 Franklin
24 Excelsior Hotel
34 Gracie Inn
36 Broadway American Hotel
40 Carlyle Hotel
44 Hotel Olcott
48 Inn New York City
68 Mayflower Hotel
69 Pierre Hotel
70 Lowell Hotel
79 Sherry-Netherland Hotel

PLACES TO EAT & DRINK

1 Saints
3 Night Cafe
11 Kinsale Tavern
12 Carmine's
21 Cafe Lalo
22 Tibet Shambala
25 Lexington Candy Shop
26 Zabar's
28 Cafe con Leche
29 Dublin House
30 The Evelyn
35 Ruby Foo's
37 Fairway Market
39 Park View Restaurant at the Boathouse
40 Bemelman's Bar
41 Empire Szechuan
46 Cafe Greco
49 Cafe Luxembourg
52 Empire Szechuan
53 Cafe des Artistes
54 Tavern on the Green
58 Picholine
64 La Goulue
65 Gourmet Garage
72 Madame Romaine de Lyon
73 Subway Inn
74 Favia Lite

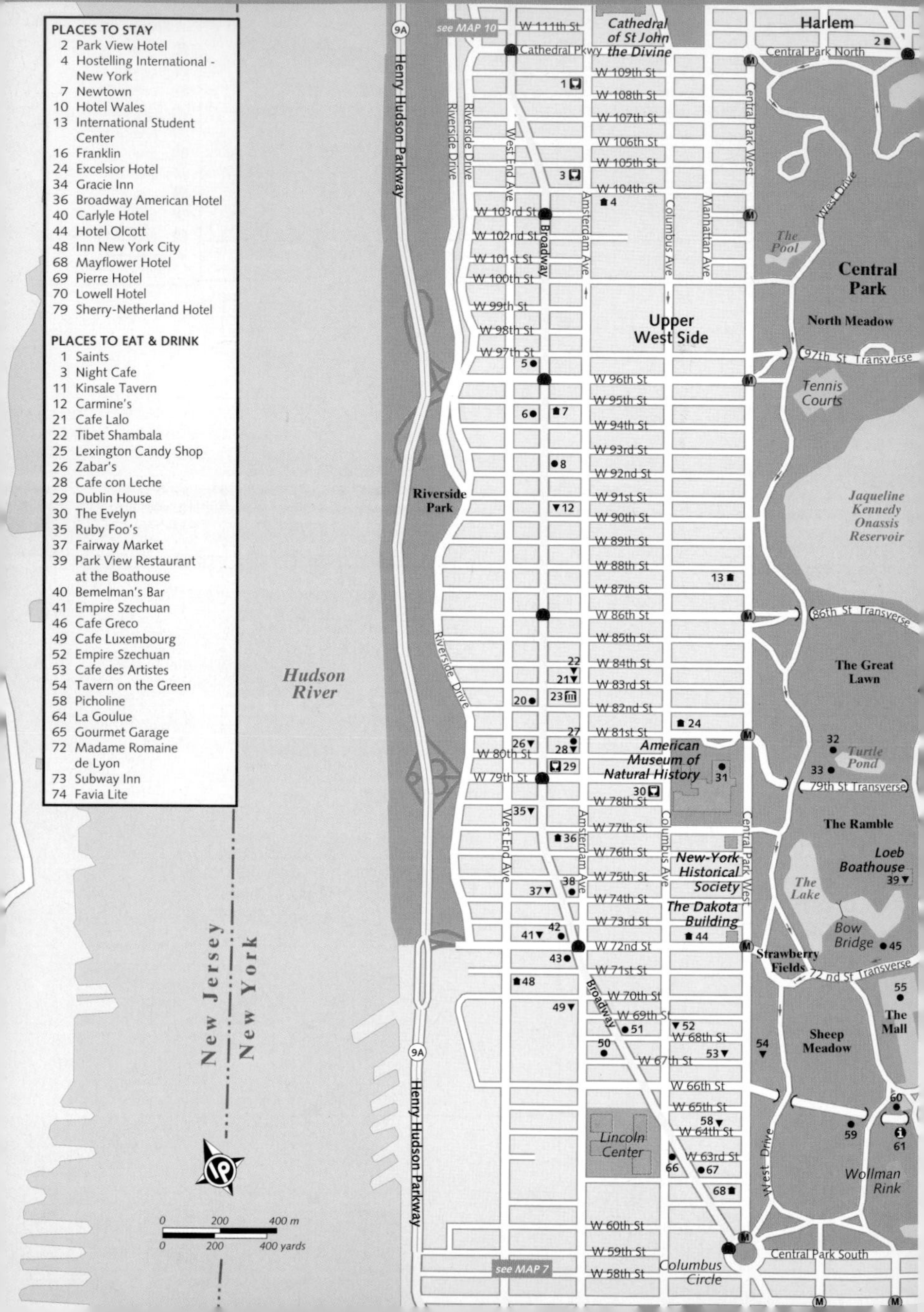

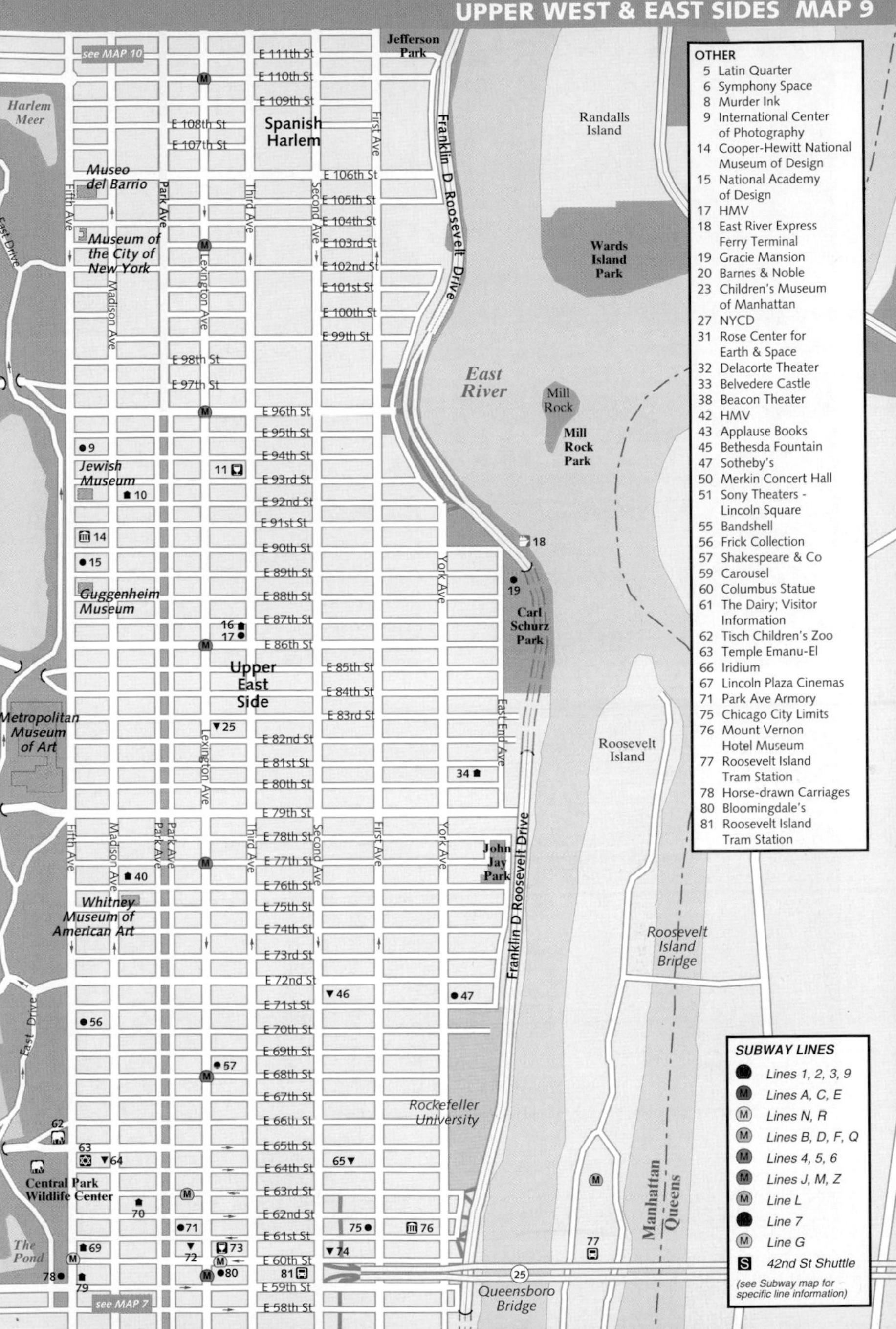

OTHER
5 Latin Quarter
6 Symphony Space
8 Murder Ink
9 International Center of Photography
14 Cooper-Hewitt National Museum of Design
15 National Academy of Design
17 HMV
18 East River Express Ferry Terminal
19 Gracie Mansion
20 Barnes & Noble
23 Children's Museum of Manhattan
27 NYCD
31 Rose Center for Earth & Space
32 Delacorte Theater
33 Belvedere Castle
38 Beacon Theater
42 HMV
43 Applause Books
45 Bethesda Fountain
47 Sotheby's
50 Merkin Concert Hall
51 Sony Theaters - Lincoln Square
55 Bandshell
56 Frick Collection
57 Shakespeare & Co
59 Carousel
60 Columbus Statue
61 The Dairy; Visitor Information
62 Tisch Children's Zoo
63 Temple Emanu-El
66 Iridium
67 Lincoln Plaza Cinemas
71 Park Ave Armory
75 Chicago City Limits
76 Mount Vernon Hotel Museum
77 Roosevelt Island Tram Station
78 Horse-drawn Carriages
80 Bloomingdale's
81 Roosevelt Island Tram Station
SUBWAY LINES
Lines 1, 2, 3, 9
Lines A, C, E
Lines N, R
Lines B, D, F, Q
Lines 4, 5, 6
Lines J, M, Z
Line L
Line 7
Line G
42nd St Shuttle
(see Subway map for specific line information)
see MAP 10
see MAP 7
Jefferson Park
Harlem Meer
Spanish Harlem
Museo del Barrio
Museum of the City of New York
Jewish Museum
Guggenheim Museum
Upper East Side
Metropolitan Museum of Art
Whitney Museum of American Art
Central Park Wildlife Center
The Pond
Rockefeller University
Randalls Island
Wards Island Park
East River
Mill Rock
Mill Rock Park
Carl Schurz Park
John Jay Park
Roosevelt Island
Roosevelt Island Bridge
Queensboro Bridge
Manhattan
Queens
Franklin D Roosevelt Drive
East Drive
Fifth Ave
Madison Ave
Park Ave
Lexington Ave
Third Ave
Second Ave
First Ave
York Ave
East End Ave
E 111th St
E 110th St
E 109th St
E 108th St
E 107th St
E 106th St
E 105th St
E 104th St
E 103rd St
E 102nd St
E 101st St
E 100th St
E 99th St
E 98th St
E 97th St
E 96th St
E 95th St
E 94th St
E 93rd St
E 92nd St
E 91st St
E 90th St
E 89th St
E 88th St
E 87th St
E 86th St
E 85th St
E 84th St
E 83rd St
E 82nd St
E 81st St
E 80th St
E 79th St
E 78th St
E 77th St
E 76th St
E 75th St
E 74th St
E 73rd St
E 72nd St
E 71st St
E 70th St
E 69th St
E 68th St
E 67th St
E 66th St
E 65th St
E 64th St
E 63rd St
E 62nd St
E 61st St
E 60th St
E 59th St
E 58th St

KIM GRANT

ANGUS OBORN

NEIL SETCHFIELD

The many museums of the Upper East Side (clockwise from top left): the Jewish Museum, Cooper-Hewitt National Museum of Design and the Metropolitan Museum of Art

ANGUS OBORN

JENNIFER STEFFEY

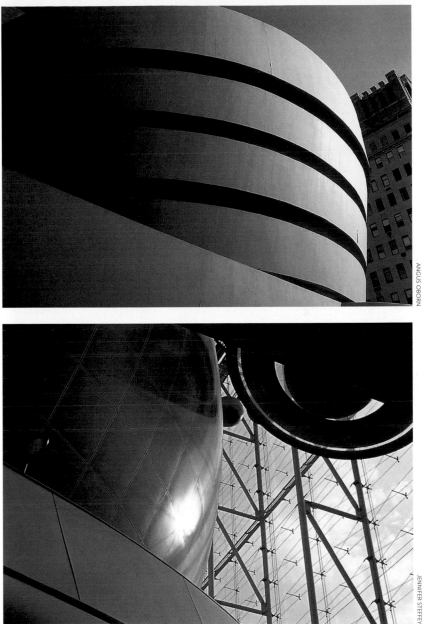

Top: Solomon R Guggenheim Museum, Upper East Side
Bottom: Rose Center for Earth & Space at the American Museum of Natural History

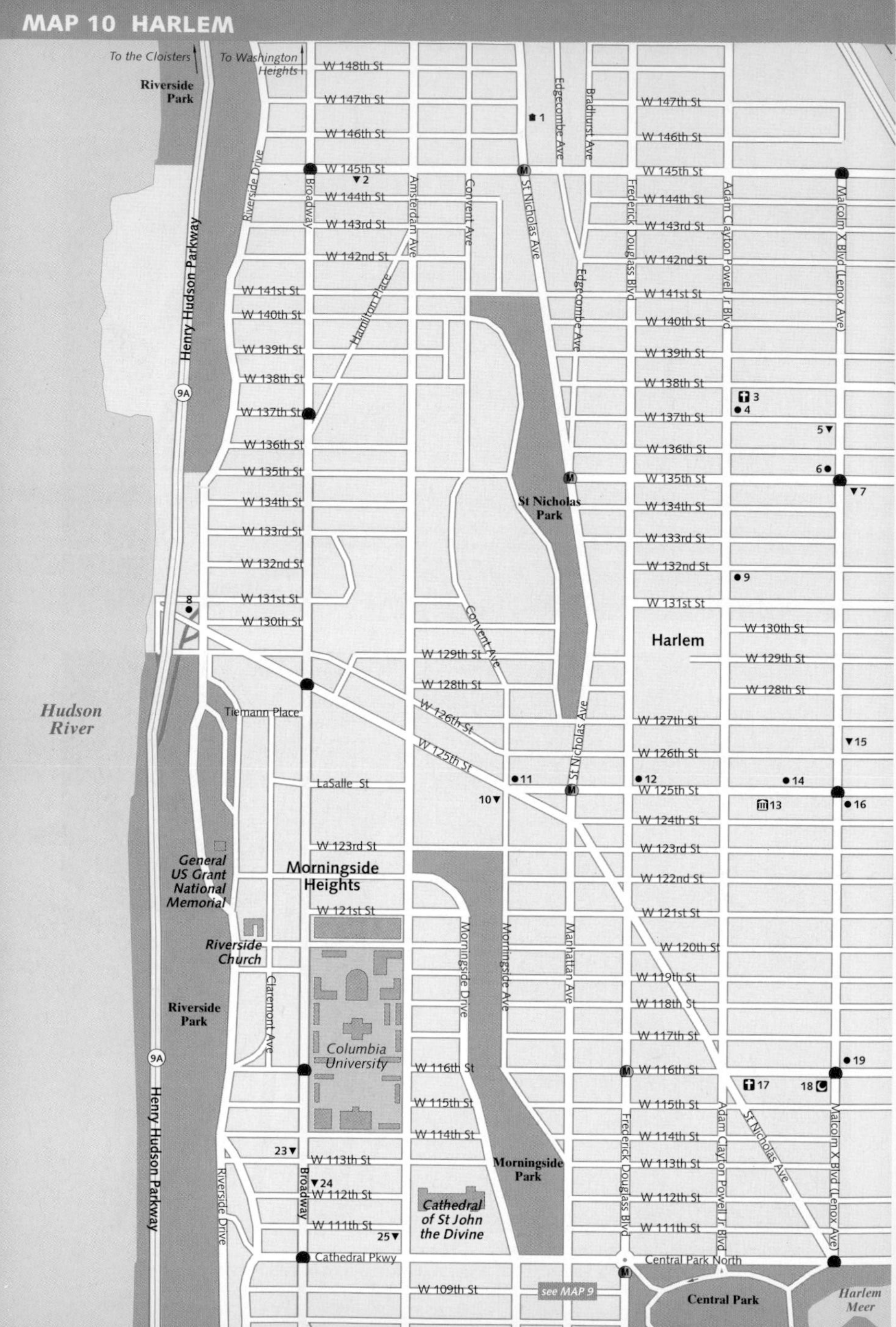
To the Cloisters
To Washington Heights
Riverside Park
Henry Hudson Parkway
9A
Riverside Drive
Broadway
Amsterdam Ave
Convent Ave
St Nicholas Ave
Edgecombe Ave
Bradhurst Ave
Frederick Douglass Blvd
Adam Clayton Powell Jr Blvd
Malcolm X Blvd (Lenox Ave)
Hamilton Place
W 148th St
W 147th St
W 146th St
W 145th St
W 144th St
W 143rd St
W 142nd St
W 141st St
W 140th St
W 139th St
W 138th St
W 137th St
W 136th St
W 135th St
W 134th St
W 133rd St
W 132nd St
W 131st St
W 130th St
W 129th St
W 128th St
W 127th St
W 126th St
W 125th St
W 124th St
W 123rd St
W 122nd St
W 121st St
W 120th St
W 119th St
W 118th St
W 117th St
W 116th St
W 115th St
W 114th St
W 113th St
W 112th St
W 111th St
W 109th St
St Nicholas Park
Harlem
Hudson River
Tiemann Place
LaSalle St
Manhattan Ave
Morningside Drive
Morningside Ave
Morningside Heights
General US Grant National Memorial
Riverside Church
Claremont Ave
Columbia University
Morningside Park
Cathedral of St John the Divine
Cathedral Pkwy
Central Park North
Central Park
Harlem Meer
see MAP 9
1
2
3
4
5
6
7
8
9
10
11
12
13
14
15
16
17
18
19
23
24
25

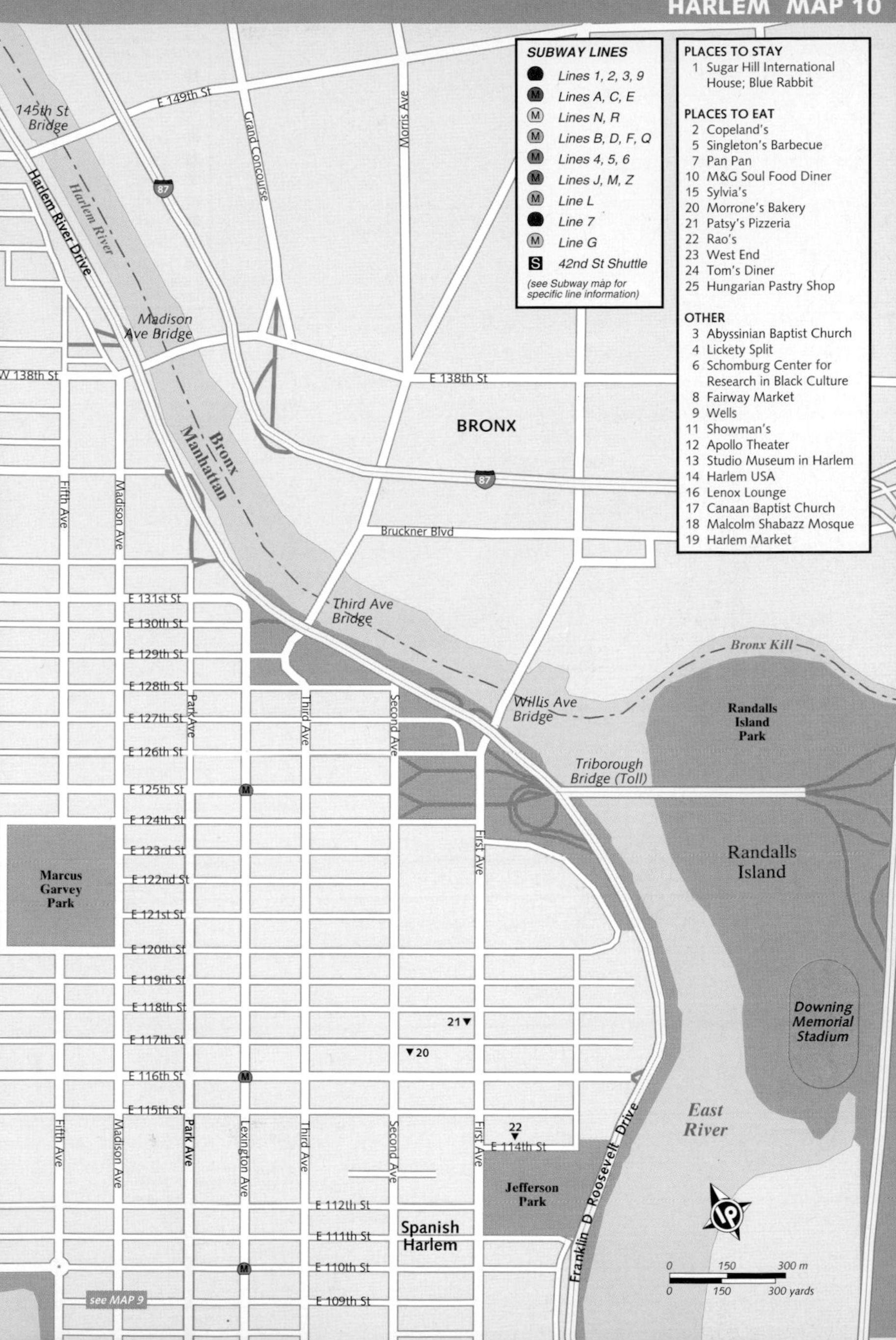
SUBWAY LINES
Lines 1, 2, 3, 9
Lines A, C, E
Lines N, R
Lines B, D, F, Q
Lines 4, 5, 6
Lines J, M, Z
Line L
Line 7
Line G
42nd St Shuttle
(see Subway map for specific line information)
PLACES TO STAY
1 Sugar Hill International House; Blue Rabbit
PLACES TO EAT
2 Copeland's
5 Singleton's Barbecue
7 Pan Pan
10 M&G Soul Food Diner
15 Sylvia's
20 Morrone's Bakery
21 Patsy's Pizzeria
22 Rao's
23 West End
24 Tom's Diner
25 Hungarian Pastry Shop
OTHER
3 Abyssinian Baptist Church
4 Lickety Split
6 Schomburg Center for Research in Black Culture
8 Fairway Market
9 Wells
11 Showman's
12 Apollo Theater
13 Studio Museum in Harlem
14 Harlem USA
16 Lenox Lounge
17 Canaan Baptist Church
18 Malcolm Shabazz Mosque
19 Harlem Market
145th St Bridge
E 149th St
Grand Concourse
Morris Ave
Harlem River Drive
Harlem River
Madison Ave Bridge
W 138th St
E 138th St
BRONX
Bronx
Manhattan
Fifth Ave
Madison Ave
Bruckner Blvd
E 131st St
E 130th St
E 129th St
E 128th St
E 127th St
E 126th St
E 125th St
E 124th St
E 123rd St
E 122nd St
E 121st St
E 120th St
E 119th St
E 118th St
E 117th St
E 116th St
E 115th St
E 114th St
E 112th St
E 111th St
E 110th St
E 109th St
Park Ave
Lexington Ave
Third Ave
Second Ave
First Ave
Third Ave Bridge
Willis Ave Bridge
Bronx Kill
Randalls Island Park
Triborough Bridge (Toll)
Randalls Island
Marcus Garvey Park
Downing Memorial Stadium
East River
Franklin D Roosevelt Drive
Jefferson Park
Spanish Harlem
21
20
22
0 150 300 m
0 150 300 yards
see MAP 9

MAP 11 BROOKLYN HEIGHTS & SURROUNDING NEIGHBORHOODS

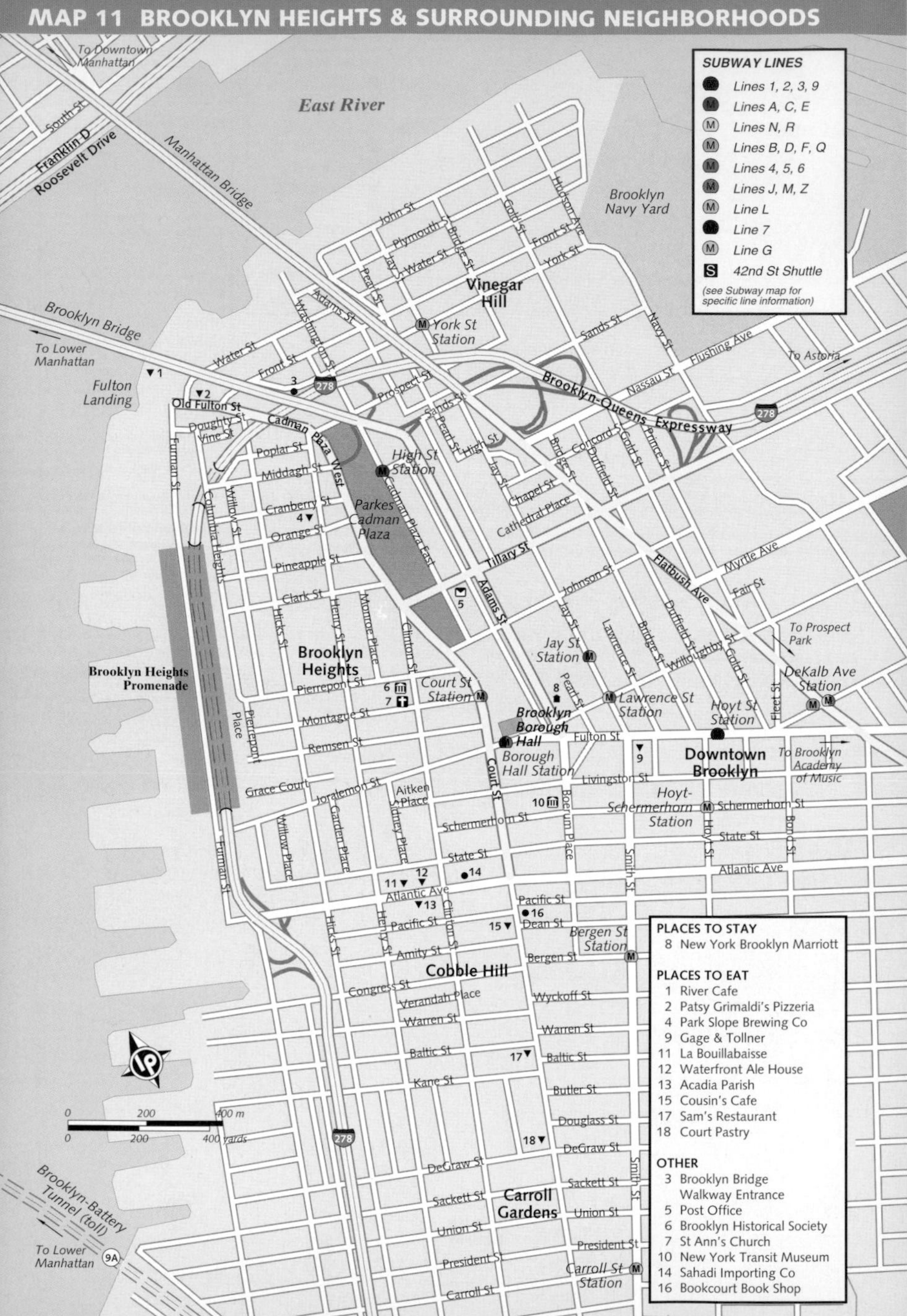

SUBWAY LINES
Lines 1, 2, 3, 9
Lines A, C, E
Lines N, R
Lines B, D, F, Q
Lines 4, 5, 6
Lines J, M, Z
Line L
Line 7
Line G
42nd St Shuttle
(see Subway map for specific line information)
PLACES TO STAY
8 New York Brooklyn Marriott
PLACES TO EAT
1 River Cafe
2 Patsy Grimaldi's Pizzeria
4 Park Slope Brewing Co
9 Gage & Tollner
11 La Bouillabaisse
12 Waterfront Ale House
13 Acadia Parish
15 Cousin's Cafe
17 Sam's Restaurant
18 Court Pastry
OTHER
3 Brooklyn Bridge Walkway Entrance
5 Post Office
6 Brooklyn Historical Society
7 St Ann's Church
10 New York Transit Museum
14 Sahadi Importing Co
16 Bookcourt Book Shop
East River
To Downtown Manhattan
Franklin D Roosevelt Drive
Manhattan Bridge
Brooklyn Bridge
To Lower Manhattan
Fulton Landing
Brooklyn Navy Yard
Vinegar Hill
York St Station
High St Station
Parkes Cadman Plaza
Brooklyn-Queens Expressway
To Astoria
Brooklyn Heights
Brooklyn Heights Promenade
Court St Station
Jay St Station
Lawrence St Station
Hoyt St Station
DeKalb Ave Station
To Prospect Park
Brooklyn Borough Hall
Borough Hall Station
Downtown Brooklyn
To Brooklyn Academy of Music
Hoyt-Schermerhorn Station
Bergen St Station
Cobble Hill
Carroll Gardens
Carroll St Station
Brooklyn-Battery Tunnel (toll)
To Lower Manhattan
0 200 400 m
0 200 400 yards

SUBWAY LINES

- Lines 1, 2, 3, 9
- Lines A, C, E
- Lines N, R
- Lines B, D, F, Q
- Lines 4, 5, 6
- Lines J, M, Z
- Line L
- Line 7
- Line G
- S 42nd St Shuttle

(see Subway map for specific line information)

PLACES TO STAY & EAT

1 Ozzie's
2 Lemongrass Grill
4 Tom's Restaurant
9 Park Slope Brewing Co
10 Bed & Breakfast on the Park

OTHER

3 JFK Memorial
5 Community Bookstore
6 Soldiers' and Sailors' Monument
7 Brooklyn Public Library
8 Brooklyn Museum of Art

ANGUS OBORN

ROBERT REID

Top and bottom: Getting around New York City in the fast and slow lanes

TOM SMALLMAN

RICHARD I'ANSON

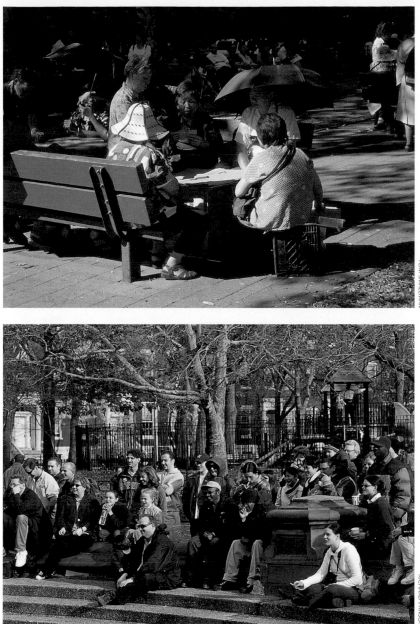

Top: Playing cards in Chinatown
Bottom: Watching some street theater in Washington Square Park

MAP 13 ASTORIA & SURROUNDING NEIGHBORHOODS

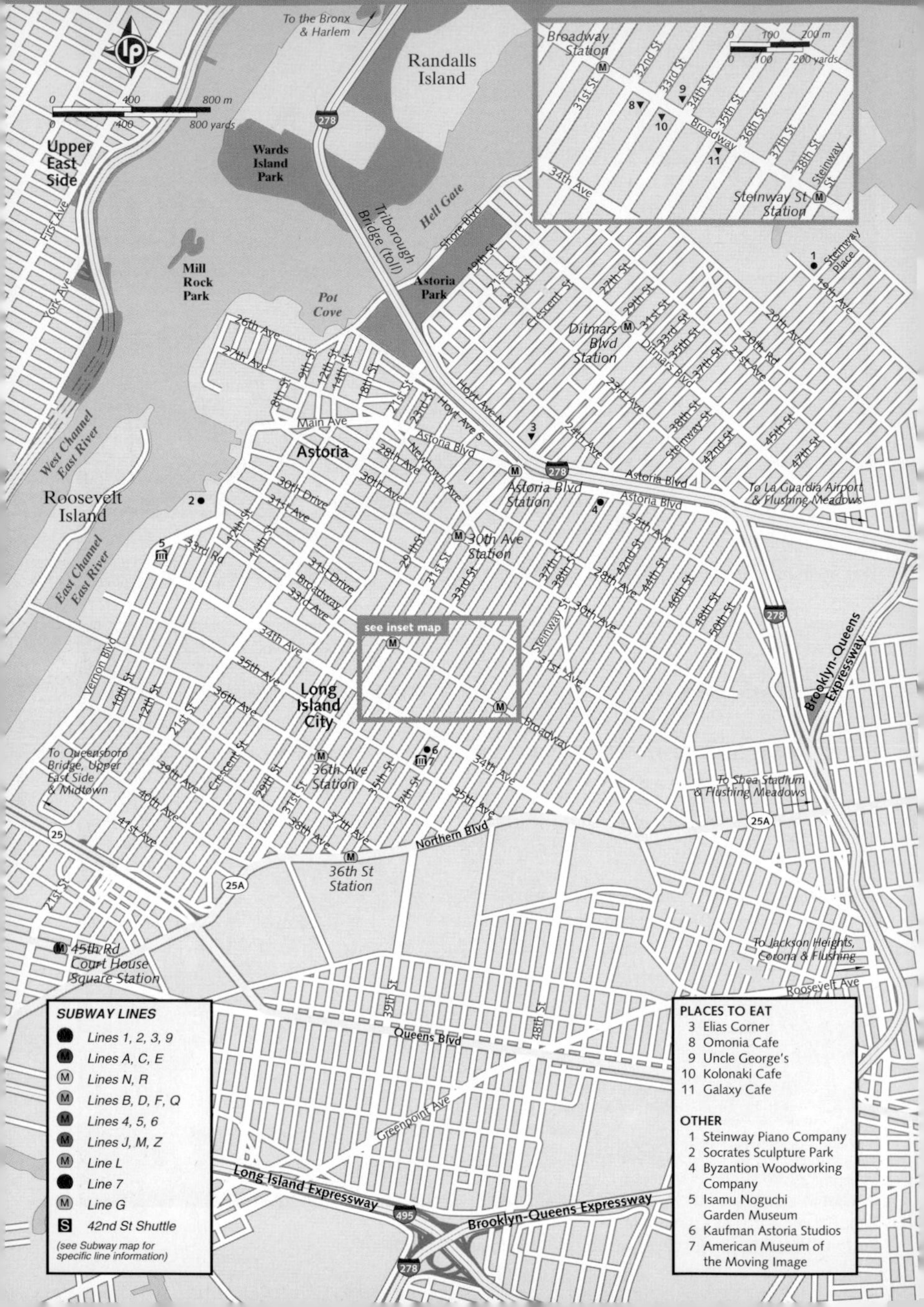

To the Bronx & Harlem
Randalls Island
Wards Island Park
Upper East Side
Hell Gate
Triborough Bridge (toll)
Shore Blvd
Mill Rock Park
Pot Cove
Astoria Park
First Ave
York Ave
West Channel East River
Roosevelt Island
East Channel East River
Astoria
Long Island City
Ditmars Blvd Station
Astoria Blvd Station
30th Ave Station
36th Ave Station
36th St Station
45th Rd Court House Square Station
To La Guardia Airport & Flushing Meadows
To Shea Stadium & Flushing Meadows
To Jackson Heights, Corona & Flushing
To Queensboro Bridge, Upper East Side & Midtown
Brooklyn-Queens Expressway
Long Island Expressway
Northern Blvd
Queens Blvd
Greenpoint Ave
Roosevelt Ave
Broadway
Steinway St
Vernon Blvd
see inset map
Broadway Station
Steinway St Station
SUBWAY LINES
Lines 1, 2, 3, 9
Lines A, C, E
Lines N, R
Lines B, D, F, Q
Lines 4, 5, 6
Lines J, M, Z
Line L
Line 7
Line G
42nd St Shuttle
(see Subway map for specific line information)
PLACES TO EAT
3 Elias Corner
8 Omonia Cafe
9 Uncle George's
10 Kolonaki Cafe
11 Galaxy Cafe
OTHER
1 Steinway Piano Company
2 Socrates Sculpture Park
4 Byzantion Woodworking Company
5 Isamu Noguchi Garden Museum
6 Kaufman Astoria Studios
7 American Museum of the Moving Image

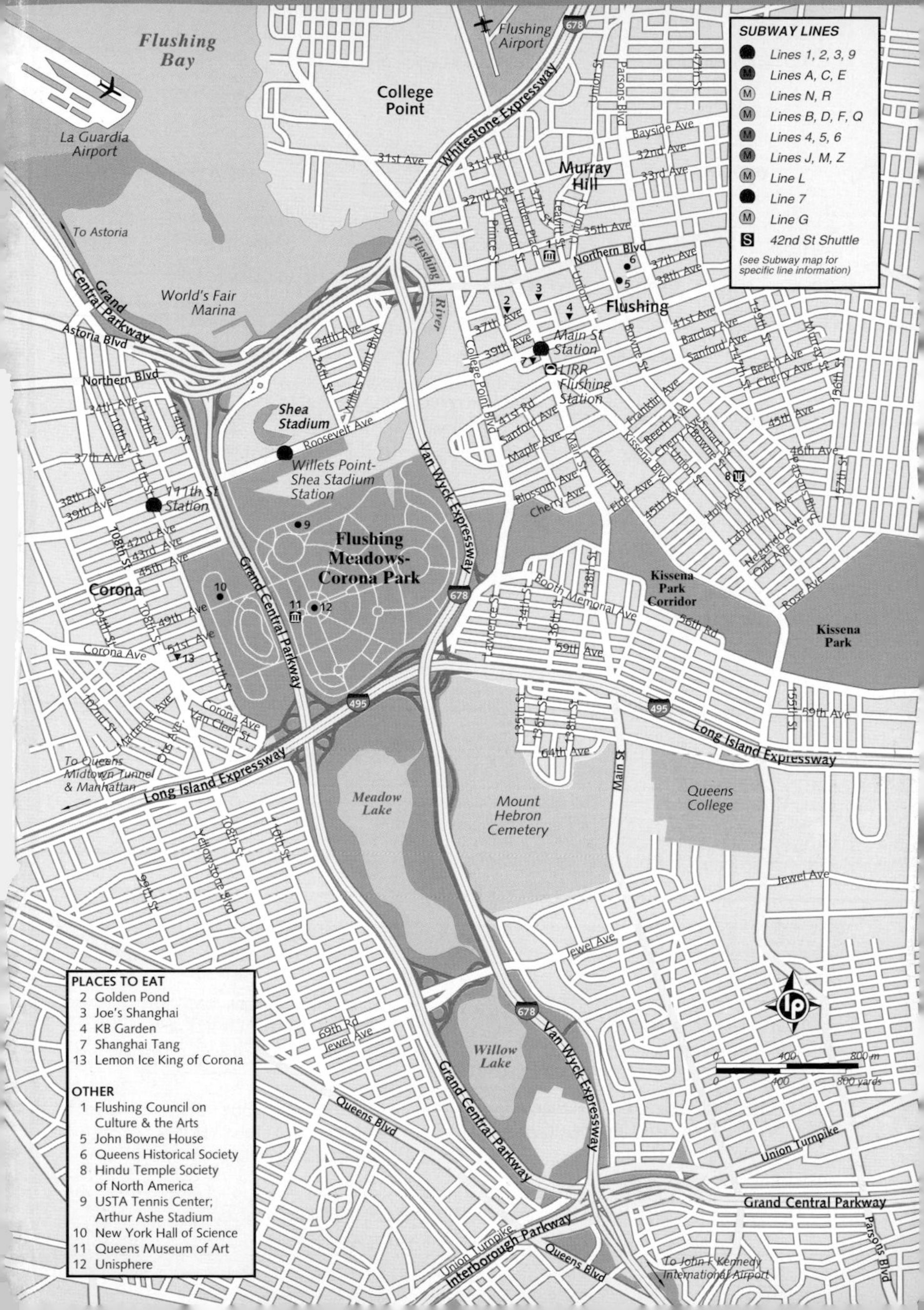

MAP 14 FLUSHING

SUBWAY LINES

- Lines 1, 2, 3, 9
- Lines A, C, E
- Lines N, R
- Lines B, D, F, Q
- Lines 4, 5, 6
- Lines J, M, Z
- Line L
- Line 7
- Line G
- S 42nd St Shuttle

(see Subway map for specific line information)

PLACES TO EAT

2 Golden Pond
3 Joe's Shanghai
4 KB Garden
7 Shanghai Tang
13 Lemon Ice King of Corona

OTHER

1 Flushing Council on Culture & the Arts
5 John Bowne House
6 Queens Historical Society
8 Hindu Temple Society of North America
9 USTA Tennis Center; Arthur Ashe Stadium
10 New York Hall of Science
11 Queens Museum of Art
12 Unisphere

MAP LEGEND

BOUNDARIES

- International
- State, Province
- County

ROUTES & TRANSPORT

- Freeway
- Toll Freeway
- Primary Road
- Secondary Road
- Tertiary Road
- Unpaved Road
- Pedestrian Mall
- Trail
- Walking Tour
- Ferry Route
- Railway, Train Station
- Metro Line, Metro Station

ROUTE SHIELDS

- 495 Interstate Freeway
- 25 New York State Highway
- 1 US Highway
- 46 County Road

HYDROGRAPHY

- Water
- Coastline
- Beach
- River, Waterfall
- Swamp, Spring

AREA FEATURES

- Building
- Park
- Plaza
- Cemetery
- Campus
- Golf Course, Zoo

MAP SYMBOLS

- NATIONAL CAPITAL
- STATE, PROVINCIAL CAPITAL
- Large City
- Medium City
- Small City
- Town, Village
- *Point of Interest*

- Place to Stay
- Campground
- RV Park

- Place to Eat
- Bar (Place to Drink), Nightclub

- Airfield
- Airport
- Archaeological Site, Ruins
- Bank
- Baseball Diamond
- Beach
- Border Crossing
- Bus Station
- Bus Stop
- Cathedral
- Church
- Embassy, Consulate
- Ferry
- Footbridge
- Garden
- Gas Station
- Hospital, Clinic
- Information
- Internet Access
- Lighthouse
- Lookout

- Monument
- Mosque
- Mountain
- Museum
- Park
- Parking
- Pass
- Picnic Area
- Police Station
- Pool
- Post Office
- Shipwreck
- Shopping Mall
- Stately Home
- Synagogue
- Temple
- Toilet
- Train Station
- Transport
- Tunnel
- Winery

Note: Not all symbols displayed above appear in this book.

LONELY PLANET OFFICES

Australia
Locked Bag 1, Footscray, Victoria 3011
☎ 03 8379 8000 fax 03 8379 8111
email talk2us@lonelyplanet.com.au

USA
150 Linden Street, Oakland, California 94607
☎ 510 893 8555, TOLL FREE 800 275 8555
fax 510 893 8572
email info@lonelyplanet.com

UK
10A Spring Place, London NW5 3BH
☎ 0171 428 4800 fax 0171 428 4828
email go@lonelyplanet.co.uk

France
1 rue du Dahomey, 75011 Paris
☎ 01 55 25 33 00 fax 01 55 25 33 01
email bip@lonelyplanet.fr
www.lonelyplanet.fr

World Wide Web: www.lonelyplanet.com *or* AOL keyword: lp
Lonely Planet Images: lpi@lonelyplanet.com.au